Paul's Pisidian Antioch Speech

Paul's Pisidian Antioch Speech (Acts 13)

JOHN EIFION MORGAN-WYNNE

☙PICKWICK *Publications* · Eugene, Oregon

PAUL'S PISIDIAN ANTIOCH SPEECH (ACTS 13)

Copyright © 2014 John Eifion Morgan-Wynne. All rights reserved. Except for brief quotations in critical publications or reviews, no part of this book may be reproduced in any manner without prior written permission from the publisher. Write: Permissions, Wipf and Stock Publishers, 199 W. 8th Ave., Suite 3, Eugene, OR 97401.

Pickwick Publications
An Imprint of Wipf and Stock Publishers
199 W. 8th Ave., Suite 3
Eugene, OR 97401

www.wipfandstock.com

ISBN 13: 978-1-62564-0505

Cataloging-in-Publication data:

Morgan-Wynne, John Eifion

    Paul's Pisidian Antioch Speech (Acts 13) / John Eifion Morgan-Wynne.

    xiv + 260 p. ; 23 cm. —Includes bibliographical references and index(es).

    ISBN 13: 978-1-62564-0505

1. Bible. N.T. Acts XIII—Criticism, interpretation, etc. 2. Direct discourse in the Bible. I. Title.

BS2625.6 S6 M77 2014

Manufactured in the U.S.A.

Translations of New Testament passages are the author's. Other quotations from the Bible and the Apocrypha are from the text of the Holy Bible, New Revised Version, copyright 1987, by the Division of the Christian Education of the National Council of the Churches of Christ in the USA, is used by permission.

Dedicated to Professor Jimmy Dunn,
in gratitude
for both his guidance as my 'Doktorvater,'
and his enormously helpful and stimulating contributions
to the understanding of the message of the New Testament.

Contents

Preface ix
Abbreviations xi

Chapter 1
Survey of Scholarship from Cadbury to the Present 1

Chapter 2
Setting the Context of the Speech 34

Chapter 3
The Structure of the Speech 62

Chapter 4
Did Luke Use Sources for the Speech? 69

Chapter 5
The Theological Emphases of the Speech 139

Chapter 6
The Speech and Luke's Community 206

Chapter 7
Summary and Conclusions 209

Appendix: Other Summaries of Israel's History 217
Bibliography 225
Biblical and Extra Biblical Writings Index 245
Authors Index 257

Preface

While still a history undergraduate at Oxford, I purchased a copy of C. H. Dodd's *The Apostolic Preaching and Its Developments*. That first sparked off my interest in the speeches in Acts, and this interest was further stimulated when I was a theological student and attended a lecture series entitled *Kerygma and Didache*, given by the late Revd. D. E. H. Whiteley, chaplain-fellow of my old college, Jesus College. Soon after my appointment as NT Tutor at Regent's Park College, Oxford, the syllabus for the Theology degree was revised and Acts ceased to have a prominent place in the NT papers. Despite this, I continued to read what had been written and continued to be written on the speeches as a whole and individual speeches in particular. Over time I began to concentrate on Paul's speech at Pisidian Antioch. Eventually I chose this speech as the topic of my presidential address to the Bristol Theological Society delivered in May 1992. This paper remained in a drawer until in retirement I was drawn back to it and had the time to devote to expanding it into a book.

There has been no full-scale treatment of this speech in English since the two volumes by C. A. J. Pillai published in America in 1979 and 1980 (and long since out of print), and this really still applies to W. Zhang's work *Paul among the Jews* which was published in 2011, though several monographs in German have been devoted to it. I hope that his volume may fill a gap for English readers.

It is my hope, as a life-long preacher myself, that the examination of this speech and how Luke presented the preaching of the apostle Paul may also stimulate reflection on the communication of the Gospel today.

I would like to express my thanks to my daughter, Leri-Anne Morgan-Wynne, for help in matters to do with the computing of this work; to my friend and former colleague, the Revd. Dr. Rex A. Mason, for help at one particular juncture; and, as ever, to the encouragement of my dear wife,

Enid, who has borne with my long hours in the study and has helped in proofreading and preparing the indexes.

I would like to thank all at Pickwick Publications who have helped in preparing this book for publication: Justin Haskell, Dr. Christopher Spinks and especially my typesetter, Ian Creeger.

Abbreviations

AB	Anchor Bible
AcBib	Academia Biblica (Society of Biblical Literature)
AGAJU	Arbeiten zur Geschichte des antiken Judentums und des Urchristentums
AJEC	Ancient Judaism and Early Christianity
AnBib	Analecta Biblica
Apg.	Apostelgeschichte
APOT	The Apocrypha and Pseudepigrapha of the Old Testament in English. Volume 1—Apocrypha. Volume 2—Pseudepigrapha.
ASNU	Acta Seminarii Neotestamentici Upsaliensis
BAG	W. Bauer, A Greek-English Lexicon of the New Testament. Translated and adapted by W. F Arndt and F. W. Gingrich. Chicago: Chicago University Press and Cambridge: Cambridge University Press, 1957.
BBB	Bonner Biblische Beiträge
BDF	F. Blass and A. Debrunner, A Greek Grammar of the New Testament and Other Early Christian Literature. Translated and revised by R. W. Funk Cambridge: Cambridge University Press and Chicago: Chicago University Press, 1961.
BETL	Bibliotheca Ephemeridum Theologicarum Lovaniensium
Bib	Biblica
BJRL	Bulletin of the John Rylands Library
BRS	Biblical Resource Series

BSL	Biblical Studies Library	
BU	Biblische Untersuchungen	
BWANT	Beiträge zur Wissenschaft vom Alten und Neuen Testament	
BZ	Biblische Zeitschrift	
BZNW	Beiträge zur Zeitschrift für neutestamentliche Wissenschaft	
CBET	Contributions to Biblical Exegesis & Theology	
CN	Coniectanea Neotestamentica	
CNT	Commentaire de Nouveau Testament	
DSSE	The Dead Sea Scrolls in English. Translated by G. Vermes. Penguin Classics.	
EHPR	Études d'Histoire et de Philosophie Religieuses	
EKKNT	Evangelisch-Katholischer Kommentar zum Neuen Testament	
ESEC	Emory Studies in Early Christianity	
ET	Evangelische Theologie	
EV	English Version	
ExT	Expository Times	
FRLANT	Forsuchungen zur Religion und Literatur des Alten und Neuen Testaments	
FzB	Forschung zur Bibel	
GN	The Good News for Modern Man. The NT in Today's English Version	
GNS	Good News Studies	
HJ	Hibberd Journal	
HTKNT	Herders theologischer Kommentar zum Neuen Testament	
HTR	Havard Theological Review	
HTS	Havard Theological Studies	
ICC	International Critical Commentary	
JB	Jerusalem Bible	
JBL	Journal of Biblical Literature	
JSNT	Journal for the Study of the New Testament	
JSNTSS	Journal for the Study of the New Testament Supplement Series	

JSOTSS	Journal for the Study of the Old Testament Supplement Series
JSPSS	Journal for the Study of the Pseudepigrapha Supplement Series
JTS	Journal of Theological Studies
KEKNT	Kritisch-Exegetischer Kommentar über das Neue Testament
LA	Luke-Acts
LD	Lectio Divina
LNTS	Library of New Testament Studies
LSJ	H. G. Liddell, R. Scott & H. S. Jones, A Greek-English Lexicon. Revised and augmented by H. S. Jones with the assistance of R. McKenzie. Oxford: Clarendon, 1968.
n.	Footnote
NA	Neutestamentliche Abhandlungen
NCB	New Clarendon Bible
NCB	New Century Bible
NEB	New English Bible
n.f.	Neue Folge
NICNT	New International Commentary on the New Testament
NIGNC	New International Greek Testament Commentary
NIV	New International Version
NRSV	New Revised Standard Version
NT	Novum Testamentum
NTC	New Testament in Context
NTD	Das Neue Testament Deutsch
NTOA	Novum Testamentum et Orbis Antiquus / Studien zur Umwelt des Neuen Testaments
NTS	New Testament Studies
OTKNT	Ökumenischer Taschenbuch Kommentar zum Neuen Testament
OTL	Old Testament Library
OTP	Old Testament Pseudepigrapha
PA	Pisidian Antioch

PBTM	Paternoster Biblical and Theological Monographs
REB	Revised English Bible
RNT	Regensburger Neues Testament
RSR	Revue de Science Religieuse
RV	Revised Version
SANT	Studien zum Alten und Neuen Testament
SBL EJIL	Society for Biblical Literature: Early Judaism and Its Literature
SBS	Stuttgarter Bibel-Studien
SBT	Studies in Biblical Theology
SBLMS	Society of Biblical Literature Monograph Series
SHAWPK	Sitzungsberichte der Heidelberger Akademie der Wissenschaften, philosophisch-historische Klasse
SNTA	Studiorum Novi Testamenti Auxilia
SNTSMS	Society of New Testament Studies Monograph Series
SP	Sacra Pagina
SPB	Studia Post-Biblica
SR	Sciences Religieuses
TDNT	Theological Dictionary of the New Testament. 10 vols. Edited by G. Kittel and G. Friedrich. Translated by G. W. Bromiley. Grand Rapids, Michigan: Eerdmanns, 1964–76.
TF	Theologische Forschung
TP	Theologie und Philosophie
TPINTC	Trinity Press International New Testament Commentary
TU	Texte und Untersuchungen
WBC	Word Bible Commentary
WMANT	Wissenschaftliche Monographien zum Alten und Neuen Testament
WUNT	Wissenschaftliche Untersuchungen zum Neuen Testament
ZNW	Zeitschrift für Neutestamentliche Wissenschaft
ZSNT	Zacchaeus Studies: New Testament

Chapter 1

A Survey of Scholarship from Cadbury to the Present

THE SO-CALLED KERYGMATIC SPEECHES IN GENERAL

I

H. J. Cadbury, who devoted much of his scholarly work to studies on Luke-Acts (hereafter LA), wrote a short essay in 1933 on "The Speeches in Acts."[1] Cadbury dealt entirely with the issue of whether Luke relied on oral sources for the speeches or whether they were his own composition. He set out the arguments for and against Luke's reliance on traditional material, and came to the conclusion that Luke "attempted to present what the speakers were likely to have said" and that the speeches "indicate at least what seemed to a well-informed Christian of the next generation the main outline of the Christian message as first presented by Jesus' followers in Palestine and in the cities of the Mediteranean world."[2]

In 1936, C. H. Dodd published his influential *The Apostolic Preaching and Its Developments* (originally three lectures given at King's College, London, in 1935),[3] the first chapter of which dealt with "The Primitive Preaching." Dodd sought to construct "the outlines of an apostolic gospel which

---

1. Lake and Cadbury, *Beginnings*, 5:402–27. For Cadbury's other works on LA, apart from his contributions to *Beginnings*, see the bibliography.
2. Ibid., 5:426–27.
3. It was reset towards the end of the Second World War in 1944 and reprinted several times after that. All quotations are from the reset edition.

Paul's Pisidian Antioch Speech (Acts 13)

Paul believed to be common to himself and other Christian missionaries."[4] He listed seven items culled from Paul's writings (Rom. 1.3; 1 Cor. 15.3–4; Rom. 8.34; 1 Thess. 1.10) in an attempt to restore its outline:

- The prophecies are fulfilled and the new Age is inaugurated by the coming of Christ.
- He was born of the seed of David.
- He died according to the scriptures, to deliver us out of the present evil age.
- He was buried.
- He rose on the third day according to the Scriptures.
- He is exalted at the right hand of God, as Son of God and Lord of the living and dead.
- He will come again as Judge and Saviour of men.[5]

Then Dodd analysed the Petrine speeches in Acts and came up with the following scheme for the kerygma of the Jerusalem church:[6]

- The age of fulfilment has dawned (2.16; 3.18, 24).
- This has taken place through the ministry and death of Jesus, of which a brief account is given—his Davidic descent (2.30–31); ministry (2.22; 3.22); his death (2.23; 3.13–14); his resurrection (2.24–31; 3.15; 4.10); by virtue of the resurrection, Jesus has been exalted at God's right hand, as Messianic Head of the new Israel (2.33–36; 3.13; 4.11; 5.31); the Holy Spirit in the church is the sign of Christ's present power and glory (2.33); the Messianic Age will shortly reach its consummation in the return of Christ (3.21; 10.42).
- The Kerygma closes with an appeal for repentance, the offer of forgiveness and of the Holy Spirit (2.38–39; 3.19, 25–26; 4.12; 5.31; 10.43).

As a further step, Dodd outlined the differences which existed between his outline of Paul's preaching of the common gospel and that of the preaching of the Jerusalem church in Acts. In the Jerusalem kerygma, Jesus is not called "Son of God;" it is not said that Christ died for our sins; nor that the exalted Christ intercedes for us.[7] Dodd pointed out in respect to the

---

4. Dodd, *Apostolic Preaching*, 16.

5. Ibid., 17.

6. Ibid., 21–24. Note that Dodd expressly said that these speeches represented "not indeed what Peter said upon this or that occasion, but the kerygma of the Church at Jerusalem at an early period" (21).

7. Ibid., 25–26.

stress in Acts on the Holy Spirit that the idea of the Spirit in the Church is very prominent in the Pauline epistles, even if not included explicitly in his "Gospel;"[8] while it would be rash to conclude from Paul's silence about the facts of Jesus' ministry in his letters that he ignored the life of Jesus in his preaching.[9]

Dodd thus defended the substantial agreement between Paul's version of the kerygma and that recorded in Acts, and felt that this led to "a fairly clear and certain outline sketch of the preaching of the apostles."[10]

A number of questions are left in the reader's mind after Dodd's handling of the topic. In the first place, he did not press rigorously enough the issue of the atoning nature of Christ's death in the pre-Pauline formula quoted at 1 Cor. 15.3–5 (7) and the lack of any such reference in the Acts speeches. This is no slight difference. Did Luke edit such an interpretation out, or were there a number of ways of interpreting the death of Jesus in the early years of the church and Luke has opted for one of these—the contrast between human condemnation of Jesus leading to his death and divine vindication in the resurrection and exaltation?

Secondly, while Dodd admitted that the formula of Rom. 1.3–4 is not Pauline in origin, he does not press this point. How is it that Davidic descent is stressed so much in the speech attributed to Paul at Pisidian Antioch [hereafter PA] in Acts 13.16–41, while in Paul's own letters, apart from Rom. 1.3, it is mentioned only at Rom. 15.12 in a catena of scripture passages, the main point of which is that Gentiles should praise God or hope in the Messiah?[11]

In the third place, there is the issue of the Son of God Christology of Rom. 1.4—did the original pre-Pauline formula used here think of Jesus' becoming Son of God on the basis of the resurrection from the dead (with Paul adding "in power" to introduce a modification) and is this the position which Acts 13.32–33 also assumes? What, then, of the Christological pattern discernible in Paul's letters (preexistence, earthly life, postexistence)? Arguably, Dodd glossed over this issue.

Finally, Dodd missed the importance of apostolic witness in the Acts speeches, and, as a result, failed to discuss Acts 13.31 and its relationship to Paul's statements about the origin of his gospel and apostleship in Galatians 1–2; 1 Corinthians 9; 2 Corinthians 10–13.

8. Ibid., 26.
9. Ibid., 28–29.
10. Ibid., 31.
11. I leave on one side the probably Trito-Pauline 2 Tim. 2.8 (itself probably an adaptation of Rom. 1.3–4).

4 Paul's Pisidian Antioch Speech (Acts 13)

M. Dibelius had in his pioneering work on form criticism in 1919 briefly alluded to the outline of the preaching of the early Christians—he reduced it to a tripartite scheme of Kerygma or message of what God has done in the life and ministry of Jesus; scriptural proof that these events fulfilled prophecy; and the exhortation to repentance and conversion.[12] Later, in the thirties and forties before his death in 1947, he wrote several essays on the Acts, including a famous essay on the speeches in Acts: "The Speeches in Acts and Ancient Historiography."[13]

Dibelius argued that Luke needed to be judged against the background of ancient classical historiography. There, the speeches were "an artistic device to achieve the author's aims" and the interpreter must, therefore, ask "what is the function of the speeches in the whole work;"[14] similarly with Luke, the speeches are "the work of an author who was consciously creating, rather than renouncing, literary devices."[15] The so-called kerygmatic speeches seek to show "how the gospel is preached and ought to be preached!"[16] There is "no distinction between Peter and Paul as speakers."[17] The repetition in the speeches of Acts 2–13 "is intended to offer the same material in constantly new variation, to summarise what is essential in the message and to produce the same impression which Paul, also speaking of the kerygma, formulated in 1 Cor. 15.11: 'Whether it is I or they, thus do we preach and thus have you come to believe.'"[18] In another essay, Dibelius wrote that these speeches in Acts "are intended not for the audience who actually heard them but for the readers."[19]

Dibelius makes out a strong case for his position, but there are questions which arise. Firstly, his treatment of the kerygmatic speeches is not very detailed. They call for discussion at greater length than Dibelius actually gives them. Secondly, he never deals with the question whether there might be "primitive" tradition within the speeches. Thus, he says the question of "a dependence upon older texts . . . can only be raised, not answered,"[20] which is hardly satisfactory. It would not be impossible for Luke to have

---

12. Dibelius, *From Tradition to Gospel*, 17.

13. In Dibelius, *Studies in the Acts of the Apostles*, 138–91 (originally submitted in 1944 and published in the *Sitzungsberichte der Heidelberger Akademie der Wissenschaften, philosophisch-historische Klasse*, 1949).

14. Ibid., 144, 145.

15. Ibid., 150

16. Ibid., 165.

17. Ibid., 165

18. Ibid., 166

19. Ibid., 133.

20. Ibid., 166.

pursued the overall literary aims which Dibelius suggests and made use of old material.

Dibelius makes no reference to Dodd's work, though the two scholars were friends and, in fact, when Dibelius had first visited Britain after the 1914–18 war, Dodd was involved in discussions with Dibelius about his lectures.[21]

To some extent, it would not be an exaggeration to say that for some while afterwards, scholarship lined up behind either Dodd or Dibelius,[22] espousing the view either that Luke has given substantially accurate summaries of the early preaching of the gospel or that he has freely composed the speeches to indicate how he thought the Christian message should be preached and adapting that to the particular circumstances where he placed these speeches in his narrative. Indeed, a number of scholars of a conservative persuasion did in fact go somewhat further than Dodd and maintained the substantial accuracy of the speeches in Acts 2–13, attributing the differences between Peter and Paul to the individuality of the speakers.

II

F. F. Bruce, who was still a classical scholar and lecturer when he was invited to give the Tyndale Lecture in 1942, chose as his theme "The Speeches in the Acts of the Apostles."[23] Bruce defended the substantial accuracy of the Lucan speeches. He saw them as basic summaries of what had been said, and explained the similarities in the kerygmatic speeches of Peter (chaps. 2–10) and Paul (chap. 13) as due to the fact, stressed by Paul in 1 Corinthians 15.11, that they did share a common kerygma. At the same time, the differences in the speeches were an indication of the individuality of the speakers: into this category fell the reference to law and justification at the close of the PA speech (13.33–39).

Bruce went on to become Professor of the Department of Biblical Studies at Sheffield and then succeeded T. W. Manson in the Rylands Chair of Biblical Exegesis at Manchester from 1959 till his retirement. He returned to the theme of the speeches off and on during his career—he wrote two commentaries on Acts, one on the Greek text (1951) and the other on the

---

21. See the reference to this occasion in an extract from a lecture Dodd gave in Union Seminary, New York, and quoted in Dillistone, *C. H. Dodd*, 172.

22. Dupont, *Nouvelles Études*, 91, said that Dibelius and Dodd opened up "a decisive stage" in the study of the missionary discourses of Acts, and that the results of their work "exercised a determinative influence on a whole generation of exegetes" (92).

23. Bruce, *Speeches in the Acts of the Apostles*.

English text (1954), and then, his contribution to the Leon Morris Festschrift *Reconciliation and Hope*, bore the title "The Speeches of Acts—Thirty Years After."[24] Bruce really added no new arguments, reviewed some intervening works and saw no reason to change his basic position.

E. Trocmé, although not treating the speeches in any detail in his survey of scholarship on Acts, expressed his opinion to the effect that, while "the speeches have been chosen and positioned with care by the author and have in the work a role which largely surpasses the immediate effect which the story attributes to them," nevertheless it was "hardly probable that [Luke] has invented entire parts of any episode and composed the majority of his speeches without a traditional core."[25]

Although not concerned with the accuracy of the speeches in Acts as such, O. Cullmann in his *The Christology of the New Testament* (1959), argued for a Pais-Christology characteristic of the apostle Peter, based on the occurrences of παις [servant] in Acts 3–4 and 1Peter 2.21–25 and the experience of Peter at Caesarea Philippi (Mark 8.27–33),[26] though Cullmann acknowledges that this hypothesis cannot be proved.

Like Bruce, the Dutch scholar, H. Ridderbos, in 1961, also delivered the Tyndale lecture, and chose as his theme "The Speeches of Peter and Paul in Acts."[27] He dissented from the position of Dibelius and reached similar conclusions to Bruce. The same can be said of I. H. Marshall in his Tyndale commentary on *The Acts of the Apostles* (1980),[28] which replaced the earlier volume in the series by E. M. Blaiklock.

In 1975, M. Wilcox, in a general discussion of methodology concerning the speeches, posed the issue of whether, if Luke treated Jesus' words rather faithfully, he might also do so in respect of information about the apostles. He thought that the material in the speeches sometimes does not fit the context (e.g., Stephen's speech in chap. 7) or does not tally with Luke's own interpretation (e.g., the glossolalia of Acts 2 and Luke's view of a linguistic miracle), or the material is not homogeneous (e.g., Acts 2 and 3). This led Wilcox to suggest that it may be the framework which is secondary rather than the speeches.[29]

---

24. Bruce, "The Speeches in Acts," 53–68.
25. Trocmé, *Actes*, 110 and 121 respectively.
26. Cullmann, *Christology*, 73–75.
27. Published in 1962.
28. Marshall, *Acts*, 39–42.
29. Wilcox, "Foreword," 206–25.

G. Schneider in his commentary on Acts argued that Luke, in the speeches to Jews, had worked over a *schema* of preaching from his tradition, but not written sources (vorgegebene Texte).[30]

In the series entitled The Book of Acts in its First Century Setting,[31] published jointly by Eerdmans in America and Paternoster in Britain, C. Gempf contributed an essay on "Public Speaking and Published Accounts" in the first volume, which bore the title *The Book of Acts in Its Ancient Literary Setting* (1993).[32] After pointing out that to the ancients rhetoric was power and that the record of a speech was not regarded in antiquity as a transcript but should preserve faithfully the strategies behind the speech viewed as event, Gempf looks at the approach of various Graeco-Roman historians from Thucydides to Lucian of Samosata, and also Jewish writers. His conclusion is that speeches are the compositions of an author, but at their best are representative of the speaker, the situation and the contents of the original, with Josephus being an exception. He does not think that the coherence of a speech with the author's own purposes is sufficient grounds for dismissing the record of the speech as invention. Gempf speaks of "literary and historical appropriateness." "We must learn to think of the public speeches not as (accurate or falsified) transcript/summaries of the words of famous people, but rather as records (faithful or unfaithful) of historical events."[33]

R. Bauckham took up the issue of the kerygmatic speeches in Acts in an essay published in 1996.[34] He believed that Luke followed a kerygmatic summary which was very traditional but also very flexible and variable. The form was hospitable to variation and innovation. He believed that traces of this kerygmatic summary were to be found in three places of the Ascension of Isaiah (incorporated into its highly developed mythological-Christological framework); in the letters of Ignatius of Antioch; the Kerygma Petrou (as quoted by Clement of Alexander in his Stromateis); Justin Martyr; and Irenaeus. He also suggested that the formula quoted by Paul in 1 Corinthians 15.3 may have begun earlier. In the speeches of Acts, Luke chose not to begin with the birth of Jesus, but with the ministry of John the Baptist. The speeches in Acts 2–13 exhibit both correspondences and variation, and show some augmentation from gospel traditions as well as the fulfilment of

30. Schneider, *Apg.*, 1:95–103, esp. 102.

31. Originally six volumes were planned. Five were published between 1993 and 1996. The sixth volume, *Witness*, edited by Marshall and Peterson, was published for some reason separately in paperback form by Eerdmans in 1998

32. Gempf, "Public Speaking," 259–303.

33. Ibid., both quotations on 303.

34. Bauckham, *Kerygmatic Summaries*, 185–217.

prophecy theme. For Bauckham, then, the kerygmatic summary was essentially an oral form, capable of various adaptations and of being filled out by writers and especially Christian preachers with their knowledge of Gospel traditions and scriptural testimonia. What we have in Acts are "literary representations of sermons."[35]

In his commentary on Acts of 1998, B. Witherington denied the, for him, all too common assumption that Luke created the speeches in Acts. Luke used sources for his speeches, presenting summaries, editing them according to his own agendas and sometimes rendering portions in his own words for stylistic purposes. The similarities between Peter and Paul were due to the use of the basic kerygma and testimonia. Witherington believes that Luke stands in the same tradition as Thucydides who reported in his own style a selection of ideas and thoughts (γνώμη) expressed in a speech, seeking to make them clearer and in a way that served his own particular purpose.[36]

J. Jervell wants to go further than scholars who accept that in the speeches there are elements from tradition. He believed that in some speeches Luke worked with "pre-found speeches or fragments of speeches." Of the different types of speeches in Acts, he maintained that the mission speeches contained the oldest material which probably reproduced the scheme at the basis of the oldest mission preaching to the Jews.[37]

III

Turning now to works which have followed in the trail marked out by Dibelius, mention must first be made of H. Conzelmann's seminal work on Luke, *Die Mitte der Zeit* ("The Centre of Time"), published in 1953, and translated into English with the colourless title *The Theology of St Luke* (1960), which heralded a new epoch in Lucan studies, with the emphasis on Luke as a creative theologian. Although in this volume Conzelmann does not treat the speeches in Acts as a topic, it is clear, as his later commentary on Acts[38] was to confirm, that he sided with the view that saw the speeches as Luke's own creation.[39]

---

35. Ibid., 216.
36. Witherington, *Acts*, 39–49, 116–20.
37. Jervell, *Apg.*, 71.
38. The English translation was published in the Hermeneia series in 1987.
39. Cf. Conzelmann's comments on the Areopagus speech: *Studies*, 217–30, esp. 218.

In an article entitled "The Kerygma" (1956), which virtually coincided with the translation of Dibelius' work into English, C. F. Evans criticized Dodd's views and basically mediated Dibelius' position to the English-speaking world. Evans was later to return to the speeches in an essay entitled "'Speeches' in Acts."[40] Here Evans raised the question of whether speeches or missionary sermons was the better designation. He decides firmly in favour of the former, and believes that the character of defence in the face of attack attaches in some measure to all the speeches in Acts[41] (e.g., those in chaps. 2; 3.1—5.42; 7; 17; 20; 24–25), though that in chapter 13 is more an exhortation or exposition. Evans points to the close knit argument in 2.14–36 and 17.23–31, while the most constant component of the speeches, and the Christian message, is the resurrection by which Jesus is alive and shown to be active in preaching and healing and by which Israel is warned.[42] By repetition in the early speeches Luke establishes his case in Jerusalem—the Jews destroyed a man approved by God and asked Pilate for a murderer.[43]

A monograph on the kerygmatic speeches appeared in 1961 from U. Wilckens: *Die Missionsreden der Apostelgeschichte*, swiftly followed by a slightly corrected second edition in 1963. After an introductory survey of previous studies, Wilckens then proceeds firstly to a detailed analysis of the structure of the speeches, which reveals an overall similar scheme, though each speech is related to the narrative situation.[44] He then analyses the framework of the speeches. These are fitted into the context, related to it and "stamped" by it in details, from which Wilckens concludes Lucan authorship of the whole, the context and speech.[45] Thirdly, he looks at the schema. While Luke did have a traditional schema for the speeches in chapters 14 and 17 (cf. 1Thess. 1.9–10; Hebs. 6.1–2), he did not for those in chaps. 2–13, but adapted the schema for the speeches in chaps. 14 and 17, for preaching to the Jews. These speeches are a means of expressing the witness to Jesus of the apostles at decisive turning points in the movement of the mission. The form and schema of the speeches is throughout understandable from the total theological standpoint of Luke.[46] Fourthly, Wilckens turns to the individual motifs—John the Baptist; Jesus' activity before his death; his condemnation and death; statements concerning his resurrection and

---

40. Evans, "'Speeches' in Acts," 287–302.
41. Ibid., 293–94.
42. Ibid., 297–99.
43. Ibid.
44. Wilckens, *Missionsreden*, 32–55
45. Ibid., 56–71.
46. Ibid., 72–100.

exaltation; Christological titles.[47] For most of these, Wilckens' analysis leads him to postulate Lucan creation. Occasionally, as with the statements on the resurrection and exaltation or a Christological title like ἀρχηγός or υἱός in 13.33, he accepts traditional material. He summarises: "The apostolic speeches of Acts are in a pre-eminent sense summaries of (Luke's) theological conception; they are not to be evaluated as witnesses of an old or indeed oldest early Christian theology but of Lucan theology at the end of the first century."[48]

In terms of literary analysis Wilckens is in the tradition of Dibelius, and in terms of theological analysis he is akin to Conzelmann and Haenchen.

However, in the third edition of his work which appeared in 1974, Wilckens modified his position concerning the traditio-historical background of the mission speeches.[49] Luke's share in the composition of the speeches is still great, but he has taken over from Jewish Christian preaching to Jews a schema modelled on the Deuteronomist preaching of repentance, to which O.H. Steck had drawn attention in *Israel und das gewaltsame Geschick der Propheten* (1967). This is particularly so of Stephen's speech, to which the speech at PA shows the greatest similarities. But whereas the speech of Stephen is a Deuteronomistically shaped speech of reproach (Scheltrede), the apostolic speeches are sermons which offer salvation and which see the OT history only as prehistory and promise of the perfect salvation in Jesus. This represents a considerable modification of Wilckens' original position in 1961.

In the wake of Conzelmann's influential work, E. Haenchen's commentary on Acts appeared in 1956, revised and enlarged in 1961[50] He was emphatic that Dodd was in error, even more so the view that the speeches represented Peter's original train of thought, and that Dibelius' thesis was right: "Peter's speeches go back to Luke himself."[51]

In 1966 came the publication of another important contribution on the speeches in Acts. In the *Festschrift* for P. Schubert, *Studies in Luke-Acts*,[52]

---

47. Ibid., 100–186.

48. Ibid., 186; cf. 188, 193.

49. The introduction and first two sections remained the same, but a supplement was added in which Wilckens goes into criticism and deals with new literature.

50. Published in 1956, this was originally the 10th edition of Acts in the Meyer series. It was revised several times. The work was translated into English in 1971 from the 15th edition (1968); the quotation is from 185. All references hereafter are to the English translation.

51. Haenchen, *Acts*, 185. Compare his opinion on the Pisidian Antioch speech that "Luke does not hesitate to invent a long speech and put it in [Paul's] mouth," 415.

52. Keck and Martyn, *Studies in Luke-Acts*.

E. Schweizer wrote an essay "Concerning the Speeches in Acts."[53] He also believed that Dibelius was right in seeing the speeches as "basically *compositions by the author of Acts*."[54] He analysed the speeches of Peter and Paul and showed that they exhibit "a *far-reaching identity of structure*"[55] which shows that "*one and the same author* is decisively involved in the composition of all the speeches here investigated."[56]

E. Krankl's monograph of 1972, *Jesus der Knecht des Gottes*, dealt with the speeches in Acts. The work was divided into two parts. The first part gave a very detailed survey of trends in the scholarly discussion of the speeches in Acts from the beginnings of critical study to the time of publication. As a result of this survey, which reveals that a majority of scholars take the speeches to be the work of Luke, Krankl assumes this as his starting point for part two, which discusses nine individual themes: Jesus as son of David; John the Baptist and Jesus; Jesus' public work; the death of Jesus; his resurrection; his exaltation; witnesses; the role of the exalted one in God's saving work for human beings; Jesus and the eschatological event. Krankl's conclusion is that, while the speeches do contain a variety of traditions of different age and origin, on the whole they are genuine witnesses to Lucan theology.

E. Plumacher devoted a section of his work on *Lukas als hellenistischer Schriftsteller* (1972) to the theme of the missionary speeches in Acts in their relation to Hellenistic literature.[57] At the outset he expressed his agreement with the (earlier) position of Wilckens that the missionary speeches reflected Luke's own theological conceptions. Luke, in accordance with the conventions of Hellenistic historiography as exemplified by Dionysius of Halicarnassus, wanted to show preaching as the decisive moving force at key points of the mission of the Church (the speeches are the *movens* of events in the history of salvation).

Just as Hellenistic historiographers imitated famous predecessors—for example, Dionysius of Halicarnassus imitated Thucydides, Xenophon and Demosthenes,—so Luke deliberately coloured what he wanted to say in a Biblical manner with the help of Septuagintalisms. As for Luke, the beginnings of the church in Palestine are a unique, unrepeatable era, a holy time,

---

53. 208–16.

54. Ibid., 208 (Schweizer's italics).

55. Ibid., 210 (Schweizer's italics). Schweizer listed 9 points in a general scheme.

56. Ibid., 212 (Schweizer's italics). Schweizer also analysed the two speeches to Gentiles in 14.15–17 and 17.22–31, and compared and contrasted them with the previous analysis of the so-called kerygmatic speeches, the main difference being that the testimony for Jesus is replaced by the proclamation about God because of the Gentile audience (212–13).

57. Plumacher, *Lukas*, 32–79.

and he lets its representatives speak with a holy language—that of the Bible used by the church, the Septuagint. Plumacher thinks that Luke saw the ideal early time echoed in Paul's speech at Miletus before the breaking in of heresy. Luke also uses archaic titles and formulae to evoke in the reader the idea of the "old time." Far from indicating the age of the tradition, this is a technique of archaicizing deliberately used as a literary technique by Luke, to which the Roman historian, Livy, offers a parallel. Plumacher, then, rejects the view of Dibelius that the mission speeches in Acts have no connection with ancient historical writing.

Plumacher returned to this theme in an article entitled "Die Missionsreden der Apg. und Dionysius von Halikarnass,"[58] later enlarged with an addendum and translated into English.[59] Plumacher showed how Luke had indicated the connection of the preaching by Peter of the kerygma about Jesus and the gift of the Spirit to Cornelius and others, which led to their baptism and admission to the church, and Paul and Barnabas' preaching at PA and the turning to the Gentiles. For Luke, it is preaching the keygma which sets in motion the development towards the Gentile church. Dionysius of Halicarnassus also believed that it was speeches which determined the course of history at important turning points and Plumacher illustrates this conviction from Dionysius' own works. Without postulating any direct dependence of Luke on Dionysius, Plumacher believes that both were convinced that speeches were the *movens* of events which possessed the power to lend legitimacy to circumstances of their present.

Delling's article, "Die Jesusgeschichte in der Verkundigung nach Acta," reviewed the material in the speeches concerning the ministry of Jesus, his death and resurrection, the role of the witnesses of the resurrection, the exaltation and Jesus' activity as the exalted one. He concluded that because God has acknowledged Jesus in his earthly activity and resurrection, preaching must include the story of Jesus (and hence also the need of certainty about that story, as evinced in Lk.1.2–4).[60] Luke makes that clear not only in his Gospel but also in the speeches composed by him in Acts, in which he varies the amount of material about Jesus according to context.[61]

Probably the latest monograph on the speeches in Acts comes from the pen of the American scholar, M.L. Soards, *The Speeches in Acts: Their Content, Context and Concerns*. What strikes Soards most about the speeches is

58. *NTS* 39 (1993) 161–77.
59. In Moessner, *Jesus*, 251–66.
60. Delling, "Jesusgeschichte," 386.
61. Ibid., 389.

their sheer repetitiveness,[62] which, he claims, has often gone unrecognized.[63] By this repetitiveness, Luke unifies the story of Acts and advances his theme of divinely commissioned, unified witness to the ends of the earth.[64] Chapter two, the largest chapter, looks at 36 speeches in Acts, examining the way phrases constantly recur in the speeches as well as major ideas like God's authority and plan, the status of Jesus in God's plan, the importance of the time in which the speaker speaks, the witness theme, etc. These major ideas are taken up and discussed in chapter 4.

Another scholar who has written extensively on LA is L.T. Johnson. In his commentary on Acts, he wrote: "Luke may have structured some of these discourses on the foundation of traditional preaching patterns, but the specific rhetorical turns in each speech come from him rather than from some source. The speeches sound authentic because of his artistry. . .The speeches in Acts provide authorial commentary on the narrative."[65] In one of his latest contributions to the study of LA, Johnson reiterated his position clearly: "All the speeches in Acts are Luke's speeches . . . Luke's speeches, in short, contain not only his language but also his perceptions."[66]

IV

As the second half of the century wore on, many scholars began to tread a middle way between Dodd and Dibelius. They acknowledged that the language and style of the speeches were often thoroughly Lucan, but also believed either that Luke was faithfully transmitting earlier traditions, or, at any rate, had in places woven earlier tradition into the speeches. As an example, we may cite J. Dupont who was a prolific writer on Acts. Two volumes of his collected articles were published, each of them over 500 pages: *Études sur les Actes des Apôtres* and *Nouvelles Études sur les Actes des Apôtres*.[67] For Dupont, the literary contribution of Luke in the speeches was very great.[68] They are too brief to be literal reproductions. They betray literary devices

---

62. Soards, *Speeches*, 11, 143, 161.
63. Ibid., 15.
64. Ibid., 15–16, 182, 204.
65. Johnson, *Acts of the Apostles*, 53. Johnson is the author of the commentaries on both Luke and Acts in the Sacra Pagina series and has written extensively on Luke-Acts.
66. Johnson, *Septuagintal Midrash*, 8.
67. Published in 1967 and 1984, they were nos. 45 and 118 respectively in Lectio Divina.
68. Dupont, *Nouvelles Etudes*, 84, 11.

like interruptions. Yet Luke did make use of older traditions[69] (e.g., a Pais Christology[70]). In a similar way R. Pesch argued that we ought not to rule out a priori that Luke used traditional material. The alternative "really delivered speech" or "speech created by the author of Acts" was overdrawn and he pleaded for a more nuanced and differentiated picture.[71]

One of the boldest attempts to reconstruct a tradition behind all the speeches in Acts 2–17 and to disentangle it from Lucan redation is the 1975 work of K. Kliesch.[72] He strongly emphasises the role of tradition behind the speeches and seeks to reconstruct a tradition about God's activity in the history of Israel mainly from Stephen's speech with some material from Paul's PA speech.[73] He then goes in quest of what might have been the beginning and end of such a history, and, after examining Paul's speeches at Lystra and Athens, he obtains statements about God's action in Creation in Acts 17.24a and 25b. As a possible conclusion, only the experience of some new saving act of God can come into consideration and Kliesch believes that 13.34b,33a and 23 furnished just such a conclusion. This leads him on to the tradition about God's action in Jesus, and he extrapolates from the various speeches a brief set of Christological statements beginning with the miracles of Jesus and mentioning his death, resurrection, the appearances seen by witnesses, his exaltation and his destiny to be Judge at the End.[74] These two parts, the account of God's activity from Creation to the fulfilment of His promise and the affirmations about Jesus, belong together in what Kliesch calls the Credo. The former did not exist by itself, but was drawn up as a result of the experience of what God had done in Jesus. Kliesch also looks at the use of the OT in the speeches and seeks again to disentangle pre-Lucan material from Lucan. Then Kliesch devotes a chapter to looking at where Luke has redacted the speeches in Acts 2–17. Finally, he considers the Credo which he has constructed, as a key to understanding the speeches. Luke is a master of composition. He is true to tradition and yet actualises it. The speeches broaden, interpret and ground statements of the Credo through Scripture. Luke aimed to illuminate events by shaping the confession into speeches. Kliesch comments that the speeches are Lucan and yet scarcely a sentence has been formed without a traditional background. Each speech has its own

---

69. Ibid., 111.
70. Ibid., 90.
71. *Apg.* 1.42–45.
72. Kliesch, *Heilsgeschichtliche Credo*.
73. Ibid., 45–47, where Kliesch prints his reconstruction.
74. Ibid., 102, where Kliesch prints his reconstruction.

profile and yet deals with the activity of God as confessed in the Credo without needing to transcribe the whole of it in every speech in the same form.

Luke shows what the content of preaching was, is and should be—God's word on the basis of the Credo and, as such, the announcement of God's activity in history. Christianity has to remember its historical origins in order not to lose its bearings and, therefore, become incomprehensible in changing times. Although the speeches are a literary creation, yet Luke is dependent, both formally and contentwise, on pre-given tradition to a far greater extent than has been generally accepted.

Part of G.N. Stanton's study, *Jesus of Nazareth in New Testament Preaching* (1974) was devoted to an examination of pre-Lucan traditions about Jesus in the speeches in Acts, with particular reference to Peter's address to Cornelius and his household. Stanton came to the conclusion that pre-Lucan material lay at the heart of Peter's speech. "In Acts 10.36–39 we have the 'fossils' of three passages [Psa. 107.20; Isaiah 52.7 and 61.1] which may have been linked together at a very early period."[75] He also thinks that Psalm 107.19–20 is alluded to in Acts 13.26.[76]

In 1981, the new edition of Acts in the NTD series by J. Roloff appeared. While agreeing that the speeches of Acts are not "vessels" for the preservation of traditions but narrative instruments to illustrate situations, Roloff believes that different traditions have been preserved in individual statements and formulations within the speeches. Luke has attempted in many places to bring the traditional basic scheme into harmony with his own theological conception.[77]

G. Lüdemann in his *Early Christianity according to the Traditions in Acts. A Commentary*, assumes that the speeches come from the pen of Luke, but this does not exclude the possibility that the scheme of the speeches (which Lüdemann does not usually discuss) and individual elements in them derive from traditions.[78]

C. K. Barrett reviewed the issue of the speeches in Luke after his exegesis of Peter's Pentecost speech. He came to the conclusion that Luke in composing this speech and others made use of some traditional material. Luke wrote the whole of the speeches, but use of sources or traditions was not thereby excluded. "It can fairly be said that nothing [in the speeches] requires a post-Pauline or Johannine date; but this in no way proves that

---

75. *Jesus of Nazareth*, 77.
76. Ibid., 83.
77. *Apg.* 49–51.
78. *Early Christianity*, 47–48.

Christians were not still preaching in this manner at the time when Acts was written."[79]

In the introduction to his commentary on Acts, J. A. Fitzmyer did not offer a firm conclusion. On the one hand he wrote "Neither the narratives nor the speeches can be regarded as mere *creatio ex nihilo* on Luke's part," while he also asserted that the speeches are "ultimately Lucan compositions."[80]

J.D.G. Dunn, in the second volume of his *Christianity in the Making*, entitled *Beginning from Jerusalem* (2009), examined the sources for someone wishing to write a history of Christianity's beginnings. In this chapter he devoted a section to the speeches in Acts. He made the following points. The style of the speeches is thoroughly Lucan. There is a combination of brevity and roundedness, and he likened the speeches to cameos, finely crafted miniatures. He noted their individuality and distinctiveness of material, which suggested that Luke had been able to draw on and incorporate tradition.[81] By tradition Dunn did not mean written sources, nor that some fixed or stable forms were still current in Luke's day. He pleaded for a recognition of the fact that Luke lived in an oral society[82] and that it was possible that Luke could have found older teachers and elders who could still recall the emphases and arguments of earlier days, even though the living tradition of the churches had left them behind.[83][84]

V

Overlapping some of the more recent discussions just discussed, a trend (from the late nineties into the twenty-first century), associated particularly with Daniel Marguerat, his colleagues and students at Lausanne and other scholars,[85] needs to be mentioned. Using the tools of narrative criticism especially, this approach focuses on the ways in which Paul was heard,

---

79. *Acts* 1.129–133, esp. 133.

80. *Acts,* 103–8, quotations from 102 and 103 resp.

81. 89.

82. See the first volume of Dunn's *Christianity in the Making*, entitled *Jesus Remembered*, 173–254, esp. 192—254, for his reflections on the traditioning process as oral tradition.

83. *Beginning*, 96–98.

84. The monograph by M. Cifrak, *Die Beziehing zwischen Jesus und Gott nach den Petrusreden der Apg.* assumes that Luke has used traditions and concentrates on the Christological issue mentioned in his title.

85. S. Butticaz, Claire Clivaz, J.-F. Landolt, Odile Flichy, together with A. Dettwiler (Geneva) and J. Schröter (Berlin).

Received, read, re-read, and reinterpreted after his death.[86] In different ways, particular authors select aspects of the apostle's persona[87] most amenable to their viewpoint and the needs of the community/ies for which they were writing.[88] It is a case of authors exploiting a potential within the Pauline traditions available to them.[89] It has been called "reception history."[90] This "reception" of the Pauline tradition is characterized by continuity and discontinuity, by coherence and displacement,[91] and not distortion or falsification or betrayal of Paul's original gospel, as represented by scholars such as e.g., Vielhauer, Käsemann and Marxsen.[92] Luke represents one such way of handling the Pauline tradition. His way can be characterized as "a narrative transformation of the Pauline legacy."[93] He was dependent on narrative recollections preserved by communities within the sphere of Paul's mission[94] and he may even have lived and worked within "a community of interpretation in which numerous texts from Israel's scriptures were read through the lens of the message of Jesus' death and resurrection."[95]

This approach draws a distinction between what Paul's own writings disclose to us and the biographical memories preserved in the congregations where Paul had worked or which had been founded by him. This is put sharply by maintaining that the canonical letters were not the sole means of

---

86. Moessner et al., *Paul*, xvi.

87. Thus, Marguerat, *First Christian Historian*, 74–75, suggests what he calls a documentary "pole" (Paul as writer of letters); a biographical one (Paul as missionary to the nations); and a doctoral pole (Paul as teacher of the church)—later there is the hagiographical pole (represented by the Acts of Paul). Flichy, *Figure*, 33, speaks of a canonical pole; a biographical pole; and a doctoral pole. Butticaz, "Has God Rejected," 152, cautions against compartmentalizing too sharply these modes of reception—they often overlap or interact with each other.

88. Marguerat, *First Christian Historian*, 75. Cf. Flichy, *Figure*, 13, 41, 44; Schröter, "Founder," 197.

89. Marguerat, "Paul after Paul," 82, cf. Schröter, "Founder," 206, 210, 217–18.

90. Moessner, *Heritage*, 320; cf. the title of the work edited by D. Marguerat, *Reception of Paulinism in Acts/Réception du Paulinisme dans les Actes des Apôtres* (2009).

91. Marguerat, "Paul after Paul," 89; Butticaz, "Has God Rejected," 155; Flichy, "The Paul of Luke," 33.

92. Butticaz, "Has God Rejected," 151, puts it in this way: "It is no longer a question of the 'distortion' or 'falsification' of the Pauline tradition, but of its 'legacy' and 'creative treatment.'" Cf. Flichy, "The Paul of Luke," 34; and Moessner, *Heritage*, 321.

93. Butticaz, "Has God Rejected," 157; Flichy, "The Paul of Luke," 33, also speaks of Luke's decision to render the Pauline tradition into narrative form; Schröter, "Founder," 199.

94. Butticaz, "Has God Rejected," 152.

95. Hayes, "Paulinism," 44. Cf. the views of B. Reicke, quoted by Moessner, *Paul and the Heritage of Israel*, 321 n.1.

preserving the memory of the apostle. They did not necessarily constitute the norm of the Pauline tradition.⁹⁶

Narrative criticism as its name suggests deals with narrative, so what about the speeches? In general terms, Marguerat sees the speeches in Acts as a way Luke has of lifting God's incognito (God hides Himself in history) and so move people from misunderstanding to knowledge, to replace the ἄγνοια from which soteriological lack both Jews and pagans suffer (Jewish errors concerning messiahship and the lack of success in the Hellenistic religious quest, respectively) with the word of salvation for all people. Through the words of His messengers, the hidden God is revealed. There is an alternation of narrative (which describes history) and speech (which deciphers the action of God within history). The speeches of God's witnesses "decode the signs of the eschatological work of God in the chaos of history."⁹⁷ Moessner describes the speeches as "medial links" that carry the continuity of the narrative and motivate the plot to its intended purpose.⁹⁸

A drawback is the fact that we do not possess an example of Paul's preaching to a congregation in a Synagogue—a precursor text—which might in the PA speech be in the process of being appropriated and reapplied in a different situation.

In spite of many new insights and stimulating interpretations, one is left with an uneasy feeling that some practitioners of narrative criticism are in danger of presenting us with a model of readers poring over a written manuscript and able to go back and consult previous passages and so on. Thus, for example, Marguerat himself constantly refers to *the reader* or *readers*. Thus, in a chapter headed "The Unity of Luke-Acts: the Task of Reading," he wrote that to discern the unity "*is devolved as a task to the reader who must construct this unity in the course of reading.*"⁹⁹ Odile Flichy says "The act of reading the text is a dynamic act requiring the participation of the reader in elaborating the meaning of the text, as a response to the indication of interpretation set down by the narrator in his narrative."¹⁰⁰ Now it is absolutely clear that by readers Marguerat and Odile Flichy mean those in Luke's own day, not the modern reader. But what if the majority of Christians of Luke's day would not have possessed manuscripts and only *heard* a writing like LA

---

96. Marguerat, "Paul after Paul," 75; Flichy, *Figure*, 320.

97. Marguerat, *First Christian Historian*, 103; cf. the remark of Flichy, *Figure*, 47–48, who says that the reader should respond to clues which the narrator sets down in his narrative and which are to lead the readers to decode the meaning of history told to them, a remark which could apply inter alia to the speeches.

98. Moessner, "Luke's 'Witness of Witnesses,'" 128.

99. Marguerat, *First Christian Historian*, 45 (italics original).

100. Flichy, *Figure*, 47–48.

and possibly only heard portions (however lengthy[101] compared to modern lectionary practice) periodically on the occasions of formal assembly for worship or informal meetings for prayer and fellowship,[102] at the house of a more wealthy fellow Christian? Gamble has maintained that "We must assume, then, that the vast majority of Christians in the early centuries of the church were illiterate, not because they were unique but because in this respect they were typical."[103] While illiteracy does not mean that Christians would be totally ignorant or unfamiliar with the contents of the Scriptures and some early Christian texts, it does mean that we should be very cautious about making assumptions based on modern reading and study habits and reading these back into antiquity. Gamble makes the general comment on the period of the Roman Empire, and he is including members of Christian congregations: "The capacity to read, the interest and leisure to do so, and the financial means to procure texts, belonged to the few."[104]

PAUL'S SPEECH AT PISIDIAN ANTIOCH

While commentaries obviously deal with this speech in Acts 13, there have been seven monographs devoted to it in the last fifty years and numerous articles dealing with specific points within the speech, while several works have discussed it as part of a treatment devoted to a specific theme like the use of the OT in Acts or Luke's use of the Davidic messiah theme.

In his work on *Jewish Hermeneutics in the Synoptic Gospels and Acts* (1953), J.W. Doeve touched on the PA speech of Paul in Acts 13.17–41. Doeve believed that the promise of v. 23 was 2 Sam 7.6–16, which "forms the background of the speaker's entire argument so far." The transition from 2 Sam 7 to Psalm 2 at 13.33 was easy, since 2 Sam 7.14a had said that David's seed would be the son of Yahweh. For the speaker, Psalm 2.7 is a reference to the resurrection. Doeve believes that the next OT passage quoted at 13.34, namely Isaiah 55.3, only speaks of resurrection if one connects it with Psalm 16.10 which in fact follows it in the speech at v. 35. The hasdhe of Isaiah 55.3, here rendered as τὰ ὅσια (elsewhere by ἔλεος), is interpreted via hasidka of Psalm 16.10 as resurrection. "In these two striking instances where the root hsd appears, the meaning of the one is determined by the other"[105] (on

---

101. See Justin Martyr's comment in 1 Apology 67.
102. See Delling, *Worship*, 104–27, for a review of passages germane to the latter possibility.
103. Gamble, *Books*, 6.
104. Ibid., 39.
105. Doeve, *Jewish Hermeneutics*, 174.

the principle that one word in a passage may be explained by its occurrence in another passage).[106] According to Doeve, the argument of Acts 13 is the work of a schooled rabbi: "If the author of Acts composed the discourse in chapter 13 himself, then he must have had an excellent command of hermeneutics as practiced in rabbinic Judaism."[107]

E. Lövestam published *Son and Saviour: A Study of Acts, 13.32–37* (1961). Lövestam assumes from the start that the speech is a genuine one by Paul. The bulk of the book is primarily devoted to the three scriptural quotations in 13.33–35: Ps. 2.7 in v. 33 (8–47); Isa. 55.3 in v. 34 (48–80); and Ps. 16.10 in v. 35 (81–83).[108]

Lövestam points to the fact that the promise of everlasting power for the Davidic house was closely connected with the idea of divine sonship, as shown in Pss. 2 and 89 and 2 Sam. 7.1–16. The use of Ps. 2.7 constitutes the scriptural evidence that God has fulfilled the promise to David by raising Jesus from the dead and exalting him as Son to universal sovereignty.

According to Isa. 55.3, God renews the Davidic covenant (so prominent in the OT and Judaism) with His people. But how can Isa. 55.3 be used here to support the idea that God raised Jesus from the dead? Part of that covenant with David was the promise of everlasting rule and dominion: Lövestam takes τὰ ὅσια to mean the blessings and gifts from God within the framework of the Davidic covenant, specifically everlasting dominion. By the resurrection Jesus has been installed in that everlasting dominion, and that benefits Israel (hence the ὑμῖν in v. 34; cf. v. 23 ἡμῖν). God's promise was reliable (τὰ πιστά).

Since David died (v. 36), Ps. 16.10 cannot apply to him (cf. 2.29). The one whom God raised, however, saw no corruption (cf. v. 34a).

Lövestam's conclusion is that the object of Paul's sermon is the announcement and presentation of the complete salvation in Jesus the messiah.[109] He maintains that the whole wealth of the NT message of salvation is implied: the forgiveness of sins and complete salvation, with freedom from death and all the powers of evil, and participation in the kingdom of God with the risen and exalted Jesus.[110]

The use of the OT in the PA speech, which dominated Lövestam's monograph, has continued to be a source of major interest for scholars.

---

106. Ibid., 67, discusses this when explaining examples of the scriptural exegesis of the early Tannaitic rabbis.
107. Ibid., 172.
108. *Son and Saviour*, 8–47, 48–80, and 81–83 resp.
109. Ibid., 84.
110. Ibid., 87.

As already mentioned, J. Dupont made the study of Acts a major part of his prolific scholarly activity over the years.[111] Of the large number of his essays on Acts gathered together and published in 1967 as *Études sur les Actes des Apôtres*, two especially have considerable bearing on the PA speech, namely "L'Interpretation des Psaumes dans les Actes des Apôtres"[112] and "ΤΑ ΟΣΙΑ ΔΑΥΙΔ ΤΑ ΠΙΣΤΑ (Actes 13, 34 = Isaie 55, 3),"[113] and, to a lesser extent, "Utilisation apologetique de l'ancien testament dans les discours des Actes."[114]

The "promise" of v. 32 can only be the "promise" mentioned in vv. 22–23, i.e., Nathan's oracle to David. God has fulfilled His promise that a descendant of David should be His Son—Ps. 2.7 quoted in v. 33. The resurrection of Jesus is his royal investiture. As to the use of Ps. 16.10 in v. 35, Dupont points to the fact that the argument in vv. 34–37 is particularly interested in "corruption" from Ps. 16. Verse 36 sets out the negative consideration—the psalm does not apply to David, and v. 37 gives the positive side—Jesus whom God raised is the real object of the messianic promise.

Dupont believed that what we witness in the use of the psalms in chapter 13 and elsewhere in Acts is, above all, a Christological exegesis: "Christians sought Christ above all in the Psalms,"[115] which gave access to a deep understanding of the Easter mystery.

As to Isa. 55.3 quoted in 13.34, Dupont argues for "the blessings which one can expect from God" as the meaning of τὰ ὅσια. These have become available through the resurrection of Jesus, and the hearers themselves can benefit (hence the phrase "I will give to you"). The blessings are the forgiveness of sins, justification, holiness and eternal life.

J. W. Bowker wrote an article "Speeches in Acts: A Study in Proem and Yelammedenu[116] Form."[117] Tentatively,[118] Bowker suggested that Acts 13.16–41 was a synagogue sermon based on the reading from the Pentateuch ("seder")—Deut. 4.25–46, with the summary of the exodus, wilderness and conquest seeming to rest on this passage; the reading from the Prophets ("haftarah")—2 Sam. 7.6–16; and a text ("proem" = introductory text)—1

---

111. He was responsible for Acts in the Jerusalem Bible and published *The Sources of Acts: The Present Position* (1964).

112. *Études*, 283–307.

113. Ibid., 337–59.

114. Ibid., 245–82.

115. Ibid., 306

116. Yelammendenu-rabbenu = let our rabbi teach us.

117. *NTS* 14 (1967–68) 96–111.

118. *Speeches*, 103—"a reasonable guess."

Sam. 13.14 (quoted in the Targum form "The Lord has sought him, a man doing His wills"). Bowker believed that vv. 23–41 are the homily preached. Interpretation is made by quoting a series of other texts of scripture which carry the theme forward, viz. Ps. 2.7; Isa. 55.3; and Ps. 16.10. The theme is that Jesus is the meaning of the various texts of scripture.

D. Goldsmith contributed a short article on "Acts 13.33–37: A Pesher on II Samuel 7."[119] As the title suggests, Goldsmith regarded the OT quotations in vv. 33–37 as a pesher on 2 Sam. 7. They had been carefully chosen to show the Jews how God fulfilled His promise to David in 2 Sam. 7, by raising Jesus from the dead.

Also in 1968, T. Holtz published his investigations of the OT quotations in LA: *Untersuchungen über die alttestamentliche Zitate bei Lukas*. On the Acts 13 speech, Holtz believed that Luke worked over a presentation of the history of salvation which existed before him. He views 1 Sam. 13.14 as the basis of 13.22, embellished with other phrases from the OT—Isa. 11.1, 10; Ps. 89.21 and Isa. 44.28. As to vv. 33–35, Holtz is of the opinion that Luke has taken over the Isa. 55.3 passage—he would not himself have rendered Isaiah 55.3 so freely nor would he have suppressed the covenant idea. Isaiah 55.3 does not refer to the resurrection, whereas Pss 2.7 and 16.10 do. Holtz conjectures a collection which began with the quotation in 13.22, and followed by the rendering of Isa. 55.3 to prove the legitimacy of the application of a promise for David to the heir of his rule, the messiah, who will not see corruption (Psa. 16.10). He further suggests that Luke inserted Ps. 2.7 between 1 Sam. 13.14 and Isa. 55.3 or changed a quotation from 2 Sam. 7.12–14 with that of Ps. 2.7. This collection was a late Jewish messianic testimonium, introduced by a brief historical retrospect.

The following year (1969), in the Matthew Black *Festschrift*, E.E. Ellis contributed an essay entitled "Midrash, Targum and New Testament Quotations."[120] Ellis briefly refers to the PA speech. Second Samuel 7.6–16 is probably the "haphtarah text." Its application to Jesus is confirmed by other Scriptures, and by Jesus' Davidic descent and his resurrection. The early church not only appropriated 2 Sam. 7, but established its interpretation by means of midrash.[121] A year later (1970), Ellis continued his interest in this topic in a similar contribution to another Festschrift. He gave it the title "Midrashic Features in the Speeches of Acts."[122] He began by expressing support for the work of J.W. Doeve and J. Bowker on features of midrashic

---

119. *JBL* 87 (1968) 321–24.
120. *Midrash*, 61–69.
121. Ibid., 68.
122. *Melanges Bibliques*, 303–12

A Survey of Scholarship from Cadbury to the Present

exegesis in the Acts speeches. He pointed out that in the Qumran pesher the OT text-form often undergoes an interpretative alteration (often in the form of word-play), in order to apply it to the eschatological fulfillment in the present. He believes that the same thing has happened in the PA speech, and instances εὗρον and Δαυὶδ in the textually altered quotation at v. 22 which are repeated in the subsequent commentary and applied to Jesus, and also the use of ἐγείρειν/ἀνιστάναι in vv. 22, 30, 33 and 37. He then goes on to concentrate on the use of Ps. 118.22 in Acts 4.11, which he sees as drawn from a traditional midrash.

A Canadian scholar, M. Dumais, wrote a work on the PA speech. He conceived a project of examining this speech and Paul's speech at Athens with a view to learning lessons for how to adapt the preaching of the gospel to different cultural audiences. In the end, the treatment of the PA speech took up so much detail that he abandoned the original aim and published his treatment of the Acts 13 speech under the title *Le Langage de l'Evangelisation: l'Annonce missionaire en milieu juif (Actes 13, 16–41)* (1976).[123] Dumais maintained that the PA discourse is a homiletical midrash, of the pesher type, based on the promise to David in 2 Sam. 7. The résumé of Israel's past history (13.17–22) is an introduction to the midrash proper, being a commentary or paraphrastic reprise of 2 Sam. 7.6-9. Verse 22, which quotes 1 Sam. 13.13-14, a passage which itself alludes to 2 Sam. 7 and Ps. 89, is the "text." Then Dumais treats the scriptural quotations of vv. 32–37. Here we have a midrashic interpretation of 2 Sam. 7, the key term ἀνίστημι being reinterpreted as resurrection, by drawing in other scriptural quotations to illuminate it and draw out its hidden meaning. The first passage quoted is from Ps. 2.7 which had been messianically interpreted in Judaism. There is a link via υἱός between Ps. 2.7 and 2 Sam. 7, and this means that the promise of universal lordship promised to the descendant of David has been fulfilled through the resurrection of Jesus. The application of Ps. 16 to the messiah was something new. It is a case of the Easter event shedding new light on the text. The promise that God would "raise up" a descendant of David is assumed and interpreted in a richer way of resurrection. In the light of Ps. 16.10, the previously quoted Isa. 55.3 refers to resurrection. Blessings will flow from the resurrection of the descendant of David.

Now Dumais turns back to deal with vv. 23–31, about Jesus. He comments on the Lucan character of the verses dealing with the condemnation of Jesus and does not feel that the true Paul would have spoken the words

---

123. Dumais wrote after C. A. J. Pillai had completed his doctoral thesis on the Pisidian Antioch speech but before Pillai published his two works on the speech. Dumais had access to Pillai's thesis.

of v. 31 about the witness of the Galilean followers, which are attributed to him.

In the second part of the book, Dumais turns to "Hermeneutics" and is concerned with the whole issue of the language of missionary preaching as the church pursues its task in the world at any given period, and he engages with the ideas of Heidegger, Gadamer and Riccoeur.

M. Wilcox's article "Upon the Tree—Deut. 21.22-23 in the New Testament,"[124] argued for the existence of a midrashic treatment of Deut. 21.22-23 in NT times and that the three instances in Acts referring to the cross as a tree derive from this traditional material. Deut. 21.22-23 became another OT passage in which the death and burial of Jesus were regarded as portrayed and prefigured.

The papers at the Louvain Colloquium on Acts were published in 1979,[125] and two of its contributions are of interest to us, those by M. Rese and J. Schmitt. M. Rese wrote on "Die Funktion der alttestamentliche Zitate und Anspielungen in den Reden der Apostelgeschichte." After reviewing previous scholarly opinion, Rese looked at Acts 2.25-28 and then 13.47, which used Isa. 49.6 as a word of Jesus the Lord who takes Paul and Barnabas up into the task of being witnesses to the ends of the earth (cf. Acts 1.8). What was true of Jesus in Luke 2.32 is transferred to Paul and Barnabas (cf. Acts 26.16-18 for something similar: the use of OT allusions as a word of the risen Lord).[126] J. Schmitt entitled his essay "Kerygme pascal et lecture scripturaire dans l'instruction d'Antioche (Act. 13, 23-37)" (155-67). He regards vv. 32-37 as the remnants of a Jewish-Christian re-reading of ancient royal messianism. In the first Jewish-Christian generation, 2 Sam. 7.11-14 was one of the scripture readings at Easter. These verses from Acts 13 are a witness to "the unique tenacity of ancient royal messianism and its near disappearance."[127] Schmitt thinks that v. 33 is based on 2 Sam. 7.11-14, Ps. 2.7 being a variant of it. This verse gives the motive for the exaltation of Jesus to the status of Son of God (later, the exaltation was linked with Psalm 110.1). He further maintains that Isa. 55.3 was a key scriptural quotation for Jewish messianism (cf. Sir. 47.11, 22; 1 Macc. 2.57; 4Q PB 1/2.4); here Luke omitted the reference to "eternal covenant" and took God's "favours" to David in the sense of the event of Easter. Psalm 16.10 spoke of the definitive incorruption of Jesus. There is thus a triple reference to the superiority of Jesus over David.

---

124. *JBL* 96 (1977) 85-99.
125. Kremer, *Les Actes des Apôtres*.
126. *Die Funktion*, 61-79.
127. *Kerygme pascal*, 107.

In successive years, the Canadian scholar C.A.J. Pillai produced two volumes on the PA speech: *Early Missionary Preaching: a study of Luke's report in Acts13* (1979), followed by *Apostolic Interpretation of History: a Commentary on Acts 13.16–41* (1980).[128] It is not unfair to say that a major concern of Pillai is to reject the view that the speech is a purely Lucan composition and to argue for the view that the speech is authentically Pauline, because Luke had access to units of oral tradition, probably used in Paul's preaching (with vv. 23 and 32 being Luke's editorial activity). What we are given is not a stenographic record of all that Paul said on this occasion, but a summary of the main themes of Paul's preaching.

In 1980, a German scholar, M.F-J. Buss, devoted a monograph to the speech: *Die Missionspredigt des Apostels Paulus im pisidischen Antiochen: Analyse von Apg. 13, 16–41 im Hinblick auf die literarische und thematische Einheit der Paulusrede.*[129] Buss opts for a fivefold division of the speech: vv. 16a–23; 24–26; 27–31; 32–37; 38–41, and sees its overall aim as demonstrating that the event of Jesus belongs to the history of Israel, which is guided by God's faithfulness to His promise. Verse 23 has central significance, and it is linked to vv. 26 and 32–33. Key concepts in the speech are promise, saviour and raise up. Unlike Dumais and others, Buss does not see 2 Sam. 7 as underlying this speech:[130] for example, neither saviour nor salvation occur in 2 Sam. 7, but they are key ideas in the speech.

Subsequent chapters exegete the speech according to the fivefold division just mentioned. Buss points out that all negative aspects of Israel's history are omitted in vv. 16a–23. The whole of the OT is crystalized in the one promise, which is the message of the resurrection of the messiah. Verse 26 contains both the heavenly origin and the universal direction of the message of salvation (it is "sent" and it is addressed to God-Fearers). The choice and presentation of scenes from the Passion Story are determined by the preaching situation, with Luke being concerned to set Jesus' Passion in relation to Scripture. The twelve apostles are a guarantee of continuity between the time of Jesus and the post-Easter time.

The longest chapter in the work is devoted to vv. 32–37, the resurrection of Jesus in the witness of the OT. The content of God's promise which

---

128. They both grew out of Pillai's doctoral thesis, which had actually been consulted and referred-to by Dumais. Of these two works, *Apostolic Interpretation of History* was not available to me despite efforts to obtain access to it via Inter-Library Loan.

129. While Buss knew of Dumais' work, he does not refer to Pillai's.

130. About the only other scholar not to accept that 2 Sam. 7 is at the basis of the speech is Doble, *Paradox*, 222, who threw out the suggestion, without pursuing it, that the whole PA sermon might be woven around its unexpressed text, Hab. 2.4 (he refers the reader to his PhD thesis accepted by Leeds University in 1992).

God has fulfilled is the resurrection. The aim of the three scriptural quotations is not to offer scriptural proof of the resurrection, but that Scripture linked fulfilment of the promise with resurrection. Buss seeks to offer a coherent explanation for the sequence of the OT quotations as they occur in vv. 33b–35. The "today" of Ps. 2.7 in v. 33b is the day of Jesus' resurrection, his birth to eternal life as Son of God, and, therefore, his entry into his eternal and universal role as saviour. Through resurrection he did not see corruption (v. 34a—the language anticipates the use of Ps. 16.10 in v. 35), and his resurrection has soteriological consequences, for God's mercies shown to David are the eternal blessings of salvation and these are now being offered to all (Isa. 55.3 used in v. 34b). Finally, in v. 35, Ps. 16.10 is quoted to show why salvation is now being offered—God's Holy One, Jesus, did not see corruption but was raised, and, therefore, he is the one who is permanently alive and immortal and can bestow the "blessings promised to David" on all.

In his exegesis of vv. 38–41, Buss denies the views of those who see here a two stage justification: forgiveness cannot be worked through the law of Moses, but comes through Jesus alone and opens the way to eternal life.

In a final chapter, Buss looks at what he considers the leading theological themes of vv. 16–41: the Biblical view of history led by God controls the thought. God initiated the history of Israel with a view to salvation of all people. Salvation in Jesus and the history of Israel are connected. Buss looks at Luke's understanding of the place of the cross in God's saving plan and the schema of promise and fulfilment as these themes emerge in the speech.

The American scholar, G.A. Kennedy, in his *New Testament Interpretation through Rhetorical Criticism* (1984), claimed that the rules of classical rhetoric ought to be applied to the speeches of Acts. As regards the PA speech, he suggested that 13.16b was the proem (introduction); vv. 17–25, the narratio (narrative); v. 26, the propositio (proposition); vv. 27–37, the probatio (proof); and vv. 38–39 [sic—presumably, vv. 38–41 was intended], the peroratio (final exhortation).[131] Overall, he classified the PA speech as an example of epeideictic rhetoric, i.e., a speech intended to induce belief. He was followed in this analysis of the structure by B. Witherington in his commentary on Acts (1998), except that Witherington classified the speech as deliberative rhetoric, i.e., it seeks to persuade to some action.[132]

---

131. For a similar five-fold division applied to a Pauline letter, see Betz, *Galatians*, 16—23 (Betz actually adds a sixth category—Epistolary Postscript [Conclusio] to cover 6.11–18).

132. Witherington, *Acts*, 407.

In the Heinrich Greeven Festschrift (1986),[133] C.K. Barrett dealt with "OT History according to Stephen and Paul."[134] (57-69). Barrett notes the surprising omission of any reference to Moses and the law in the PA speech, an omission which he attributes to the fact that Luke had fully treated this theme in chapter 7. He suggests that the speech of Acts 13 "contains what may be called Luke's Jewish understanding of the OT—for it is Jewish, with the one additional conviction that Jesus of Nazareth was the promised Messiah." (66-67). The survey of Israel's history stops with David because "the essential factors have all been disclosed: gracious election, deliverance, organized society, and a human king whose reign puts into effect the reign of God" (67). David foreshadowed and foretold the true king and the resurrection established his identity—Jesus in whom the whole story finds its fulfilment. The Jews must either accept or deny the destiny to which their history points (67).

In 1988, J. Killgallen wrote an article on "Acts 13.38-39: Culmination of Paul's Speech in Pisidia."[135] He also maintained that Jesus' resurrection was the fulfillment of the promise made to the fathers and the means by which God intended to fulfil His promise of providing a successor for David. The resurrection means that salvation can now reach the Pisidian Antiochenes (the ὑμῖν of v. 34[136]). God has prepared Jesus by resurrection and incorruptibility to be a saviour to Israel of every time and place. In vv. 38-39, the τὰ ὅσια Δαυὶδ become the offer of forgiveness and justification. The Antiochenes are the beneficiaries of what God planned, promised, and carried out. They need to respond in faith to the God who is offering this forgiveness and justification through Jesus.[137] Thus, the Acts 13 speech sets forth the message of salvation offered to the Diaspora Jews.

In 1990, R.C. Tannehill published *The Acts of the Apostles*, the second of his two volume *The Narrative Unity of Luke-Acts: A Literary Interpretation*.[138] Tannehill aimed to take advantage of the development of narrative criticism and its borrowing from non-biblical literary criticism, and apply this to a study of LA as a unified work. He sees the theme of God's purpose as unifying the narrative. Themes will be developed, dropped, then

---

133. Schrage, *Studien*.

134. *Old Testament History*, 57-69.

135. *Bib* 69 (1988) 480-506. Killgallen was also the author of a monograph, *The Stephen Speech*.

136. Kilgallen, "Culmination," 483, sees the καταγέλλεται of v. 38 as responding to the request by the synagogue leaders for a λόγος παρακλήσεως at v. 15.

137. Ibid. 482, suggests that the summons to remain in God's grace at v. 43 fits vv. 38-39 rather than the earlier announcements.

138. Volume 1, *The Gospel according to Luke*, had appeared in 1986.

presented again. Internal connections lead to a considerable movement back and forward in LA. Tannehill points out that the grand vision of salvation for all peoples through Jesus announced in Luke 2.32 and 3.6 appears to lead to disappointment, with resistance and rejection especially by the Jews being major factors in the unfolding story, and this is emphasized by Paul's remarks in the final scene in Acts. LA shows itself keenly aware of the problem, without being able to resolve it.

Tannehill believes that Paul's PA sermon has central significance for understanding Paul's work in Acts. The review of Israel's history, with its stress on God's election of Israel and David, affirms a community of relationship between the speaker and the audience. The speech announces the fulfilment of God's promise to the Jewish people to bring them salvation. Paul identifies the promised Davidic messiah with Jesus who has been installed as messiah through the resurrection. Because the messiah has been enthroned by resurrection, he is no longer threatened by corruption and his reign will have no end. The effects of what God has done in Jesus are, however, limited by rejection. While the salvation of the Gentiles is shown to be firmly rooted in Scripture (Isa. 49.6), and is certainly not a "second choice" on the part of God, we are not allowed to forget Jewish rejection (13.50).

Tannehill's work makes a useful contribution by its challenge to set the PA speech in its overall setting in the whole of Acts.

M.L. Strauss devoted a detailed monograph to *The Davidic Messiah in Luke-Acts: The Promise and its Fulfillment in Lukan Christology* (1995), during which he examined Paul's PA speech (148–80).[139] The promises to David in 2 Sam. 7 form the conceptual framework of the sermon (150, 153), with two key word groups (ἐπαγγελία and ἐγείρειν/ἀνιστάναι being significant). In a first climax (v. 23), Jesus' arrival is announced to be the culmination of God's choice of, and providential care for, Israel. Jesus' crucifixion is the God-ordained opposition to the Davidic messiah predicted beforehand in scripture. The second climax is vv. 32–33. The quotation of Ps. 2.7 both confirms Jesus as God's Son to be the messiah and introduces the resurrection argument which follows (The "Today" is the day of Jesus' resurrection). Strauss argues that it is inconceivable that the author of Isa. 55.3 could affirm the continuing reliability of the Davidic covenant without the renewal of the Davidic throne. In the Acts 13 sermon, verse 34 proclaims the reliable and enduring nature of the promises to David. Through David's heir, all of God's people receive the blessings of salvation which the messiah and saviour of Israel brings. The use of Ps. 16.10 forges a relation between resurrection to incorruption and the eternal nature of the Davidic

---

139. Strauss, *Davidic Messiah*, 148–80.

covenant. Jesus' resurrection proves that God has fulfilled the promise to David of an eternal reign.

In the volume *Witness to the Gospel: The Theology of Acts* (1998),[140] G.W. Hansen contributed an essay entitled "The Preaching and Defence of Paul." He devoted a few pages to the PA speech.[141] After noting the frequent references to the word (of God) in chapter 13, which fits in with a Lucan emphasis on the productive power of the word of God as preached by Jesus and his witnesses, Hansen stressed the centrality of the resurrection in the speech. It is set forth as the climax of the story of God's acts in history; as the fulfilment of the promise to David (2 Sam. 7); as the basis for the offer of forgiveness and justification; and it is "the amazing work" of God mentioned in the Hab. quotation at v. 41.[142]

J. Pichler, *Paulusrezeption in der Apostelgeschichte: Untersuchung zur Rede im pisidischen Antiochen* (1997) investigates the PA speech and then goes on to consider how Luke has portrayed Paul as a means of answering certain problems in the post-apostolic period. After pointing out the similarities between the preaching of Peter and Paul, which, by demonstrating a church consensus (Paul's positions are legitimized by Peter), can give assurance to his readers in a time of uncertainty, Pichler devotes three longish chapters to an analysis of the structure, of the contents of the PA speech and then an exegesis of the speech and its sequel. Then he examines the emphases in the teaching on salvation of Paul, Luke and the Pastorals, before turning his attention to the "Paulinism" of Acts. Pichler believes that Luke had already sought to anchor the tendencies of the Pauline gospel in his own Gospel (Luke 7.35; 16.15; 18.9–14) and thus to demonstrate that Paul was in agreement with Jesus. The Lucan church recognises Paul's interpretation as the norm. Paul becomes a representative as it were of the Lucan church in its conflicts with Gentile society, while the charges which are made against Paul from the Jewish side are also part of the reality which Luke's church faces. The Lucan Paul is "an integration figure," helping to show Gentile Christians how they must be true to the Jewish heritage of the church.

J. Jeska's monograph, *Die Geschichte Israels in der Sicht des Lukas: Apg 7, 2b–53 und 13, 17–25 im Kontext antik-judischer Summarien der Geschichte Israels* (2001) has filled a gap in the secondary literature on the PA speech. Prior to him there had not been a really exhaustive study of summaries of Israel's history in the OT and early Jewish literature. After his introductory two chapters, Jeska looks at a total of 27 summaries of Israel's history. He

---

140. In Marhsall and Peterson, *Witness to the Gospel*.
141. Hansen, "Preaching and Defence of Paul," 297–306, out of 295–324.
142. Ibid., 306, in agreement with Pillai, *Apostolic Interpretation*, 71–73.

comes to the conclusion that these summaries cannot be classified as a *Gattung*, but they form a structural element in addresses, prayers, hymns/songs, accounts of visions and prophetic/divine speech.¹⁴³ The choice of material is determined by the context, and this material is applied ("actualized") to the present situation of the writer. Jeska maintains that none of these summaries is without a *Tendenz*.¹⁴⁴ Passing over what Jeska says about the speech of Stephen, we pick up his comments on the PA speech. He believes that the summary of Israel's history grounds the beginning of the Christian mission in the Synagogue and among the Jews.¹⁴⁵ The summary stresses God's action in favour of His people, with the sending of Jesus being an integral part of the history of Israel and indeed its climax. While the particularity of the message of salvation is stressed (it is for Israel), there is a hint of universalism, and Jeska takes the ἔργον of the Habbakuk quotation to indicate not only the message of justification by faith in Jesus but also the Gentile mission.¹⁴⁶

As far as Jeska is concerned, Luke is the author of this summary of Israel's history. No prior summary could be said to have acted as a literary source for Luke, who has reached back into the historical narratives of the LXX to formulate his own summary. Indeed, Luke conceived and shaped the summaries of Israel's history both in Acts 7 and 13 for their present function within their nearer and farther contexts. The different choice of material in Acts 7 and 13 shows to what extent Biblical texts can be reproduced in an altered way in summaries of Israel's history.¹⁴⁷

The last treatment known to me specifically on the PA Speech is that by the Chinese scholar, Wenxi Zhang, *Paul among Jews. A Study of the Meaning and Significance of Paul's Inaugural Sermon in the Synagague of Antioch in Pisidia (Acts13.16-41) for His Missionary Work among the Jews* (2011). The title is perhaps a little misleading as, after a very brief review of some recent treatments of the speech, the next two chapters deal with what Zhang calls Jesus' inaugural sermon in the Nazareth Synagogue and Peter's inaugural sermon on the day of Pentecost.¹⁴⁸ Chapter four deals with the PA speech (110-51).¹⁴⁹ Zhang compares these two "inaugural speeches" with Paul's inaugural speech at PA. In all three speeches Luke gives a sample of how

---

143. Jeska, *Geschichte*, 21-22.
144. Ibid., 44-86, 94, 100, 115, 126.
145. Ibid., 243, 246.
146. Ibid., 233, 237, 239, 242, 246.
147. Ibid., 253, 269-71.
148. *Paul's Inaugural Sermon*, 34-109, i.e., more than half the book.
149. Ibid., 110-51

Jesus, Peter and Paul preached to the people of Israel. Zhang is concerned to argue that Luke presents Paul as much a preacher to Israel as to Gentiles[150]

How narrative criticism handles the PA speech is probably best seen in the work of Odile Flichy, in whose *La Figure de Paul dans les Actes des Apôtres* (2008) two chapters are devoted to discussing Acts 13–14.[151] Noting that there is an inclusion between the beginning of the first missionary journey of Paul and Barnabas (13.2) and its conclusion (14.26) via the concept of the work (ἔργον) to which God through the Spirit had called and appointed them,[152] she sees elements of the story which have proleptic significance—the opening of the door of faith to Gentiles as seen in the conversion of the Roman pro-consul, Sergius Paulus, and the proclamation made to the pagan crowd at Lystra, while nonetheless the mission among the Jews at PA is the centre of this missionary journey.[153] She sees typological nuances present in the speech in "exalted" (ὕψωσεν, v. 17), "raised up" (ἤγειρεν, v. 22) and in the David-Jesus typology, and believes that the concentration on the rejection and death of Jesus in vv. 27–29 is due to the need to defend the assertion that Jesus is the Messiah-Saviour although he ended up on a cross.[154] In the events surrounding the cross the Scriptures have been fulfilled, while God has confirmed the identity of Jesus in the resurrection and also, thereby, fulfilled the promise made to their ancestors.[155] While the offer of forgiveness and justification is, within the framework of the discourse an offer to Jewish hearers, for the reader this has undeniable universal significance, extending beyond the PA synagogue.[156] In the events on the next sabbath, Scripture shows that the turning to the Gentiles is faithful to the traditions of Israel and is required by obedience to the will and plan of God.[157]

Luke insists on *both* the links between the new stage of Christian preaching and what has gone before (the Davidic typology as a means of reading Israel's history and the Scriptural roots of the entire argument) *and* the legitimacy of the offer of God's reconciliation made to all people (the

---

150. Ibid., 152–90.

151. Flichy, *Figure*, 167–221. Schröter, "Founder," 217, says that Luke, through the speeches at PA and Athens in Acts 13 and 17, stresses that certain aspects of Paul's theology are fundamental, and that for Luke Paul's teaching is absolutely important.

152. Flichy, *Figure*, 174

153. Ibid., 174, 176–80, 224.

154. Ibid., 198.

155. Ibid., 199, 201, 206.

156. Ibid., 210.

157. Ibid., 217–18.

mission to the pagan world was written into the vocation of Israel from the start).[158]

SUMMARY

Our survey has revealed how in the last sixty years the Speeches in Acts generally have been the focus of a good deal of scholarly attention and research, and the same holds good of the PA speech in particular. The latter has been treated in monographs together with articles both long and short on various aspects of the speech, while there have been references to it within general treatments of the speeches, Lucan theology or early Christianity. However, until recently, there had been no monograph on the PA speech in English since the works of Pillai which were published in America in 1979 and 1980 and which are now virtually unobtainable, and even Zhang's treatment of the PA speech published in 2011 is not all that detailed and passes over a number of issues which the speech raises.

While that might seem sufficient justification for a new treatment of the PA speech, our survey has shown that there is a wide range of opinion on whether Luke is reproducing the gist of what Paul preached in the PA synagogue or whether he has composed entirely himself or whether he has used some traditional material in composing the speech. This applies to all the sections of the speech: the review of Israel's history (13.17–22); the reference to the ministry of John the Baptist (vv. 23–25); the so-called kerygmatic section on Jesus (vv. 26–31); the use of the OT passages in connection with Jesus' resurrection (vv. 32–37); and the final appeal and warning (vv. 38–41). A particular facet of this discussion is, of course, whether in this speech we hear the genuine voice of the apostle Paul or do we have here a Lucan Paul speaking? New voices are now heard which break the mould of "genuine Paul versus Lucan Paul," and speak in terms of a reception of Pauline tradition which entails both continuity and discontinuity, as the tradition is reinterpreted for a new generation.

A specific issue is the centrality of the resurrection in the speech, and how, if at all, does this emphasis fit in with Paul's emphasis on the cross? Is the latter implied in the reference to the cross as the "tree"?

By far the majority of scholars believe that a key point of reference of the speech is the famous divine promise conveyed to King David via the prophet Nathan as recorded in 2 Sam. 7.1–16. Often the term midrash or pesher is used, though these seem at times to be used in a somewhat loose fashion, almost to the extent that they lose their cutting edge. Some scholars

---

158. Ibid., 221.

believe that Luke has given us the gist of a sermon actually preached on this passage in the synagogue and which reflects Jewish modes of interpretation, while others believe that the speech reflects classical rhetorical models.

The review has shown that "promise" (ἐπαγγελία) and "to raise up" (both the two Greek verbs ἐγείρειν/ἀνιστάναι being employed) are key terms, and the discussion about the OT quotations in vv. 33–35 has raised the question of the precise function of the quotation from Isaiah 55.3 in its present position.

In what follows, as we seek to let the text yield up its riches, we propose to use various approaches, believing that such methods are complementary, rather than contradictory. In this way we hope to be able to make a modest contribution to understanding the importance of this speech both in its own right and in the setting of the book of Acts itself, and of the whole work, LA.

Chapter 2

Setting the Context of the Speech

THE STORY OF PAUL'S FIRST MISSIONARY JOURNEY (ACTS 13-14)

At Acts 13.1, Luke resumes the story of the church at Antioch. Earlier, at 11.19-26, he had described its founding by members of the Hellenist group and its initial phase, helped and guided by Barnabas and Paul, together with a brief account of the generosity of these new Christians towards their fellow Christians in Jerusalem when they heard about an impending famine from the lips of a prophet called Agabus (11.27-30). After reporting the persecution of the church at Jerusalem by Herod Agrippa I and his sudden death (12.1-24), Luke gets Barnabas and Paul back to Antioch from their visit to Jerusalem to deliver the aid (12.25).

Initially, we learn that, in addition to Barnabas and Paul, three others share the leadership of the church, namely Simeon (nicknamed "Black"); Luke, a Cyrenaean; and Manaen, a former steward of Herod the Tetrarch. These five are called "prophets and teachers." During a time when they[1] were worshipping the Lord and fasting, they received a revelatory command from the Holy Spirit (in the way in which Luke tells the story, the emphasis falls entirely on what was believed to be the divine origin of the command, any human agency of this divine command being passed over, as

---

1. Grammatically, the plurals of the verbs relate naturally to the five prophets and teachers. On the other hand, when Paul and Barnabas returned, they gathered together the church and gave them a report of what God had done through them, so that it is entirely possible that Luke might have thought of the involvement of the church as a whole in their being commissioned, even if the original impetus came through the prophets and teachers as a group.

is any possible prior discussion of "outreach" work): they were to set apart Barnabas and Paul for the work to which the Spirit had called them (13.2). No geographical area is designated in the word from the Spirit, nor actually that missionary work is specifically in mind.

At the end of his Gospel, Luke had the risen Jesus explaining that God's plan contained in the OT was that the message of repentance and forgiveness of sins should be proclaimed to all nations, beginning from Jerusalem, and commissioning his disciples to be his witnesses in this task (24.45-49). Then, the risen Lord repeated this commission at the beginning of Acts in what has so often been described as the programmatic statement of the book (Acts 1.8). Luke had also in the course of his story informed the reader that Paul is the "chosen vessel" appointed by the risen Lord Jesus to proclaim the name of Jesus "before Gentiles and their kings and before the people of Israel" (9.15). So, although Peter is in Luke's story the first to admit a Gentile to the Christian church (Acts 10.1-11.18)[2] and although the Hellenists were the first to preach to non-Jews in Antioch (11.19-21), it cannot be said that the reader receives the impression that the risen Lord's strategy has really got under way. Now, however, this is to change. There is going to be a mission-outreach from the church at Antioch, ordered by the Spirit and to be spear-headed by Barnabas and Paul. Luke reported that the two men were duly sent out after the rest had laid hands on them (13.3-4a). Again, Luke concentrated on the divine origin of the venture, by stating that the two were sent out by the Holy Spirit (v. 4a).

The two (we learn a little later at v. 5b that they were accompanied by John Mark, whom they had brought with them from Jerusalem after their visit there with the famine relief contribution—12.25) set sail for Cyprus and preached in the synagogues in Salamis, the capital of the island (13.4b-5). They crossed over the island to reach Paphos on the south-west corner (v. 6). Here the pro-consul, Sergius Paulus, sent for them to hear the word of God. At his court, there was a Jewish magician, a false prophet, called Elymas bar-Jesus, who sought to prevent the proconsul's being influenced by Barnabas and Saul into accepting the Christian faith (vv. 6b-8).

---

2. The status of the Ethiopian eunuch is ambiguous. According to Deut. 23.1, he could not be admitted to the assembly of the Lord, but a more open and liberal approach is evinced by Isa. 56.1-8, which envisages both foreigners and eunuchs [both true of the official] who obey the law of Yahweh as being welcomed into the House of the Lord, though whether Isa. 56 would take precedence over Deut. 23 in the Judaism of the first century AD is another matter. Barrett, *Acts*, 1:426, concludes that we must be content to take the story as a piece of tradition about Philip which Luke placed here not because it fitted into his scheme of Christian expansion but because this was the point at which he was dealing with Philip. As many have rightly emphasized, *Luke* clearly saw the conversion of Cornelius as the admission of the first Gentile.

Paul, under the inspiration of the Spirit, not only sternly rebuked Elymas, but also struck him with temporary blindness (vv. 9–11). This made a deep impression on Sergius Paulus, who is described as an intelligent man (v. 7), and he became a believer. "When the pro-consul saw what had happened he believed, because he was astonished at the teaching of the Lord" (v. 12). The first convert mentioned by Luke is thus a Gentile.

From Cyprus, Luke has the missionaries sail to the mainland of Asia Minor, to Perga, from where they went to Antioch in Pisidia (vv. 13–14). From this point on, Luke made Paul the leading figure: e.g., at v. 13 he says "Paul and his companions;" at v. 16 it is Paul who preached; and now Luke uses the order "Paul and Barnabas" eight times[3] (and only once, at 14.14, "Barnabas and Paul" as previously), though it is true that at Lystra, the locals called Barnabas "Zeus" and Paul "Hermes," because Paul was the chief speaker (14.12).

At the synagogue in PA, the chief officials asked the missionaries whether they had a message of παράκλησις, which may be translated as "encouragement" or "exhortation."[4] Either sense or both/and could be the meaning here, but Lucan usage perhaps favours "encouragement."[5]

Paul began by a selective review of the story of God's dealings with Israel (vv. 16b–25). The emphasis is on God: He chose the Hebrew "fathers;" exalted Israel while in Egypt and led them out of that land; nourished them in the desert; drove out those who lived in Canaan; and settled the Israelites there (vv. 16b–19). God gave the people judges and, even when the people requested a king, He gave them Saul (vv. 20–21). God, however, set him aside and raised up David, who is described as a man after God's own heart and dedicated to doing His will, to be king (v. 22). The speech then leaps to

---

3. 13.42, 43, 46, 50; 14.1, 3, 20, 23.

4. See BAG, 623, for a list of the various shades of meaning for παράκλησις.

5. Luke uses παράκλησις twice in his Gospel and four times in Acts. The occurrences in the Gospel both have the nuance of "comfort" or "consolation;" Simeon was looking for the eschatological salvation of Israel (2.28) and the Woe on the rich is justified because they have already received their comforts now (6.24). In Acts, Barnabas is called "the son of encouragement," i.e., he was a man who encouraged others (4.36), while the churches in Judea and Galilee grew through "the encouragement supplied by the Holy Spirit" (9.31). The members of the church at Antioch rejoiced at the encouragement of the letter sent by the Jerusalem church to them (15.31). If we could assume that Luke could use the word in a similar way to Paul at 1 Cor. 14.3, where Paul says that someone prophesying speaks what builds up (οἰκοδομὴ), exhortation (παράκλησις) and comfort (παραμυθία), then "exhortation" might be preferred. However, since context does not demand a sense contrary to Lucan usage elsewhere, probably "encouragement" should be favoured if we have to make a choice. Barrett, *Acts*, 1:629, however, assumes a "*word of exhortation*, hortatory discourse, sermon," as does Flichy, *Figure*, 185.

a descendant of David, Jesus, whom God had brought on the scene to be a saviour for Israel (v. 23). The coming of this Jesus in fulfillment of God's promise was announced by John the Baptist who preached a baptism of repentance for all the people of Israel. John the Baptist declared the imminent coming of one far greater than himself (vv. 24–25).

Having mentioned Jesus, the speech now turns specifically to him and the message of salvation which flows from him and his ministry (v. 26). Attention is focussed on the fact that the inhabitants of Jerusalem and their leaders, through failure to recognise him for what he was and their failure to understand the prophetic Scriptures, paradoxically fulfilled those very Scriptures when they condemned him and, although they found no real cause for the death sentence, went on to request that Pilate put him to death. He was then taken down from the cross and buried in a grave (vv. 27–29). But God raised him from the dead. Thus raised to life, Jesus appeared over a period of many days to those who accompanied him from Galilee to Jerusalem. They are now his witnesses to the people (vv. 30–31). The focus is now directed specifically to the congregation, and the speaker asserted that he was announcing the good news that God had fulfilled for the congregation the promise made to the fathers, by raising Jesus from the dead (vv. 32–33). Then there follows three passages from the OT which help to elucidate the significance of the resurrection of Jesus. Firstly, Ps. 2.7 is used to show that Jesus had been begotten as God's Son through the resurrection (v. 33b). As one raised and, therefore, immortal (never to suffer corruption), Jesus is the one through whom God will give to the congregation the reliable, holy blessings promised to David (as predicted by Isa. 55.3), for, finally, as Ps. 16.10 asserted, God will not let His Holy One see corruption (vv. 34–35). God had promised eternal rule to David's descendant, and only one who is immortal could receive and fulfill such a promise. The promise was clearly not meant for David, who died and did see corruption. But the one whom God raised did not see corruption, and is, therefore, able to impart the blessings of his eternal rule to men and women (vv. 36–37).

The speech climaxes in both promise (vv. 38–39) and warning (vv. 40–41). Through this Jesus, forgiveness of sins and justification (something the Mosaic Law could not achieve) are offered to everyone who believes. On the other hand, the congregation should not despise and reject the work which God was doing in their day, a work so unusual that there will be the temptation not to believe. The work which God is doing probably includes both the actual ministry of Jesus, now in the past, but also what flows from that ministry, and specifically from the resurrection of Jesus, which has been stressed from v. 30 onwards, namely the universal spread of the good news of God's salvation to everyone who is prepared to believe, irrespective of race (like the Roman centurion, Cornelius; the people of Antioch; or the Roman proconsul, Sergius Paulus).

Paul and Barnabas received a request to address the synagogue on the next sabbath (v. 42). Many Jews and proselytes accompanied them as they left the synagogue and received encouragement to continue in God's grace (v. 43). While the language may be somewhat muted, there are certain hints that it is not inappropriate to regard what Luke says in v. 43 as the founding of a Christian community in PA: there is the use of the verb "to follow" which can have religious overtones given the context of preaching by Paul; the use of the verb "to persuade" which Luke can use elsewhere as a synonym of "to believe;"[6] and the use of the phrase "to continue in the grace of God" with its suggestion that the hearers were already *in* the grace of God.[7]

Luke says that all the city gathered at the synagogue a week later to hear God's word (v. 44), a fact which re-ignited zeal for the law[8] in some[9] of the Jews who spoke against and slandered what Paul and Barnabas were saying, because, in their estimation, by admitting Gentiles on the basis of faith the two missionaries were compromising the purity of Israel. Paul and Barnabas then made a solemn assertion that it was necessary first to proclaim God's word to the Jews, but, since the Jews rejected it and, thereby, proved themselves unworthy of eternal life, they would turn to the Gentiles. For the Lord had commanded them to do so. Isa. 49.6—the task of the Servant of the Lord to be a light to the nations so that God's salvation might reach to the ends of the earth—is quoted to substantiate this turning to the Gentiles (vv. 46–47).

This assertion filled the Gentiles with joy and they praised the Lord for his word. Those ordained for eternal life believed. The word of the Lord spread through the whole area (vv. 48–49).

The unbelieving Jews resorted to stirring up pious women of noble birth and the leading men of the city, and they succeeded in instigating a persecution against Paul and Barnabas, and, indeed, as a result of these efforts, Paul and Barnabas were expelled from the region. But the two shook the dust from their feet as a symbolic prophetic witness against their opponents[10] and moved on to Iconium (vv. 50–52).

---

6. See 17.4; 28.24 (on the latter text, see 53n44).

7. See Deutschmann, *Synagoge*, 92–95.

8. Taking ζῆλος in this sense (rather than as envy or jealousy), with Hengel, *Zealots*, 181; Roloff, *Apg.*, 205; Pesch, *Apg.* 2.45; Dunn, *Acts*, 184; Klinghardt, *Gesetz*, 236; Koet, *Five Studies*, 102–6; Deutschmann, *Synagoge*, 96–99, esp. 97, 99; Marguerat, *First Christian Historian*, 137; and Flichy, *Figure*, 214.

9. These are to be distinguished from those who believed according to v. 43.

10. Strathmann, μάρτυς *TDNT* 4.503: "The fact that they leave their hearers

Luke opens his account of events at Iconium with the phrase ἐγένετο δὲ ἐν Ἰκονίῳ κατὰ τὸ αὐτό. While most scholars interpret this phrase as Luke's indication that a visit to the Synagogue was the customary first step in the method of the missionary work pursued by Paul and Barnabas,[11] it is possible that Luke meant that the same pattern occurred at Iconium as at PA. This would suggest that the events at PA had a typical character about them.[12] Initially at Iconium, Paul and Barnabas made many converts from both Jews and Gentiles through their preaching in the synagogue there. But once again those Jews who were unconvinced stirred up the Gentiles and turned them against the Christians (14.1-2). Paul and Barnabas continued an effective ministry of word and deed, with the Lord enabling them to perform miracles to confirm the message. In the end, however, when a plot to set upon and stone Paul and Barnabas became known, they left the town and went on to Lystra and Derbe and that district, preaching the gospel there[13] (14.3-7).

At Lystra[14] the missionaries encountered a purely pagan crowd (Luke does not mention any visit to a Synagogue). Paul healed a man who was a cripple from birth (vv. 8-10), and this produced an attempt to worship Paul and Barnabas as gods visiting the earth (Barnabas being taken for Zeus in human form and Paul for Hermes, the messenger of the gods, because he was the chief speaker). Paul and Barnabas only just managed to prevent the priest of Zeus from sacrificing to them (vv. 11-14).

Paul exclaimed that he and Barnabas were just human beings like them and called on the Lystrans to turn from such idolatrous activity to the living God. God had made heaven and earth and sea and everything in them. In previous generations He allowed the Gentiles to behave in such an idolatrous fashion, although He did not leave them without a witness to His powerful and benevolent activity, for He gave them rain and fruitful

with this gesture will be a witness against their resistance and unbelief on the day of judgment."

11. So Haenchen, *Acts*, 409; Marshall, *Acts*, 233; Schneider, *Apg.* 2.150; Roloff, *Apg.*, 211; Lüdemann, *Early Christianity*, 159; Pesch, *Apg.* 2.51; Barrett, *Acts* 1:667; Jervell, *Apg.*, 368; Fitzmyer, *Acts*, 527; Kee, *Acts*, 171.

12. This seems to be implied by Johnson, *Acts*, 250 and Witherington, *Acts*, 418; and is forcefully stated by Flichy, *Figure*, 183-84 (the events at PA have the significance of a typical example). See the NRSV "The same thing occurred at Iconium."

13. As they do in Derbe in the transitional v. 21. Flichy, *Figure*, 225, comments that this shows that the presence of the missionaries in this new region is always under the sign of the "proclamation of the Good News."

14. For a full-scale study of what happened at Lystra and the mini-speech delivered there, see Béchard, *Paul*. See also Lerle, "Predigt," 46-55; Flichy, *Figure*, 223-42; Kezbere, *Umstrittener Monotheismus*, 152-63.

seasons from heaven. He also provided food and He filled people's lives with gladness (vv. 15–17).

Then some Jews from PA and Iconium arrived at Lystra and won over the Lystrans. The result was that the people stoned Paul and left him for dead outside the city. Paul, however, revived and the Christians brought him back into the town (vv. 19–20b).[15] On the morning of the next day, he and Barnabas left for Derbe, where they continued to preach the gospel and make disciples for Christ (vv. 19–21a).

The two missionaries returned the way they had come and revisited Lystra, Iconium and Antioch, strengthening the new converts, encouraging them to remain in the faith and warning them that it would be through tribulations that we enter the Kingdom of God. In all the churches which they had established, they appointed elders and committed them to the Lord in whom they had believed (vv. 21b–23).

They continued southwards through Pisidia to the coast and embarked at Attalia on board ship for Antioch, from where the church had committed them to the grace of God "for the work which they had fulfilled" (this phrase picks up the words of the Spirit about "the work to which I have called them" at 13.2).[16] There they reported to the church on all that God had done through them and how He had opened the door of faith to the Gentiles (vv. 24–28).

THE PLACE OF PAUL'S SPEECH WITHIN THE JOURNEY ACCOUNT

Within this first missionary journey, Paul's speech at Pisidian Antioch occupies a key place.[17] It is true that Luke does record some words of Paul to the (pagan) people of Lystra (14.15–17), but this is hardly a full-scale address[18]

---

15. Bechard, *Paul*, 141, 165, maintains that the episode at Lystra constitutes the dramatic climax of the journey. While there is some truth in this, it should not be maintained at the expense of the importance of Paul's PA speech.

16. In grammatical parlance, there is an inclusio here (Note also that at the end of PA speech there is a reference to the "work" which God is doing, 13.41); cf. Maloney, *God*, 118, 127, 129; cf. Flichy, *Figure*, 174. Compare too how Luke says at 13.5 that the two missionaries proclaimed "the word of God" in the synagogues of Cyprus and at 14.25 that Paul and Barnabas spoke "the word" in Perga on the return journey to the coast before embarking for Syrian Antioch.

17. Compare Wilckens, *Missionsreden*, 70; Buss, *Missionspredigt*, 17; Tyson, *Death*, 39; Strauss, *Davidic Messiah*, 149–50. Korn, *Geschichte Jesu*, 150, describes it as the center (Schwerpunkt) of the activity of Paul with Barnabas in PA.

18. We may agree with Jervell, *Apg.*, 377–79, that this is not "a missionary sermon."

and, indeed, could be said to be a "curtain-raiser" or preliminary sketch for Paul's speech at Athens (17.22–31). The speech at PA really dominates: it is the centerpiece of this section of Acts.[19] Quantitatively, out of 80 verses in these two chapters, the speech occupies 26 verses, which is virtually a third of the material. In this important turning point in the Christian mission, Luke has chosen to give Paul a major speech.

Although Luke has previously reported how Paul engaged in preaching (Acts 9.20–22, 28–29; 11, 26), he has only given the barest summary of the theme of Paul's preaching, so that this is the first occasion we experience a speech "in full" from him.[20] Thus, Luke gives us a speech from the character who is from now on to be the dominant figure in Acts 13–28. As we have already seen, Barnabas is of secondary importance compared with Paul in chapters 13–14. Throughout these chapters Paul is the leading figure of the two (one could say that just as Peter in the early chapters of Acts is accompanied by John, so here Paul is accompanied by Barnabas).

The speech is one delivered in a synagogue and addressed to Jews plus those who fear God (vv. 16, 26). After the conclusion of the address, as Paul and Barnabas were leaving the building, Luke tells us that many Jews and God-fearing proselytes attached themselves to the missionaries (v. 43). On first impression, then, Luke seems to have in mind an audience of Jews and full converts rather than Jews and those Gentiles attracted by Jewish monotheism and ethical teaching, without having taken the step of converting fully to Judaism.[21] Nonetheless, Gentiles are attracted to hear "the word of God" on the following sabbath (13.44).

One could say that Paul is shown to be a loyal, not a renegade, Jew. He goes to the synagogue and he addresses the congregation and shows himself to be one capable of handling the sacred scriptures. He is mindful of the election of Israel (13.17) and of Israel's prior claim to receive good news from God (vv. 32–33a,46). He can describe his ministry in terms of the commission to the Servant of Yahweh (in Isaiah 49.6) at v. 47.

While the flow of the sermon seems to involve Israel, for God has now fulfilled the promise which He originally made to the fathers and renewed to David, yet in the closing section of the speech there is the seed of the universal implication of the good news: "By this man *everyone* who believes will be justified." This comes out unambiguously on the following sabbath

---

19. We may, therefore, query the claim made by some scholars that the episode at Lystra represents the climax of the first missionary journey—see Bechard, *Paul*, 141, 165 n. 15 and Flichy, *Figure*, 224 (both quote Beutler, *Heidenmission*, 360–83 as also making this point).

20. Zwang, *Paul*, 122–23, 151 153, 188, 194, stresses this point frequently.

21. See chapter 4 below for a discussion of this question.

when, in the face of Jewish opposition, Paul declares the intention of Barnabas and himself to turn to the Gentiles. The positive reason for this is the fact that Gentiles are included in God's age-old plan as recorded in the OT. "Light" and "Salvation" are, in God's purposes, meant for the Gentiles, even at earth's farthest bounds (Isa. 49.6, quoted at v. 47). Thus, while Jesus is the fulfillment and climax of God's dealings with Israel, he is also the destined Saviour of the Gentile world as well. Nevertheless, there is truth in the observation made by Odile Flichy that the actual sermon at PA does not give such a central place to the point stressed in Luke's summary of the report made by Paul and Barnabas to the church at Antioch, viz. that God had opened the door of faith to the Gentiles (14.27).[22]
The implications of this will be considered later in our study.

Although the speech stresses that God has fulfilled His promise to His people, we come up against the problem of Jewish rejection of this claimed fulfillment. There is, first, the warning issued at the end of the speech, via the quotation from Hab. 1.5, not to despise the work which God is doing. This is followed by the opposition of many Jews and their rejection of the message. Then, the declaration of turning to the Gentiles is the first of three declarations to the same effect (the others are at 18.6 and 28.28). This may be said to be like the first occurrence of a musical theme which recurs in a symphony with ever-increasing insistence. It feeds into the readers' awareness both that the Christian message is not finding favourable response with the Jewish people and that this message must be proclaimed to all and sundry, for that has been the divine intention all along. As Tannehill has stressed, "we are not allowed to forget Jewish rejection. . . Acts does not mitigate the problem and reduce the tension by weakening the witness to God's saving purpose and the scriptural promise to the Jewish people."[23]

THE RELATION OF THE SPEECH TO WHAT HAS PRECEDED IN CHAPTERS 1-12

Luke has, of course, introduced us to the figure of Paul before chapter 13. We have learned how he agreed with putting Stephen to death (8.1); how he wreaked havoc on the Christian community in Jerusalem by hauling off

---

22. Flichy, *Figure*, 175-76. In accordance with her narrative critical approach, she suggests that this constitutes what she calls the "program" in advance of what Luke proposes to narrate concerning the activity of Paul still to come. Some events in chapters 13-14 (the conversion of Sergius Paulus and the speech to the pagan crowd at Lystra) have a significant proleptic dimension.

23. Tannehill, *Narrative Unity*, 2:174-75.

members to prison (8.3); and how he was authorized by the High Priest to proceed against Christians at Damascus (9.1-2); and how, while on the way to Damascus, he was "stopped in his tracks" when the risen Jesus confronted him. Temporarily blinded by the vision, Paul was led to Damascus where a devout Jewish Christian, Ananias, came to him, on the orders of the risen Jesus. Paul received his sight and was baptized (9.3-9, 17-19).

In the way that Luke tells the story, we, the readers, learn of Paul's future role via the risen Jesus' conversation with Ananias. When the latter demurs at going to meet one with such a bad reputation as a persecutor of Christians, he is overruled and told to go, for Paul "is a chosen vessel for me, to take my name before the Gentiles and kings and the sons of Israel. For I will show him what he must suffer for my name" (9.15-17). Having been baptized at Ananias' command, Paul immediately engaged in preaching that Jesus was the messiah, the Son of God, in the synagogues of Damascus to the amazement of those who heard him (9.20-22).

The risen Lord's prediction of suffering soon started to be fulfilled, as the Jews of Damascus plotted to kill Paul and, indeed, they kept watch at the city gates to prevent his escaping. However, the Christians lowered him down the walls in a basket, and Paul got away and returned to Jerusalem (9.23-25). There, the Christians were suspicious of him, but one Barnabas took Paul "under his wing" and acted as a kind of guarantor for Paul and brought him to the apostles and vouched for him (9.26-27). Paul took up preaching among the Greek-speaking Jews—just as Stephen before him had done—but also, like Stephen, aroused murderous designs among them, which resulted in the Jerusalem Christians sending him out of the city and away to Tarsus (9.28-30).

It is from Tarsus that later on Barnabas persuaded Paul to join him in a ministry to strengthen the comparatively recently formed congregation at Antioch. Barnabas and Paul taught for a whole year in the church (11.25-26). Indeed, the church sent relief to the Jerusalem Christians, adversely affected by famine, by Barnabas and Paul, an evident sign of the respect and honor in which they were held, plus, of course, the fact that Barnabas had originally come to Antioch at the instigation of the Jerusalem Christians (11.27-20; 12.25).

In spite of all this, chapters 13-14 are our first proper, extended look at Paul. We have had summary type statements of his activity as a Christian preacher in Damascus, Jerusalem and Antioch. Now we see him in action. Luke gives us an extended glimpse of him, and the sermon at PA is a sample of his preaching to Jews. We were told through the risen Jesus' words to Ananias that Paul would bear the name of Jesus before Gentiles, kings and the sons of Israelites. At PA, Paul addressed the "sons of Israel" and Gentiles

(13.16, 44), while Paul also had spoken earlier before Sergius Paulus, who, even though not a king, was a very high ranking Roman official and a member of the highest order of Roman society.

The way in which Paul and Barnabas faced opposition, not only at PA (13.45, 50), but also at Iconium (14.2, 5) and Lystra (14.19), picks up the theme of Paul's suffering for the sake of Jesus mentioned in Jesus' conversation with Ananias (9.16).

Many have rightly pointed out that each of Luke's main characters in his double volume commence their ministry with an important inaugural sermon—Jesus in the Nazareth sermon (Lk.4.18-21); Peter on the Day of Pentecost (Acts 2.14-38); and Paul at PA.[24] Paul's speech at PA has links with both of the others.

Here we will look at the links with Peter's speech in Acts 2.[25] Both speeches assume the Davidic descent of Jesus (2.30 and 13.23); emphasise the responsibility of the Jerusalemites for the death of Jesus (2.23,[26] 36 and 13.27-29); operate with a contrast scheme of what men did in putting Jesus to death and how God reversed that in raising Jesus from the dead (2.23-24, 36 and 13.28-30); make liberal use of the OT with both using Psa. 16 as a proof text for the resurrection of Jesus, with Peter's speech giving a fuller discussion (2.25-32 and 13.34-37); mention the theme of witnesses to the resurrection (2.32 and 13.31); refer to Jesus' exaltation (2.33-35 and 13.33-34), though the Christological titles they use are different; and end in varying ways with the same offer of forgiveness (2.38 and 13.38). There are differences too, an obvious one being that Peter's speech mentions the Spirit (2.14-21, 33), whereas Paul's speech does not. Paul's speech, on the other hand, has a brief, selective résumé of Israel's history, which does not figure in Peter's speech. Nevertheless, despite these differences, when it comes to fundamentals, Luke's picture is that these two leading figures of the early church were in agreement. There was a basic similarity of message.[27]

---

24. "Commmence" would not be strictly accurate, since Paul had been preaching earlier. Yet in a sense, from a Lucan perspective, the journey of Acts 13-14 is the beginning of Paul's ministry as a missionary sent out. See Tannehill, *Narrative Unity*, 2:160-61.

25. For the latest handling of this theme, see the extremely thorough treatment of Clark, *Parallel Lives*, esp. 230-60.

26. Here, we need not discuss whether the phrase "at the hand of lawless men" refers to the Romans or the Jewish leaders.

27. Paul himself strongly maintained that there was a fundamental unity of message between him and those who were apostles before him—see 1 Cor. 15.11. In Gal. 2.6, he vehemently maintained that the Jerusalem triumvirate of James, Peter, and John "added nothing to my gospel" and, indeed, his argument in 2.1-10 assumes that there was a core agreement on "the gospel." At Antioch, he rebuked Peter for not acting in

We may also mention two further links with material in chapters 1–12. The reference to the risen Jesus' appearing over a period of many days to those who had come up to Jerusalem with him from Galilee (13.31) recalls to the reader the earlier mention at 1.3 that the risen Jesus had shown himself to be alive by many proofs over a period of forty days. Likewise, the phrase "to the ends of the earth" in the Isa. 49.6 quotation at 13.47 would remind the reader of the similar phrase, likewise dependent on Isaiah 49.6, in the risen Lord's commission to be his witnesses at 1.8. We have, therefore, two reminders of the "prologue" of Acts in chapter 13.

THE RELATION OF THE SPEECH TO WHAT FOLLOWS IN CHAPTERS 15–20

Luke has Paul and Barnabas telling the church at Antioch on their return "how God had opened the door of faith to the Gentiles" (14.27). The activity of Paul and Barnabas had raised this issue, as the sequel to the PA speech makes clear (vv. 44–49). Later, in Lystra, the two men speak directly to non-Jews who worshipped pagan gods, whatever contact they may or may not have had with Judaism previously (14.15–17).

The whole issue of the relation of non-Jews to the Christian faith surfaced immediately in Luke's next block of material, commonly referred to as the "Jerusalem Council." Some Jewish Christians from Judea arrived in Antioch and taught members of the church that unless they were circumcised in accordance with the law of Moses, they could not be saved, provoking thereby a good deal of discussion and dispute with Paul and Barnabas. Eventually, the Antioch church decided to send Paul and Barnabas and others to Jerusalem to discuss the matter (15.1–2). At Jerusalem, some Pharisaically-inclined believers asserted the same viewpoint—that converts must be circumcised and told to keep the Law of Moses (15.5). Presumably, those mentioned in 15.1 and 5 were members of an ultra-conservative wing of the Jewish Christian community in Jerusalem and Judea. The issue, then, is one of salvation: can Gentiles be saved by faith (as Paul claimed at 13.39) or do they have to become Jews in order to become members of the people of God?[28]

---

accordance with the truth of the gospel, and, again, the assumption of his argument is that Peter accepted that both Jews and Gentiles alike were justified on the basis of faith in Jesus Christ (Gal. 2.11–16).

28. In this section, on the level of narrative criticism, we are not required to discuss the historical questions surrounding the Jerusalem Council and whether, e.g., there was (as Jervell believed, *Unknown Paul*, 23, 26–38) a resurgence of Jewish Christian militancy as a reaction to the success of the Antioch mission and whether the conservatively

In the discussion at the meeting between the apostles, elders and members of the church at Jerusalem and the Antiochene delegation, Peter emphatically supported the position of Paul and Barnabas. Peter refers to how God had chosen him to bring the word of the gospel to the Gentiles—a reference to the Cornelius episode recorded in Acts 10.1–11.18. On that occasion, God had made no difference between Jews and Gentiles: He had given the latter the Holy Spirit, just as He had to the former on the day of Pentecost, and had cleansed their hearts by faith (15.7–9). We may note two points in what Peter subsequently is recorded as saying, where there is agreement with the position taken by Paul in the PA speech. Peter says to impose the Law on Gentile converts would be equivalent to putting God to the test and placing on Gentile converts a yoke which neither Jews in the past nor present had been able to bear (v. 10). In his PA speech, Paul had said that only through Jesus could one be justified before God from the things from which one could not be justified by the Law of Moses (13.38). The wording may be different, but there is agreement in essence. Then Peter says "But we believe that we [Jews] shall be saved through the grace of the Lord Jesus in a way similar to them [the Gentiles]" (15.11). Paul had said through Jesus everyone who believes will be justified (13.39). Thus, in respect to Law and Salvation, the stance taken by Paul is that also taken by Peter at the Jerusalem Council.

We note that the σωθῆναι of Peter's final words (15.11) picks up the σωθῆναι of 15.1 and enunciates a different approach to that put forward there; grace from the Lord Jesus and faith from human beings are the twin poles of salvation.

Luke does not report what Paul and Barnabas said, since he has already narrated the signs and wonders which God had done through them among the Gentiles, in chapters 13–14 (though Luke is not *per se* averse to repetition as 10.1–48 and 11.1–18; and 9.1–19, 22.1–21 and 26.2–23 clearly show).

James then took up the discussion and supported Peter's position by quoting Amos 9.11–12.[29] James asserted that God had planned the admission of the Gentiles to His people all along. There are two stages in this process. Firstly, the "fallen tent of David" would be restored. Probably there is both a personal and a corporate dimension to this idea. The everlasting rule promised to the Davidic house will be restored through the resurrection

---

inclined members at Jerusalem saw the conversion of someone like Cornelius as an exception, a "one-off" incident, without establishing a precedent or principle.

29. While the quotation in Acts 15.16 differs from the MT and the LXX of Amos 9.11, at 15.17 it is much closer to the LXX of Amos 9.12. See the careful discussion of Sabrine Nägele, *Laubhütte Davids*, 81–107, esp. 81–89.

of Jesus and his consequent entry into lordship at God's right hand. But the resurrection and exaltation of Jesus, the descendant of David, have corporate implications—the renewal of the people of God. This takes place through the outpouring of the Spirit of God. This renewal of the people of God through the Spirit of God is the necessary preliminary step towards the incorporation of Gentiles into the people of God.[30] This is, secondly, precisely what the scriptural quotation says: the rest of humanity will seek God, i.e., Gentiles on whom His name has been called.[31] Calling a name over someone is a biblical idiom indicating ownership.[32] The perfect tense of the verb indicates a past action with continuing consequences, whether God's calling His name over them took place in creation or in the saving ministry of His Son, Jesus Christ. The idea of God's name being called over the non-Jewish world picks up James' opening remark that God recently acted through Peter to take a people from among the Gentiles for His name (v. 14). So, the recent experience of God's action through His Spirit in the Cornelius story and the testimony of Scripture cohere to indicate what God's will was in relation to Gentiles and to show that this purpose was known from of old.

Since James said that the prophetic scriptures agreed with what Peter had reminded them about God's action to secure a people for Himself from the Gentiles, then the way in which "the rest of humanity" seeks God can only be on the basis of the grace of the Lord Jesus and the exercise of faith.

Thus, whatever may be the purpose of the abstention from certain things proscribed by Mosaic Law, *in Luke's narrative* they cannot affect the point that to be saved rests on the grace of the Lord Jesus and faith from human beings. In other words, the decision of the Council vindicates the mission of the Antioch church led by Paul and Barnabas. Thus, we might say that the outcome of the Jerusalem Conference on the issue of how we receive salvation had already been adumbrated in the PA speech. We may set out the links as follows. Paul and Barnabas recount "how God had opened the door of faith to the Gentiles" (14.27); Peter declares that we believe that we shall be saved by the grace of the Lord Jesus in a similar way to them (15.11). James said that "With this the words of the prophets agree...so that the rest of humanity might seek [i.e., by faith] the Lord."

The letter sent by the Jerusalem church confirms this approach, because it begins with a total repudiation of those from within their own ranks

---

30. For a fuller discussion of this passage and the meaning of "David's fallen tent," see 170–75.

31. This assumes that ἐπικέκληται is a perfect indicative passive.

32. The REB sacrifices the Biblical idiom and freely renders "whom I have claimed for my own."

who had unsettled the Antioch church members and denies that they had received any authorisation to do so (15.24). One could not ask for the matter to be put more clearly. Whatever the intention behind the request to abstain from certain things listed in 15.29, this does not appertain to salvation.

The reception of the letter and its bearers further confirms our argument. "When they had read (it), they rejoiced at its encouragement" (15.31). The verb "rejoiced" (ἐχάρησαν) is the same verb which Luke used to describe the reaction of the Gentiles when Paul and Barnabas said that they were turning to the Gentiles and quoted the words addressed to the Servant of the Lord "I have appointed you to be a light to the nations, that you may be (the means of bringing) salvation to the ends of the earth" (13.46–48). The encouragement received from the letter is the encouragement that salvation rests on the grace of the Lord Jesus to be received by faith, and not on being circumcised and keeping the Law.

The immediate sequel to the PA speech showed that Paul and Barnabas' pronouncement that the Jews had proved themselves unworthy of eternal life and that they would turn to the Gentiles, was not absolute. At the very next town, Iconium, Paul and Barnabas went to the synagogue (14.1).[33] This pattern continues in Paul's second missionary journey: at Philippi (16.13), where Paul and his companions search for a place of prayer (i.e., Jewish) on the sabbath; Thessalonica (17.1-2, where Luke writes "according to his custom"); Berea (17.10); Athens (17.17); Corinth (18.4; where Paul also made the solemn asseveration "From now on I will go to the Gentiles" 18.6); Ephesus (18.19). It continues to be the case for the third missionary journey: Ephesus (19.8); Greece—?Corinth (20.2-3—if the Jews plotted against him, this suggests that he was trying to convert them to belief in Jesus as messiah). We note also that in his speech to the Ephesian elders at Miletus Paul said that he had declared the need to repent and believe in the Lord Jesus, to both Jews and Greeks (20.21). In other words, Luke wants the reader to understand that Paul did not give up his attempts to bring Jews to faith in Jesus, wherever he went.

The inference is clear: neither 13.46 nor 18.6 is meant in an absolute and final manner. Paul continues to have a concern for his own people. He still has a mission to them in accordance with his commission from the risen Jesus (9.15).

Although the title "the Christ/Messiah" does not figure in the PA speech, nonetheless Jesus is described as a descendant of David; he is part of

---

33. The point is reinforced if the phrase κατὰ τὸ αὐτό means "as usual"—so Barrett, *Acts* 1:667; NIV (BAG, 123, 408, however, takes it as "together," "in the same place"). It is difficult to see why Wilckens, *Missionsreden*, 71, has said that this is the last call to repentance addressed to the Jews.

the story of Israel and the fulfillment of the promise made to the fathers; and it is to him and his resurrection that the OT refers. The PA speech can give the background, therefore, against which Luke's bare remarks about Paul's preaching to Jews can be seen. At Thessalonica, Paul spent three sabbaths in the synagogue reasoning with the people from the Scriptures and seeking to prove that the messiah had to suffer and rise from the dead and that Jesus whom Paul was preaching was the messiah (17.2–3). The Berean Jews were of a more noble character and they listened eagerly to what Paul said and they "examined the scriptures daily to see if Paul's message was true" (17.11). At Corinth, Paul testified to the Jews that Jesus was the messiah (18.5). Alleging that Jesus was the messiah is a summary type statement of the kind of preaching Paul gave as exemplified in the PA speech.

We saw that the result of Paul's PA speech and the subsequent sabbath session was a mixed one. That repeated itself in so many places which Paul visited subsequently on his second and third journeys. There was often fierce opposition, frequently from the Jews, sometimes necessitating a speedy departure. Some Jews did believe in spite of this opposition from their own people. Gentiles, very often from the group of non-Jews who were loosely attached to the synagogue, believed. Dupont has commented that what happened at PA sets a pattern for the future: in a sense, the mission at PA is "a sort of prototype of the Pauline mission."[34]

As we come to the close of this sub-section, it is worth pointing to a fact which is, from the point of view of Luke's narrative, an interesting feature. If we take chapters 13–20 as a whole, i.e., the section of Acts which covers the missionary career of Paul as a free man, we observe that Luke has allocated (so to speak) three major speeches to Paul,[35] of which the first is the PA speech, addressed to members of the synagogue there, primarily to Jews, but also including some proselytes. The second major speech of Paul is that delivered before a wholly Gentile audience at Athens (17.22–31), a speech which many see as epitomising the encounter of Christianity and Greek philosophy, the Gospel and Greek culture.[36] The third major speech given to Paul is that delivered to the Ephesian elders at Miletus, i.e., a speech

---

34. Dupont, *Nouvelles Études*, 344. See also Deutschmann, *Synagoge*, 137–41 (cf. 167, 215), for a summary of the pattern discernible in Luke's descriptions of Paul's ministry to Jews in the Diaspora and see 89–90 for Deutschmann's assertion that 13.42–52 has an "ideal" or "typical" character—it is typical of Paul's mission experience in the Diaspora.

35. Cf. Witherington, *Acts*, 408.

36. E.g., Dibelius, *Studies*, 79–83. See Jervell, *Apg.*, 445, 451, 452–53, for his view that this speech is not a missionary sermon, but a speech addressed to philosophers and expressing judgment on paganism.

addressed to Christians, specifically the leaders of a major Pauline congregation and giving through them a pastoral "last will and testament" to a church founded by him.

Thus, in Paul's time as a Christian missionary in Acts 13–20, we have sermons to Jews (primarily), Gentiles and Christians. From the point of view of our study, Luke has in effect given his readers a sample of Paul's preaching to a primarily Jewish audience in the PA speech. We do not subsequently in Acts get a detailed account of the actual content of Paul's preaching on his many visits to the synagogue during the remainder of his mission. This further underlines the importance of the PA speech in the structure of Acts.[37]

THE RELATION OF THE PA SPEECH TO THE WHOLE BOOK

To a large extent, this theme has already been touched on in the previous subsections, and we shall seek to avoid duplication. It is a perennial danger to read Acts in the light of what Paul says about himself and not to let Acts speak for itself. Thus, Paul claims to have been called to take the gospel to the Gentiles (Gal. 1.16; Rom. 1.5; 11.13), though he also was deeply concerned for his own people as Romans 10.1 amply testifies, and, indeed, he did say in Romans 11.13–14 that he saw his ministry to the Gentiles as designed to provoke his own people to jealousy (at Gentiles' receiving salvation) and so save some of them, and he affirmed that in the end God's mercy would triumph and all Israel would be saved (Rom. 11.26). Furthermore, he enunciated his famous principle of "accommodation" in 1 Cor. 9.19–23, which included becoming like a Jew to win Jews. Despite these important statements, we tend naturally to think of Paul as the apostle to the Gentiles.

Luke's picture of Paul on this issue could be said to be more nuanced than this "popular" view of Paul. We have already mentioned Acts 9.15 where those to whom Paul is sent to take the name of Jesus include "the sons of Israel" in addition to "Gentiles and kings." Alongside this passage we must now consider others.

In the second account of his call in Acts 22, we read that Ananias conveyed the risen Jesus' message to Paul: "You will be his witness to all people concerning what you have seen and heard." Later, after returning to Jerusalem, Paul had had a vision from the risen Jesus within the holy precincts of the temple. He received an order from Jesus: "Go: I will send you far away to

---

37. Von Bendemann, "Paulus und Israel," 296, goes so far as to describe the PA speech as a "lexicon" (*Lexikon*), containing the developed Christological witness (Zeugnis) of the witness (Zeugen) to the Diaspora Synagogue.

the Gentiles," at which point the crowd interrupted him and prevented his continuing (22.21). From a literary point of view, the speech is interrupted at a vitally significant point. So, there is no doubt that Luke here wishes to stress that Paul's commission definitely includes going to the Gentiles.

The emphasis in the defense speeches of Paul during the various trial scenes (Acts 23–26) is, however, very much on Paul's Jewishness and his faithfulness to the basic tenets of Israel's faith, specifically, the hope of resurrection from the dead (e.g., 23.6). Paul claims that he "believes all that has been written in the Law and the prophets, having hope in God . . . that there will be a resurrection of the righteous and unrighteous" (24.14–15). Before the governor Festus he protests "I have done nothing wrong against either the Law or the temple or against the Emperor" (25.8). Then, in a session before both Festus and the Jewish king, Herod Agrippa II, Paul emphasises his strict Jewish upbringing and that he is on trial for the hope contained in the promise made by God to their ancestors ("our fathers"). As he goes on to narrate the story of his call to be a servant of and witness to the risen Lord, received on the road to Damascus [the third occasion that the readers/hearers have heard this], he reports the promise that the Lord Jesus will rescue him from his own people and the Gentiles—a promise which assumes a ministry to both (26.16–17). In obedience to that call, Paul has preached to those in Jerusalem and Judea and to the Gentiles (26.20). Paul also goes on to say that the scriptures foretold that the messiah should suffer, be the first to rise from the dead and proclaim light to the people and to the Gentiles (26.22–23). The risen Jesus will do this proclaiming through his servants like Paul (e.g., 22.2–5, 12–14, 17–18). The light motif picks up this same theme from the final scene at PA, where Paul and Barnabas say that their preaching to the Gentiles corresponds to the command of the Lord in scripture "I have appointed you to be a light to the Gentiles" (13. 47). At PA, the allusion is to Isa. 49.6, while at 26.17–18 the combination of phrases suggests Isa. 42.6–7, 16; nevertheless, this light theme links the PA speech and that before Festus and Herod Agrippa II.[38]

All this fits in with the picture which the PA speech of Paul conveys of a man committed to the Scriptures and the promise contained therein which God made to the fathers and which He has fulfilled through a descendant of David, who was himself a man after God's heart and the recipient of a renewal of the promise made to the fathers, and in this respect a kind of prototype of his descendant to come, namely Jesus, the Saviour of Israel and the source of forgiveness and life to all who believe.

---

38. Cf. Marguerat, "Saul's Conversion," 152.

But if Paul does have a ministry to his own people as well as to Gentiles, what success does he have among them? It is clear that Paul's message has a mixed reception and divides the Jewish communities to which he goes. At the end of the PA preaching, the situation is that while some Jews have responded (v. 43), many have rejected the message, and not only rejected but have actively spoken against what Paul said. Luke uses the verb ἀντιλέγειν at 13.45. This reminds us of what Simeon had said about Jesus—that he was a sign which would be spoken against (σημεῖον ἀντιλεγόμενον, Lk. 2.34), and anticipates what Luke has Paul saying twice at the very end of the Book of Acts: firstly, Paul said that it was when the Jews of Jerusalem spoke against him (ἀντιλεγόμεντων δὲ τῶν Ἰουδαίων) that he was compelled to appeal to Caesar at Rome (Acts 28.19), and, secondly, the leaders of the Roman Jews reported that all that they knew about Christians was that everywhere people spoke against the movement ([ἡ αἵρεσις] πανταχοῦ ἀντιλέγεται, 28.22).[39]

The issue of a picture of Paul who carries on a ministry to Jews as well as to Gentiles brings us now to the disputed issue of the main episode at the end of Acts. When Paul eventually arrived at Rome, Luke's account makes no mention of Paul's contact and dealings with Christians (apart from their meeting him at the Appian Forum and the Three Taverns—28.15), but has Paul inviting the leaders of the Jewish community to his hired lodgings to explain why he has arrived in Rome as a prisoner. They agreed to meet him again to consider his message at depth, and, on that occasion, for the whole day, Paul carried on discussions with them, based on the Law and the prophets, about the kingdom of God and the things concerning Jesus (28.17-28). The Jewish leaders in Rome were divided by what Paul had maintained. Some were persuaded; others did not believe. Then, Paul quoted Isa. 6.9-10[40] to them and concluded: "Let it be known to you, therefore, that

---

39. Luke uses the verb ἀντιλέγειν 5 times (out of 9 occurrences in the NT). The other occurrence is at Luke 20.27, where he reports that the Sadducees spoke against the idea of the resurrection of the dead.

40. Isaiah 6.9-10 seems to have been an early Christian *testimonium* to explain Jewish refusal of the message both of Jesus himself and their own proclamation of him as messiah, and to justify taking the Christian gospel to the Gentiles. See e.g., Lindars, *NT Apologetic*, 159-67; Gnilka, *Verstockung Israels*.

this salvation[41] of God has been sent to the Gentiles. They—yes they[42]—will listen" (28.25b-27, 28).

Is this third and last pronouncement definitive? Coming so close to the end of the entire book,[43] it might well seem to have an ominous note, as if "the end of the road" had been reached. Has Luke deliberately ended Acts with this assertion as an indication that he has written off the Jewish people? Have they for Luke forfeited their role as the elect people? Is the church now for Luke a Gentile church? Is Rome now the center and no longer Jerusalem? It is understandable if some scholars have assumed an affirmative answer to these questions. These concluding verses seem to sound a dark and sombre note.

Yet the following points need to be borne in mind. In the first place, not all the Jews in Rome refused to believe—some were convinced. It is entirely possible to take the clause καὶ οἱ μὲν ἐπείθοντο τοῖς λεγομένοις in a positive sense (v. 24).[44] The opposite reaction (οἱ δὲ ἠπίστευουν) is "not believing."[45] Secondly, according to 28.30, Paul under house arrest received all who came to him. It is difficult to exclude all Jews from this "all."[46]

---

41. Note the rare neuter form, σωτήριον, which also occurs strategically at Luke 2.32; 3.6 (this occurs elsewhere in the NT only at Eph. 6.17) and then at the very end of his two volume work. See Dupont, *Études*, 398-401, for a discussion of the way Luke has balanced the beginning of his gospel and the end of Acts through the use of this rare form, σωτήριον. (See further 58 n. 75, 93-94, 189-92).

42. How should v. 28b be translated? The JB, GN, REB, and NRSV simply ignore the καί. The NIV is probably in the wrong with "and they will listen," because καί comes second, not first. The translation offered attempts to get the nuance of the καί which strengthens the pronoun αὐτοί (Cf. J. B. Phillips: "and they at least will listen to it!"). Delebecque, *Actes*, 140, quoted by Barrett, *Acts* 2:1247, translated "Eux, oui, ils écouteront." On the other hand, Schröter, "Heil," 300, argues for taking the καί with the verb, not the pronoun.

43. Wasserberg, *Israels Mitte*, 102, stresses this point to counter what he calls the optimism of Tannehill's interpretation of this closing scene of Acts (Tannehill, *Narrative Unity*, 2:350).

44. So Barrett, *Acts*, 2:1244; Witherington, *Acts*, 801; Franklin, *Christ*, 114; Wainwright, *Restoration*, 76; Koet, *Five Studies*, 127, 133; Evans, *Scripture*, 208; Evans, "Luke's View," 37; Mutzner, "Erzählintention," 37; Merkel, "Israel," 396; Rapske, *Paul*, 362-63; Ravens, *Restoration*, 238-39 (who shows that Luke's use of πείθειν "can, on occasions, have the sense of conversion and a corresponding change of belief" (he gives as examples Lk. 16.31; 20.6; Acts 5.36-37; 17.4; 18.4; 19.26; to which could be added Acts 19.8; 26.28; and also 14. 2 in a negative sense); Prieur, *Verkündigung*, 65; Deutschmann, *Synagoge*, 194-95, 229; Sellner, *Heil Gottes*, 372. On the other hand, many stress that Luke does not actually say that they believed—Haenchen, *Acts*, 723; Marshall, *Acts*, 424; Schneider, *Apg.*, 2.417; Fitzmyer, *Acts*, 795.

45. Raven, *Restoration*, 239; Deutschmann, *Synagoge*, 195.

46. In agreement with Barrett, *Acts*, 2:1252; Fitzmyer, *Acts*, 797; Witherington, *Acts*, 803; Dupont, *Nouvelles Études*, 479-82; Brawley, *Luke-Acts*, 77; Koet, *Five Studies*,

Thirdly, would Luke have gone out of his way to stress Paul's commitment to his ancestral faith and the hope of Israel in chapters 22–26 (just reviewed), only then to have him go back on this simply because some of the Roman Jews had not believed?[47] Fourthly, would Luke have included such massive promises in Luke 1–2, only to write them off at the end of Acts?[48] Tannehill's contention that Luke does not minimise the tension between God's promises to Israel and Israel's failure to respond is surely correct.[49] Fifthly, we should bear in mind that the idea of a Gentile mission had already been legitimized by the risen Jesus with reference to God's plan revealed in Scripture (Luke 24.46–47; Acts 1.8); confirmed to both Paul (Acts 9.15) and Peter (Acts 10.1–11.18); and accepted by the Jerusalem Council on the advice of James and his exposition of Scripture (15. 13—21).[50] Paul is not enunciating something new at the end of the story recorded in Acts. Sixthly, we may note that Barrett believed that the ending of Acts reflects not so much whether the Jews have a continuing place in the purposes of God, as Luke's "triumphalism of the word:" even if the Jews as a whole reject the word, others will take it up.[51] Seventhly, Dunn maintains that just as in its original context the hardening statement was part of Isaiah's commission and was in no way intended to mean that he should not preach to his fellow countrymen and women, so it may be assumed that neither did Luke think that the quoted verses from Isaiah meant that Paul should no longer preach to the Jews.[52]

137; Evans, *Luke*, 209; Ravens, *Restoration*, 241–42, 246; Prieur, *Verkündigung*, 71, 74; Wolter, *Israel's Future*, 319; Stenschke, *Gentiles*, 237, who quotes Weiser, *Apg.* 2.377, "Luke means . . . predominantly Gentiles, but does not exclude Jews."

47. Cf. Franklin, *Christ*, 114–15.

48. Cf. the comment of Farris, *Hymns,* 159, that it is more reasonable to suppose that Luke placed the "hymns" [Magnificat, Benedictus and Nunc Dimittis] of Luke 1–2 at the head of a book which sees an Israel repentant and restored, at least partially, rather than an Israel rejecting the gospel and therefore rejected by its God. He believes that these hymns are like an overture which sets out motifs which recur in the body of compositions and he singles out the themes of promise and fulfillment and the restoration of Israel (151) and he believes that there is no reason to suppose that Luke had given up all hope for unrepentant Israel or that Acts 28 represents the end of a mission to Israel (199 n. 39). Mittmann-Richet, *Sühnetod*, 275, maintains that the initial picture in the Gospel of Israel welcoming its Messiah with open arms points to the End.

49. Tannehill, *Narrative Unity*, 2:174–75. See Ravens, *Restoration*, 49, 211, 246, 255, for a strong defense of the view that Luke still held on to a belief in the restoration of Israel.

50. Von Bendemann, "Paulus und Israel," 299–300.

51. Barrett, *Acts*, 2:1246. Prieur, *Gottesherrschaft*, 83, says that in Acts 28.17–31 Luke is not concerned about Paul but his message.

52. Dunn, *Acts*, 355.

Finally, we might mention the view more recently put forward by a number of scholars, that the end of the quotation from Isa. 6.9-10 in Acts 28.26-27 contains a note of hope that despite Israel's hardening God will heal them. The arguments which they put forward may be summarized as follows. The adverb καλῶς is not intended in an ironical sense, but indicates that the Holy Spirit has spoken so well that what was said in the past also applies in the present.[53] Grammatically, the future καὶ ἰάομαι αὐτούς is not equivalent to a subjunctive after μήποτε of v. 27d, but a genuinely independent clause.[54] The LXX has translated the Hebrew in a positive sense—God will heal the Israelites as an act of grace reversing the hardening.[55] The assumption of a positive sense for καὶ ἰάομαι αὐτούς fits in with the other notes of hope for Israel to be found in LA.[56]

Perhaps the safest conclusion is that for Luke the obdurate part, the unrepentant part, of the nation as a whole had forfeited for the time being its special status,[57] but that individual Jews continued to be welcome if they came to believe in Jesus as messiah and lord.[58] Those Jews who believed provided the link with the history of salvation in the past and guaranteed the continuity of Israel, the true people of God.[59]

Does Luke go any further than this? Does he still hold on to the hope that the Jewish people might one day welcome their messiah? Or, to put the matter another way, would Luke think that God would somehow fulfill His promises? There are hints, one cannot put it more strongly, that he had not surrendered the hope of such an eventuality. As mentioned, the promises within the birth narrative seem strategically placed. There is the word of

---

53. Bovon, *Studies*, 118-19.

54. Bovon, *Heilige Geist*, 230; Karrer, *Verstockungsmotiv*, 257-59 (he denies that a change to the future indicative in a series is the rule, rejecting the view of BDF, para. 442).

55. Karrer, *Verstockungsmotiv*, 260-63, 271. In that Karrer stresses that in the LXX God will heal the Jewish people, his position is more forcefully put than Bovon, *Oeuvre*, 150; Steyn, *Quotations*, 228; and Koet, *Five Studies*, 129-30, who think more of the possibility of Israel's repentance.

56. Karrer; *Verstockungsmotiv*, 271. Cf. Butticaz, "Has God Rejected," 163 who cautiously says that these verses in LA are not to be overemphasized but neither underestimated.

57. Cf. Gnilka, *Verstockung*, 154; Talbert, *Martyrdom*, 101. That could be taken as the thrust of the parable of the guests invited to the supper in Luke 14.15-24, esp. v. 24.

58. Cf. Franklin, *Christ*, 114; Brawley, *Jews*, 77; Tannehill, *Narrative Unity*, 2:357; Korn, *Geschichte Jesu*, 52-54; Prieur, *Verkündigung*, 71; Marguerat, "Saul's Conversion," 155 n. 72; And "Enigma," 299; Deutschmann, *Synagoge*, 233-51, 260. This seems to be the view also of Bock, *Proclamation*, 219.

59. Cf. Brawley, *Jews*, 151, "The only Church Acts knows still has the umbilical cord attached" to Israel.

Jesus in Luke 13.35—did Luke only apply it to the entry into Jerusalem (as many scholars believe)[60] or had he the Parousia in mind?[61] And, if the latter, does it imply a positive response[62] or a "Too late"?[63] Does the reference to a limit on the "times of the Gentiles" in Luke 21.24 hold out the implication that God's mercy might save Jerusalem in the deepest sense of the word?[64] Did Luke understand the promise of Jesus to the twelve at 22.28-30 only in terms of their leadership of the group of disciples in Jerusalem in the early days after the resurrection and ascension, or did he think of the eschatological completion of the purposes of God which would embrace Jews and Gentiles?[65]

Dogmatism is out of the question. But we may affirm that to say that Luke has written off the Jews is to go too far.[66] The Christian message is still "the hope of Israel" (Acts 28.20).[67] It is noteworthy that Luke never transfers the concept of Israel to the church nor does he use some such phrase as "the true Israel" or "the new people of God" of the church.[68]

A second theme to be explored is the relation of Acts to the promises of Luke 1-2. The angel Gabriel promised Mary that her son would be great and would be called Son of the Most High and that he would receive the throne of his ancestor David and would reign over the house of Jacob

---

60. E.g. Evans, *Luke*, 565.

61. So Grundmann, *Lukas*, 290; Marshall, *Luke*, 577; Nolland, *Luke*, 2:742; Bock, *Proclamation*, 121; Chance, *Jerusalem*, 131-32.

62. Grundmann, *Lukas*, 290; Caird, *Luke* 174 (though taking the reference to God); Marshall, *Luke*, 577 (a live possibility); Nolland, *Luke*, 2:742; Franklin, *Christ*, 130; Bock, *Proclamation*, 121. Ellis, *Luke*, 192, leaves the question open.

63. Manson, *Sayings*, 128; Fitzmyer, *Luke*, 2:1036.

64. Borgen, "From Paul to Luke," 168-82, and Marshall, *Historian*, 187, see Luke close to Paul here.

65. So, e.g., Marshall, *Luke*, 818.

66. In agreement with Dunn, *Acts*, 183, 354-56; Koet, *Five Studies*, 139, 150-53; Deutschmann, *Synagoge*, 119, 166-67 188, 200-201, 203, 209-10, 212-13, 215, 219, 224; Mittmann-Richert, *Sühnetod*, 274-75; Anderson, *God Raised Him*, 271, who comments: "Jewish rejection of the gospel in Luke-Acts should not be interpreted as the grounds for a dismissal of all Jews for all time, but neither should it be trivialized so that no long-term consequences for disbelieving Jews are envisioned."

67. Franklin, *Christ*, 115. He describes Acts 28.28 as "less a program for the future than a justification of what has happened." A not dissimilar position is taken by Bendemann, "Paulus und Israel," 300-302. Deutschmann, *Synagoge*, 258, affirms that the hope of conversion of Jews has not been given up by Luke, while Denova, *Things Accomplished*, 175, asserts that the view that Acts 28.25-29 means the ultimate rejection of the Jews as a nation cannot be sustained.

68. This is stressed very strongly by Deutschmann, *Synagoge*, 84, 200-201, 209-10, 212-13, 215, 219, 224.

forever (Luke 1.32–33). He would be holy and the Son of God (v. 35). In the PA speech, Ps. 2.7 is used to reveal that Jesus at his resurrection became Son of God, while the language of Ps. 16 about God's "Holy One" is used of Jesus (admittedly, ὅσιος is used and not ἅγιος as at Luke 1.35). There is the strong hint, therefore, that, having been raised from the dead never to return to corruption, i.e., immortal and eternal, the risen Jesus is now sharing in the life of God.[69] In other words, the promise to Mary about her son's eternal reign is fulfilled by being transcended. The eternal reign is not on earth, but in heaven: there the Son is with the Father. The promise made by Gabriel to Mary about Jesus is fulfilled in such a way as to eclipse and transform the original promise completely.

The promise to the fathers is a key point in the PA speech (13.32–33; cf. v. 23): it is now fulfilled in Jesus, especially his resurrection. Though "promise" does not occur in Luke 1–2, the idea of God's oath sworn to the fathers does, and this must be taken as a synonym of promise.[70] In the Benedictus, we hear of the oath which God swore to Abraham that He would deliver Israel from her enemies so that they might worship and serve him in holiness (ἐν ὁσιότητι) and righteousness (1.73–75). The Magnificat paraphrases this idea when it says "as He spoke to our fathers," i.e., to remember to show mercy to Abraham and his seed forever.[71] Promise, oath, speech, whatever the language used, the idea is the same. God made a promise to Abraham and his descendants[72] and now He has fulfilled that promise in Jesus, especially in his resurrection, since in his risen, immortal state Jesus the Holy One (ὁ ὅσιος) can mediate the reliable, holy things promised to David.

Via the use of the light theme from Isaiah 49.6, there is a link between the oracle of Simeon and the PA episode taken as a whole. Simeon had predicted that the babe in his arms was destined to be a "light for revelation to the Gentiles" (Luke 2.31). The Gentiles need revelation in order to recognise the God of Israel as the God of all the earth and of all nations. Their hearts and minds need to be illuminated: they need the light of the revelation which Jesus will bring. In the sequel to Paul's sermon, on the following sabbath, after the Jews of the synagogue had for the most part rejected "the

---

69. Peter's speech at Pentecost explicitly said that Jesus was exalted and received from the Father the promised Spirit whom he has poured out on believers, 2.33; cf. 5.31.

70. See also the discussion in Sellner, *Heil Gottes*, 49–50.

71. The syntax of Luke 1.54b-55 is awkward. The καθὼς ἐλάλησεν πρὸς τοὺς πατέρας ἡμῶν may be a parenthesis with τῷ Ἀβραὰμ καὶ τῷ σπέρματι αὐτοῦ the indirect object of remembering mercy of v. 54b.

72. See Gen. 22.16; 26.3; 32.13; Deut. 4.31; 7.8, 12; 8.1, 15, for reference to God's oath to Abraham.

word of salvation," Paul quoted Isa. 49.6 with its mention of "light for the Gentiles."[73]

Salvation is another theme which links the PA speech with the rest of LA.[74] From David's descendants, God has brought on the scene Jesus as a Saviour for Israel (13.23). The word of God's salvation has, accordingly, been sent to the present generation (13.26). On the following sabbath, Paul and Barnabas quote Isa. 49.6 to justify their taking the message to Gentiles—the Lord had appointed them to be his instruments in taking salvation (σωτηρία) to the ends of the earth. In the birth narratives, Simeon had predicted that the babe in his arms was the salvation (σωτήριον) which God had prepared "for all the peoples" (Luke 2.30-31)

Luke sets this theme going in the birth stories when Zachariah praises God because He has raised up for Israel "a horn of salvation" in the house of David (1.68). The angel of the Lord announces to the shepherds the birth of a Saviour (2.11). Peter declared to the Sanhedrin that there is salvation in no one else but Jesus, the rejected but vindicated stone (4.12), and later to the same body proclaimed the risen Jesus as a saviour for Israel (5.31).

It is probably highly significant from a literary artistic standpoint that Luke uses three times the rare neuter form σωτήριον (he usually employs σωτηρία): twice at the beginning of his work (Luke 2.30 and 3.6) and once at the very end of his work (Acts 28.28).[75] The aged Simeon declared that in the infant Jesus he had seen the σωτήριον of God, which God has prepared in the presence of all peoples. A little later, Luke (alone among the Synoptics) extends the quotation from Isa. 40 to include the line "And all flesh will see the σωτήριον of God." Finally, at the end of Acts, Paul said to the Jews at Rome: "Be it known to you, therefore, that this σωτήριον of God has been sent to the Gentiles" (28.28). This "inclusio" is hardly accidental, but is a deliberate linkage between the beginning and end of a carefully planned work.[76]

While the verb "to save" is not used in the PA speech, it is used frequently by Luke of the activity or results of Jesus' activity. If we leave on

---

73. Von Bendemann, "Paulus und Israel," 300, goes so far as to say that with Acts 28.28 (which with the phrase σωτήριον τοῦ Θεοῦ echoes Isa. 49.6 and Luke 2.32) Luke has reactualized the oracle of Simeon, which speaks of the glory of Israel along with the universal promise of God's saving action.

74. For a detailed study of the themes of salvation, to save and saviour in respect of God and Jesus in LA, see Marshall, *Historian*, 77-216. Marshall (93) calls salvation "the central motif of Lucan theology," "this central, guiding motif."

75. Dupont drew attention to this in "Salut," 132-55 (=*Études*, 393-419, esp. 398-401).

76. See the previous note.

one side the phrase "Your faith has saved you" in healing stories (Luke 7.50; 8.48 [cf. 8.50]; 17.19; 18.42; cf. Acts 4.9; 14.9) and the two instances of the verb in the shipwreck story (Acts 27.20.31), there are still some impressively important statements. In the explanation of the Parable of the Sower, Luke rewrites what Mark says about the first group of seeds which fell on the path and were eaten by the birds: "When they have heard (the word of God), then the devil comes and takes the word from their hearts lest they believe and are saved" (8.12). Clearly, Jesus' word conveys salvation. At the end of the incident involving Jesus' visit to the house of Zaccheus and the transforming effect on his host, Jesus said "Now salvation has come to this house, because he also is a son of Abraham. For the Son of Man came to seek and to save the lost." (19.9–10).

There is an inclusio in Peter's speech on the Day of Pentecost. The quotation from Joel finishes with "Whoever calls on the name of the Lord will be saved" (Acts 2.21) and at the end of his speaking, Peter calls on the crowd "Save yourselves from this crooked generation" (2.40). Luke rounds off his account with the comment "The Lord added daily to their number those who were being saved" (2.47). To be saved is clearly something of the highest importance for men and women. Even the highest in the land, the members of the Sanhedrin, need to be made aware that only through the name of Jesus can we be saved—there is none other beside him who can save us (4.12).

In defense of his action in baptising Cornelius and others at Caesarea, Peter recounted how the centurion had been told by an angel to send for Peter "who will speak to you words by which you and your whole household will be saved" (11.14). The Philippian jailor cried out to Paul and Silas "Sirs, what must I do to be saved?" and was told that he and his household should believe in the Lord Jesus and they would be saved (16.31).

The theme of salvation and its recipients also links the PA episode to the programmatic sentence at the beginning of Acts. The Lord Jesus, on the point of ascending to heaven, said to his disciples: "You will receive power when the Holy Spirit comes upon you, and you will be my witnesses in Jerusalem and all Judea and Samaria and to the ends of the earth" (ἕως ἐσχάτου τῆς γῆς 1.8). When they reproached the Jews of PA with proving unworthy of eternal life by refusing their message, Paul and Barnabas said that they would turn to the Gentiles, for the Lord had commanded them in this way, and they quoted Isa. 49.6: "I have appointed you to be a light to the nations so that you might be (the bearer of) salvation to the ends of the earth" (ἕως ἐσχάτου τῆς γῆς 13.46–47).

Now the eleven disciples addressed in Acts 1.8 do not in actual fact fulfill the commission "to the ends of the earth." For Luke, the discharge of that part of the commission fell supremely to Paul. Arguably, we see this beginning to happen in earnest in Acts 13-14. In his PA speech, Paul acknowledged the role of the original witnesses (13.31): significantly, though, they are witnesses "to the people," i.e., of Israel. Later, in Paul's speech before the infuriated crowd outside the temple, he said that Ananias had said to him in Damascus: "The God of our fathers has appointed you to know His will and see the Righteous One and hear his voice, because you will be his witness to all people concerning the things which you have seen and heard" (22.14-15). In this way, Paul is linked with the original disciples as a witness to the Lord Jesus.[77]

Forgiveness of sins is another important theme for Luke. The risen Jesus asserts that the Scriptures (Law, Prophets and Psalms) had taught that the messiah should suffer, that he should rise from the dead on the third day and that repentance leading to the forgiveness of sins should be proclaimed in his name to all the nations, beginning from Jerusalem' (Luke 24.46-47). In three of his speeches, Peter mentions the gift of forgiveness. He challenges the crowd on the day of Pentecost to repent and be baptized in the name of Jesus Christ (faith is "collapsed into" the submission to baptism) for the forgiveness of sins (Acts 2.38). Before the Sanhedrin, Peter maintained that God has exalted Jesus as Leader and Saviour at His right hand, in order to give repentance to Israel and forgiveness of sins (5.31). Peter concluded his address to Cornelius and his household by saying that all the prophets bore witness to Jesus, that everyone who believes in him should receive forgiveness of sins through his name (10.43).

Thus, when Paul announces forgiveness of sins through Jesus (13.38), going on to explain this in the next clause as justification from sins, he is preaching in a manner faithful to scripture, to Jesus and to the Jerusalem disciples led by Peter. In the light of 26.18, we may also say—in a manner faithful to the commission received directly from the risen Lord Jesus who had said to him that he was sending him "to open their [that is, the (Jewish) people and the Gentiles[78]] eyes, to turn them from darkness to light and from the power of Satan to God, that they might receive forgiveness of sins and a place among those sanctified by faith in me" (26.18).

---

77. Cf. Dupont, *Nouvelles Études*, 455-56: Paul "appears as the executor of the mission entrusted to the apostles . . . On Paul falls the task of assuring to the church its universal dimension announced by the prophets." For a similar viewpoint, see also Jervell, *Apg.*, 283, 288, 595, 639.

78. So Pesch, *Apg.*, 2.278; Roloff, *Apg.*, 353; Fitzmyer, *Acts*, 760; and Witherington, *Acts*, 744. Barrett, *Acts*, 2:1160, appears to accept a double reference in the οὔς, though concedes that it is possible that the reference is only to the Gentiles. Haenchen, *Acts*, 686; Schneider, *Apg.*, 2.374; and Johnson, *Acts*, 436-37, refer it to the Gentiles.

Previously, we mentioned that Luke had each of his three main characters begin their ministry with an inaugural speech. We turn now to examine some of the links between the speech of Jesus at Nazareth and Paul's PA speech. If Jesus was commissioned to preach the good news in fulfillment of Isa. 61.1, so too Paul with Barnabas preached the good news of God's fulfillment of His promise to the fathers (Acts 13.32). If Jesus believed himself "sent" to preach, so Paul said that the word of salvation had been sent to the people (Acts 13.26) and backs up his sense of being sent with the use of Isa. 49.6 at 13 47. Jesus uses ἄφεσις in respect of captives and downtrodden twice (Luke 4.18—Luke has probably taken these statements in a metaphorical or spiritual sense[79]), while Paul's speech climaxed in the offering of the ἄφεσις of sins (Acts 13.38—forgiveness being a spiritual release). At Nazareth there is a hint that the blessings of Jesus' ministry will go eventually to Gentiles, recourse being made to the stories of the dealings of Elijah and Elisha with foreigners (Luke 4. 25–27). Paul began within the synagogue, but, as a result of the rejection by the Jews at PA, he turned to the Gentiles and backed this up as corresponding to the will of God by reference to Isa. 49.6, having earlier proclaimed that everyone who believes will be justified before God by Jesus.

There is, then, a web of threads which link the PA speech and episode to the rest of Luke's twofold volume. These threads attest the importance and significance of the speech and episode within Luke's overall plan and strategy for his work.

---

79. In agreement with Rese, "Alttestamentliche Motive," 146, and Korn, *Geschichte Jesu*, 77, who interpret the "oppressed" to be sinners.

Chapter 3

The Structure of the Speech

I

How should this speech be divided up? What is the structure intended by Luke? Should linguistic considerations or the contents determine our divisions?

It is possible to make the address ἄνδρες Ἰσραηλῖτες / ἄνδρες ἀδελφοί καὶ φοβούμενοι τὸν Θεόν into a structure-forming device and so divide the speech into three parts—verses 16–25, 26–37 and 38–41. We could then define the contents in this way: first, a review of "sacred" history; then, the kerygma about Jesus as the fulfillment of God's promise; finally, the concluding peroration consisting of both appeal and warning. This is the division preferred by Dumais,[1] Dupont,[2] Pesch,[3] Lüdemann,[4] Barrett,[5]

---

1. Dumais, *Langage*, 57–58.
2. Dupont, *Nouvelles Études*, 387–88n13.
3. Pesch, *Apg.*, 2.30.
4. Ludemann, *Early Christianity*, 153.
5. Barrett, *Acts*, 1:623.

Fitzmyer[6], Hall[7] Strauss,[8] Pilcher,[9] Schröter,[10] Pietsch,[11] Anderson,[12] Odile Flichy[13] and Zhang.[14]

Bruce also accepted a tripartite structure, but he divided the speech into verses (16) 17–22, 23–37 and 38–41. By this means, Bruce secured the initial reference to Jesus at v. 23 within his second section.[15] Jervell[16] too proposed a tripartite division, though again along different lines: vv. 17–25, 26–31 and 32–41. He stressed the personal emphasis in v. 32 "And *we* proclaim to *you* the good news that. . .," but merges vv. 38–41 into the third section with vv. 32–37. Verses 38–41 should be accorded a separate section. In his comment on v. 38, however, Jervell said: "And now the conclusion, which is a consequence from the resurrection of Jesus," as if he actually acknowledged that vv. 38–41 formed a separate section.[17] Wills offers a tripartite division according to Authoritative Examples (*exempla*) from the Past or Present (vv. 16b–37), Conclusion (vv. 38–39) and Exhortation (vv. 40–41).[18] Quite apart from separating vv. 37–39 and 40–41 in a somewhat unnatural manner, his first section is too long, creating a somewhat unbalanced structure.

Soards divided the actual speech itself into four, splitting vv. 38–41 into two: vv. 38–39 and vv. 40–41 (he actually counted vv. 46–47 as a fifth section, calling it an epilogue). Otherwise, he also divided the rest of the speech into two parts: vv. 16b–25 and 26–37.[19]

Klinghardt seems to be unique in dividing the speech in a tripartite manner, but treating verses 16–31 as *narratio*, verses 32–39 as *argumentatio*, and verses 40–41 as *peroratio*.[20] The weakness of this is that it ignores verse

---

6. Fitzmyer, *Acts*, 507.
7. Hall, *Revealed Histories*, 185.
8. Strauss, *Davidic Messiah*, 153–57.
9. Pilcher, *Paulusrezeption*, 118–19, 125–27, 140, 161, and 186.
10. Schröter, "Heil," 295.
11. Pietsch, *Sprotz Davids*, 297–98.
12. Anderson, *God Raised Him*, 238–39.
13. Flichy, *Figure*, 186–87.
14. Zwang, *Paul*, 122–23.
15. Bruce, *Acts*, 271–79.
16. Jervell, *Apg.*, 354, 357, and 358
17. Ibid., 360.
18. Wills, "Sermon," 277–99, esp. 278–79.
19. Soards, *Speeches*, 79–80.
20. Klinghardt, *Gesetz*, 99n6. Actually, he does refer to K. Berger, *Formgeschichte des Neuen Testaments*, 72.

26 and its division-forming character, and by keeping verses 38–39 in the argument section, Klinghardt has made the peroration end on a very negative note. The double οὖν statements of verses 38 and 40 are better taken together as forming an effective antithetical conclusion, summing up the two possibilities depending on whether the message evokes belief or refusal.

Schneider also like Bruce began a second section with v. 23, but he split vv. 23–37 into two parts—23–30 and 31–37: i.e., he put Jesus' earthly ministry up to his death and burial inside his second section (23–30) and began the third section with the resurrection and took in the OT proof-texts for this (31–37). With vv. 38–41 as the conclusion of the speech, Schneider has a four-part division. A number of other scholars have also divided the speech into four parts, but in a different way from Schneider. Thus, Kliesch,[21] Weiser,[22] Roloff,[23] van de Sandt,[24] and Steyn[25] preferred to divide the speech into vv. 16b–25, 26–31, 32–37, and 38–41. They divide vv. 26–37 into two, taking in God's raising of Jesus and the apostolic witness into their second section, and beginning a third section with Paul's announcement of the good news of God's fulfilling His promise and with OT proof texts backing this up.

Kennedy[26] takes the speech as an example of epideictic rhetoric aiming at belief, not action, and divides it along lines of Greek rhetorical style into a rather formal proem (v. 16b); narration (vv. 17–25); proposition (v. 26); proof (vv. 27–37); and epilogue (vv. 38–39).[27] Witherington acknowledged his indebtedness to Kennedy and followed him in his fivefold division of the speech: exordium v. 16; narratio vv. 17–25; propositio v. 26; probatio vv. 27–37; peroratio vv. 38–41.[28] Both Kennedy and Witherington are open to the charge of having applied too rigidly rules from the Greek rhetoricians to the PA speech. Thus, verse 16 hardly merits the label proem or exordium: it is hardly an introduction in any sense of introducing or presenting a summary of the facts. It is difficult to believe that a Greek or Roman orator would have recognized v. 16 as a genuine proem/exordium. As to vv. 17–25 being a narratio, one has considerable hesitations. Arguably, a greater con-

---

21. Kliesch, *Credo*, 163.
22. Weiser, *Apg.*, 322–23.
23. Roloff, *Apg.*, 202–3.
24. Van de Sandt, "Quotations," 26.
25. Steyn, *Quotations*, 160–63.
26. Kennedy, *Rhetorical Criticism*, 124–25.
27. Presumably, Kennedy actually intended the epilogue to include vv. 40–41 as well.
28. Witherington, *Acts*, 407.

centration on the story of David and explicit quotation of the promise of God through Nathan would be better suited to a narratio. There is some merit in saying that v. 26 is the propositio, though one might argue that v. 23 would also qualify for that classification. In respect of vv. 27-37, it could be argued that both categories of narratio and probatio are to be found and that only labelling this unit as probatio is to be guilty of forcing the material too much into a strait-jacket.[29] All in all, considerable reservations must attach to the attempt to use these categories from ancient rhetoricians in analysing the PA speech.[30] These are increased if the speech is seen to be more of a midrashic exposition of God's promise to David through Nathan in 2 Samuel 7.

Whether it is correct to apply the rules of Greek and Roman rhetorical style or not, the division favoured by Kennedy and Witherington in the end comes fairly close to the tripartite division accepted by Barrett and Fitzmyer, with the major exception being that v. 26 has been separated as a proposition from its proof in vv. 27-37. However, the γάρ (for) of v. 27 surely requires taking v. 27 and what follows closely with v. 26.

Buss argued for a five-part division: vv. 16a-23; 24-26; 27-31; 32-37; 38-41. Grammatically, however, as he himself pointed out, v. 24 belongs with v. 23 and v. 25 belongs with v. 24. This seems to be a weakness of his dividing v. 23 off from vv. 24-25. The γάρ (for) of v. 27 suggests that a separation of v. 26 and v. 27 is rather harsh and not outweighed by Buss' argument that "Jerusalem" forms an inclusion between vv. 27 and 31. While a direct address, whether ἄνδρες Ἰσραηλῖται or ἄνδρες ἀδελφοί, opens sections at vv. 16 and 38, on this analysis ἄνδρες ἀδελφοί concludes a section at v. 26.

Wilckens analysed the speech into six parts: vv. 16-23; 24-25; 26-31; 32-37; 38-39; 40-41,[31] as did Pillai.[32] We have already pointed out the grammatical link of vv. 24-25 with v. 23. It is perhaps an over-refinement

---

29. Cf. the reservations about confining the structural development of the speech into a precise form found in ancient rhetorical handbooks, expressed by Anderson, *God Raised Him*, 239.

30. Pilcher, *Paulusrezeption* (see n. 9) used the terms narratio, argumentatio, and peroratio for his threefold division (vv. 16b-25, 26-37, 38-41). Flichy, *Figure*, 187-89, in addition to the tripartite division mentioned earlier, also mentions a rhetorical structure with exordium (v. 16), narratio (vv. 17-25) and then the propositio in two stages, each followed by a probatio (26 with 27-31 and 32-33 with 34-37); concluding with the peroratio (vv. 38-41).

31. Wilckens, *Missionsreden*, 54.

32. Pillai, *Missionary Preaching*, 63, 72-75, 121, was also prepared to argue for a broader covenant pattern—historical recital of God's mighty acts followed by the appeal for fidelity to and confidence in Yahweh (here vv. 16-37 and 38-41) as found in Exodus and Deuteronomy.

to divide 38–41. Like those who propose a fourfold division Wilckens has divided vv. 26–37 into two sections.

The advantage of the tripartite division is the agreement between form and content, even if as regards the former the mode of address is not absolutely constant. Although the name of Jesus is mentioned in v. 23, there is no need to make a division at that point. On the tripartite division, John the Baptist is included in the review of sacred history, and the report of what he said about the coming one forms a suitable end to one section and the preparation for the section actually on Jesus.

Should the second section vv. 26–37 be subdivided? A case can be made for a break between vv. 31 and 32. With v. 31, we reach the end of the kerygma about Jesus, while vv. 32–37 deal with OT proof texts. However, these proof texts deal with the resurrection which is the theme of v. 31, and so really ought not to be separated from it. Accordingly, we have opted to adhere to the overall tripartite division. Its very simplicity is satisfying and does not resort to over-subtle refinements.

The speech intends to persuade and convince. The survey of Israel's history functions as an introduction to help show that Jesus, a descendant of David, is not only part of the story of Israel, but is also the climax and culmination of that history. He is the savior who gathers up the hopes and longings of what has gone before. He is the savior who fulfils what God had promised in Israel's story. The section on Jesus is brief and concentrates on his death and resurrection, for the resurrection is crucial. Not only did it reverse the—tragically sad—rejection of Jesus by Jerusalem and its leaders, but by ensuring that he would not see corruption also meant that he could dispense the blessings inherent in the promise made by God to David. The OT is called on to substantiate the significance of the resurrection of Jesus. The conclusion or peroration sets before the hearers/readers the possibility of salvation (expressed as forgiveness or justification) or taking offence at this and not believing the work which God was doing at the time (which attitude is tantamount to proving oneself unworthy of eternal life).

In technical terms drawn from Greco-Roman rhetoric this speech is epideictic rhetoric:[33] it is a speech which seeks to persuade the hearer/reader of the claims on behalf of Jesus, son of David.

---

33. So Kennedy, *Rhetorical Criticism*, 124–25; Soards, *Speeches*, 79; against Witherington, *Acts*, 407, who classifies it as deliberative rhetoric.

II

We turn now to examine the PA speech from the angle of how far do the three sections proposed interlock with one another. What is the evidence of careful crafting of the speech to dovetail the three sections into each other and into the framework?

Right at the beginning of the speech there is a reference to the "fathers" elected by God (v. 17). In the second section, verse 32 refers to the promise made to "the fathers." Twice in vv. 20–21 in the first section there are two references to God's *giving* judges and Saul as king. In the second section the verb "to give" figures twice, both times in OT quotations: God 's promise to give the holy, reliable blessings promised to David (v. 34), and the assertion that God will not give His Holy One to see corruption (v. 35). In the first section, in v. 22, the verb ἤγειρεν is used in the sense of God's bringing on the scene David as king for Israel; in the second section, twice God is said to have raised up (ἤγειρεν) Jesus from the dead (vv. 30, 37). If the story of God's dealings with Israel before Jesus climaxes with David who is described as someone after God's own heart and who does God's will (v. 22) and the promised savior is a descendant of David (v. 23), in the second section David and Jesus are set in a relationship of contrast—David died whereas Jesus was raised from the dead (vv. 34–37). One might well describe this as a typological relationship.[34]

At verse 23 Jesus is described as a savior for Israel, while at the beginning of the second section, Paul announced that "the word of *this* salvation has been sent to us" (v. 26).

The concept of promise is mentioned in the first section at v. 23 ("God brought Jesus to Israel as savior κατ' ἐπαγγελίαν"); this is taken up in the second section when Paul announced that God had fulfilled the promise (ἐπαγγελίαν) made to the fathers (vv. 32–33).

There may also be one further link. In the review of God's dealings with Israel, God is the subject of the verbs except at v. 21 where it is said that the people asked for (ἠτήσαντο) a king, and this probably carries a pejorative nuance, because according to one strand in the OT (e.g., 1 Sam. 8) Saul was not really the king whom God had in mind for Israel. In the second section, the Jerusalemites and their rulers are said to have asked (ᾐτήσαντο) Pilate that Jesus should be executed (v. 28), which is clearly a totally wrong action, because they have refused their true king.[35]

---

34. Cf. Pichler, *Paulusrezeption*, 150, 162, 221; Miura, *David*, 186 (Miura also links the Davidic messiah model and the Isaianic New Exodus model in his interpretation of Paul's PA Speech—see 181, 185, 241).

35. Cf. Pietsch, *Sprotz Davids*, 303.

Thus, there are several cross-links between the first and second sections.

Are there any links of a similar kind between the third section and the other two? The use of the demonstrative adjective οὗτος αὕτη τοῦτο does occur in all three sections in key verses. Thus, at verse 23 it is from this man's seed [τούτου ... ἀπὸ τοῦ σπέρματος] that God has brought a savior to Israel; at verse 26 the word of this salvation [τῆς σωτηρίας ταύτης] has been sent to the hearers; at verse 33a God has fulfilled the same [ταύτην, viz the promise made to the fathers]; and finally, the double "through / by this man" occurs at verse 38–39 [διὰ τούτου ... ἐν τούτῳ]. In addition, we might mention also that "the word of this salvation" at the beginning of the second section has something of an echo in the Isaiah 49.6 quotation in the sequel to the speech, with the reference to "salvation" to be taken to the ends of the earth (v. 47).

Certainly, the forward position of the demonstrative in verses 23 and 38–39 and the structure of the sentence in verses 32–33a means that "this" carries emphasis in the Greek, which may often be lost in modern English translations.

Thus, we may say that there are enough signs that the speech has been carefully composed in order to link its three main sections together and enable the reader's attention to be focused on the things that the author wished to emphasise.

Chapter 4

Did Luke Use Sources for the Speech?

PART 1 OF PAUL'S SPEECH AT PISIDIAN ANTIOCH: VERSES 16–25

Verse 16: The Address

The speech opens with the direct address "Israelites and you who fear God." The term "Israelites" is chosen no doubt because the speaker is about to review the history of Israel, however selectively. What he is going to speak about is their history, their story. They are a part of it. Is a second group envisaged with "and you who fear God" or is the καὶ epexegetic (explanatory)—"that is, you who fear God"? And if a second group is envisaged, who are they—are they proselytes or those non-Jews who were sympathetic to Jewish beliefs, felt drawn by its monotheism and high ethical standards, and worshipped in the synagogue, but had not taken the actual step of becoming full converts to Judaism (the need to be circumcised and to follow the food laws being a disincentive to them)?

In recent years there has been considerable discussion as to whether this latter group of people was actually known by a quasi-technical term "God-Fearers." Most would accept that there were such people;[1] the issue is whether there was a fixed or a semi-technical term for them. Certainly, the stele listing Jews and God-Fearers found at Aphrodisias, and dated by its editors to the early third century AD, seems to have tilted the scales of the balance in favour of the view that θεοσεβής at any rate had become

---

1. Exceptions are Kraabel, "Disappearance," 113–26, and Wilcox, "God-Fearers," 102–22.

something of a technical term by then.² But we need to exercise some care in arguing back from the early third century AD and assuming that this was so in the second half of the first century AD, though Wander believes that this is legitimate.³

However, the issue in 13.16 and 26 is not whether in general there were such people, nor whether there might have been a technical term for them outside the NT, but *what did Luke intend by the phrase which he used in the context of the whole episode?* Consideration has to be taken of Luke's description of what happened immediately after the synagogue service and a week later. Luke says that when the service ended and people began to disperse, "many of the Jews and the devout proselytes [πολλοὶ . . . τῶν σεβομένων προσηλύτων]⁴ followed Paul and Barnabas who spoke to them and sought to persuade them to continue in the grace of God" (v. 43). This suggests that back at vv. 16 and 26 proselytes were in mind in the phrase "you who fear God"/ "those among you who fear God."⁵ It is a week later that Gentiles come into the picture: Luke says that *almost the whole city* was gathered to hear the word of God, which provoked opposition from the Jews as a result of which Paul and Barnabas indicated their intention to turn to the Gentiles who, when they heard these words, rejoiced and glorified the word of the Lord. Those ordained (by God) to eternal life believed (v. 48). At v. 50, Luke describes the Jews as enlisting the help of devout women [τὰς σεβομένας γυναῖκας] and the leading men of the city in their campaign against Paul and Barnabas. The "devout women" appear to be at the very least sympathisers and supporters of Judaism. The assistance of "the leading

---

2. See Levinskaya, *Diaspora Setting*, 51–126, esp. 51, 70–80; also Gempf, "God-Fearers," 444–47; Trebilco, *Jewish Communities*, 145–66; de Boer, "God-Fearers," 50–71; Barclay, *Jews*, 279n50, 403n6; Wander, *Gottesfürchtige*; Witherington, *Acts*, 341–44; Riesner, *Early Period*, 109n5; Hirschberg, *Das eschatologische Israel*, 109n385. For a bibliography of the discussion over God-Fearers, see Wander, *Gottesfürchtige*, 247–57, and Fitzmyer, *Acts*, 450.

3. Wander, *Gottesfürchtige*, 127.

4. The articular participle is here used as the equivalent of an adjective.

5. Barrett, *Acts*, 1:639 interprets the phrase to indicate proselytes and takes the phrase "among you" to mean those who have joined the ranks of the synagogue rather than those who are in the same building. Wassenberg, *Israels Mitte*, 48–51, also argues that proselytes are in mind at vv. 16, 22, and 43 (he points out that Luke distinguishes between those born-Jews and proselytes at 2.11 and that otherwise we would have to distinguish between the circle of those addressed *in* the synagogue and those outside *in front of* the synagogue); see also Pietsch, *Sprotz Davids*, 298. Schneider. *Apg.*, 1:131, poses the question whether proselytes are intended at v. 16 but does not answer his question. Deutschmann, *Synagoge*, 59, thinks that non-Jews are in mind, but that they play only a peripheral or passive role and merely have the status of observers.

men" may have been solicited by these devout women,[6] or these men may have been the husbands of the devout women who enlisted their help[7] or who were themselves along with their wives sympathetic to Judaism but did not express it openly.

On this interpretation, then, the following picture emerges: up to v. 44, Luke has in mind as Paul's audience both native Jews and Gentile converts ("proselytes"). Though the inclusion of Gentiles within the people of God who receive salvation was part of God's purpose from the beginning, as the reader/hearer has been informed by Simeon's prophecy (Luke 2.28-32), in practice it is Jewish unbelief and rejection of the gospel which leads to that gospel being proclaimed to the non-Jews (a pattern which repeats itself often hereafter in the narrative of Acts).

There remains, however, a substantial body of scholarly opinion which assumes that at vv. 16 and 26 two groups are being addressed: those born Jews and those Gentiles attracted by the Jewish faith but not proselytes, not converts in the full sense of the word.[8] They argue that Luke seems to have used ὁ φοβούμενος / οἱ φοβούμενοι τὸν Θεόν as an equivalent to the claimed technical use of σεβομένος.[9]

Now, outside of the PA speech, Luke uses φοβούμενος τὸν Θεόν of the Roman centurion Cornelius at Acts 10.2, 22. In both instances, Luke does not employ the definite article, and the participle seems to be used synonymously with εὐσεβής and δίκαιος at vv. 2 and 22 respectively, i.e., adjectivally. When Peter speaks to Cornelius, he says that God has shown him that in every nation the person who fears Him [ὁ φοβούμενος αὐτὸν] and does what is right is acceptable to Him (v. 35). As Barrett rightly says: "Here at least it seems that Luke is not employing a technical term ('God-Fearer') but uses his word descriptively in a way that could be applied to a Jew, to a proselyte, or to any kind of Gentile who possessed the qualities and observed the practices that are commonly in mind when the term 'God-Fearer' is used as a technicality."[10]

6. Haenchen, *Acts*, 414; Kee, *Every Nation*, 169; Wander, *Gottesfürchtige*, 192.

7. Marshall, Acts, 231; Roloff, *Apg.*, 210; Deutschmann, *Synagoge*, 132 (could perhaps be the husbands).

8. So Bruce, *Acts*, 274; Haenchen, *Acts*, 409; Roloff, *Apg.*, 202; Schneider, *Apg.*, 2:135; Pesch, *Apg.*, 2.31; Fitzmyer, *Acts*, 514; Witherington, *Acts*, 411; Buss, *Missionspredigt*, 35; Koch, "Proselyten," 95; Zwang, *Paul*, 127.

9. Cf. de Boer, "God-Fearers," 63-65.

10. Barrett, *Acts*, 1:519. Wander, *Gottesfürchtige*, 189, maintains that in general "God-fearing" could apply to three groups: as a designation of the attitude and conduct of Jews and of Gentiles close to Jews, in order to specify their piety; as a synonym for proselytes; and as a term for a special group between pure Gentiles and proselytes. See also Deutschmann, *Synagoge*, 52-53.

As to the verb to worship σέβεσθαι, Luke uses it seven times, all in Acts and all from chapter 13 onwards.[11] The present participle middle is used twice at 13.43, 50 adjectivally, with the sense, as already seen, of "devout." Luke uses the phrase σεβομένη τὸν Θεόν of Lydia at 16.14. Paul met her at a place for prayer on the Sabbath outside the city of Philippi. She is clearly a Gentile woman who is sympathetic to Judaism. At Thessalonica Paul discussed with worshippers in the synagogue for three consecutive sabbaths. "Some of the Jews were persuaded and joined Paul and Silas, as were (te) a large crowd of devout Greeks [τῶν τε σεβομένων Ἑλλήνων πλῆθος πολύ], and several of the leading women" (17.4). The noun "Greeks" distinguishes them from "Jews," and, since they are described as devout, they are probably sympathisers. Luke adds that several of the women of high standing also believed. Having arrived in Athens, Paul discussed with Jews and the devout persons [τοῖς σεβομένοις] in the synagogue and in the market place every day with those who happened to be there (17.17).[12] The σεβομένοι here are clearly distinguished from born Jews. Probably, in the absence of the noun "proselytes," they are non-Jewish sympathisers, like Lydia at Philippi. Finally, for our purposes,[13] Luke mentions that at Corinth Paul met resistance from the Jews and decided to separate from the synagogue (18.6). He was welcomed into the house of Titius Justus, whom Luke describes as one who was a σεβόμενος τὸν Θεόν (v. 7). Again, the probability is that Titius Justus was a non-Jewish sympathiser with Judaism who responded positively to the preaching of the message about Jesus, and opened his home, as had Lydia, to Paul and, possibly, as a "house church" for the new Christian converts.

This brief survey suggests that Luke has no technical term by which he describes those non-Jews who were sympathetic to Judaism but who did not become proselytes. He can use the phrase "fear God" adjectivally of Cornelius and in a general descriptive way of those who are acceptable to God in every nation. He can use the participle of σέβεσθαι adjectivally of proselytes (13.43) and of non-Jewish supporters of the synagogue (13.50), and of those non-Jewish worshippers at the synagogue present when Paul preached

11. Wander, *Gottesfürchtige*, 192, points this out. He explains the change of usage as due, not to the use of different sources, but to the transition to the different cultural milieu of Europe compared with Syria-Palestine; cf. the brief comment of Cadbury, *Making*, 225.

12. This third group are presumably those described as δεισιδαιμονεστέροι at 17.22 (with its possible double nuance—very religious or very superstitious).

13. Acts 18.13 (the accusation that Paul and his companions are teaching the people to worship God contrary to to the law) and 19.27 (the statement made by the leader of the silversmiths, Demetrius, that the pagan goddess Diana is worshipped throughout the Roman province of Asia) are not relevant for our enquiry.

(17.17) and of those non-Jewish worshippers who responded positively to Paul's preaching (17.4); he can use it, with τὸν Θεόν as an object, of those non-Jews who had been sympathetic to Judaism and became converts to Christ (Lydia, 16.14; and Titius Justus, 18.7). The variety of groups covered by the phrases "fear God," "worship God," and "devout" tells against any attempt to describe any of these terms as a technical term in *Luke's* vocabulary. We may accept that for Luke the terms "fear God" and "worship God" are overlapping concepts. Context must decide what is in Luke's mind in each given occurrence.[14]

Verses 17–23: The Review of Sacred History

After the direct address "Men of Israel and you who fear God" and the appeal for attention (ἀκούσατε) in v. 16, the speech reviews selectively Israel's history, from God's election of the patriarchs to the appointment of David, son of Jesse, as king in succession to Saul.

The history naturally begins with the patriarchs. "God of this people, Israel, chose our fathers" (v. 17a). In this short half-sentence a good portion of Gen. 12–50 is summarized. God called Abraham (Gen. 12.1–3) and promised him, among other things, descendants (Gen. 15-4–5; 17.5–6, 15–16); promised His covenant to Isaac (Gen. 17.19–21); and renewed it to Jacob (Gen. 27.13–15; 35.10–12). The next phrase leaps over the Joseph saga and the subsequent enslavement of the Hebrews in Egypt, to their deliverance: "God ὕψωσεν the people in a foreign land, in Egypt" (v. 17b). The verb could mean "exalted," in the sense of "gave them victory" over the Egyptians,[15] or "make great" in the sense of "increase their numbers and power."[16] While the latter could appeal to Exod. 1.6–10, in general the former sense probably fits the context better with its emphasis on God's pow-

---

14. Wander, *Gottesfürchtige*, 197–200, attempts a schematic presentation of "God-fearers" in Acts in five categories: i) the φοβούμενος / σεβόμενος τὸν Θεόν who combines affinity and quality description (e.g., Cornelius, Lydia); ii) the same Greek phrases used as an affinity description (e.g., 13.26; 17.17; 18.7); iii) σέβομαι used both of Gentiles who were more than sympathisers but had no fixed participation in the Synagogue (13.50; 17.4; cf. the centurion of Luke 7.4) and of proselytes as especially worthy (13.43); iv) "sympathisers"—politically influential people of the upper class who helped the synagogue (13.50; 17.4, 12); v) the public present as hearers of Paul's preaching (13.44, 48).

15. Roloff, *Apg.*, 204; Johnson, *Acts*, 231; Barrett, *Acts*, 1:631; Pichler, *Paulusrezeption*, 213. Flichy, *Figure*, 191–92, believes that the reader is being invited to read the history of Israel from the resurrection of Christ (ὑψόω is used of the exaltation of Christ at Acts 2.33 and 5.31).

16. BAG 858; Marshall, *Acts*, 223; Pesch, *Apg.*, 2.34; Witherington, *Acts*, 409.

erful intervention on behalf of His people: "and led them out of it with an uplifted arm" (v. 17c),[17] which summarises the Exodus from Egypt (Exod. 12.29-36; 13.17-15.21).

The period in the desert is referred-to in v. 18: "and for a period of about[18] forty years God cared for[19] them in the desert" (Exod. 15.22-17.11), and the occupation of the land of Canaan is compressed into "and He destroyed seven nations[20] in the land of Canaan and made [the Israelites] inherit their land over a period of four hundred and fifty years"[21] (the Book of Joshua). The review passes quickly over the period of the judges ("and

17. The picture of God's uplifted or mighty arm as a symbol of His effective power in connection with the Exodus from Egypt is frequently employed in the OT: e.g., Exod. 6.1, 6; 13.3, 9, 16; 32.11; Deut. 3.24; 4.39; 5.15; 6.21; 7.8; 9.26.

18. Probably Luke was responsible for the ὡς—so Schneider, *Apg.*, 2:132; Barrett, *Acts*, 1:631; Buss, *Missionspredigt*, 39.

19. The reading ἐτροφοφόρησεν ("cared for"—the reading of P74, the corrector of A, E, d e g) is to be preferred, with Ropes, *Beginnings*, 3:120; Haenchen, *Acts*, 408; Marshall, *Acts*, 223; Pesch, *Apg.*, 2:35; Barrett, *Acts*, 1:632; Witherington, *Acts*, 410; Johnson, *Acts*, 231; Pillai, *Missionary Preaching*, 30, 40; Dumais, *Langage*, 143; Hall, *Revealed Histories*, 188; Strauss, *Davidic Messiah*, 158 n. 1; Pilcher, *Paulusrezeption*, 145-46; Pietsch, *Sprotz Davids*, 302; Flichy, *Figure*, 192; and Zwang, *Paul*, 130; against ἐτροποφόρησεν ("put up with"—the reading of ℵ B D lat; and defended by BAG 835; Schneider, *Apg.*, 2.132. Steyn, *Septuagint Quotations*, 164 accepts "endured"). (Interestingly, the manuscript tradition of the passage in Deut. 1.31, to which Acts 13.18 seems indebted, shows similar textual variants). The context emphasises the positive side of God's actions on behalf of the people, and this favours the reading "cared for." See the study by Gordon, "Targumic Parallels," 285-87, who has indicated that, while dependence on the LXX must remain as the probable explanation of Luke's use of ἐτροφοφόρησεν, nevertheless the Targumic phrase swphq ṣwrkh' which occurs at Deut. 2.7; 32.10 in Targum Onkelos; and at Hos. 13.5 and Zech. 9.11 in Targum Jonathan, offers a parallel to ἐτροποφόρησεν and is at least worthy of consideration, especially in view of Wilcox's suggestion on v. 22 (see below on 75-76), which Gordon appears to accept.

20. The reference to seven kings seems to be dependent on Deut. 7.1 (Deut. 20.17 mentions six, not referring to the Girgashites. Ps. Philo *Biblical Antiquities* 20.9 mentions 39 kings!). Flichy, *Figure*, 192, sees a death-resurrection theme hinted at here, but this seems rather a strained interpretation.

21. The reference to "about 450 years" is something of a puzzle. The time references in the Hebrew text of Judges add up to 410 years, which, plus the 40 years of 1 Sam. 4.18, gives 450 years, but the LXX has 20 in the 1 Samuel text which results in only 430 years. 1 Kgs 6.1 calculates 480 years from the Exodus to the founding of the Temple (the LXX again differs—440), but the reigns of Saul and David plus the first 4 years of Solomon's reign would need to be subtracted and these would bring the figure to well below 450. Pesch, *Apg.*, 2:35 takes v. 20b to refer to the period from the capture of the land to the exile—ca. 1150 to 700 BC, but this view is not convincing as the Judeans were still in occupation of their portion of the land after the demise of the northern kingdom, and, furthermore, the phrase "and after these things He gave them judges" hardly tallies with a reference to the exile of the northern Hebrews. Probably, the reference to 450 years is an approximate rather than an exact date.

after these things He gave[22] them judges until Samuel the prophet" v. 20a) and God's giving to the Israelites, in response to their request, a king in the person of Saul (1 Sam. 8-10), who reigned for forty years (1 Sam. 11-31)[23] (see v. 21). All that is mentioned about Saul, apart from the length of his reign, is that God removed him[24] and "raised up" David to be a king for the people (v. 22).[25]

Later in the speech, David will again be referred to and his death and burial will be contrasted with what God did to and for Jesus by raising him from the dead (vv. 34-37).

That David is a crucial point of the review is shown by the solemn assertion that God had borne witness to him (v. 22): εὗρον Δαυὶδ τὸν τοῦ Ἰεσσαί ἄνδρα κατὰ τὴν καρδίαν μου ὃς ποιήσει πάντα τὰ θελήματά μου. ("I found David, the son of Jesse, a man after my own heart, who will do all my will(s)").

Taking these phrases individually, εὗρον Δαυὶδ is drawn from Ps. 89.21 (LXX 88), while τὸν τοῦ Ἰεσσαι seems to echo 2 Sam. 23.1 (cf. 1 Sam. 16.1) or even Isa. 11.1, 10 (though here the phrase "root of Jesse" is used). The words ἄνδρα κατὰ τὴν καρδίαν μου are very similar to LXX 1Kgdms.13.14 (= EV 1 Sam. 13.14) which runs ἄνθρωπον κατὰ τὴν καρδίαν αὐτοῦ, the αὐτοῦ being changed here to μου of direct speech and ἄνθρωπον to ἄνδρα.

The final phrase ὃς ποιήσει πάντα τὰ θελήματα μου has often been thought to come from Isa. 44.28 (with the verb placed first instead of last), which would entail a transfer of what was there said about Cyrus the Persian king to David.[26] There is, however, an alternative suggestion, that put forward by M. Wilcox, an Aramaic specialist, who suggested that what we have here is the use of 1 Sam. 13.14 followed by its rendering in the Targum to the Prophets, which may be translated "a man (who) does his wish (or, wishes)," i.e., two alternative renderings of the same verse, and he points to the way that this is done in several of the manuscripts of the Palestinian

---

22. Buss, *Missionspredigt*, 43, suggests that "gave" is used instead of "raised up," in order to keep ἐγείρειν, used in the LXX in the Book of Judges (e.g., 3.9, 15), for the climax at v. 22 (Buss adds v. 23, wrongly in our view—see 91-94).

23. Josephus, *Antiquities* 6.378, has 40 years, but in *Antiquities* 10.143 he has 20 years.

24. Cf. 1 Sam. 13.13-14 (15.11-35, esp. 23; 16.1).

25. The verb ἐγείρειν can mean to raise up in the sense of "bring on the scene" or "to raise up—from the dead." The former is the sense here, but later in the speech the latter sense will be uppermost.

26. E.g., Fitzmyer, *Acts*, 512; Johnson, *Acts*, 232; Witherington, *Acts*, 410; Holtz, *Untersuchungen*, 134, though he says that it is not clear why such a transfer should have happened; Jeska, *Geschichte*, 228.

Pentateuch Targum, Codex Neofiti and in the Geniza Fragments published by Paul Kahle.[27]

If Wilcox is right, then this procedure is hardly likely to go back to Luke himself, but would rest on very early exegetical work in Christian circles. Such an idea, pointing to a possible testimonium source, may receive some support from the fact that Ps. 89.20 and 1 Sam. 13.14 are quoted together in 1 Clem. 18.1 (which also has ἄνδρα for ἄνθρωπον) and this might suggest that Luke and Clement drew on a common testimonium,[28] with Clement or his tradition dropping "who will do all my wills."[29]

While Barrett urges caution about Wilcox's thesis and Fitzmyer is dismissive,[30] it remains a suggestion which needs to be borne in mind,[31] as we move on to the next stage of our enquiry. If the examination of the review as a whole has left us without a clear answer on whether it is based on pre-Lucan material or is a Lucan composition, this verse 22 has raised a significant possibility of the former.

Irrespective of the correctness or otherwise of Wilcox's suggestion, Holtz is right in declaring that the embellished sentence from 1 Sam. 13.14 in the PA speech receives a messianic nuance not present in the original.[32] In the use of this phrase "who will do all my will(s)," David is being seen as a type or symbol of the one of his descendants who will come to be a savior for Israel (see v. 23).[33]

Within this review of God's dealings with Israel, there are six "moments" which are highlighted:
the election of the patriarchs, v. 17a;

27. Wilcox, *Semitisms*, 21–24.

28. Knopf, *Clemensbrief*, 72; Bruce, *Acts*, 265; Haenchen, *Acts*, 4; Roloff, *Apg.*, 205; Barrett, *Acts*, 1:35; Holtz, *Zitate*, 135; Bock, *Proclamation*, 243.

29. Buss, *Missionspredigt*, 47, and Bruce, "Paul's Use," 72, accept the use of a testimonium at v. 22. Roloff, *Apg.*, 205, refers to a tradition.

30. Barrett, *Acts*, 1:636 (this more correctly describes Barrett's position than the claim of Miura, *David*, 170, that Barrett accepts Wilcox's proposal); Fitzmyer, *Acts*, 512. Holtz, *Zitate*, 135, rejects the suggestion. Steyn, *Septuagint Quotations*, 166, does not discuss Wilcox's suggestion at all, while Jeska, *Geschichte*, 228–29, does not seem to be aware of it. Strauss, *Davidic Messiah*, 158, broadly accepts Wilcox's proposal, but suggests the influence of Isa. 44.28 LXX in the word πάντα, since "all" does not occur in the Targum of 1 Sam. 13.14; similarly, Bock, *Proclamation*, 243.

31. If it is accepted, it would automatically rule out the suggestion of Miura, *David*, 181, that the Lucan Paul has in mind the image of the Davidic Messiah who is the Isaianic New Exodus deliverer like Cyrus, but who accomplishes God's will, not by military means like Cyrus but through suffering.

32. Holtz, *Zitate*, 135.

33. Miura, *David*, 181, emphasises the David-Jesus typological perspective. Cf. Flichy, *Figure*, 194.

the deliverance and exodus from Egypt, v. 17b;
the period in the wilderness, v. 18;
the conquest of the land of Canaan, v. 19;
the period of the judges up to Samuel, v. 20;
the establishment of the monarchy in the person of Saul, his rejection by God and his replacement by David, vv. 21–22.

The speech then leaps over the centuries to a descendant of David, Jesus, who, it is claimed, is God's promised savior for Israel, who appeared during the ministry of John the Baptist (vv. 23–25). Why these six "moments," with king David as the climax, and why does the review then pass on to a descendant of David? The clue why the review of Israel's story stops with David is the interest in "the promise" given to David and concerning his "seed." What is the promise which is in mind? The passage in 2 Sam. 7 comes into consideration as a major candidate. We shall have to return to this point later, but for the moment we shall assume that this is the case.

Looking at the span of this historical review, we are struck by the absence of any mention of Moses and the covenant and giving of the law at Sinai.[34] The focus is very much on David and the "promise" made in 2 Sam. 7 and now fulfilled in a descendant of his. In fact, it is possible that the choice of the six moments has been influenced by the promise of 2 Sam. 7 made by God via the prophet Nathan to David.[35] In Nathan's words, there is a reference to "the tribes of Israel" (2 Sam. 7.7), a phrase which recalls the sons of Jacob, the grandson of Abraham. The Exodus is mentioned at the beginning of God's message (2 Sam. 7.6). The inheritance of the land is behind the reference to God's planting His people in their own land and their enjoying rest without the need to be on the move, as they were in the desert (2 Sam. 7.10). God had given commands to "the judges" who were appointed over Israel (2 Sam. 7.11). There is a reference to the rejection of Saul (2 Sam. 7.15). God promises David that his descendant and successor will be like a son to Him and He will be like a father to him (7.14) and the Davidic throne will be established and made sure forever (7.16)—note that the PA speech goes on to mention Jesus' sonship at Acts 13.33 and that he, raised from the dead by God, will never see corruption—that is, will enjoy an eternal rule.

---

34. Barrett, "OT History," 67, thinks that this was perhaps due to the fact that they had been "covered" in Stephen's speech, which he sees as a Hellenistic Jewish sermon taken over and adapted by Stephen (and not a Lucan composition). Cf. Haenchen, *Acts*, 415.

35. See the table of verbal links between Acts 13.16–22 and 2 Sam. 7.6–16 in Dumais, *Langage*, 90–91.

There is, then, a case for thinking that the review of God's dealings with Israel was to a considerable degree "controlled" by the passage from 2 Sam. 7, which was the charter of the Davidic dynasty, and that it was not put together haphazardly, nor that its "omissions" were due to the fact that Luke had already in Stephen's speech mentioned Moses and the Law and so felt no need to mention them here in Paul's speech at PA.[36] Arguably, there is a coherence between the choice of the six moments and the passage which contained the "promise" to David in 2 Sam. 7.

In the OT and Jewish literature, there are a number of surveys or reviews of Israel's history. They are of varying length and, arguably, amount to a sufficient number to say that this type of survey or review constituted a specific genre, or, if this seems to claim too much, to a sub-genre or a recognisable *topos*.[37] Jeska investigated twenty-seven summaries of Israel's history. We wonder whether he has cast his net too widely for the purpose of a comparison with Paul's PA speech. The review of Israel's history in the PA speech is crisp and succinct in style and theocentric in character and content. There is no verbosity or long-windedness, and the theme might be summarized as "the mighty acts of God" in favour of his people. There is no discussion of the reaction of the people of Israel. The spotlight falls on divine action, not on human response, whether positive or negative.

In the light of this, we may legitimately reduce the material for comparison on the following grounds. Firstly, we may set aside those reviews where the interest is in a series of *individuals*, who either displayed immense heroic courage in the face of dangerous situations or pre-eminent virtue when confronted by temptation or difficult circumstances. In some cases, there is a blending of divine action for Israel and Israel's disobedient, ungrateful and disloyal response, with the emphasis being placed on the latter in order to evoke repentance from the contemporary addressees. Into this category we would place Sir. 45–50; 1 Macc. 2.52–60; 2 Bar. 56–74; and, indeed, Heb. 11.[38]

Secondly, there are passages where the interest is limited to examples of divine punishment inflicted on people who flagrantly transgressed divine

---

36. Against the suggestion mentioned as a possibility by Barrett, "OT History," 67 (see n. 34).

37. Jeska, *Geschichte*, 22, maintained that the summaries of Israel's history do not represent an independent literary *Gattung*, but, since they occur embedded in many different *Gattungen* (address, prayer, hymn, account of a vision, prophetic/divine speech), he argued that they constitute a "structural element" (*Strukturelement*). Perhaps we could say that a survey of Israel's history is a *topos* which could be used for different purposes according to the author's overall plan.

38. Assuming a "source" used by the author, as maintained by Michel, *Hebräerbrief*, 245.

law or who were guilty of arrogant self-assertion over against the divine will. Here we would place 3 Macc. 2.2-20 and the Damascus Document 2.14-6.11. Possibly also Jdt. 5.6-18 should be included, though we have some doubts about this.

Thirdly, there are reviews of Israel's history which are set forth in a verbose and prolix manner and/or where the review is governed more by the thought of a divine fixing of the periods of history than the mighty intervention of God in history, though the latter is sometimes mentioned. Probably, the Apocalypse of Weeks in 1 Enoch 93; 91.12-17 and the Animal Apocalypse in 1 Enoch 85-90 should be assigned to such a group.

Based on the above negative criteria, we have isolated ten from the OT and one from the Apocrypha, together with two from Josephus[39], to which might be added Acts 7. These are Deut. 6.20-24 and 26.5-9; Josh. 24.2-13; 1 Sam. 12.8-13; Neh. 9.6-31; Pss. 78, 105, 106, 135 and 136; possibly, Jdt. 5.6-18; and two passages from Josephus' *Jewish Antiquities*.

We shall summarise extremely briefly these reviews, listing the main "moments" of Israel's history mentioned in them.[40]

Deuteronomy 6.20-24:
the slavery in Egypt, v. 21a;
the exodus, vv. 21b-22;
the occupation of the land, v. 23.

Deuteronomy 26.5-9:
Jacob goes into Egypt, v. 5
slavery in Egypt, vv. 6-7
exodus, v. 8
conquest, v. 9

Joshua 24.2-13:
Pre-Abraham period, v. 2
Abraham, Isaac and Jacob, vv. 3-4
Descent into Egypt, v. 4c
Plagues, v. 5
Exodus, the Reed Sea and Wilderness, vv. 5b-7
Entry and conquest of the land, vv. 8-13.

---

39. Originally, I had included thirteen plus Acts 7 and Heb. 11. I then read Jeska's fine study, and, stimulated by his work to further reflection, revised my list as a result. I added some and pruned others. See the appendix for a brief look at some of the passages rejected from my survey but which have some claim to be the respective authors' use of the *topos* of a summary of Israel's history.

40. It lies beyond the scope of this study to discuss the question of whether the confessional statements of God's redemptive activity eventually developed into the Hexateuch as we have it, as argued by Rad, *Problem*, 1-78; *OT Theology*, 1:121-25, 166-67.

1 Samuel 12. 8–13
Jacob entered Egypt, v. 8
(Implied) Israelites were oppressed, v. 8b
God delivered them through Moses and Aaron, v. 8cd
And brought them to the Land, v. 8e
Pattern of people's disobedience, punishment
and then God's deliverance of them through the judges -
Jerubbaal [Gideon], Barak, Jephthah and Samuel, vv. 9–11.
Israelites' request for a king, vv. 12–13.

Nehemiah 9.6–31:
Creation, v. 6
Abraham, vv. 7–8
Slavery in Egypt and Exodus, vv. 9, 10
Reed Sea and Wilderness, vv. 11, 12.
Sinai and the Law, vv. 13–14
Miracles in the Wilderness, v. 15
Disobedience of the Israelites (Golden Calf), vv. 16–18
Yet God's faithfulness, vv. 19–21
Conquest of the land, vv. 22–25
Cycles of disobedience-judgment-salvation, vv. 26–35.

Psalm 78:
Exodus through the Reed Sea; Wilderness; Water and
Manna provided; Israel's continual disobedience, vv. 12–53.
Conquest of the land, vv. 54–55
Israel's rebellion and God's judgment, vv. 56–64
God's election of Judah, Zion and David, vv. 65–72

Psalm 105:
Covenant with the patriarchs and promise of the land, vv. 8–11
Rise of Joseph in Egypt, vv. 16–22
Jacob/Israel enters Egypt, vv. 23–24
God causes the Egyptians to hate the Hebrews, v. 25
Rise of Moses, signs/plagues, vv. 26–36
Exodus, God's provision in the wilderness, vv. 37–41
The land, vv. 42–45

Psalm 106 (which is really a catalogue of Israel's ingratitude in the face of God's mighty acts and gracious provision):
Plagues in Egypt, vv. 6–7
Reed Sea, vv. 8–12
Wilderness, including the Golden Calf, vv. 13–22
Intercession of Moses, v. 23
Baal-Peor incident, vv. (24–) 28–31

Meribah incident, vv. 32–33
Lack of fidelity to God in Canaan, vv. 34–39, 40–43
God's anger[41] and His mercy, vv. 44–46
Psalm 135:
Creation, vv. 6–7
Exodus (signs and wonders), vv. 8–9
God overcomes the nations, vv. 10–11
and gives the land to Israel, v. 12
Psalm 136:
Creation, vv. 5–9
Exodus through Reed Sea, vv. 10–12
God's provision in the Wilderness, vv. 13–16
God overcomes nations and gives the land to Israel, vv. 17–22
Jdt[42] 5.6–19
Origin of the people in Mesopotamia, vv. 6–8
Divine revelation leading to Canaan, v. 9
Famine leading to journey to Egypt, v. 10a
Enslavement, vv. 10b–11
Exodus, vv. 12–13
Sinai-Kadesh-Barnea, vv. 14–15a
Conquest of the land, vv. 15b–16
Key theme of obedience bringing prosperity and disobedience bringing suffering in the land, vv. 17–18b
Exile and return, vv. 18c–19
To these we may also add –
Josephus, *Jewish Antiquities* 3.86:
Plagues
Reed Sea
Provision of meat and water
Adam
Noah escaped the flood
Abraham was settled in Canaan
Isaac was born
Jacob was graced by twelve sons
Joseph rose to lordship in Egypt

---

41. While v. 46 does not by itself demand the exile, v. 47 certainly assumes that people have been scattered among the nations.

42. Nicklesburg, *Literature*, 108–9, suggests that *Judith* is a tale originating in the Persian period but rewritten in the Hasmonean period, the late second to first century BC. Our passage is actually placed on the lips of a pagan, Achior, leader of the Ammonites, addressing Holophernes, the Assyrian commander-in-chief.

Josephus, *Jewish Antiquities* 4.43–45
God showed fire on Sinai
Enabled Moses to produce prodigies
Helped Israel to escape from Egypt
Delivered them at the Reed Sea
Sweetened the water
Provided quails and manna
Acts 7 (Stephen's Speech):
God called Abraham, vv. 1–7
Isaac and Jacob, v. 8
Joseph in Egypt, vv. 9–10
Jacob goes to Egypt, and dies there,
but is buried in Shechem, vv. 11–16
Enslavement of the Hebrews, vv. 17–19
Moses and his early career, vv. 20–34
Moses sent back to Egypt, vv. 30–34
He delivers the people at the Reed Sea
And is with them in the wilderness, vv. 35–38
Golden Calf incident, vv. 39–43
Entry into Canaan under Joshua, vv. 44–45
David's wish to build a residence for Yahweh, v. 46
Solomon builds the temple, vv. 47–50
The following comments may be made:

a) Creation as a work of God is not often mentioned. It does receive mention in two Pss. (135.6–7; 136.5–9) and Neh. 9.6.

b) The major focus in the OT passages is from Egypt to Canaan, including the Exodus (whether or not Moses, the Reed Sea deliverance and the care of God for His people in the wilderness are specified) and the Conquest (God drives out the nations before His people and so the promise to the fathers is fulfilled).[43]

c) Some OT passages stress the disobedience and ingratitude of Israel. These are Pss. 78.12–72; 106.6–46; 1 Sam. 12.8–13 and Neh. 9.6–31.[44]

d) In the main, in OT passages it is the entry into the land which is seen to be the fulfillment of God's promise to Abraham, a promise renewed to the other patriarchs.

---

43. Cf. Holtz, *Zitate*, 101.

44. This is true of Ezek. 20.5–29 which Jeska, *Geschichte*, 82–83, includes in his survey.

e) Of OT passages, only Ps. 78 mentions God's demand, and this in connection with the choice of Judah and, within Judah, of Zion as God's sanctuary and of David to "feed" and guide Israel.

f) There is no hint in Stephen's speech that the Davidic monarchy was the goal and focus of the history of God's dealings with the descendants of the fathers. David is mentioned as someone who found favour with God (7.46 = Ps. 132.5) and who asked to be allowed to "build a dwelling [=Temple] for [i.e., to be used by] the house of Jacob,[45] and[46] Solomon built a house for Him" [God]—there appears to be some tension between this enterprise and what was God's intention as revealed in Isa. 66.1-2, quoted at verses 48b-50, to which we shall return.[47] There is no sense, however, that the Davidic monarchy was the climax of God's plan and purpose in relation to the Israelites descended from Abraham.

Thus, as a conclusion, we have a negative result. The speech in Acts 13 does not seem directly indebted to any extant example within this genre or topos of "survey of Israel's history." It seems unique within examples of such a genre or topos in seeing the establishment of the Davidic monarchy as the goal to which God was moving in fulfillment of His promise. Psalm 78 does, of course, mention the choice of David (vv. 70-72), but the major emphasis is on the fact that the "tent of Joseph" went astray in spite of all that God had done for them in Egypt, in the Exodus, the wilderness, and in bringing them to the promised land, and were "given up" by Yahweh who chose "the tribe of Judah," Mount Zion for His sanctuary, and David to "feed" and guide His people. That Yahweh let His people be consumed by the sword stands as a warning for future generations not to forsake His ways (vv. 1-8).

The uniqueness of the review of Israel's history in the PA speech may lie in the very fact that the review of Israel's history is determined by the fact of Jesus and the conviction that he is the one in whom the promise made

---

45. Reading τῷ οἴκῳ Ἰακωβ with P74 Aleph* B D cop (sah). This is the harder reading: why would anyone alter τῷ Θεῷ Ἰακωβ ("for the use of the God of Jacob")? So Schneider, *Apg.*, 1:466; Fitzmyer, *Acts*, 383; Barrett, *Acts*, 1:372 (adding that the difference between the two readings is not as great as is sometimes thought); Witherington, *Acts*, 272-73. On the other hand, Haenchen, *Acts*, 285; Roloff, *Apg.*, 125; Pesch, *Apg.*, 1:244, 256; Johnson, *Acts*, 132-33; Bihler, *Stephanusgeschichte*, 74; Holtz, *Zitate*, 91; and Kilgallen, "Culmination," 29-30, prefer θεῷ. Penner, *Christian Origins*, 313, 322, is undecided, quoting different translations on two different pages.

46. Whether δὲ has full force here is debated; see 163-65. For the rest, the language picks up 1 Kgs 6.1.

47. See 164-65 for further discussion of this issue.

to David has attained its real fulfillment. As already mentioned,[48] it may be that the promise to David through Nathan now contained in 2 Sam. 7 has exerted a considerable influence on the shape of the review of Israel's history.

If this is accepted as a working hypothesis, there are two possible explanations of how it actually arose: either Luke composed this survey himself by reflection on 2 Sam. 7 or he drew on a pre-Lucan tradition,[49] possibly within a Jewish tradition which has not come down to us, or, more likely, within early Christianity itself. Let us see how far we can proceed in an attempt to decide between these alternatives.

In the first place, there is the reference to Jesus' Davidic descent in the opening section of Romans. With some exceptions, most scholars accept that Paul is here quoting a formula current before him:

"who was born of the seed of David according to the flesh;

declared Son of God in power according to the Spirit of holiness on the basis of the resurrection of the dead" (Rom. 1.3-4).

Whether or not Paul added "in power" to soften or reinterpret the aorist participle passive with which the second member begins (ὁρισθέντες), the first clause undoubtedly declares Jesus' Davidic descent. The formula lived on in the Pauline congregations and is quoted in the Trito-Pauline 2 Tim (2.8), albeit in the reverse sequence and in an abbreviated form.[50]

Later, in Romans, Paul can list among the privileges of Israel "the messiah τὸ κατὰ σάρκα" (9.5). Even if the phrase τὸ κατὰ σάρκα strongly emphasises a limitation,[51] and, in Dunn's estimation, denotes a seriously inadequate understanding of the term or relation so qualified limited,[52] and even if we must remember that Paul understands Jesus not only as not only as Israel's messiah but as the risen Lord of all, Gentiles as well as Jews (e.g., Rom. 10.9-13), the fact remains that Jesus was born within the Hebrew-Jewish people and is related to them in that way. Of itself, Rom. 9.5 does not demand Davidic descent, but after 1.3 Davidic descent is the natural assumption.

---

48. See 77-78.

49. Holtz, *Zitate*, 109, argued for a source which had its place in the Judaism of the first centuries BC and AD.

50. That it did live on must be an indication of its acceptable currency and tells against the view that Paul merely quoted it in Romans for tactical reasons to gain favour with the congregation(s) at Rome (which, it is often held, were primarily Jewish-Christian in outlook—a view which may be queried for the time of the writing of Romans).

51. BDF, 266(2).

52. Dunn, *Romans*, 2:528.

Finally, in Rom. 15, in a string of OT quotations, we meet Isa. 11.10 with its reference to "a root from Jesse" who is "appointed to reign over the Gentiles, in whom they will hope" (v. 12). The reason why Paul quotes this verse and the others in the catena is not actually for the purpose of stressing Jesus' Davidic descent, but to show that God's age-old purpose was that the Gentiles should praise Him (v. 9 "that the Gentiles should glorify God for His mercy, as it is written. . ."). Nonetheless, Jesus is still a Jew, indeed "he became a servant of the circumcision for the sake of the truth[53] of God, to confirm the promises made to the fathers" (v. 8)—we note that the perfect infinitive active γεγενῆσθαι implies that the now risen Jesus continues in this role as well as at the same time being the hope of the Gentiles.

In this collection or catena of quotations in Rom. 15.9-12, we have words drawn from the Law (Deut. 32.48 in v. 10), the Prophets (Isa. 11.10 in v. 12) and the Writings (Pss. 18.49 in v. 9 and 117.1 in v. 11). The quotations are taken from the LXX, which speaks against the collection's having come from Aramaic speaking Christians. Either Paul composed the catena himself or he came across it among Greek-speaking Jewish Christians open to the Gentile mission. Since the quotations fit the argument perfectly, there seems no reason for not accepting that Paul himself linked these passages together.[54] If this is a correct conclusion, then it reinforces the impression left by 1.3 and 9.5: Paul accepted the Davidic descent of Jesus. Even if Paul would argue strongly against any attempt to ground salvation on "fleshly" grounds (descent from Abraham), nevertheless he was not only aware of but also accepted that God's working through the Jewish people entailed certain factors, one of which was the birth of the messiah within the people of Israel, and, of all the possibilities, that within the Davidic house was the most significant.[55]

We should not fall into the trap of thinking that, because Paul distinguished between the Jew who is one externally and the true Jew who is one inwardly (Rom. 2.28-29), he totally devalued the advantages that had been given to Israel (Rom. 3.1-2) or that because he believed that the Spirit was the blessing for the nations in the promise made to Abraham (Gal. 3.14), Paul dismissed the human channels by which that blessing had come into

---

53. ἀλήθεια Θεοῦ carries the connotation of the faithfulness of God: so Cranfield, *Romans*, 2.741; Käsemann, *Romans*, 385; Dunn, *Romans*, 2:847.

54. Käsemann, *Romans*, 386, in agreement with Michel, *Paulus und seine Bibel*, 87. This is assumed by Barrett, *Romans*, 272; Black, *Romans*, 173; Cranfield, *Romans* 2:744-47.

55. I have phrased this in a deliberately general way, given the varieties of Jewish messianic hopes—a prophet like Moses, Davidic descendant, Elijah redivivus, Melchizedek, Enoch, a priestly messiah. See Neusner, et al., *Judaisms and their Messiahs*.

being; or that because for Paul salvation-history revolved round the Adam-Christ contrast, he set at nought the importance of Jesus' being the seed of Abraham, to which David also belonged (so Matt. 1.1–17; Luke 3.23–38).[56]

Add to all this, the famous principle of accommodation, enunciated in 1 Cor. 9.19–23, that he was ready to be all things to all men and women in order to save some, makes it *a priori* possible that Paul would seek to utilise Davidic descent at some point in his commendation of Jesus to his fellow Jews. (It could be one way in which he might seek to compensate for the "stumbling block" of the cross, even if not the main way[57]).

We might also mention briefly here the fact that Paul quotes "David" in Rom. 4.6–8 about the blessedness of those persons who experience God's gracious forgiveness of their sins; while prior to this he has used a quotation from Psa. 51, which in the tradition of Israel had come to be associated with David's repentance after his adultery with Bathsheba and the forgiveness of his sins by God mediated through Nathan the prophet. This quotation is designed to support Paul's declaration of the integrity of God's justice/righteousness and of the lack of any grounds for human challenge to or protest against this, but Hays has convincingly argued that the confession of guilt and the plea for forgiveness in the Psalm "sound subliminally beneath the overt argument" and that there are complex resonances between the Davidic Psalm and the Pauline kerygma.[58]

Our lack of a clear indication from Paul as to how he preached to his fellow countrymen and women is a handicap, but we cannot dogmatically rule out that he could stress Jesus' Davidic descent when preaching in the synagogue. All this is not mere speculation in the hope of bolstering up a pre-conceived position. Mention might be made to the approach of N.T. Wright, among others, to Paul. Wright has argued that Paul's theology was basically a redefinition, by means of Christology and pneumatology, of two key Jewish doctrines, monotheism and election, God and Israel, and that the messiahship of Jesus was important for Paul, for he treats Jesus as Israel's anointed representative.[59] If this is at all on the right lines, then it would be entirely reasonable to assume that Paul would have reflected on the promises made to David in the OT Scriptures.[60]

---

56. Paul's negative and positive statements about the Law are a warning not to reduce his view on the issue of Jesus' messiahship to an either-or position

57. In Rom. 4.7–8, Paul quotes "David" (Ps. 32.1–2) as a supportive text for his justification-by-grace-through-faith approach!—see the whole section of Rom. 4.1–9.

58. Hays, *Echoes*, 48–50.

59. Wright, *Climax*, 1, 43.

60. Cf. Hays, *Faith*, 294 "the centrality of Israel/covenant themes in Paul's theology."

What of other Christians before and contemporary with Paul? One of the points of agreement between the birth stories of Luke and Matthew is that Joseph was of the house of David (Luke 1.27; 3.31; Matt. 1.20), which suggests—given their complete independence of one another[61]—that they each drew this from traditions in circulation prior to them. This, of course, would not necessarily take us back to a time before Paul. The idea of Jesus' Davidic descent occurs in Rev. 3.7; 5.5; 22.16, but how old this tradition was is difficult to say. There certainly was a strong Jewish population in Asia Minor.

If Acts gives us a faithful picture of the earliest Jerusalem community, then we could confidently state that the earliest preaching did refer to Jesus' Davidic descent (e.g., 2.24–36; compare 15.16), though, interestingly, it could also utilise the prophet like Moses from Deut. 18.15 (according to Acts 3.22; compare 7.37). But, of course, the value of Acts is in debate and would be dismissed out of hand by many scholars.

Finally, we turn to consider whether Luke himself might have composed this review of Israel's history, climaxing initially in the establishment of David as king, and then, ultimately and definitively, in a descendant of his, Jesus.

Certainly, Luke in his birth narratives stresses the link between Jesus and David. Gabriel tells Mary that her son will be great:
"and he will be called the Son of the Highest and the Lord God will give him the throne of his father, David, and he will reign over the house of Jacob forever and there will be no end to his kingdom" (1.32–33).

Whether Luke is personally composing or taking over some birth narrative source, the language remains within a this-worldly framework, although clearly Luke himself would interpret the words spiritually, and see a fulfillment of these words in the session to God's right hand and Jesus' enthronement in heaven (Acts 2.32–36).

The link between Jesus and David emerges again in the journey of Joseph to Bethlehem, the city of David, for the census (2.4)[62] and in the angelic message to the shepherds: Jesus, the Savior, the messiah, the Lord, is born in the city of David (2.11). The genealogy contains the link too (3.31). Luke has made his point and the reader/ hearer is expected to bear in mind that the hero of the ensuing story is the fulfillment of ancient promises to the house of David. But this of itself is not enough to make out a case for Luke's having

---

61. I am aware that a minority of scholars would dispute this assertion, but it remains very much the majority point of view.

62. The historical problems of the statement of Luke 2.4 concerning the census do not affect the point being made!

constructed a history of Israel with David as an initial climactic point. We proceed further.

Luke could have read Gen. 12, 15 and 17[63] and deduced that the Davidic monarchy was the fulfillment of the promises made to Abraham. Thus, Gen. 12.2 (from the J stream of tradition) speaks of Abraham's becoming "a great nation," and Jewish tradition did look back at the Davidic era as the time when Israel was a great nation. Gen. 15.18 (from the E stream of tradition) mentions boundaries which recall the Davidic-Solomonic empire (1 Kgs.4.21), while Gen. 17.6 (from the P stream of tradition) states that kings shall descend from Abraham and that God's covenant will be an everlasting one. In additional to this, there is the fact that both Abraham and David were linked with Hebron (Gen. 13.18; 23; 25.7-10; and 2 Sam. 2.1-4; 5.1-5).

Even more striking is 2 Sam. 7, regarded as the charter of the Davidic monarchy. God sends a message via the prophet Nathan to David when he had expressed a desire to create a permanent dwelling for Yahweh in place of the (moveable) Tent of Meeting.[64] God promises to make David's name great (v. 9) and to give him peace and to establish David's house on the throne of His people. One of David's sons will succeed him (vv. 11-12). Even if this son does wrong and God will punish him, God will not take away His love from him as in the case of Saul (vv. 14-15). "Your house and your kingdom shall endure forever before me; your throne shall be established forever" (v. 16).

In Ps. 132 there is a link between Yahweh's choice of Zion (Jerusalem) and David. The psalm begins with an account of David's desire to find a dwelling for Yahweh and his bringing the ark into the city (vv. 2-9). Then comes Yahweh's irrevocable oath to David in vv. 11-12: "I will place one of your own descendants on the throne: if your sons keep my covenant and the statutes I teach them, then their sons shall sit on your throne forever and ever" (note the condition here). This is followed by "For the Lord has chosen Zion, He has desired it for His dwelling" (v. 13).

In Ps. 89, the major focus of the first part (vv. 1-37) is on Yahweh's choice of David (in the light of which His treatment of the existing anointed Davidic descendant is bewildering and calls forth a lament, vv. 38-51). Yahweh's oath to establish David's line forever is stated (vv. 3-4) and from verse 9 onwards Yahweh's choice of David and His promises to him are reiterated,

---

63. That these chapters are attributed to differing "streams of tradition" by modern scholars (J, E, and P respectively) is not relevant for our purposes. Their inclusion by the final editor of Genesis underlines the importance of the promise to Abraham. See Williamson, *Abraham*.

64. Here, reconstructing the possible historical background behind Nathan's actions is no concern of ours.

culminating in "I will establish his line forever, his throne as long as the heavens endure" (v. 29). If any of his descendants do not keep Yahweh's commands, He will punish him:

> "but I will not take my love from him,
> Nor will I ever betray my faithfulness.
> I will not violate my covenant
> Or alter what my lips have uttered.
> Once for all, I have sworn by my holiness –
> That his line will continue forever
> And his throne endure before me like the sun;
> It will be established forever like the moon,
> The faithful witness in the sky" (vv. 33, 37).

No wonder that this royal ideology created problems when the state and monarchy ceased to exist with the destruction of Jerusalem by the Babylonians in 586 BC.

To any devout worshipper, however, *these words would have to have a fulfillment*. God's word cannot fail; His promises are reliable. Such a worshipper would hang on to these promises through thick and thin. We see this in the so-called messianic interpretation of many passages like Isa. 9 and 11, while the idea of someone from the line of David to rule over God's people remained within the treasure store of Israel's traditions over the centuries after the exile, and was available to be reactivated by, e.g, the author of the Pss. of Solomon 17–18.[65]

All this does no more than say that an early Christian *could* have composed something like the review of Israel's history, given a conviction that Jesus was the messiah of God and that he was a descendant of David. It does not, of course, in any way prove that Luke did so.

We now turn to look further at the role of verse 22 discussed above. Bowker[66] made the suggestion that this verse was the text for the sermon, taken from outside the set passages to be read for the day in the service, but linked verbally to the reading from the haphtarah [the reading from the prophets] which he believed was 2 Sam. 7.1–16, with Deut. 4.25–46 being the seder reading [the reading from the Law]. Inevitably there is a good deal of uncertainty about this thesis, since we are not sure of how soon the lectionaries in synagogue worship were fixed. However, Luke does mention

---

65. See especially Psa. Sol. 17.5, 23–51; 18.6. I have phrased this sentence carefully, aware of the disagreement between scholars as to whether the Davidic tradition continued alive throughout the post-exilic period or whether it was "revived" by the author of the Pss. Sol. in reaction to the rise of the Hasmonean House.

66. Bowker, "Speeches," 96–111; followed by Dumais, *Langage*, 95–98, 151; Pesch, *Apg.*, 2:34, 36.

that there were readings from the Law and the prophets (Acts 13.15). There would be little disagreement that 2 Sam. 7.1-16 is in the background of the flow of the speech.[67] The choice of Deut. 4.25-46 as the seder passage is more open to question. A century ago, W.M. Ramsay said that Deut. 1 and Isa. 1 had been suggested, and he gave as the reason for these suggestions the fact that Deut. 1 suggests the historical retrospect and Isa. 1 the promise of the remission of sins.[68] Isa. 1 is far less suitable than 2 Sam. 7.1-16, however, in view of the stress in the speech on David and the theme of promise. A major weakness of Bowker's thesis is that verse 22 does not seem to contain any verbal link with the haphtarah reading, conjectured to be 2 Sam. 7.1-16.[69] Even more damaging is the claim made by Aune that the Yelammedenu homilies are much later than the end of the Tannaitic period (first two centuries AD).[70]

We hesitate, therefore, to endorse Bowker's thesis. An alternative suggestion is that of an interpretation of 2 Sam. 7.1-16, the fruit of early Christian reflection on the passage and part of the dialogue of Christian Jews with fellow Jews in the synagogue.[71] This could be combined with a belief that the PA speech could represent the kind of sermon preached by Christian preachers, without being tied to the assumptions that Bowker put forward. Since, however, 2 Sam. 7.1-16 is not actually quoted explicitly, we would have to assume that this is an interpretation of a passage, of which audience

---

67. Buss, *Missionspredigt*, 48, 82, is a noteworthy exception. Pietsch, *Sprotz Davids*, 304 n. 253, while accepting that the references to "promise" in the speech are related to the Nathan promise of 2 Sam. 7, does not believe that this passage has exercised any influence on the sketch of salvation-history in vv. 17-25, which he is inclined to see as a Lucan composition.

68. Ramsay, *St. Paul*, 100—it is clear that Ramsay is picking up the opinion of others before him. Cadbury, *Beginnings*, 5:409, refers to the conjecture of Deut. 1 and Isa. 1 without elaboration, as does Pillai, *Missionary Preaching*, 85. More recently, Aileen Guilding, *Jewish Worship*, 78, suggested *en passant* that it is possible that the seder was Deut. 1 and the haphtarah was Jer. 30.

69. Correctly noticed by Buss, *Missionspredigt*, 49. Dumais, *Langage*, 96, is not very convincing when he states that the links are "David" and "a man after my heart" which is an explanatory reprise of 2 Sam. 7.9a and 15a. The former is too general, while the latter phrase is not really supported by either of the two verses from 2 Sam. 7, which Dumais mentions.

70. Aune, *Literary Environment*, 202.

71. Among the many scholars who endorse this view are Marshall, *Acts*, 221; Pesch, *Apg.*, 2.34; Doeve, *Jewish Hermeneutics*, 168-76; Lövestam, *Son and Saviour*, 7; Goldsmith, "Pesher," 321-24; Bowker, "Speeches," 96-111; Dumais, *Langage*, 67-114; Ellis, "Midrashic Features," 304, 307; Strauss, *Davidic Messiah*, 150.

and speaker/author and readers/hearers were aware.[72] For that assumption to be credible, the exegesis of the next verse is crucial.

First Pivotal Verse—Verse 23

> Τούτου [=David] ὁ Θεὸς ἀπὸ τοῦ σπέρματος κατ' ἐπαγ‐
> γελίαν ἤγαγεν τῷ Ἰσραὴλ σωτῆρα Ἰησοῦν.

The τούτου, placed emphatically at the beginning of the sentence, refers back to David, whom God had described as a man after His own heart, someone who would do His will (v. 22). It is from this man's seed, from his descendants, that God has brought on the scene a savior for Israel. With this verse, we reach the climax of the review of the story of God's dealings with Israel. It is very much a key verse in the speech. We may legitimately call it the first "pivotal verse" in the speech.

The use of σπέρμα recalls God's promises both to Abraham and David. At Gen. 17, God made a covenant with Abraham and promised to multiply him and promised also that kings would come out of him. This was to be an everlasting covenant with Abraham and his seed, and God would be their God (17.2, 6–7).[73]

Now, the genealogy at the end of the book of Ruth begins with Perez, who was a son of Judah, a grandson of Jacob and, therefore, a great-great-grandson of Abraham, and ends with David. So David is very much of Abraham's seed. Furthermore, he is himself a beginning of the fulfillment of that promise that kings should emerge from Abraham's descendants. According to 2 Sam. 7.12, God promised to establish David's seed on the throne of Israel forever. This is enshrined also in Ps. 89 (LXX 88): God has made a covenant with David and will establish his seed on the throne forever (vv. 3–4, 28–29, 36–37). Even if his descendants break God's statutes, while God will chastise them, He will not withdraw His favour from David's line (vv. 30–35).

---

72. Note the comment by Butticaz, "Has God Rejected," 155, speaking as a proponent of narrative criticism and taking over the view of Gérard Genette, that the derivation from a source by imitation or borrowing "does not necessarily imply the mention or explicit borrowing of the source text." That could apply in the case of the PA speech, particularly as the reference to "promise" in relation to the descendant of David is a reasonably strong reminder of 2 Sam. 7. See the discussion of v. 23 which follows.

73. Flichy, *Figure*, 195, also sees beyond the promise to David the promise to Abraham (she specifically thinks of Gen. 17.7 and 16).

Anyone acquainted with these two areas of Scripture (the promise to Abraham and to David) could well envisage one covenant, first made with Abraham, and partially fulfilled and renewed with David the King of all Israel. This could be the background to the phrase κατ' ἐπαγγελίαν in our verse. God's promise starts with Abraham and runs through David on into the present.

This attempt to include Abraham with David in the concept of "promise" would do justice to the affirmation that God "chose" our fathers (i.e., the patriarchs) at the beginning of the speech (v. 17), and it is in harmony with the fact that the audience is addressed in v. 26 as "sons of the race of Abraham." Finally, in vv. 32–33, God is said to have fulfilled the promise made to the fathers, this being the good news which is now being announced.

It is in accordance with this promise—one promise in essence[74]—that God ἤγαγεν for Israel a Savior, Jesus. There is another reading: ἤγειρε. The former is attested by ℵ A B E lat; the latter, by D 33 614 d g sy sa. Buss opted for ἤγειρε.[75] This would echo v. 22 ("God raised up [brought on the scene] David as king for them") and anticipate the use of ἤγειρεν as "raised up from the dead" in vv. 30 and 37. It is, however, possible to reverse this argument and suggest that a scribe early spotted the potential appropriateness of using ἤγειρε. It is also possible that two passages in the Book of Judges where ἐγείρειν σωτῆρα occurs (3.9, 15) may have exerted some influence and helped to cause a change from ἤγαγεν to ἤγειρε. But, in the end, one has to ask why would anyone seek to change ἤγειρε into ἤγαγεν? It is easier to see ἤγαγεν being changed into ἤγειρε than vice versa. Accordingly, we opt for ἤγαγεν with the sense of "brought on the scene."[76]

The beneficiaries of God's action are Israel. This note also occurs in the next verse. There it is said that John the Baptist in his work of preparing for the entry of Jesus on the scene preached a baptism of repentance to *the entire people of Israel* (v. 24). The message of salvation is sent "to us" (ἡμῖν at v. 26 is emphatic). Those to whom the risen Jesus appeared are now his witnesses "to the people" (v. 31). There is, however, in v. 38 the affirmation that everyone who believes will be justified by Jesus. We might assume that this meant everyone in Israel. It is not till after the speech, a week later, and in the face of Jewish opposition, that Paul and Barnabas assert that, in view

---

74. Buss, *Missionspredigt*, 46, has aptly remarked that for Luke the whole of the Old Testament crystalises in the one promise.

75. Buss, *Missionspredigt*, 47. The JB with "raised up" seems to have preferred ἤγειρε.

76. Among those who opt for ἤγαγεν are Cadbury, *Beginnings*, 4:152; Barrett, *Acts*, 1:620 (translation); Johnson, *Acts*, 232–33; Strauss, *Davidic Messiah*, 159; Pichler, *Paulusrezeption*, 157.

of this opposition, the Jews have proved themselves unworthy of eternal life, and so the two of them are turning to the Gentiles (vv. 44–47). Luke comments that the Gentiles rejoiced and those who were appointed to eternal life believed.

That Jesus is God's appointed Savior both for Israel and for Gentiles is a theme which has already been adumbrated by Luke before. The orientation upon Israel in the canticles in the birth stories is well known (1.54–55 in the Magnificat; the entire Benedictus, 1.68–79; 2.32b in the Nunc Dimittis). But Luke also began to insinuate the theme that Jesus is the savior intended by God for all people right at the beginning of his gospel: in the birth narratives in the words of Simeon (Luke 2.30–32a); then in the extension of the quotation from Isa. 40 to include "And all flesh shall see the salvation of our God" (Luke 3.6); and in the use of how Elijah and Elisha brought blessing to non-Israelites, in what Jesus said in the synagogue at Nazareth (Luke 4. 25–27). The risen Jesus shows his disciples that the Old Testament scriptures had already announced that repentance and forgiveness of sins should be preached to all nations in the name of the Messiah who should suffer and rise from the dead on the third day (Luke 24.46–47) and according to Acts 1.8 he commissioned his disciples to be his witnesses to the ends of the earth.

The two themes—Jesus as Savior for Israel and for the nations—continue to be developed in Acts. At the beginning of Christian preaching in Jerusalem on the day of Pentecost, Peter announced that God's promise was "to you and your children" as well as "to all who are afar off," which alludes to Gentiles as those afar off and not just to Diaspora Jews (2.39). His second sermon ends with the reminder that his hearers are the sons of the prophets and of the covenant made with Abraham (Gen. 12.3 and 22.18 are quoted): "To you first God has raised up His Servant and sent him to bless you, by turning everyone of you away from your iniquities" (3.25–26). Before the Sanhedrin, Peter's words are for its members and "all the people of Israel" (4.10, 11–12). On a second occasion before the Sanhedrin, Peter says that God exalted the Jesus whom they had slain, to be Leader and Savior, to give repentance and forgiveness of sins to Israel (5.31).

We learn that Saul, halted in his tracks as a persecutor of Christians on the Damascus Road, has been destined to bear the name of Jesus before the Gentiles and kings as well as before the children of Israel (Acts 9.15). Even to the Roman centurion and his household, Peter says that the word (τὸν λόγον) was sent by God to the sons of Israel, preaching the good news of peace by Jesus Christ (10.36). Those who were witnesses of Jesus' resurrection were commissioned "to preach to the people" (10.42). It is the pouring out of the Spirit on these Gentiles who respond to the message which convinces the Jewish Christians with Peter that they should baptise Cornelius and his household (10.44–48).

At the Apostolic Council in Jerusalem, James quotes Amos 9.11–12 (LXX) which speaks of the restoration of the fallen tabernacle of David, in order that the rest of humanity, i.e., all the Gentiles on whom God's name has been called, may seek after the Lord (15.15–17). David-Israel is first restored,[77] with the aim that Gentiles might be induced to seek God. A renewed Israel can receive Gentiles who seek God.

To return to Acts 13.23: Jesus is described as Savior (σωτήρ) for Israel. This was one of the titles given him by the angel in the message to the shepherds at his birth (2.11). In the Benedictus, Zechariah praised God for visiting and redeeming His people, for raising up "a horn of salvation for us in the house of David, His servant" (Luke1.69; cf. v. 71). Salvation is to be obtained in no other name than Jesus, said Peter to the Sanhedrin (Acts 4.12).[78] Peter used the title "Savior" along with Leader (ἀρχηγός) at Acts 5.31, also in addressing members of the Sanhedrin.

The theme of salvation re-emerges in the PA speech at v. 26, another pivotal verse (as we shall see): "The word of this salvation has been sent to us." In a completely derivative sense, the messengers of Jesus the Savior are the means of salvation through the proclamation of the good news, as can be seen when Paul and Barnabas apply Isa. 49.6 to themselves: the Lord has appointed them to be the means of bringing light to the Gentiles, the means of bringing salvation to the ends of the earth (Acts 13.47).

What, then, is the overall message of verse 23? There is the theme of promise and fulfillment contained in κατ' ἐπαγγελίαν. This will emerge more fully at verses 32–33. Clearly, Jesus is seen to be part[79] of, indeed the climactic, part of Israel's history. He cannot be understood apart from that story nor can that story be fully understood without him.[80] There is an arc, so to speak, from Abraham via David to Jesus. Jesus, the climax of Israel's history, is the promised Savior and brings God's salvation.

It is clear from this survey that verse 23 is a crucially important verse in the PA speech. That 2 Sam. 7 was in mind may be confidently asserted, even if it has not been specifically quoted.

---

77. See below 170–75 for a justification of this interpretation.

78. For the theme of salvation as a key theme of Lucan theology, see Marshall, *Historian*, 77–102.

79. Cf. Hall, *Revealed Histories*, 185.

80. Buss, *Missionspredigt*, 48; cf. the general remark of Pokorny, *Theologie*, 62: "The church has recognized Jesus as the messiah, to whom the whole of scripture refers."

Additionally, words and concepts which this verse 23 uses will reappear in yet another pivotal verse (v. 26), which we will consider in due course.

verses 24 –25: The Ministry of John the Baptist

v. 24 προκηρύξαντος Ἰωάννου πρὸ προσώπου τῆς εἰσό
δου αὐτοῦ[81]

βάπτισμα μετανοίας παντὶ τῷ λαῷ Ἰσραήλ.

v. 25 ὡς δὲ ἐπλήρου Ἰωάννης τὸν δρόμον, ἔλεγεν

Τί ἐμὲ ὑπονοεῖτε εἶναι; οὐκ εἰμὶ ἐγώ· ἀλλ' ἰδοὺ ἔρχεται μετ' ἐμὲ

οὗ οὐκ εἰμὶ ἄξιος τὸ ὑπόδημα τῶν ποδῶν λῦσαι.

Luke 3

v. 3 κηρύσσων βάπτισμα μετανοίας εἰς ἄφεσιν ἁμαρτιῶν...

v. 6 ἔρχεται δὲ ὁ ἰσχυρότερός μου,

οὗ εἰμὶ ἱκανὸς λῦσαι τὸν ἱμάντα τῶν ὑποδημάτων αὐτοῦ.

Grammatically, verse 24 is linked to v. 23 by the genitive absolute construction. Thereby, a close link is established between the Savior Jesus, mentioned at the very end of v. 23, and the forerunner John the Baptist,[82] whose ministry verses 24-25 discuss briefly, although a number of scholars see vv. 24-25 as having a parenthetical character.[83]

Both general usage and the context probably mean that προκηρύσσειν in verse 24 means to speak forth or declare publicly.[84] The object of the verb is βάπτισμα μετανοίας, so that prediction of something to come in the future is ruled out, as John the Baptist was in fact preaching and baptising people! The phrase κηρύσσειν βάπτισμα μετανοίας occurs in Luke 3.3

---

81. While the meaning is clear—John the Baptist preceded Jesus—the Greek is unusual. There is a combination of προσώπου and εἰσόδου, where one of these words on its own would have sufficed, either πρὸ προσώπου αὐτοῦ or πρὸ τῆς εἰσόδου αὐτοῦ. The former phrase reflects the Septuagint's translation of the Hebrew לפני.

82. There is a danger of exaggeration in the assertion of Wilckens, *Missionsreden*, 102, that the Baptist is *detached* from Jesus.

83. Schneider, *Apg.*, 2:134; Wilckens, *Missionsreden*, 101; Dumais. *Langage*, 230. Marshall, *Acts*, 224 and Strauss, *Davidic Messiah*, 160, call it a "short digression." Barrett, *Acts*, 1:637 deems verses 24-25 as almost an afterthought.

84. See Friedrich, κῆρυξ, κηρύσσω κτλ, *TDNT* 3.717-18; Buss, *Missionspredigt*, 53-54.

(= Mark 1.4), where Luke takes over from Mark the accompanying phrase εἰς ἄφεσιν ἁμαρτιῶν. Luke did not feel the need to drop this phrase, as did Matthew. John the Baptist is a true servant of God and his baptism was administered with the imminent eschatological judgment in mind. Clearly, for Christians, after the ministry, death, resurrection and exaltation of Jesus, forgiveness was the gift of Jesus (see Acts 13.38 for the emphasis that forgiveness comes through Jesus and was conveyed to the person who repented and believed and was baptised, according to Acts 2.38).[85]

We note how all-embracing the focus of John's ministry was: he preached a baptism of repentance "to all the people of Israel" (13.24). It is important for Luke that all Israel should have had the opportunity to hear and see Jesus. The ministry of John the Baptist assisted in this. This stress on Israel links up with v. 23, where, as we have seen, God is said to bring Jesus on the scene as a savior for Israel. This is a further, small confirmation of taking verses 24-25 with what precedes them.

The speech then includes at verse 25 a reference to John the Baptist's witness which he is said to have made when he was on the point of finishing "his course," i.e., before his death.[86] Wilckens sees this as a further sign of Luke's tendency to distance John and Jesus and points to Luke 3.19-20,[87] but the position of the note about the Baptist's death at Luke 3.19-20 may be due to Luke's desire to round off his account of John before proceeding with the story of Jesus, beginning with his baptism and genealogy.[88]

---

85. See Nolland, *Luke*, 1:142-43, for a careful discussion of the issue of repentance and forgiveness in relation to John and Jesus. Acts 18.25-19.6 presents us with what appears to be conflicting evidence. Apollos, though he knew only John the Baptist's baptism, does not appear to have received Christian baptism; whereas the twelve Ephesian "disciples," who had only been baptised with John's baptism, were baptised in the name of the Lord Jesus. No doubt things were "untidy" in the earliest days of the Christian movement. On the other hand, Apollos was "teaching accurately the things about Jesus" (19.25) and was already preaching that the messiah expected by the Jews was in fact Jesus (18.28), whereas the twelve at Ephesus seem ignorant of what was basic to early Christianity, namely the Holy Spirit. Note, firstly, how Matthew drops the phrase "for the forgiveness of sins" in his account of John the Baptist and has John saying that he baptised with water εἰς μετάνοιαν (? to mark their repentance, Matt. 3.11. Compare Gundry, *Matthew*, 48, who comments "'For repentance' implies that baptism enabled people to actualise their repentance by carrying it out in symbolic action") and then, secondly, Matthew adds the phrase "for the forgiveness of sins" to the cup saying at the Last Supper from Mark 14.24 at 26.28.

86. δρόμος also occurs at Acts 20.24 about Paul in his speech to the Ephesian elders at Miletus (elsewhere in the NT only at 2 Tim. 4.7).

87. Wilckens, *Missionsreden*, 104.

88. See Robinson, *Weg*, 11.

The idea that people may have been speculating about John's place in God's purposes (this is the implication of v. 25b) is found in Luke 3.15, which may be Luke's own composition but based on tradition, because this is a place where Luke and John's Gospel have an agreement in sense, if not in exact wording, for the Fourth Gospel has John the Baptist denying that he was the messiah (cf. John 1.19-28). Dodd maintained that there was "a reasonable degree of probability that the author of Luke-Acts had some traditional authority for the statement that there was, if not a belief, at least a suggestion of a possibility, that John the Baptist might be the Messiah, and that he expressly repudiated it."[89]

As to the prediction that a greater than John was coming, Acts 13.25 is very different from Luke 3.16. Both have ἔρχεται; οὐκ εἰμὶ; λῦσαι; and a reference to sandals. But Luke does not have ὁ ἰσχυρότερός μου after ἔρχεται but has μετ' ἐμὲ; and, whereas Luke 3.16 says that John the Baptist was not ἱκανὸς to untie τὸν ἱμάντα of the coming one's sandals, Acts 13.25 has John the Baptist saying that he was "not ἄξιος to untie the sandals on his feet" (John 1.27 also uses ἄξιος, but otherwise has the same words as Luke 3.16). If John the Baptist was unworthy even to untie the sandals of the One coming after him, that Coming One was clearly vastly superior to him, so no loss of meaning is incurred by the omission of ἰσχυρότερός.

Of course, Luke may have chosen to vary the phraseology of the words which he used about John the Baptist in his Gospel,[90] but he might also be in touch with a tradition which differed slightly from what he used in his Gospel. (This tradition need not have been in written form, but could have been in oral form).[91]

A major issue, following Conzelmann's work, used to be whether for Luke John the Baptist was the last of the OT prophets and belonged to the old era and not to the actual time of salvation[92]. Many scholars have criticised Conzelmann's theory[93] that Luke divided the history of salvation into three epochs (the time of Israel; the middle time—the ministry of Jesus; and the time of the church after the ascension) and especially the way in which he ignored the Birth Stories, the way he sought to use Luke 16.16 to argue the case for three periods in the history of salvation, and his use of Luke

---

89. Dodd, *Historical Tradition*, 257.

90. What Dunn, *Jesus Remembered*, 173-254, calls "oral retelling" or "oral performance."

91. Again, see Dunn, *Jesus Remembered*, 202, 250

92. Conzelmann, *Theology*, 18-27. In agreement with Conzelmann, see Wilckens, *Missionsreden*, 102-6; Schneider, *Apg.*, 2:134.

93. Conzelmann, *Theology*, 16-17.

22.35-38.⁹⁴ It is not impossible that for Luke John the Baptist was in a real sense both the last of the prophets and also the forerunner on the threshold and within the time of salvation.⁹⁵ No doubt Luke was aware of a certain tension between Jesus' own words contrasting John the Baptist and the least in the Kingdom of God on the one hand and Jesus' fulsome praise of John as the greatest born of woman on the other hand (Luke 7.26-28a). If Jesus could hold the two views together, why not an evangelist? Luke 1.76 is quite clear that John "will go before the Lord to prepare his ways," in the spirit and power of Elijah (1.17). Luke extends the Isa. 40 quotation which had been applied to John the Baptist's ministry, in order to include the reference that "all flesh shall see the salvation of God" brought by Jesus (Luke 3.4-6; 4.18-21). No wonder Luke could say that "with many other exhortations he [John] proclaimed the good news to the people" (3.18).⁹⁶

The mention of John the Baptist as a forerunner preparing for Jesus' entry on the scene is akin to Mark's inclusion of John the Baptist as the beginning of the gospel (Mark 1.1), whereas Luke puts the beginning (ἀρχή) of the gospel as Jesus' virginal conception by the Holy Spirit and accompanies that birth with remarkable signs (Luke 2). The Q tradition, whether oral or written or partly both, appears to have started with an account of the preaching of John the Baptist (see Luke 3.7-9 / Matt. 3.7-10).

Even the Fourth Gospel, which, we believe, was independent of Mark but drew on a tradition parallel to Mark, also begins his story with John the Baptist (1.19-34), and even mentions John the Baptist twice in the prologue at John 1.6-8, 15, verses which are possibly the author's own insertions in a previously composed hymnic confession.

---

94. See especially, Minear, "Birth Stories," 111-30; Kümmel, "Gesetz und Propheten," 398-415; and also Minear, "Luke xxii.36," 128-34. See Marshall, *Historian*, 84-102, for general criticisms of Conzelmann and others who shared Conzelmann's approach.

95. See e.g., Roloff, *Apg.*, 295.

96. Note the use of εὐηγγελίζετο at Luke 3. 18. Since Luke uses this verb of Jesus (4.18, 43; 7.22; 8.1; 16.16; 20.1; Acts 10.36) and of the disciples (9.6; and no less than 14 times in Acts of various Christian preachers), it seems unlikely that he wished to separate the different periods too rigidly.

Wilckens, *Missionsreden*, 101-2, argues that Luke placed great emphasis on John the Baptist's preaching. While there is clearly a degree of truth in this, it should not be over-exaggerated. Luke at 3.9 refers to the crowds who came out to John *to be baptised by him*, and at 3.3 he has taken over Mark 1.4 which has John the Baptist "preaching a *baptism* of repentance," which clearly implies that John baptised those who repented, just as in the verse under consideration at Acts 13.24.

Given the esteem in which John the Baptist was held among the Jewish people,[97] it would not be surprising if very early Christian apologetic sought to get John the Baptist on the Christian side.

We have no means of knowing what Paul may have thought about John the Baptist. It beggars belief, however, that he did not know anything about John or that he was ignorant that the gospel story mentioned the Baptist's ministry or that Jesus was baptised by John. These are the kinds of things which would also have formed part of the tradition passed on to him when he was instructed in the faith following his baptism at Damascus and would have been in all likelihood touched upon in his conversations with Peter during the fortnight he spent in Jerusalem (Gal. 1.18). Furthermore, if he encountered John the Baptist's disciples in the course of his missionary work, he would have had to have worked out what he needed to say to such people in order to commend Jesus.[98]

Arguably, Luke did not need to include any reference to John the Baptist, since he had already mentioned him and his role in God's plan of salvation sufficiently, though, of course, it could possibly be maintained that he might wish to show Paul preaching very much the same themes as Peter who, in his sermon at the household of Cornelius, had referred to John the Baptist as the beginning of what God was doing for Israel (Acts 10.37), but if that was in Luke's mind why omit the kind of reference to the ministry of Jesus which Acts 10.37–39a includes?

All in all, a good case can be made out for the fact that the mention of John the Baptist at vv. 24–25 may owe its position to the firm place which he had, in early Christian tradition, as the beginning of the gospel of Jesus.

There is some problem of how to translate John the Baptist's response to the implied speculation of the people about himself. The initial τί may be taken as an equivalent of a relative and its clause taken as a predicate and translated "I am not what you think me to be."[99] Alternatively, the τί can be taken as the interrogative pronoun and the phrase translated "What do you think that I am? I am not he [? the messiah or promised savior]."[100] In the end, on either translation, the meaning is clear—John the Baptist

---

97. E.g. Josephus, *Jewish Antiquities* 18.116–19.

98. Cf. the story recorded at Acts 19.1–6, whether or not the "some disciples" were followers of John the Baptist or not (Luke normally uses μαθητής / μαθηταί for Christians, but 19.1 may just be an exception).

99. So BDF, paras. 298(4) and 299(2); followed by Haenchen, *Acts*, 409; Schneider, *Apg.*, 2:134; Pesch, *Apg.*, 2:28.

100. Moule, *Idiom Book*, 124, 132; Bruce, *Acts*, 269; Barrett, *Acts*, 1:638. In fact, P45, C, D, latt, have τινά, probably a secondary reading to secure a personal masculine sense.

disclaimed any higher status than that of a servant of one who was to be far greater than he and who was none other than the savior whom God was bringing on the scene for Israel.[101] John the Baptist himself recognized Jesus as the savior mentioned in v. 23. Strauss suggested that verses 24–25 offer "an historical testimony to the identity of Jesus."[102] The Jesus who came after John the Baptist is the one greater than he, the messiah, who, John said, would come after him (μετ' ἐμὲ).

PART 2 OF PAUL'S SPEECH AT PISIDIAN ANTIOCH: VV. 26–37

The Second Pivotal Verse: v. 26

ἄνδρες ἀδελφοί, υἱοὶ γένους Ἀβραὰμ
καὶ οἱ ἐν ὑμῖν φοβούμενοι τὸν Θεόν
ἡμῖν ὁ λόγος τῆς σωτηρίας ταύτης ἐξαπεστάλη.

We describe verse 26 as the second pivotal verse primarily because of the announcement which it makes: "To us the word of this salvation has been sent." The ἡμῖν, placed emphatically at the beginning of the announcement, directly addresses the audience. The first section of the speech had begun with a reference to "*our* fathers;" now at the beginning of the second section, the audience is once again specifically drawn in.

The word or message (ὁ λόγος) of this salvation (τῆς σωτηρίας ταύτης) picks up the reference to "Savior Jesus" in v. 23. The Savior promised long ago has come. God has brought him on the scene. The forerunner, John the Baptist, has borne witness to him and prepared for his appearance (vv. 24–25). The message of salvation which he has brought is now to be passed on to those present. As Barrett points out,[103] no attempt is made here to define what salvation means (for this, see vv. 38–39).

The language has a Biblical flavour to it. Ps. 107 (LXX 106).20 runs ἀπέστειλεν τὸν λόγον αὐτοῦ.[104] There may be a slight echo of the herald who brings good news (εὐαγγελιζόμενος ἀγαθά) in Second Isa.:

ὅτι ἀκουστὴν ποιήσω τὴν σωτηρίαν σου.

---

101. Johnson, *Acts*, 233, comments "On either case, the sense is the same."
102. Strauss, *Davidic Messiah*, 160.
103. Barrett, *Acts*, 1:639.
104. Stanton, *Jesus*, 72–74, accepts that Ps. 107.20 is used here; Steyn, *Septuagint Quotations*, 167, alludes to it; Pillai, *Early Missionary Preaching*, 40, calls it a "minor citation."

("because I will make your salvation to be heard:" 52.7).[105]

Those addressed are described in a unique and more elaborate way than at v. 16b:
ἄνδρες ἀδελφοί υἱοί γένους Ἀβραὰμ καὶ οἱ ἐν ὑμῖν φοβούμενοι τὸν Θεόν.

The Jews present are described as the sons[106] of the race of Abraham. They were reminded of their "fathers" in v. 16; now they are reminded of the father of the race, Abraham himself. Descent from Abraham was a matter of pride for the Jew (cf. Matt. 3.9/Luke 3.8[107]). The mention of Abraham can also serve as a reminder of the promises to Abraham, which provide that wider context for the theme of the promise of a Davidic descendant who would be a savior.[108]

The message of salvation is for them, but also those addressed include some who are differentiated from those who are ethnically descendants of Abraham: those among them who fear God (It would be well nigh impossible to take this part of the address as it now stands to mean born Jews, that is, those Jews among them who really fear God). Having argued for Gentile proselytes in v. 16, it is logical to assume the same people are being addressed here.[109] Why otherwise speak of those who fear God *"among you"*? Without that phrase, the καὶ could have been taken as explanatory or epexegetic and introduce a further description of the descendants of Abraham.

We take "those who fear God" to refer to those who were proselytes, not sympathisers or "fellow travellers," who had not taken the step of conversion to Judaism. Though ethnically from a different race, they have become converts to Judaism and are included in the offer of the message of salvation. Salvation is being offered to them also.

---

105. Less likely is Isa. 55.11: οὕτως ἔσται τὸ ῥῆμά μου ὃ ἐὰν ἐξέλθῃ ἐκ τοῦ στόματός μου (against Buss, *Missionspredigt*, 64).

106. That is, members of Abraham's race (The υἱοί represents the Hebrew "ben" of classification).

107. Compare how Paul argued against a purely physical descent from Abraham in both Rom. 4 and Galatians 3; see also Rom. 2.28-29.

108. Cf. Dahl, "Abraham," 148.

109. Barrett, *Acts*, 1:639, and Wasserberg, *Israels Mitte*, 48-51, take them as proselytes, but Haenchen, *Acts*, 409n6; Fitzmyer, *Acts*, 514; Witherington, *Acts*, 411, assume that they are God-Fearers.

Verses 27–31: The Message about Jesus

οἱ γὰρ κατοικοῦντες ἐν Ἰερουσαλὴμ καὶ οἱ ἄρχοντες αὐτῶν
τοῦτον ἀγνοήσαντες καὶ τὰς φωνὰς τῶν προφητῶν
τὰς κατὰ πᾶν σάββατον ἀναγινωσκομένας
κρίναντες ἐπλήρωσαν,
καὶ μηδεμίαν αἰτίαν θανάτου εὑρόντες
ᾐτήσαντο Πιλᾶτον ἀναιρεθῆναι αὐτόν
ὡς δὲ ἐτέλεσαν πάντα τὰ περὶ αὐτοῦ γεγραμένα
καθελόντες ἀπὸ τοῦ ξύλου
ἔθηκαν εἰς μνημεῖον
ὁ δὲ Θεὸς ἤγειρεν αὐτὸν ἐκ νεκρῶν·
ὃς ὤφθη ἐπὶ ἡμέρας πλείους τοῖς συναναβᾶσιν αὐτῷ
ἀπὸ τῆς Γαλιλαίας εἰς Ἰερουσαλήμ,
οἵτινες νῦν εἰσιν μάρτυρες αὐτοῦ πρὸς τὸν λαόν.

That verses 27–31 go closely with v. 26 is shown by the γὰρ ("for") at the beginning of verse 27.

The personal name "Jesus" occurred at v. 23, and is not used thereafter at all in the speech. In v. 24, *his* εἴσοδος refers back to Jesus and with "salvation" in v. 26 picking up Jesus' title "Savior" from v. 23, the reader/hearer will assume that the personal pronoun αὐτός (in various cases) from now on does in fact refer to Jesus.

No details of his parents, birth, early life, baptism, ministry or preaching are given.[110] The speech begins at the end of Jesus' earthly career, with events in Jerusalem, and then refers to them only sparsely. Presumably, this is another instance of Lucan abbreviation: the reader/hearer of LA had already been given in the Gospel an account of Jesus' ministry and preaching, and, more recently, a general summary of it in Peter's speech to Cornelius (10.37-39a). On the level of an actual sermon before a PA synagogue congregation, a considerable amount of detail about Jesus of Nazareth would have had to be given to substantiate any claim that he was the climax and fulfillment of Israel's history.

This section of 13.27-31 is constructed around the contrast scheme, which is a feature of the Acts' speeches to Jews and proselytes, the contrast between what people did to Jesus (vv. 27-29) and what God did (v. 30).

---

110. A sure sign that the speech is not a verbatim report, but that Luke has chosen to concentrate on the death of Jesus. A messiah who had been put to death, never mind who had been raised from the dead, was not something that Judaism contemplated.

Schenke has made out a strong case for seeing this contrast formula as belonging to old kerygmatic tradition.[111]

In verses 27-29, the role of the people of Jerusalem and their leaders is singled out and commented on. They are charged on three accounts. Firstly, there is a double failure of understanding: they failed to recognise who Jesus really was (τοῦτον ἀγνοήσαντες) and failed to understand the prophets who are read every sabbath (καὶ τὰς φωνὰς τῶν προφητῶν τὰς κατὰ πᾶν σάββατον ἀναγινωσκομένας).[112] Secondly, they are charged with condemning Jesus, although he was innocent and they found no evidence to substantiate the death penalty (κρίναντες . . . καὶ μηδεμίαν αἰτίαν θανάτου εὑρόντες). They thereby unconsciously fulfilled the prophetic scriptures (ἐπλήρωσαν, the object of which is "the voices of the prophets" earlier in v. 27). Thirdly, in spite of not finding anything worthy of the death sentence, they requested Pilate that he should be put to death (ᾐτήσαντο Πιλᾶτον ἀναιρεθῆναι αὐτόν, v. 28). We shall look at these points now in more detail.

There is a more accusatory note in the charge of failing to recognise who Jesus was and the prophetic voices in scripture than seems to be the case in Peter's speech in Acts 3.17. There, Peter had said that the people of Jerusalem (addressed as ἄνδρες Ἰσραηλῖται in v. 12 and ἀδελφοί in v. 17) had acted in ignorance, as had their leaders (οἶδα ὅτι κατὰ ἄγνοιαν ἐπράξετε, ὥσπερ καὶ οἱ ἄρχοντες ὑμῶν). This seems to offer some extenuation for the action of bringing about the death of Jesus. Here in PA, no such mitigation is offered. The people of Jerusalem and their leaders were guilty

---

111. Cf. Schenke, "Kontrastformel," 1-20, and see 6-9 for criticism of Wilckens' view that Luke is entirely responsible for this contrast scheme. Among those who also argue for its being traditional are Schneider, *Apg.*, 1.271; Roloff, *Apg.*, 49-51; Pesch, *Apg.*, 1:121; Jervell, *Apg.*, 153. Pietsch, *Sprotz Davids*, 287 n. 159, accepts the possibility of traditional material; he thinks that it not only fits so well into Luke's composition but also that it has shaped it.

112. The sentence is rather overloaded. ("Few are likely to think that it is tolerable Greek," according to Lake and Cadbury, *Beginnings*, 4:153). The translation offered assumes that ἀγνοήσαντες governs τὰς φωνάς κτλ as well as τοῦτον: so Bruce, *Acts*, 274; Haenchen, *Acts*, 410; Marshall, *Acts*, 225; Pesch, *Apg.*, 2:28, 37; Witherington, *Acts*, 411; Jervell, *Apg.*, 357; Buss, *Missionspredigt*, 68; RV, GN, REB, NRSV. However, it is possible to take τὰς φωνάς ktl as the object only of ἐπλήρωσαν, as do *Beginnings* 4.153; Schneider, *Apg.*, 2:135; Johnson, *Acts*, 228; Fitzmyer, *Acts*, 505, 514; and NIV. Even if this second translation is preferred for v. 27, the implicit idea that the prophets witnessed to Jesus occurs in v. 29. See Ropes, "Detached Note on xiii.27-29," 261-63; Metzger, *Textual Commentary*, 409-10; Barrett, *Acts*, 1:642-43, for discussion of attempts to reconstruct the original "Western" text, which, as reconstructed, simplifies the sentence construction by not having any reference to not recognising Jesus but having μὴ συνιέντες τὰς γραφὰς τῶν προφητῶν . . . ἐπλήρωσαν in v. 27 and placing κρίναντες in v. 28.

of a failure of understanding. The blame is theirs entirely. They had not in fact found anything in Jesus worthy of the death sentence, yet went ahead in pressing that charge against him before Pilate.

The implication of the reference to the prophetic voices is that the prophets had spoken about the coming of the Savior, and that is explicitly stated in v. 29 (πάντα τὰ περὶ αὐτοῦ γεγραμένα), a point which we shall discuss shortly. The fact that the prophets were being read *every sabbath* further underlines the guilty responsibility of the people of Jerusalem and their leaders. They should have known better![113]

In the Lucan Passion Story, the Sanhedrin session does not end with a formal death sentence. Throughout 22.66-70, no individual like the high priest questions Jesus. The two questions put to Jesus are introduced by a collective λέγοντες at v. 67 and εἶπαν δὲ πάντες at v. 70. After Jesus' less than straightforward reply to the second question concerning his divine sonship, we again have a collective οἱ δὲ εἶπαν: "Why do we still need evidence? For you yourselves have heard from his own mouth" (v. 71). Luke then says that the entire assembly got up and led Jesus to Pilate (23.1). They then proceed to accuse him of various acts of sedition against Roman rule (23.2, 5).

Earlier, of course, in the last section of his gospel, at 19.47; 20.19-20; 22.2, Luke had reported the determination of the chief priests and scribes to do away with Jesus.[114] So, the readers/hearers are well aware of the attitude of the Jewish leaders to Jesus. They would deduce that a death sentence had been agreed, even if it is not formally recorded by Luke.[115]

In the Lucan Passion story, it is in fact Pilate who actually uses the phrase of not finding any reason for the death sentence in Jesus' case. He does so three times:

23.4 οὐδὲν εὑρίσκω αἴτιαν ἐν τῷ ἀνθρώπῳ τούτῳ

23.14 οὐδὲν εὗρον ἐν τῷ ἀνθρώπῳ τούτῳ αἴτιαν

---

113. The comment of Marguerat, *First Christian Historian*, 103, that ἄγνοια (here the verb ἀγνοέω is used) in Luke is not a passing deficiency but rather a soteriological lack, is correct for the PA speech.

114. Interestingly, at Luke 6.11 Luke has altered the Marcan report of a joint decision of the Pharisees and Herodians to kill Jesus (Mark 3.6) into "They were furious and discussed with one another what they might do to Jesus" (6.11). Luke felt that the Marcan report had come too early in the ministry. Of course, since Mark 2.1-3.6 has been arranged thematically and not chronologically, where Mark places this block of material is no guide as to when the individual episodes actually occurred.

115. See the discussion by Weatherly, *Jewish Responsibility*, 50-89. On Luke 22.70, Weatherly 62 maintains that Luke may have regarded the sentence of death or at least the intention to seek Jesus' death as implicit. He also believes (89) that in Acts 13.27-29 Luke has condensed the passion story into brief compass.

23.22 οὐδὲν αἴτιαν θανάτου εὗρον ἐν αὐτῷ

In using similar phraseology of the people of Jerusalem and their leaders in the PA speech (μηδεμίαν αἰτίαν θανάτου εὑρόντες), Luke is probably abbreviating and condensing, rather than being in touch with a different tradition from that which he followed in his gospel.[116] He clearly felt, along with other Christians, that Jesus did not receive a fair trial before the Sanhedrin and that its members were determined to put him to death but without due cause.[117]

The statement that the people of Jerusalem and their leaders requested Pilate that Jesus should be put to death agrees broadly with the sequence of events as narrated in all the gospels, and especially in Luke. Luke specifies charges brought against Jesus at 23.2, 5, which would be construed as treason against Rome and liable to the death sentence. Furthermore, at a crucial moment in the Lucan trial scene before Pilate, Pilate summoned "the chief priests and the rulers and the people"[118] (Luke 23.13) and when he declared Jesus to be innocent, was greeted with the demand to take Jesus away and release Barabbas (23.14–19) and a little later with the demand that Jesus should be crucified (23.20–21). The people seem to revert to their former favourable attitude to Jesus from 23.27 onwards in the Passion Story, and, finally, Luke records their beating their breasts as a sign of remorse and returning home (23.48). In the early chapters of Acts, they are depicted as being favourably disposed towards the earliest followers of Jesus.

---

116. Weatherly, *Jewish Responsibility*, 240–41, however, is prepared to consider as a possibility that Luke's sources for the speeches in Acts may have been more specific than his sources for the Gospel, in attributing popular responsibility (cf. 106, below). Schenke, "Kontrastformel," 17, believes that in the half of the traditional contrast formula describing the killing of Jesus the verb was formulated mostly in the second person plural, i.e., *hearers were directly addressed*, and he sees the *Sitz im Leben* of this formula in the early Christian mission preaching of repentance using the Deuteronomist scheme. The statement in 1 Thess. 2.15–16 together with the parable of Mark 12.1–11 and the Q material like Luke 11.47–51; 13.34–35 strongly suggest that the motif of Jewish guilt was a traditional theme (cf. Pietsch, *Sprotz Davids*, 286).

117. No doubt from the Jewish side it could be argued that the claim to be son of God or the refusal to deny it would suffice as an offense worthy of death. That "cut no ice" with early Christians, for whom Jesus was the Son of God.

118. So unusual did this reference to the people appear that Rau, "Volk," 41–51, suggested emending the text to τοῦ λαοῦ instead of καὶ τὸν λαόν, but his suggestion has not received much support; Deutschmann, *Synagoge*, 241, seems prepared to accept it. While not unsympathetic to it, Lohfink, *Sammlung*, 42, pointed out that it would not have been possible to call the people to repentance in the speeches in Acts if the people were not involved. The tension with the otherwise favourable attitude of the people to Jesus before and after (i.e., up to Acts 5) the passion should be allowed to stand.

Thus, the Gospel account, Luke 23.13-23, is the basis for the accusation in the speeches of Acts that the people of Jerusalem with their leaders were culpable of bringing about the death of Jesus. Weatherly, however, has raised the possibility that the early kerygma may have included a reference to popular Jerusalem responsibility,[119] particularly as he argues both for a pre-Pauline origin for the severe passage about Jewish killing of Jesus and persecution of his followers in 1Thess.2.14-16,[120] and, on the basis of an examination of both Jewish and non-Jewish accounts of specific persecutions and martyrdoms, for some reference to opponents in the kerygma.[121]

We come to verse 29, which, as mentioned, states what v. 27 implied: that the OT points to Jesus (πάντα τὰ περὶ αὐτοῦ γεγραμμένα). In context, this refers to the death of Jesus (v. 28). It was clearly a conviction running through early Christianity that Jesus' life, death and resurrection fulfilled God's will as revealed in the OT (see 1 Cor. 15.3-4; Rom. 1.2; 1Pet.1.10-12; Heb. and Matt. *passim*). It is no less a deeply held conviction with Luke, as can be seen in his editing of Mark 10.33 in Luke 18.31, the third passion prediction, where Luke adds "and all that is written by the prophets will be accomplished on the Son of Man."[122] The theme is heavily emphasized in Luke's resurrection chapter, to the couple from Emmaus (24.25-27) and to the disciples in Jerusalem (24.44-49), and it runs through Acts like a red thread (1.16, 20; 8.30-35; 17.3, 11; 24.14; 26.22-23).

Stressing that Jesus' death was in accordance with the plan of God revealed in the scriptures would be one of the ways in which the early Christians sought to palliate the scandal of the cross and gain acceptance of their proclamation of a crucified messiah.

The ἐτέλεσαν of our verse really refers to the death of Jesus, and then follow references to the taking down of Jesus from the cross and his burial: καθελόντες ἀπὸ τοῦ ξύλου ἔθηκαν εἰς μνημεῖον.

---

119. Weatherly, *Jewish Responsibility*, 240-41. In this he had been anticipated by Schürmann, *Lukasevangelium*, 1:535 (without any discussion, however).

120. Weatherly, *Jewish Responsibility*, 176-94; compare, too, Wilckens, *Missionsreden*, 120, who argues for Paul's use of a traditional motif.

121. Weatherly, *Jewish Responsibility*, 243-69. Wilckens, *Missionsreden*, 89-90, 119, denies that such a polemical note characterised Christian Jewish preaching, without giving detailed arguments.

122. REB; also the arguments of Fitzmyer, *Luke*, 2:1209. The alternative translation of "All that is written about the Son of Man will be accomplished," offered by JB, GN, NIV, and NRSV (see the argument that the dative is equivalent to περὶ with the genitive in Marshall, *Luke*, 690), would not alter the point being made above.

The burial of Jesus was mentioned in the pre-Pauline tradition quoted at 1 Cor. 15.3-7 (ἐτάφη), though without any elaboration whatsoever. In the mention of the burial, then, the speech is utilising traditional material.

We note that the plural continues to be used in the verbs, although Luke knew full well that Joseph of Arimathea had actually taken down Jesus' body and put it in his tomb (23.50-53). Here the purpose seems to be to let the guilt and responsibility for the death and burial (the seal of death) to be laid at the door of the people of Jerusalem and their leaders. There is no need to draw from this verse a theory that the Sanhedrin leaders saw to the removal of Jesus' body and put it in a common grave.[123] It is just possible that Isa. 53.9 may have influenced the expression,[124] but this is not likely, as there is no specification in v. 29 that the grave belonged to the wicked (or the rich[125]).

The use of ξύλον for the cross is probably due to the influence of Deut. 21.23, which is the stipulation that anyone hanged on a tree for a crime punishable by death must be removed and buried that day, for anyone hung on a tree is under God's curse; otherwise, the land will be defiled. Although we cannot prove it, it is more than likely that Deut. 21.22-23 was used from the Jewish side as a counterblast to Christian claims made for Jesus. Deuteronomy 21.22-23 could be used to disprove the assertion that Jesus was the Lord's Anointed, God's Christ.[126] Indeed, there is no reason why Paul himself may not have used it in his pre-Christian period.[127]

---

123. Against Fuller, *Formation*, 54-55. Krankl, *Knecht Gottes*, 117, refers to Goguel, *Foi à la résurrection de Jésus*, 128-33, as the first among modern scholars to put forward this theory. Wilckens, *Missionsreden*, 136, firmly rejects any use here of a separate old tradition, as does Pietsch, *Sprotz Davids*, 307.

124. So Buss, *Missionspredigt*, 73.

125. Interestingly, several scholars, including Westermann, *Isa. 40-66*, 254; Whybray, *Thanksgiving*, 103, 161n146; and Hermisson, "Fourth Servant Song," 27, accept the emendation of the Hebrew from "rich" to "evil-doers" and thus secure an exact parallelism in the first two lines of Isa. 53.9. If they are right and if this were the Hebrew text around in the first century, it would make the influence of Isa. 53.9 even less likely, since Luke expressly describes Joseph of Arimathea as "a good and righteous man," who, though a member of the Sanhedrin, had not agreed with its decision (Luke 23.50-51). In any case, the LXX of Isa. 53.9 uses ταφή, not μνημεῖον as in Acts 13.29.

126. So Lindars, *NT Apologetic*, 233-36; Bruce, "Thirty Years," 61-62; Dietzfelbinger, *Berufung*, 36-37, and *Abschied*, 18-19; Lüdemann, *Early Christianity*, 71-72; Claudia Seitz, *Jewish Responses*, 179. Weatherly, *Jewish Responsibility*, 235, lists it as a possibility without deciding.

127. In agreement with Räisänen, *Paul*, 249; Dietzfelbinger, *Berufung*, 33-42; *Abschied*, 18; Dunn, *Jesus, Paul*, 99; Hengel, *Pre-Christian Paul*, 83-84; Martyn, *Galatians*, 162-63, 320.

Paul is our earliest written evidence for the Christian use of Deut. 21.22–23. He quotes the reference to someone hanged on a tree being cursed, in Gal. 3.14, having previously quoted Deut. 27.26 to the effect "Cursed is everyone who does not remain in everything written in the book of the law, to do them." Paul turns on its head the putative Jewish use of Deut. 21.22–23 by saying that "Christ redeemed us from the curse of the law, having become a curse for us (γενόμενος ὑπὲρ ἡμῶν κατάρα), as it written, Cursed is everyone who hangs on a tree." Paul goes on to say that the purpose of this was "in order that the blessing promised to Abraham might come in Jesus Christ to the Gentiles, namely that we might receive the promised Holy Spirit through faith" (v. 14).

Thus, Paul's encounter with the risen Jesus produced a change of exegesis of this text. There is, however, no hint of such a theological interpretation in Acts 13.29 when the cross is described as ξύλον; there is no overt suggestion that Jesus atoned for sins by his death on the tree.

Apart from Paul, in the NT the "atonement" use of ξύον can be seen also in 1Pet. 2.24. Jesus Christ "himself bore our sins in his own body on the tree." In some way, vicariously, representatively, Jesus "bore our sins" with the express purpose "that we might die to sins and live for righteousness." We pass from death to life, from sins to righteousness. In context, the writer of 1Peter has been influenced strongly by the language of Isa. 53, the atoning death of the Servant of the Lord.

In the Acts' speeches, ξύλον is used for the cross on three occasions, the other two besides 13.29 being in Petrine speeches. Peter says to the members of the Sanhedrin "The God of our fathers raised Jesus, whom you killed by hanging on a tree" (κρεμάσαντες ἐπὶ ξύλου), while to Cornelius and his household, he declares "The one whom they also killed by hanging on a tree (κρεμάσαντες ἐπὶ ξύλον) God raised on the third day." In both 5.30 and 10.39, the use of ξύλον is part of the contrast scheme between what men did to Jesus and what God did. Hanging Jesus on a tree is illustrative of the rejection of him by the Jews, whereas God stepped in and raised him from the dead. There is no suggestion of any atoning effect of Jesus' death.[128]

We thus have a contrast between the use of ξύλον for the cross in the Acts' speeches (Petrine and Pauline) and that in Galatians and 1Peter. Now the idea that Christ's death availed for us and dealt with our sins is asserted in the pre-Pauline formula, quoted by Paul in 1 Cor. 15.3, a formula which

---

128. Peterson, "Atonement Theology," 65, maintains that an atoning dimension to his death could easily be argued or assumed from the cumulative effect of the argument in 5.30–31, but it is precisely the lack of any such mention that is really the point at issue.

must go back to the early 30s.[129] So, why does not this idea find any place in the kerygmatic speeches in Acts 2–13? This is one of the "puzzles" with which Acts presents us.

Did Luke "edit out" the idea because he had no theology of the cross (*theologia crucis*)? This would probably be the view of the majority of scholars.[130] The strength of this view lies precisely in the contrast between the presence of the idea in the old formula of 1 Cor. 15.3 and its absence in the speeches in Acts.

More recently, there have been attempts to lessen this perceived difference. Thus, Wolter, has argued that we must take into account the difference between the genres employed by the two: Luke was writing a narrative while Paul was discussing theological issues.[131] There is a difference between the "conceptualisation" of theology addressed to those already Christians, those already on the "inside" (Paul), and the "fictionalisation" of theology in the narrated speeches addressed to those before conversion (Luke). But is it really credible that the earliest preaching to Jews would have passed over in silence the idea that in dying Jesus was atoning for the sins of Israel? If Jesus died for our sins according to the scriptures, surely this would have played a part in arguments put forward by his disciples as they sought to persuade fellow Jews. Wolter's argument that the atoning explanation of the death of Jesus played no part in mission preaching fails to convince. Wolter has also argued that 1 Cor. 15.14–17 is dealing with the situation of mission preaching and conversion, and deduces that the resurrection works forgiveness—which is partially what is said in the speeches in Acts. Clearly, an atoning explanation of Jesus' death was only possible in the light of the resurrection, seen as God's vindication of what Jesus had done in offering himself in obedience to his Father's will. But Wolter's claim that 1 Cor. 15.14–17 reflects his mission preaching also does not carry conviction. Paul is addressing Christians, "insiders," and pointing out that what they think of as their assured place in salvation is imperilled if their position on resurrection is correct. This is an internal church discussion. Too much weight should not

---

129. Paul's "conversion" or call is usually dated to 32–34 AD, by means of working back from the assumed date of the Jerusalem Council with the help of Gal. 1–2. Where did Paul "receive" the formula? The most natural assumption is at Damascus, and it would not be difficult to imagine its having originated with the Jerusalem church and its having passed from there to Damascus. See Jeremias, *Eucharistic Words*, 101–4, and Kramer, *Christ*, 19, for arguments pointing to the origin of the formula in the Aramaic-speaking earliest community.

130. As an example, we may quote the view expressed by Sellner, *Heil Gottes*, 405, 410–11, 479, that there is an unpolemical marginalisation of the motif of atonement in the Lucan writings.

131. Wolter, "Jesu Tod," 15–35.

be placed necessarily on the absence of any explicit reference to the death of Jesus in 1 Thess. 1.9-10, since it could be contained implicitly in the declaration that Jesus saves us from the coming wrath (and in 5.9-10 Paul refers to the fact that Jesus Christ died *for us*). Overall, in 1 Thess.1.9-10, Paul seems to be focussing on God and the eschatological outcome,[132] probably due to the fact that this figured large in the concerns of the Thessalonians (as 4.13–5.10 shows).[133]

However, an alternative possibility ought to be mentioned and discussed. Was "Christ died for our sins according to the scriptures" the only way of looking at and explaining the "offense" of the cross? This must surely be answered in the negative. There were other options open to the early Christians in their attempt to overcome the scandal of the cross. At least three alternative approaches may be mentioned.

In the first place, there is the concept of the suffering righteous one who is vindicated by God.[134] Suffering belongs to the lot of the righteous in this sinful world. Suffering, therefore, does not disprove, but rather proves, their righteousness. If that is so, how much more will it be true of the Righteous One *par excellence*? In this model, there is no atoning value to the suffering and/or death. Here in Acts 13, the innocence of Jesus is asserted when it is said that the Sanhedrin had found no cause for the death sentence (v. 28).

Secondly, there was the idea of the violent death of the prophets.[135] This has left its mark on the gospel tradition and was used by Jesus according to Luke 11.49-51; 13.31-35; Matt. 23.34-39. It appears in Paul at 1Thess.2.15; and also in Stephen's speech in Acts 7.52. Both Hoffmann and Klopppenborg-Verbin believe that this was how Q dealt with the problem of Jesus' violent death.[136]

---

132. See Malherbe, *Thessalonians*, 132.

133. Best, *Thessalonians*, 87.

134. For a review of the evidence for this idea, see Schweizer, *Lordship*, 22–41; Ruppert, *Leidende Gerechte*; Nickelsburg, *Genre*, 155–63. In particular, see Doble, *Paradox*, who argues that this is the concept by which Luke interprets the cross of Jesus (in the course of his book, Doble denies the translation of δίκαιος at Luke 23. 47 as "innocent" and argues strongly for "righteous," and maintains echoes of Wisd. 2–5 in Luke's Passion Story, a position which earlier Block, *Proclamation*, 341 n. 232, had espoused without detailed argumentation).

135. See Steck, *Israel*.

136. Hoffmann, *Studien*, 187–90; Kloppenborg-Verbin, *Excavating Q*, 369–74. More recently, Steeley, "Jesus's Death," 222–34, has argued for a Cynic-Stoic understanding of the true philosopher's willingness to undergo death rather than forsake his principles and morals, as the background to Q's understanding of the death of Jesus.

Finally, we may mention the idea of "the binding of Isaac," which may underlie Rom. 8.32; possibly Gal. 3.13–14; and Rom. 3.24–25 too.[137]

Of these possible "models," only the first might underlie the thought of Acts 13.29 and 5.30; 10.39, with their idea that men did their worst against the one who obeyed and served God (cf. "the righteous and holy One," Acts 3.14), but God vindicated him by raising him from the dead. It is just possible that in the speeches Luke has drawn on this tradition, present in early Christianity, of setting forth Jesus' fate in terms of the righteous one who suffers and is put to death.[138]

Luke, then, may be reproducing tradition, but rather one sidedly, since we do not meet the idea of the vicarious and/or atoning nature of Jesus' death in the kerygmatic speeches, though it does appear—in unPauline language[139]—in Paul's speech to the Ephesian elders in Acts 20.28, and, of course, in the longer text of the Lucan version of the Last Supper[140] with its twofold "for you" in connection with both the Bread saying and the Cup saying (22.19–20).

Ulrike Mittmann-Richert has maintained that we should not expect Luke to quote an atoning passage from Isa. 53 when he has already included in his narrative what he meant to say.[141] She believes that the Supper tradition with its twofold "for you" must be deemed decisive in this respect,[142] plus the fact that clearly for Luke Jesus is the Isaianic Servant of the Lord whose way lies through suffering and death which will atone for the sins of others, to exaltation and glory.[143] Mittmann-Richert argues her case forcefully and impressively, though not all allusions to the Servant passages which she claims to find are necessarily convincing, and it still remains a puzzle why we have no explicit reference to the atoning benefits of the Servant's death, neither where Isa. 53 is expressly quoted (as in Luke 22.37 and

---

137. See Vermes, *Scripture*, 193–227; Riesenfeld, *Jésus Transfiguré*, 86–96; Schoeps, "Sacrifice of Isaac," 385–92; and *Paul*, 141–49; Dahl, "Atonement," 15–29.

138. Cf. Rese, "Aussagen," 347; Doble, *Salvation* (see n. 133).

139. Acts 20.28 refers to "the church of God which He obtained (περιεποιήσατο) through the blood of His own" (Son). The only other occurrence of περιποιεῖσθαι in the Pauline corpus is in the Trito-Pauline 1 Tim. 3.13 concerning deacons obtaining a good standing for themselves if they serve well. The verb only occurs elsewhere in the NT at Luke 17.33.

140. For a defence of the longer text, see Schmid, *Lukas*, 324; Ellis, *Luke*, 254–56; Marshall, *Luke*, 799–800 (also *Last Supper and Lord's Supper*, 36–38); Fitzmyer, *Luke*, 2:1387–88; Schürmann, "Lk 22.19b–20," 364–92, 522–41(= *Untersuchungen*, 159–92); Jeremias, *Eucharistic Words*, 139–59; Böttrich, "Proexistenz," 420–22.

141. Mittmann-Richert, *Sühnetod*, 82–83, 234.

142. Ibid., 48, 54., 110, 118–20, 134, 137, 199–203, 232–34

143. Ibid., passim., but especially 55, 89–110, 176–81, 188–95.

Acts 8.32-33) nor in the kerygmatic speeches when the death of Jesus is mentioned and specifically in the PA speech from Paul.[144]

The burial of Jesus (v. 29c), as noted above, is attributed to the Jewish leaders. This has been aptly described as "the last act of the crime" against Jesus,[145] "the final insult done to him by his enemies. It was the culmination of the Jews' No to Jesus."[146] Luke has streamlined the presentation in the speech.

We may say, then, that in v. 29 there is a mixture of tradition and Lucan redaction.

With verse 30 comes the contrast and the reversal of what people did to Jesus. The verse declares briefly and succinctly: ὁ δὲ Θεός ἤγειρεν αὐτὸν ἐκ νεκρῶν.

The δὲ has full force here. This is the divine reversal of the human rejection of God's Servant and Son. God steps in to glorify and exalt Jesus. God is the author, giver and source of life, and He can give life even to the dead. Divine vindication of the dead and buried Jesus is resurrection from the dead. The resurrection proves Jesus in the right despite the condemnation and execution carried out by the Jerusalem leaders and Pilate. The assertion is effective in its brevity.

This assertion, which attributes the resurrection to an act of God, occurs at a number of places in the NT where we have strong grounds for believing that a traditional formula is being quoted: e.g., Rom. 4.24; 10.9; 1 Cor. 6.14; 2 Cor. 4.14; Gal. 1. 1; Col. 2.12; 1Thess.1.10; and compare in the Acts' speeches 3.15; 4.10; 5.30; 10.40; 13.37; and also 1Pet.1.21. Very often the passive voice of ἐγείρειν is used, as in the formula quoted by Paul at 1 Cor. 15.4, and by this means also the resurrection is being traced back to God (the divine passive).

We may at this point add a word about Luke's vocabulary in respect to the resurrection of Jesus. Luke uses the aorist active indicative of ἐγείρειν (ἤγειρεν) with God as the subject 6 times, all in Acts (3.15; 4.10; 5.30; 10.40; 13.30, 37), and the passive voice of ἐγείρειν 3 times, all in the Gospel, one of which is an alteration of his Marcan source (Luke 9.22 [ἐγερθῆναι], altering Mark 8.34), another is repeating Mark (Luke 24.6 [ἠγέρθη] = Mark 16.6), while the third instance is quite probably a traditional saying or based on a traditional saying (24.34 [ἠγέρθη]; compare 1 Cor. 15.5). Luke also uses the active voice (transitive) of ἀνιστάναι [either the aorist indicative

---

144. We await her promised second volume taking up the theme of the atoning death of the Servant of God, in Acts.

145. Wilckens, *Missionsreden*, 135.

146. Fuller, *Formation*, 54 (cf. 73).

ἀνέστησεν or the aorist participle ἀναστήσας], with God as the subject 5 times, all in Acts (2.24, 32; 13.33, 34; 17.31). There is clearly no difference in meaning from the use of ἐγείρειν in respect of the resurrection of Jesus. Luke also uses the intransitive voice of ἀνιστάναι 5 times with Jesus as the subject (Luke 18.33 [ἀναστήσεται], repeating Mark10.34; 24.7 [ἀναστῆναι], a Lucan formulation; 24.46 [ἀναστῆναι], another Lucan formulation; Acts 10.41 [ἀναστῆναι] and 17.3 [ἀναστῆναι]. In these instances, we may detect a marginal heightening of the Christology, but Luke's overall framework remains that God is the author of resurrection—He raised Jesus from the dead. As Paul in Acts 26.8 said to Agrippa, "Why is it judged something incredible that God should raise the dead?" [εἰ ὁ Θεὸς νεκροὺς ἐγείρει;]

Just as in the formula quoted by Paul at 1 Cor. 15 the mention of the resurrection is followed by reference to the appearances of the risen Jesus, so here in the PA speech verse 31 takes us on to the appearances.

ὃς ὤφθη ἐπὶ ἡμέρας πλείους τοῖς συναναβᾶσιν αὐτῷ

ἀπὸ τῆς Γαλιλαίας εἰς Ἰερουσαλήμ.

("who appeared over many days to those who had come up with him from Galilee to Jerusalem").

The relative pronoun ὅς, which stands at the beginning of the verse, may well "conceal" the demonstrative pronoun.[147] There is clearly a deliberate recall of the statement in Acts 1.3 that the risen Jesus had presented himself alive to his apostles in Jerusalem and had taught them about the Kingdom of God.

The appearances of the one raised established the fact of his resurrection and demonstrated the identity of the risen one and the crucified one.

The Paul of this speech seems in the first place to ignore the appearance of the risen Jesus to himself and seems to limit the appearances to Jesus' Galilean followers, and, in the second place, to accord priority in witness to these Galilean followers. We shall pursue these issues now.

Of the gospel writers, Mark says that there were women looking on at the crucifixion from a distance. He names three of them—Mary Magdalene; Mary the mother of James the younger and Joses; and Salome—who had followed and ministered to Jesus when he was in Galilee, and then Mark mentions also the presence of many other women who had come up with him to Jerusalem (Mark15.40-41). The nearest Lucan parallel at 23.49 runs differently:

Εἱστήκεισαν δὲ πάντες οἱ γνωστοὶ αὐτῷ ἀπὸ μακρόθεν

---

147. So Buss, *Missionspredigt*, 74. For this usage, see BAG 587; also BDF, para. 458.

Καὶ γυναῖκες αἱ συνακολουθοῦσαι αὐτῷ ἀπὸ τῆς Γαλιλαί
ας ὁρῶσαι ταῦτα.

("And all his acquaintances were standing at a distance, and the women who accompanied him from Galilee, watching these events.")

The language of the first half of the verse is akin to Pss 38.11; 88.8, both psalms of the righteous sufferer, and it means that Luke's account has the men disciples also present at the crucifixion, as well as the women.

In addition, Luke has the Galileans observe the events which follow the crucifixion: the burial (it is stressed that the two women who observed where Jesus was buried came from Galilee, 23.55); the empty tomb (many women, including Mary Magdalene, Joanna and Mary the mother of James, discovered the empty tomb, and this was verified by Peter and the other men disciples, 24.10–12,[148] 22–24); and the resurrection appearances (Luke 24.13–53; Acts 1.9–11—note the "Men of Galilee" in v. 11). Whether Luke is drawing on an L passion story or is rewriting Mark, what he says can aid his concern to establish the reliability of what he has written (Luke 1.1–4).

According to Luke in Acts, the appearances of the risen Jesus lasted for a period of forty days, at the end of which Jesus ascended to heaven (1.9–11). Formally, the appearance to Paul fell outside that limited period. Yet Luke narrates the appearance of Jesus to Paul three times, and the passive of ὁρᾶν is used for it at 9.17 (on the lips of Ananias) and 26.16 (twice, in the speech of Paul before Herod Agrippa II). So there is something of a tension within the story of Acts in this respect.

When we turn to Paul himself, we see that he passionately defended his own apostleship in 1 Corinthians by reference to the appearance of the risen Lord to him: "Am I not an apostle? Have I not seen the Lord Jesus?" (9.1), and he goes on in chapter 15, while acknowledging the rather abnormal character of the appearance granted to him (15.8: "last of all, he appeared also to me, as to one untimely born"), nonetheless to incorporate that appearance into the "official" list (vv. 5–7). In Galatians, he vehemently asserts and defends his independence from and his equality in call and message with the Jerusalem leaders (e.g., 1.10–12). One would expect Paul, therefore, to have referred to the appearance of the risen Jesus to himself in the PA speech.

We need at this point to touch on the Lucan concept of apostleship briefly as the background to v. 31. The qualification for an apostle to replace Judas is specified at Acts 1.21–22 as follows: such a person should

---

148. Accepting Luke 24.12 as part of the original text; see Grundmann, *Lukas*, 440–41; Ellis, *Luke*, 272–73; Marshall, *Luke*, 888; Fitzmyer, *Luke*, 2:1532, 1541, 1547–48; Jeremias, *Eucharistic Words*, 149–51; Fuller, *Formation*, 101–3.

have accompanied the others throughout the time during which Jesus ministered, from John the Baptist's activity until the ascension of Jesus. The person thus qualified must become a witness of Jesus' resurrection with the eleven. Reliability is guaranteed by those who have witnessed all that Jesus did and said over the whole span of his ministry. On this view, Paul is not an apostle, and he is not so described except at Acts 14.4, 14, where he and Barnabas are referred to as apostles. Luke may in these two verses be reproducing some material from an Antiochene source[149] and allowed the phrase to stand: the two had been "sent out" by the Syrian Antioch church. Although clearly Paul is the hero of the second half of Acts, these two verses in chapter 14 are something of an anomaly.

We are driven to the conclusion that verse 31a seems more Lucan than Pauline.[150]

The second half of the verse brings up the question of the witness to Jesus. In the kerygmatic speeches as a whole, the witness theme is important. Dodd missed this theme, but Glasson pointed out the omission.[151] The theme of apostolic witness occurs elsewhere as follows:

2.32: God raised this Jesus, of which we are all witness;

3.15: God raised him from the dead, of which we are witnesses;

5.32: We are witnesses of these things [the death, resurrection and exaltation of Jesus] and the Holy Spirit whom God has given to those who obey Him; 10.39-41: And we are witnesses of all that he did in the region of Judea and Jerusalem . . . God raised him on the third day and gave him to be revealed, not to all the people, but to witnesses appointed beforehand by God, to us who ate and drank with him after he had risen from the dead.

Only the very brief speech of chapter 4 does not contain the witness theme. The most detailed elaboration of it occurs in the speech to Cornelius where the witness embraces the public ministry as well as the resurrection. Because they ate and drank with him (a Lucan stress—see Luke 24.41-43; Acts 1.4[152]), they can testify to the reality of his resurrection.

In the PA speech, Paul seems to accept the position of priority accorded to the Galilean disciples: they are *par excellence* the witnesses of Jesus'

---

149. So Pesch, *Apg.*, 1:50, 52.

150. Dumais, *Langage*, 245; Barrett, *Acts*, 1:643-44.

151. Glasson, "Kerygma," 129-32.

152. If συναλιζόμενος means eating a meal with someone (rather than gathering together with someone or some others). See BAG 791, for a brief discussion. Bruce, *Acts*, 36; Williams, *Acts*, 55; Haenchen, *Acts*, 141; Marshall, *Acts*, 58; Roloff, *Apg.*, 21; Barrett, *Acts*, 1:71-72; Witherington, *Acts*, 109, all favour the meaning of eating.

resurrection to the people. Arguably, it is difficult to envisage the historical Paul accepting the seemingly inferior status accorded to him by verse 31.[153] This seems something of a "Lucanisation" of Paul.[154]

If Acts 1.22 and 13.31 seem to accord the status of "witness" pre-eminently to the twelve, in the closing section of Acts, which tells of Paul's trials before various Roman officials and the Jewish prince Herod Agrippa II, Paul—and also Stephen—is described as a witness for Jesus. At 22.15, Ananias is depicted as telling Paul that the God of their fathers has appointed him to know His will, to see and hear the Righteous One, "because you will be a witness to him to all the people about the things which you have seen and heard." Later, when Paul is describing his Damascus Road experience before Agrippa, he quotes the risen Jesus as saying to him: "I have appeared to you for this purpose, to appoint you a minister and witness concerning the things in which you have seen me and I will appear to you" (26.16). The final phrase here quoted (ὧν τε ὀφθήσομαί σοι) points to future occasions when the risen Lord will appear to Paul from heaven (e.g., Acts 18.9; 22.17-21; 23.11. In 27.23, however, Paul says that an angel appeared to him with a reassuring message about the safety of the passengers on board ship). Paul also uses the term "witness" of Stephen when speaking to the crowd outside the temple, just after they had nearly lynched him. Paul says that the risen Jesus had appeared to him when he was in a prayerful trance in the temple and had ordered him to leave Jerusalem. Paul had remonstrated on the grounds that people knew of his past career of persecuting Jesus' followers and how he had agreed with the shedding of "the blood of Stephen your witness" (22.20). Here μάρτυς still carries the connotation of a word-witness, though this verbal testimony had led to Stephen's death.

Thus, in the end, 22.15 and 26.16 serve to place Paul alongside the Twelve in terms of witness. Paul also is a witness to the alive-ness of Jesus, even if he was not in the same position as the Twelve of having accompanied Jesus throughout his earthly ministry and, therefore, in a unique sense, witnesses to the identity of the crucified and risen one.

---

153. Cf. Dupont, *Nouvelles Études*, 72. Buss, *Missionspredigt*, 74-81, seems to pass over this difficulty without discussion. Paul had his "back to the wall" in the situations reflected in 1 Cor. 9 and Gal. 1-2 and had to defend himself with vigour and passion against detractors. In a less controversial situation, he may have been prepared to express himself differently, but one suspects that the very circumstances of his pre-conversion career and the dramatic change involved in the Damascus Road episode left him sensitive and vulnerable on this very issue (see 202-4 for further discussion).

154. So Haenchen, *Acts*, 411, and Roloff, *Apg.*, 206. Cf. Barrett, *Acts*, 1:643-44. On the other hand, Tannehill, *Narrative Unity*, 2:170, followed by Witherington, *Acts*, 411-12, thinks that, far from denying witness status to Paul, verse 31 is making the earlier disciples complementary witnesses to him.

The author of Acts was perhaps on "the horns of a dilemma." He wanted to do justice to the pre-eminent role of the Twelve as the companions of Jesus and recipients of appearances from the risen Jesus, for the church depended on and lived from their witness. Yet, on the other hand, Paul, once an arch-persecutor of Christians, was by far and away the leading figure in the dissemination of the Christian message in the north-eastern arc of the Mediterranean. In Acts 13.31 the author pointed to the difference between Paul and the Jerusalem apostles: Paul had not accompanied Jesus from the time of John the Baptist to the ascension. He had not seen Jesus during the forty days between Easter and the ascension. He could not be put on exactly the same footing as they.

Perhaps in 14.4, 14, by the use of the "apostles" and in 22.15; 26.16 by the use of "witness," and, above all, by telling the story of Paul's exploits, Luke redresses the balance, and shows how, by the grace of God, Paul labored more than the Jerusalem apostles had.

The Third Pivotal Verse: Verses 32–33a[155]

καὶ ἡμεῖς ὑμᾶς εὐαγγελιζόμεθα τὴν πρὸς τοὺς πατέρας ἐπαγγελί
αν γενομένην

ὅτι ταύτην ὁ Θεὸς ἐκπεπλήρωκεν τοῖς τέκνοις ἡμῖν,[156]

ἀναστήσας Ἰησοῦν.

("And we preach to you the good news that God has fulfilled the promise made to the fathers, to us the children, by raising Jesus [from the dead]").

The speaker now joins the ranks of the preachers. The juxtaposition of ἡμεῖς ὑμᾶς helps to move the speech from the past to the present, from historical review to contemporary application and actualisation. Buss suggests that Luke may have had Paul use εὐαγγελιζόμεθα to evoke a link with Isa. 52.7. Paul himself does use Isa. 52.7 in Rom. 10.15 (of Christian preachers in general) and, apart from this instance, he uses the verb 16 times of his own preaching in the undisputed letters (with one occurrence of himself in Eph. 3.8). On the other hand, Luke is very fond of εὐαγγελίζεσθαι and uses it of John the Baptist, Jesus and the disciples (Luke has Jesus reading

---

155. It will be seen that our stress on three pivotal verses differs from the suggestion of a proposition in two stages, put forward by Flichy, *Figure*, 189 (see chapter 3).

156. Assuming that the best-attested reading of ἡμῶν was either a slip on the part of Luke or else was a very early corruption of ἡμῖν. See Metzger, *Textual Commentary*, 410–11, for a full discussion.

Isa. 61.1 with its significant use of εὐαγγελίζεσθαι and has him apply it to himself, in the synagogue at Nazareth, Luke 4.18).

Grammatically, Luke has brought forward what is strictly speaking the object of the ὅτι clause (viz. "the promise made to our fathers"), replacing it there with a resumptive ταύτην. The noun ἐπαγγελία picks up the κατ' ἐπαγγελίαν of verse 23, and this word acts as a clamp linking the two verses together.

The phrase "the promise was made to the fathers" suggests that the promise cannot be limited to God's promise through Nathan to David, and must include the promise to the patriarchs. Since David is a descendant of Abraham (see Ruth 4.18–22), there is no problem here. One might say that fundamentally there is one promise made originally to Abraham, reiterated to his son and grandson, Isaac and Jacob, and renewed to David.[157]

What Paul announced as good news is the fulfillment of the age-old promise. The story of Israel from the patriarchs on through David had been leading up to the coming and ministry of Jesus and, above all, to the resurrection of Jesus. The fulfillment has taken place ἀναστήσας Ἰησοῦν. The succeeding context makes it reasonably certain that ἀναστήσας refers to the resurrection of Jesus from the dead.[158] Some scholars, however, have argued that ἀναστήσας here means no more, and no less, than "brought on the historical scene."[159] They do so on the following grounds. Firstly, that the idea "promise" in vv. 23 and 32 should carry the same sense, and at v. 23 "God has brought (ἤγαγεν) to Israel a savior, Jesus" means "brought on the scene." But this is surely no insuperable problem. Since the total ministry of Jesus, from the beginning of his ministry to his cross, resurrection and ascension, constituted Jesus as the promised Savior, any one of these might, in any given context, be mentioned on its own. Then, secondly, it is argued that a phrase like ἐκ νεκρῶν should accompany ἀναστήσας if the resurrection were in mind; without this phrase, ἀναστήσας could mean "to raise up = bring on the scene" as at Acts 3.22. However, this is not so at Acts 2.24 and 32. In both cases, the context makes it clear that the resurrection is in

---

157. Cf. Dahl, "Abraham," 148; Buss, *Missionspredigt*, 46. For the OT background of this, see Clements, *Abraham*.

158. So Haenchen, *Acts*, 411 n. 3; Roloff, *Apg.*, 207; Schneider, *Apg.*, 2:137; Pesch, *Apg.*, 2:38; Fitzmyer, *Acts*, 516; Witherington, *Acts*, 412; Jervell, *Apg.*, 359; Wilckens, *Missionsreden*, 51; Lövestam, *Son and Saviour*, 10; Dupont, *Études*, 265, 295–96; Goldsmith, "Acts 13.33-37," 322; Schweizer, "Davidic Son of God," 186; O'Toole, "Christ's Resurrection," 365-70; Soards, *Speeches*, 86 n. 226; Bock, *Proclamation*, 245; Turner, *Power from on High*, 200, n. 39.

159. E.g. Bruce, *Acts*, 275 n. 52; Barrett, *Acts*, 1:645–46; Rese, "Altestamentliche Motive," 82-86; Pietsch, *Sprotz Davids*, 310; Miura, *David*, 183-86.

mind, and that is the case here in 13.33. Where the context makes it clear, there is no absolute need of ἐκ νεκρῶν. Thirdly, the argument runs that Ps. 2 is associated with Jesus' baptism, while the resurrection is dealt with in v. 34. But such "back-tracking" to the baptism after the death and resurrection have just been mentioned seems somewhat odd, while Rom. 1.4 (probably part of a pre-Pauline formula used by Paul) is an illustration of how Ps. 2 was associated with the resurrection in some early Christian circles of probable Palestinian provenance.[160] We assume, therefore, that the whole block of OT quotations in verses 33-35 refers to the resurrection and not just verses 34-35.

Furthermore, Dupont[161] has pointed out that when either ἐγείρειν or ἀνιστάναι is used of the historical appearance of some one in LA, a title always follows (Luke 1.69; Acts 3.22, 26; 7.37; 13.22), whereas that is not the case here.

The case for taking ἀναστήσας of the resurrection seems stronger than for taking it of Jesus' historical appearance.[162]

The use of ἀναστήσας (rather than ἐγείρας) at v. 33 may have been occasioned by the awareness that behind vv. 22-23 there was an allusion to 2 Sam. 7.12.[163] Early Christians interpreted the promise of raising up David's seed in 2 Sam. 7.12 in the sense of resurrection and saw that promise as fulfilled in Jesus' resurrection.

As we shall see, the next section of the speech (vv. 33b-37) backs up this assertion about God's having raised Jesus from the dead. Since he has been raised and did not suffer corruption, i.e., he is permanently alive and lives as God's Son, he is able to confer salvation on others (cf. v. 26).

Use of the OT in Verses 33b-37

There are three specific OT quotations in verses 33-35. They are set in the context of the third "pivotal verse" (vv. 32-33a) just discussed. The first quotation used is that of Psalm 2.7 in verse 33b. It follows on from "by raising Jesus (from the dead)," and is introduced by "as it stands written also in the second psalm":

160. Hebrews 1.5 and 5.5 associate Ps. 2 with Jesus' exaltation and glorification to God's right hand.

161. Dupont, *Nouvelles Études*, 530.

162. There is a mediating position, which combines both viewpoints—the whole career of Jesus, including his resurrection and glorification—put forward by Cadbury, *Beginnings*, 4:154-55, and accepted by Strauss, *Davidic Messiah*, 164-66.

163. The Hiphil of the Hebrew qûm in 2 Sam. 7.12 means "cause to rise or raise up"; LXX καὶ ἀναστήσω.

Υἱός μου εἶ σύ, ἐγὼ σήμερον γεγέννηκά σε.

This corresponds to the LXX, which itself is a faithful reproduction of the Hebrew text. Ps. 2, originally a coronation psalm for the Davidic kings in Jerusalem and Judah, was eventually interpreted messianically after the demise of the monarchy following the destruction of temple, city and state by the Babylonians in 586. The Seventeenth Psalm of Solomon applies the language of Ps. 2.7 to the longed-for son of David at v. 26.

We should also bear in mind that Ps. 2.7 shared with 2 Sam. 7 the idea that the descendant of David who was anointed king in Jerusalem became God's son. "I will be his father and he shall be My son" (2 Sam. 7.14a). The concept of divine sonship in Ps. 2 would, by association, evoke also God's promise through Nathan in 2 Sam. 7.

According to the PA speech, Jesus becomes Son of God at the resurrection. The resurrection becomes his "birth-day" and is an enhancement of Jesus' dignity and status. The risen Jesus is enthroned at God's side. Such a view in respect of resurrection and exaltation can also be found in Acts 2.36, and also at Heb. 1.5 (where Ps. 2.7 and 2 Sam. 7.14 are both quoted) and 5.5 (where also Ps. 2.7 is used) and Rom. 1.4 ("appointed Son of God at, or on the basis of, the resurrection of the dead").

However, this does not exactly tally with the views of Paul who operates with the concept of pre-existence and incarnation (so 1 Cor. 8.6; 10.4; 2 Cor. 8.9; possibly Phil. 2.5-11 and, if by Paul, Col. 1.15-17), nor, indeed, with the views of Luke, for whom Jesus' special birth constitutes him as Son of God ("Therefore, the holy One to be born shall be called Son of God," Luke1.30-35).

We seem to have here an early Christological assertion about the resurrection, with which Christians did not remain content for very long, pushing the "moment" of divine election further back: the baptism (Mark1.11 et par.), the birth (Luke1.30-35; Matt. 1.23; 2.15), eternity (John1.1-18).[164] Acts 13.33 seems to be very early tradition indeed.

The speech then continues in verse 34 by asserting: "as to the fact that God raised him from the dead, never to return to corruption, He has spoken in this way:

Δώσω ὑμῖν τὰ ὅσια Δαυὶδ τὰ πιστά.

---

164. This should not be taken to imply endorsement of a smooth "linear" development from a so-called "primitive" Christology to a more "developed," sophisticated Christology. After all, Luke's Gospel is not all that far in time from Mark's Gospel, while Paul and probably Hebrews predate both. A pre-existence Christology could have existed in Johannine circles a considerable time before the actual writing down of John's Gospel.

Did Luke Use Sources for the Speech? 121

In the introduction to the quotation from Isa. 55.3, the idea of never returning to corruption anticipates the use of Ps. 16.10 in v. 35. As to the quotation itself, there are a number of problems.

The MT goes as follows: w^{e}ekhr^{e}thah lakhem b^{e}erith 'ôlam, ḥasdke dawidh hane'emanim ("And I will make with you an everlasting covenant, my sure mercies to David").

The LXX runs: καὶ διαθήσομαι ὑμῖν διαθήκην αἰώνιον, τὰ ὅσια Δαυιδ τὰ πιστά.

("And I shall covenant to you an eternal covenant, the holy and reliable things of David").

The LXX has taken the Hebrew ḥasdhê ("mercies" or "steadfast love") as τὰ ὅσια ("the holy things"), where we might have expected τὰ ἐλέη ("mercies").

In comparison with the Hebrew and the LXX, Acts 13.34 has replaced "I will covenant a covenant" (of both the Hebrew and the LXX) with "I shall give," while it has retained the τὰ ὅσια of the LXX (as against the Hebrew "mercies/steadfast love"). Luke or a source before him might have abbreviated the phrase involving covenant in order to concentrate on the reference to David, but this does not appear an entirely satisfactory explanation, because the concept of covenant appears at Luke 1.72 in the Benedictus, and that in connection with the fathers; in the longer text of the Last Supper at 20.20; and in both Peter's speech at Acts 3.25 and Stephen's speech at 7.8.[165] Another possible explanation might be an alteration in order to bind the Isa. 55.3 quotation more closely with that of Ps. 16.10 in the next verse. As it is, there is now a double verbal link up between the two OT quotations:

Verse 34: δώσω   verse 35: δώσεις
          τὰ ὅσια   τὸν ὅσιόν.

This verbal link suggests that the Holy One (i.e., Jesus) of v. 35, the One raised from the dead, never to see corruption, becomes the source of the holy things, which were promised David,[166] to the present generation (ὑμῖν of v. 34).

---

165. A number of scholars do not think that Luke himself would have omitted the idea of covenant: Holtz, *Zitate*, 138.

166. This seems the sense of the genitive of the indeclinable Δαυίδ. It cannot mean the holy things belonging to David, for God is the ultimate origin and donor of them. Cf. the comments of BAG 589, though he takes τὰ ὅσια to refer to the decrees of God. Strauss, *Davidic Messiah*, 170-71, while taking the phrase as divine blessings promised to David (namely, in 2 Sam. 7.5-16 and developed elsewhere in the OT), interprets these blessings as the promise of an heir, eternal kingdom, rest, and security, and so sees a reference to Jesus, through whom all of God's people receive salvation

So what are in mind in this phrase "the holy things promised to David"? They must be things capable of being given to believers, as the ὑμῖν contained in the quotation makes clear—"I will give to you." This tells against the interpretation of Lövestam,[167] who took v. 34 as a promise of the permanent dominion of the messiah, and that of Bauer who translated the phrase as "the sure decrees of God relating to David," which have been transferred to his messianic descendant (Bauer took these decrees as the promises made in Ps. 16).[168] Thus, the drawback with both these interpretations seems to be that they apply τὰ ὅσια to Jesus and not to believers (ὑμῖν).[169]

Accordingly, it would seem reasonable to assume that in the first instance "the holy things" are best taken as all that is embraced within salvation (v 26): forgiveness, justification, holiness and sanctity of life.[170] This interpretation is strengthened by the fact that the Isaianic passage encourages the wicked to forsake their ways and turn to God, who will have mercy on them and abundantly pardon them (Isa. 55.7a).[171] As a consequence of the resurrection of Jesus, forgiveness of sins is promised through him in v. 38.

At the same time, only he who has been raised incorruptible as the Holy One can dispense these holy blessings to the current generation. Jesus is the Savior promised of old by God (v. 23), and this role of dispenser of salvation is made possible *through his resurrection and resultant incorruption.*[172] He can enable believers "to serve God in holiness and righteousness. . .all (their) days" (Luke 1.74–75). The blessings to be given by God come only through the one raised incorruptible from the dead.[173] David's heir can fulfil what God promised to David.

---

blessings. Johnson, *Septuagintal Midrash*, 45, takes the phrase to mean "all of the Davidic promises."

167. Lövestam, *Son and Saviour*, 74–81.

168. BAG 589.

169. The same applies to Zwang, *Paul*, 146, who applies the phrase to the resurrection and consequent incorruptibility of Jesus, as the fulfillment of the promise to David. The importance of the "to you" has been recognized by many scholars, including Dupont, *Études*, 351–54. See recently, Anderson, *God Raised Him*, 250.

170. So Dupont, *Études*, 337–59; Killgallen, "Acts 13.38–39," 497–502; Strauss, *Davidic Messiah*, 170–71 see n. 324; Pilcher, *Paulusrezeption*, 179; and cf. Pietsch, *Sprotz Davids*, 312–13.

171. The wicked should return to God καὶ ἐλεηθήσεται ὅτι ἐπὶ πολὺ ἀφήσει τὰς ἁμαρτίας ὑμῶν. Van de Sandt, "Quotations," 39, has drawn attention to this sense link between Isa. 55.7 and Acts 13. 38.

172. Note the double stress on Jesus in vv. 38–39 : διὰ τούτου . . . ἐν τούτῳ.

173. Anderson, *God Raised Him*, 253–54, prefers to see the holy things promised to David as the sonship and enthronement of David's heir and the perpetuity of his

It is along these lines, then, that we can see how Isa. 55.3 supports the assertion in v. 34a, that God "raised him from the dead never to return to corruption," despite the argument advanced by some that the quotation from Ps. 16.10, now at v. 35, would seem to fit better at v. 34b rather than the Isa. 55.3 quotation.[174]

The last of the three quotations from the OT comes at verse 35. "Therefore, He also says in another (passage): οὐ δώσεις τὸν ὅσιον Ἰδεῖν διαφθοράν."

("You will not give Your holy One to see corruption").

The MT goes: lō' thitēn ḥᵃsîdᵉka lirʾoth šaḥēth.

The LXX follows this : οὐδὲ δώσεις τὸν ὅσιόν σου Ἰδεῖν διαφθοράν.

There is no major difference calling for comment.

The argument proceeds in *verse 36* along these lines: David died, was buried and "saw corruption." Thus, he cannot have been speaking about himself. But "the One whom God raised did not see corruption." The comment is rather brief and terse, and Luke might have abbreviated comment, because Ps. 16.10 had already been used and commented upon in Peter's speech at greater length in 2.25-32.

Verse 37 now contrasts (δὲ balancing the μὲν of v. 36) Jesus with David. If Ps. 16 cannot apply to David because he only served God for the duration of his own lifetime and generation,[175] then died and was buried, it can

---

kingship, with the saving benefits accruing to the people of God including justification and the forgiveness of sins. Our interpretation proceeds the other way round. The "blessings" are to the fore, but these can only be given by the one raised to life incorruptible.

174. Holtz, *Zitate*, 139, indeed goes so far as to say that the quotation fulfils no purpose in its present position, but this is probably incorrect. See 147-48, 157 for further discussion of the role of Isa. 55.3 in the argument.

175. The general thrust of v. 36 probably helps to resolve the dispute as to which phrase is governed by ὑπηρετήσας (see Barrett, *Acts*, 1:648-49, who lists the various possibilities): David served the will of God (τῇ τοῦ Θεοῦ Βουλῇ) in his generation (ἰ δίᾳ γενεᾷ) and then died. This takes Ἰδίᾳ γενεᾷ as a locative dative and τῇ τοῦ Θεοῦ Βουλῇ as the object of ὑπερετήσας. See JB; GN; NIV; REB; NRSV; BAG 850; Bruce, *Acts*, 277; Marshall, *Acts*, 227; Fitzmyer, *Acts*, 506, 517; Johnson, *Acts*, 229, 235; Rengstorff, ὑπηρέτης ὑπηρετεῖν, *TDNT* 8.540. This means that David's work was confined within his own genertion, whereas the risen Jesus, freed from corruption, can continue his work as God's servant and Son.

Other scholars take Ἰδίᾳ γενεᾷ as the object of ὑπηρετήσας with τῇ τοῦ Θεοῦ Βουλῇ as an instrumental dative—David served his own generation by the will of God: see Lake andCadbury, *Beginnings*, 4:156; Haenchen, *Acts*, 412; Schneider, *Apg.*, 2:127, 139; Roloff, *Apg.*, 207; Pesch, *Apg.*, 2:29, 39; Johnson, *Acts*, 235; Pilcher, *Paulusrezeption*,

only refer to Jesus who, though he did die, was raised to life by God, and, therefore, did not see corruption.[176]

The message of verses 33-37 may be summarized: the resurrection was both God's act in rescuing Jesus from death and corruption, but also Jesus' exaltation, his new birthday, his "adoption" as God's son. As the ever-living one, whose reign will be eternal, he can dispense to believers now those blessings which God promised through David.[177] What was promised in the OT has been fulfilled. The resurrection is in line with OT promises.

Whether or not it is right to speak about a covert or implicit midrash,[178] when a passage may be in mind but not actually quoted, the importance of David in the speech, and the reference to the seed of David in v. 23, and to the promise in v. 23 in particular, would suggest that *2 Sam. 7.12 is not far from the mind of the writer*. If Acts 13.33-37 drew on material connected with an interpretation of 2 Sam. 7,[179] then Ps. 2.7; Isa. 55.3; and Ps. 16.8 would be supportive passages in what was a Christian reinterpretation of the Davidic messianic hope. For example, Holtz thought of a late Jewish messianic *testimonia*, introduced by a summary of Israel's history up to David. He believed that the collection began with the quotation now at Acts 13.22, followed by 2 Sam. 7; with Isa. 55.3 assuring the legitimacy of the application of the promise for David to the heir of his rule, the messiah who will not see corruption; Ps. 16.10. Luke introduced Ps. 2.7 instead of the 2 Sam. passage,[180] but why should he introduce it instead of rather than in addition to the 2 Sam. 7 passage?

---

184. Barrett, *Acts*, 1:648-49, accepts this "though without strong conviction."
Grammatically, τῇ τοῦ Θεοῦ βουλῇ could also be taken with the verb ἐκοιμήθη—he died through the will of God. But the translation assumed above probably suits the flow of the argument best.

176. Strauss, *Davidic Messiah*, 172-73, has pointed out that this argument in relation to Psalm 16 is similar and yet also dissimilar to the argument in Peter's Pentecost speech at Acts 2.25-31. There, the argument is designed to prove that Jesus, not David, is the Messiah, whereas here in Acts 13 the stress is on the risen, immortal Jesus' capacity to bestow on believers the blessings promised to David.

177. Cf. Strauss' somewhat longer summary, *Davidic Messiah*, 173-74. Anderson, *God Raised Him*, 253, stresses the background of the Davidic promise tradition throughout the LXX and within Second Temple Judaism.

178. Gertner, "Midrashim," 267-92, argued for the existence of covert midrashim in the New Testament, but see Alexander, "*Midrash*," 10, 16-17 n. 10, and 17-18 n. 14, for criticisms of such an idea.

179. Those who see 2 Sam. 7 as underlying the Speech of Acts 13 include Doeve, Bowker, Dumais, Dupont, Ellis, Goldsmith, Lövestam, Schmitt, Strauss, Pietsch, Miura, and Anderson. Probably, Holtz too should be included.

180. Holtz, *Zitate*, 140-42.

Schmitt suggested that vv. 33–37 were the remnants of a Jewish Christian re-reading ["relecture"] of the old royal messianism and that the Hebrew qûm/ Greek ἀνιστάναι of 2 Sam. 7 were read in the light of Easter.[181] Like Holtz, Schmitt also believed that Ps. 2.7 was substituted for 2 Sam. 7.12 to give the reason for the exaltation of Jesus to the position of Son of God.[182]

The heart of the promise to David lay in the promise of raising up seed to him and of the sovereignty of that seed. The claim being made in the PA speech is that this had been fulfilled in raising Jesus up from the dead and giving to him, as the holy and incorruptible One, the sovereignty which would enable him in turn to pour out on God's people the blessings of his saving reign. Thus, we can perceive a logic in the passages used in vv. 33–35: Jesus is raised from the dead and exalted as God's Son. The blessings promised to David will become a reality through Jesus precisely because as risen he lives forever and will never see corruption.

The idea of a pre-Lucan reinterpretation of 2 Sam. 7 for Acts 13.33–35 would be analogous to a suggestion concerning Acts 10.36–38 put forward by G. N. Stanton:[183] namely, that originally Acts 10.36–38 was part of a longer citation of Ps. 107.20 backed up by Isa. 52.7; 61.1; and Deut. 21.22.[184]

If there is merit in this suggestion of a reinterpretation of the promise to David via Nathan in 2 Sam. 7 with supportive texts for Acts 13.33–37, then acceptance of it probably tilts the balance in favour of a pre-Lucan source for the "survey of Israel's history," rather than for Lucan composition.

PART 3 OF PAUL'S SPEECH AT PISIDIAN ANTIOCH: VV. 38–41

Conclusion (or Peroration): vv. 38–41

Verse 38 begins the conclusion to the speech. The vocative, ἄνδρες ἀδελ-φοί, is the stylistic pointer to a new division. The οὖν indicates that certain consequences will now be drawn from all that has been said. The review of sacred history indicated that the promise, which had been made to the fathers and renewed to David, of a Savior for Israel, would be fulfilled in a

---

181. Schmitt, "Kerygma Pascal," 155–67. Schmitt (167) described Acts 13.32–37 as the last sub-apostolic attempt to "maintain" the ancient Jewish Christian re-reading of Nathan's oracle and Ps. 2.7.

182. Ibid., 164.

183. Stanton, *Jesus*, 70–77.

184. Ibid., 77, says that in Acts 10.36–39 we have the "fossils" of three passages which may have been linked together at a very early period to answer the question, "What did Jesus do before his crucifixion?" or "How was his earthly life significant?"

descendant of David. God has brought on the scene, Jesus, whose coming had been prepared by John the Baptist and who had suffered rejection and death at the hands of the people of Jerusalem and their leaders, but God had raised Jesus from the dead, so that he did not see corruption, and He had installed him as His Son. It is precisely in raising Jesus to permanent aliveness that God has ensured that the blessings which He promised to and through David would be available to Israel (represented by the PA congregation—the ὑμῖν of v. 34b) through His Son.

Two such blessings are specified in verses 38-39:

Διὰ τούτου ὑμῖν ἄφεσις ἁμαρτιῶν καταγγέλλεται ...
ἐν τούτῳ πᾶς ὁ πιστεύων δικαιοῦται.

The parallelism is clear: Jesus is the one through whom forgiveness of sins and justification is mediated. Or, to put it another way, forgiveness of sins and justification mutually interpret one another.[185] Forgiveness of sins is equivalent to being declared in the right with God; being set right with God means the forgiveness of sins. That which is a barrier between God and us is removed and, therefore, this makes possible a right relationship to God.

In both instances, the accompanying verbs are in the present tense. In other words, the blessings of this forgiveness-justification are being offered here and now (cf. ὑμῖν of v. 38).

Justification by grace through faith is a major theme of Pauline theology (cf. Rom.; Gal.; Phil. 3). Barrett says that Luke "elaborates the theme of forgiveness by incorporating the Pauline terminology of justification."[186] Verse 39 may, therefore, be said to be a Pauline touch. But has Luke either misunderstood Paul, or, in an effort to give a Pauline touch to the speech, not really given us the depths of Paul's thought about the law and God's gracious justification of the sinner, as some scholars allege?[187] Some even postulate that there is a two-stage justification in vv. 38b-39.

After the statement that forgiveness of sins through Jesus is being proclaimed, the Greek runs:

Καὶ ἀπὸ πάντων ὧν οὐκ ἠδυνήθητε ἐν νόμῳ Μωυσέως δικαιωθῆναι,

---

185. See 192-97 for a discussion of the issue whether interpreting justification as forgiveness involves a narrowing of Paul's thought in a negative direction.

186. Barrett, *Acts*, 1:650.

187. In recent times this view has been especially associated with Vielhauer, "Paulinism," 41-43, esp. 42. He has been followed in varying nuances by Conzelmann, *Theology*, 160, 163, 228, 230; Schneider, *Apg.*, 139-40; Roloff, *Apg.*, 208; Lüdemann, *Early Christianity*, 154; Jervell, *Apg.*, 360. See the excellent discussion in Barrett, *Acts*, 1:650-51.

ἐν τούτῳ πᾶς ὁ πιστεύων δικαιοῦται.

Two things may be said. Firstly, Buss is surely right to maintain that the main clause must determine the meaning of the subordinate clause.[188] The main clause clearly states that a person is justified through believing in Jesus. The subordinate clause has Jewish hearers in mind: they cannot achieve justification through doing the works required by the Law of Moses.

Furthermore, from the point of view of the readers/hearers of Acts, what they have read so far indicates quite clearly that Jews are sinners and need God's gracious forgiveness through Jesus: 2.36-38; 3.22-26; 4.12; 5.31; 7.51; and even the pious Cornelius who was a person who did what was right (10.2, 4, 35) was offered forgiveness (10.43). A little later, the reader/hearer of Acts will learn from the lips of Peter that Jews and Gentiles alike "will be saved through the grace of the Lord Jesus" (15.11), a position accepted by James whose suggestions dealt with facilitating table fellowship between Jewish and Gentile Christians, and not with how someone might be saved (15.14-15, 19-21).

Secondly, the καὶ in v. 38 can and should be taken as exepegetic (explanatory).[189] It functions as equivalent to the phrase "that is."

Thirdly, a number of scholars have pointed out weaknesses in the picture of Judaism given by Sanders and others, and called "covenantal nomism"viz. that God had graciously elected Israel as His people in a covenant relationship with Himself and He had provided the sacrificial system as a means of atonement for sins committed by the elect people.[190] Gathercole, for example, has pointed out that Sanders and others have not given sufficient weight to the future justification at the Last Judgment and has drawn attention to the fact that many Jewish writers do give the impression that works would be the criterion of acceptance at the End.[191] While this debate has centered on Paul's own writings, it is not without its relevance to the interpretation of this part of the PA speech and what will emerge as a fierce debate in chapter 15, when Luke reports that some Pharisaically

---

188. Buss, *Missionspredigt*, 126.

189. Rightly, Jervell, *Apg.*, 360; Klinghardt, *Gesetz*, 100.

190. See Sanders, *Paul*, 33-238, 419-28; Dunn, *Jesus, Paul*, 183-241; and Wright, *Climax*, in particular.

191. E.g., Gathercole, *Where is Boasting?*; see also Carson et al., *Justification and Variegated Nomism*, vol. 1, which looks at the whole range of second Temple Jewish writings. The debate has generated a considerable volume of secondary literature and continues unabated, with Dunn reiterating his position with some modification in *The New Perspective*, and Watson setting out his judgment on the New Perspective in the second and much enlarged edition of his *Paul, Judaism and the Gentiles: Beyond the New Perspective*.

inclined Christians at Jerusalem asserted that to be saved one needed to keep the law of Moses. Here in PA it is asserted that salvation is not to be achieved through keeping the Law of Moses.

In the light of all this, we must dismiss the charge that Luke has seriously misunderstood Paul's teaching on justification and has produced a two stage justification.[192] That seems to be hypercriticism. Whether Luke has entirely captured the whole flavour of justification is another question. We certainly miss Paul's close link between justification and the death of Jesus as the saving event in this speech.

The referent of "believe" in v. 39 is clearly understood as "Savior Jesus" (v. 23; cf. v. 26). The sense is that by Jesus (what God has done through him in raising him to life) everyone who believes in him will be justified.

What these verses say is, in effect, to give to us *the substance* of "the word of salvation" sent to the congregation ("to us," v. 26). There is an implied appeal for belief in Jesus, but it is not specifically articulated. If it is correct to see in the phrase used in 10.35 "those who fear God" a reverential attitude to the Creator God which might be found in a person of any nation, then it has also to be said that there is surely a latent universalism in the πᾶς which accompanies the articular participle of the verb to believe here in 13.39. The step of faith, and, therefore, the gift of justification, is potentially open to everyone. The reader/hearer at least, especially after the Cornelius narrative, could not fail to pick this up. With the stress on faith in Jesus, there is a clear link between Christology and acceptance of the Gentiles.[193]

At the same time, there is clearly a contrast drawn between "by this man" (Jesus) and "by the Law of Moses" (v. 38). There is a need to believe in Jesus; keeping the Law is not sufficient. What is said here does not say everything there is to say about the Law. Here, it is faith in Jesus which brings salvation, not the Law.

Balancing this "promise" of forgiveness-justification is the warning contained in the last two verses, *verses* 40-41. Once again, οὖν points to a deduction being drawn. The offer of salvation is made, but, if that should be refused, dire consequences will ensue as foretold in prophetic scripture, specifically in Hab. 1.5:

Βλέπετε οὖν μὴ ἐπέλθῃ τὸ εἰρημένον ἐν τοῖς προφήταις
Ἴδετε, οἱ καταφρονηταί, καὶ θαυμάσατε καὶ ἀφανίσθητε,

---

192. As Vielhauer, "Paulinism," 42 (who quotes Harnack and H. Braun to similar effect) argues. See also Stuhlmacher, *Gerechtigkeit*, 194-95. Among those who reject the idea of a double justification we might mention Haenchen, *Acts*, 412 (though in scarcely flattering terms to Luke's theological capabilities); Barrett, *Acts*, 2:650; Fitzmyer, *Acts*, 519; Jervell, *Apg.*, 360-61; Wilson, *Law*, 59.

193. As Schröter rightly stressed, "Heil," 297.

Ὅτι ἔργον ἐργάζομαι ἐγὼ ἐν ἡμέραις ὑμῶν,
Ἔργον ὃ οὐ μὴ πιστεύσητε ἐάν τις ἐκδιηγῆται ὑμῖν.

("See to it, therefore, lest what was said by the prophets come upon (you).
    Look, you scoffers, and wonder[194] and perish,
    Because I am doing a work in your days,
    A work which you will never believe (even) if some should describe it in detail[195] to you.")

It used to be assumed that Luke with οἱ καταφροηταί was following the LXX, whereas the MT has "Look among the nations," but the Qumran Hebrew text of Habbakuk has the word "Scoffers," not "among the nations." The LXX may have known a Hebrew text with "scoffers" and not made a mistranslation. Acts 13.41 has θαυμάσατε, where the LXX has θαυμάσατε θαυμάσια, a literal rendering of the Hebrew infinitive absolute construction, and has διότι for ὅτι; puts ἐγὼ after the verb where its unusual position calls attention to itself; and repeats ἔργον in the final line.

As applied to the audience, "in your days" means the time of fulfillment, the time of salvation. But what is "the work" which God is doing? There are two possibilities, which may not be mutually incompatible. The work could be that of raising Jesus and establishing him as the Son-Savior in fulfillment of the promise to the fathers.[196] The salvation offered by this Son-Savior is justification through faith, interpreted as forgiveness of sins, with the corollary that the Mosaic Law as such is not the necessary way of salvation.[197] Or, the work could be the work of mission, preaching the gospel,[198] for which Paul and Barnabas were sent out by God from Antioch (at 13.2, this task is actually described as "the work" to which the Holy Spirit had called them), and on their return they gave the church at Antioch a report

---

194. Anderson, *God Raised Him*, 256 n. 70, maintains that θαυμάσατε should be rendered as "Be aghast" or perhaps "Be alarmed," but neither BAG nor LSJ offer this sense for the verb.

195. This rendering attempts to get the specific nuance of ἐκδιηγῆται. See BAG 238; Maloney, *Narration*, 141–42, 163.

196. So Barrett. *Acts*, 1:652; Pillai, *Apostolic Interpretation*, 71–73; Hansen, "Preaching and Defense," 306; Anderson, *God Raised Him*, 257–58.

197. Buss, *Missionspredigt*, 132.

198. Bruce, *Acts*, 279; Haenchen, *Acts*, 413; Marshall, *Acts*, 228–29; Schneider, *Apg.*, 2:141; Roloff, *Apg.*, 208; Fitzmyer, *Acts*, 519; Wilckens, *Missionsreden*, 52; Lohfink, *Sammlung*, 88; Pietsch, *Sprotz Davids*, 315–16; Van de Sandt, "Quotations," 45.

concerning the "work" which they had completed (14.26). There could be the added nuance that this preaching is intended to bring in the Gentiles.[199]

Nanos has suggested what is a refinement of this last view. He suggests that Paul was warning the PA Jews not to fail to recognise that the restoration of Israel was taking place, which was being manifest in the gospel's going to the Gentiles as a sign of Israel's eschatological mission and thus a sign that Israel's restoration had begun.[200] Certainly, from the flow of the narrative, what Peter said to the Jerusalemites at 3.25 indicates that it is through the seed of Abraham that all the families of the earth will be blessed, while Paul will quote Isa. 49.6 on the next sabbath, a passage which reminds of the vocation of Israel (49.3!) to take light to the Gentiles. Subsequently, James will use Amos 9.11-12 to speak of the restoration of "the fallen tent of David" in order that all the Gentiles should seek God.

The context of the whole speech favours the first interpretation, while the immediate context might be held to favour the second interpretation, and the use of the present tense ἐργάζομαι ἐγώ points to the present.[201] But, since the mission and its message are dependent on the resurrection of Jesus, perhaps we should not press an either-or approach, but accept an underlying reference to the theme of Jesus' resurrection and the salvation which he can give to men and women, while seeing the surface meaning as the task of preaching the gospel to all.[202]

The "scoffers" are those who harden their hearts and refuse to accept that God has indeed fulfilled His promise by raising Jesus from the dead.[203] The stern warning of the danger of eradication is reminiscent of the warning given by Peter in Acts 3.22-23 (cf. too Peter's implicit warning to the Sanhedrin as those who had rejected the stone which had become in God's providence the cornerstone, at 4.10). At the same time, it should be noted that the Habbakuk quotation is introduced by "Beware, therefore, lest what

---

199. This is very much the emphasis of Wassenberg, *Israels Mitte*, 313; Deutschmann, *Synagoge*, 203.

200. Nanos, *Mystery*, 270-72.

201. The verb ἐκδιηγεῖσθαι, which appears in the Habbukuk quotation (ἐκδιηγῆται), is also used at 15.3, where it is said that Paul, Barnabas and others from the Antioch church, as they passed through Phoenicia and Samaria on their way to Jerusalem, reported (ἐκδιηγούμενοι) the conversion of the Gentiles to the Christians en route, giving them great joy by such news. These are the only two occurrences of the verb in LA, and indeed in the NT as a whole.

202. Deutschmann, *Synagoge*, 203, maintains that the ἔργον is not per se the repudiation of the Jewish hearers, but concerns the extension of salvation to non-Jews.

203. Later, Luke is to use the verbs ἀντιλέγειν and βλασφημεῖν of the Jewish reaction to Paul's and Barnabas' message (13.45).

was said by the prophets should happen": that is to say, the aim is to *avert* the danger which is threatened to those who disregard the warning.²⁰⁴

Since the narrator knows that a large number of Jews will in the end not respond positively to the preaching of Paul and Barnabas, but will actually actively oppose it on the following Sabbath, there is some substance in the claim that the Habbakuk quotation also serves to explain why few Jews have believed.²⁰⁵

THE SEQUEL TO THE SPEECH: VERSES 42-52

Paul and Barnabas were asked²⁰⁶ to return on the following Sabbath to speak further on these matters (verse 42). Luke uses the indefinite plural παρεκάλουν: probably we should assume that the leaders of the synagogue were those who issued the invitation (cf. 13.15). We are then told that many Jews and devout proselytes²⁰⁷ "followed Paul and Barnabas, who spoke to them and persuaded them to continue in the grace of God" (verse 43). What are

---

204. Cf. Brawley, "God of Promises," 291. Deutschmann, *Synagoge*, 202, also stressed that the prophetic threat was intended to serve as a summons to conversion, to return to God and His ways, and that this is the intention in the PA speech. He pertinently asked why should hearers respond positively (as they do at vv. 42–43) to a speech, at whose end their repudiation is announced.

205. Evans, *Scripture*, 204.

206. προσήλυτος: the subject of the verb is not expressed, but either the synagogue leaders of v. 15 (so Buss, *Missionspredigt*, 134) or those who had been present in the synagogue (so Barrett, *Acts*, 1:653), are meant.

207. Earlier (on 38) we took this phrase at its face value. But it has caused a fair amount of discussion, probably because scholars have decided that at vv. 16 and 26 Luke was referring to God-Fearers. Thus, Schneider, *Apg.*, 1:142 n. 141; Barrett, *Acts*, 1:654; Fitzmyer, *Acts*, 520; Witherington, *Acts*, 414 n. 233; Jervell, *Apg.*, 362, favour a specific reference to proselytes (earlier Jervell, *Church*, 14, had asserted the other view). On the other hand, Kuhn, προσήλυτος, *TDNT* 6.743; Klinghardt, *Gesetz*, 184, and Johnson, *Acts*, 240, assume a reference to God-Fearers. Haenchen, *Acts*, 413 n. 5, and Pesch, *Apg.*, 2:41, deem "proselytes" a Lucan gloss without really saying why Luke should have added it, while Lüdemann, *Early Christianity*, 156, ends his discussion with the comment that the problem is "still unresolved." The basic issue is whether Luke has in mind members of the same group mentioned in vv. 16 and 26 as "you who fear God." If there he had proselytes in mind, there is consistency in the flow of his story. If he had God-Fearers in mind, then he has later at v. 43 suddenly switched to distinguishing born Jews and proselytes. The flow of the narrative would seem to favour the view that proselytes are in mind up to and including v. 43. Koch, "Proselyten," 100–102, 104–5, emphasizes the narrative level, and argues that vv. 42–43 are to do with a purely Jewish reaction, while from v. 44 on Luke is dealing with ἔθνη who are open to the preaching of the missionaries and so God-Fearers need not be mentioned separately. This correct observation can in fact support the case that Luke had in mind proselytes in vv. 16 and 26.

we to infer from this phraseology? While Luke does not in fact say of them that they "believed," nonetheless three of the phrases seem to point in that direction.[208] There is, firstly, the use of the verb "follow." It can be used in a straightforward spatial sense, but it can also be used of "becoming a disciple" and that is the sense it often bears in all three Synoptic Gospels. The spatial sense could not be dogmatically excluded, but Luke may have chosen this word deliberately with its potential to suggest faith also. Then, secondly, that Paul and Barnabas "persuaded them" could well imply that Paul and Barnabas won them over to accept their message. Finally, the phrase "to continue in the grace of God" suggests that the persons concerned were already "in" the grace of God, i.e., they had believed and received the forgiveness of sins offered previously in the sermon. There is, then, a strong case for accepting that Luke intended us to understand that the sermon together with what Paul and Barnabas subsequently said was successful in gaining converts.[209]

A large crowd ("almost all the city") had gathered at the synagogue on the next Sabbath day (verse 44). This aroused increased zeal for the Law[210] on the part of the Jews who contradicted with abuse what Paul and Barnabas were saying (verse 45). Clearly, these Jews do not include those who had previously come to faith (v. 43). They thus ignored both the invitation to believe and the warning not to refuse belief issued in the sermon of the previous Sabbath (13.38–39, 40–41). Thus, here, on the first occasion which Luke reports of a preaching by Paul in the Diaspora, there takes place the kind of division among Israel which Simeon had predicted at the time of Jesus' birth (Luke 2.34–35).

Paul and Barnabas boldly responded:

> "It was necessary that the word of God should be spoken first to you. Since you reject it and condemn yourselves as unworthy of eternal life, see, we are going to turn to the Gentiles. For so the Lord has commanded us:
>
> τέθεικά σε εἰς φῶς ἐθνῶν
> τοῦ εἶναί σε εἰς σωτηρίαν ἕως ἐσχάτου τῆς γῆς "

"I have appointed you to be [or to take] light to the Gentiles,
that you might become salvation [or a means of (bringing) salvation] to the ends of the earth" (verses 46–47).

---

208. Deutschmann, *Synagoge*, 92–95.

209. Among those who do think that they had become Christians and were being urged not to give up their new faith are Barrett, *Acts*, 1:654; Jervell, *Apg.*, 361–62; Deutschmann, *Synagoge*, 92–95.

210. For this interpretation of ζῆλος, see chap. 2.

There is a divine necessity in the preaching to the Jews first (cf. πρῶτον of 3.26, and Paul's assertions at Rom. 1.16; 2.9–10). There are two reasons given for Paul and Barnabas' turning to the Gentiles, one negative and the other positive. The negative reason is the rejection of their message by the Jews who thereby prove themselves unworthy of eternal life (v. 46d). The positive explanation is the command of the Lord expressed in Isa. 49.6 (from the so-called second Servant Song). In context, Israel is the servant addressed by God (v. 3). Who is "the Lord" mentioned in the introduction to the quotation? If we take "the Lord" as God, then the σε in the quotation could, on a *Christian* interpretation of Isa. 49.6, refer to Jesus who is the Servant of God, and he would be conceived as carrying on his commission through his servants, the apostles.[211] If the "Lord" is Jesus himself,[212] he would be conceived as speaking through the prophet of the OT, and addressing his missionaries. Of course, Luke did not think of Paul and Barnabas as themselves the light or salvation. The Lord Jesus is himself the light and the universal savior (e.g., Luke 2.32; 3.6; Acts 26.23, etc.). Christian missionaries and preachers take the light and the salvation of Jesus to people—hence the translation offered in square brackets above as an alternative.[213] The Servant's commission, while uniquely applied to Jesus, passes derivatively to those commissioned by him to be his witnesses to all and sundry (cf. Acts 9.15–16; 22.14–15, 21; 26.16–18).

Since Luke uses Kyrios elsewhere in Acts of both God and Jesus, we have to turn to the context to see whether this offers a decisive clue. The stress throughout the speech is on God, both in the section on Israel's history up to David and in the section on Jesus culminating in his resurrection which is God's act (vv. 30, 37). Furthermore, in the sequel to the speech, there are references to the grace of God (v. 43) and the word of God (vv. 44, 46). In view of this, it would be natural to take the "Lord" of v. 47 to refer to God,[214] with this then influencing the use of "word of the Lord" in vv. 48–49, rather than "word of God" as at vv. 44 and 46. The meaning would be, then, that God has appointed Jesus to be light and salvation for the whole world and that Jesus is carrying out that task in the present through his chosen servants, in this case Paul and Barnabas. This would fit in with passages elsewhere in Luke's work which envisage the risen Jesus working through

---

211. Dupont, *Nouvelles Études*, 52, 56–7, 348.

212. So Roloff, *Apg.*, 209; Johnson, *Acts*, 241; Pao, *Isaianic New Exodus*, 101.

213. Buss, *Missionspredigt*, 138–39, sees in σε a reference both to the missionaries and Jesus.

214. Among those who assume the reference to be God are Schneider, *Apg.*, 2:145; Jervell, *Apg.*, 364; Fitzmyer, *Acts*, 521; Koet, *Five Studies*, 107; Deutschmann, *Synagoge*, 114.

his disciples to take the message of repentance and forgiveness to all nations (Luke 24.47 and Acts 1.8 and 26.23).[215]

Whatever the correct interpretation of "Lord" may be, the fundamental point is that God through scripture has made His will clear—He wills the Gentile mission (cf. Luke 24.47). Scripture proves that turning to the Gentiles has been part of God's plan revealed to Israel and is, therefore, in no way in conflict with the traditions of Israel.[216]

Another interpretation has been proposed for the meaning of σε, namely Israel. On this approach, Paul and Barnabas are reminding the Jews of their responsibility to be the bearers of light to the nations. They should be fulfilling the role of the Servant of the Lord. Since the Jews of PA are unwilling to do so, Paul and Barnabas claim that they will turn to the Gentiles and thus they will fulfil the divine intention that salvation should be extended to the Gentiles.[217] This is an attractive proposal. It could fit in with the interpretation espoused above that the zeal aroused in the Jews who rejected the preaching of Paul was zeal for the Law. They felt that what Paul and Barnabas were saying undermined the teaching of the Law and the primacy of Israel among the nations.

However, there are reasons for some hesitation about this interpretation stated in this form. In the first place, Luke has already indicated that for him—on the narrative level, Philip the evangelist—the Servant of the Lord in Isaiah is Jesus (see 8.30–35). Then, secondly, the reader/hearer will also recall from Simeon's prophecy that Jesus is destined by God to be light to bring revelation to the Gentiles, which will also be to the glory of His people, Israel (Luke 2.28–32, where the language is redolent of the Servant passages in Isa. 42.5 and 49.6). Thirdly, salvation is obviously a key idea in the quotation, and this surely points back to "savior" of v. 23 and "salvation" at v. 26 in the PA speech: the promised savior has come (v. 23) and the promised salvation has been realised when God raised Jesus from the dead (v. 32).

Mention may be made of Deutschmann's argument that when Paul had spoken a second time a week later (v. 45), he expanded on what he had said the first time in the direction of the extension of the message of salvation to the Gentiles. He clarified the "work" mentioned at the end of

---

215. This is a point which Dupont has stressed—see *Nouvelles Études*, 52, 56–57, 348, 494, 501, 510 (Dupont has called this the Christological significance of the evangelisation of the nations). Cf. Strauss, *Davidic Messiah*, 177.

216. Cf. Flichy, *Figure*, 217–18, 221.

217. Koet, *Five Studies*, 110–14; Jervell, *People of God*, 61, and *Apg.*, 364, who applies the σε to Israel, though Paul and Barnabas are representatives of Israel; Dunn, *Acts*, 184; Radl, "Rettung," 43–60; Deutschmann, *Synagoge*, 111–20; Flichy, *Figure*, 218.

the Habakkuk quotation at v. 41,[218] thus arousing the indignation of some Jews who refused to believe. But, Deutschmann alleges, Luke chose not to spell out in detail anything of what he reports Paul as saying (v. 45). It has to be said that Deutschmann has here filled the Lucan silence with his own creative imagination, and this is hardly a legitimate procedure.

Koet has a point when he complained that scholars have neglected the original context of the Servant passage in Isa. 49.[219] He points out that in the LXX version of Isa. 49 it is the task of Israel gathered by the Servant-Israel to be the light of the Gentiles. He believes that it is to create a false dilemma to pose the question whether the quotation refers to Jesus, Paul and Barnabas or Israel.[220]

It may well be that we should interpret the passage along the following lines. In the passage in Isa. 49, God addressed the Servant as Israel in 49.3. The initial task of this Servant is to gather Israel, and, in turn, Israel thus gathered should embrace the task of being a light to the Gentiles. For Christians in general, and Luke in particular, the Servant of the Lord in Isaiah was unquestionably Jesus himself. In Luke's presentation, Jesus confines his ministry to Israel—he does seek to gather Israel (cf. Luke 13.34). That task is initially carried on by his apostle-witnesses and others in Jerusalem (Acts 1–7). Subsequently, the message will be taken out into the non-Jewish world. As Paul puts it in front of Agrippa II, he has only preached what the prophets previously proclaimed, that the messiah should suffer and that by being the first of the resurrection of the dead he should preach light to the people and to the nations (26.22-23). Clearly, the risen Jesus proclaims light through his witnesses.

Stated thus, this interpretation would be claiming that Luke has exploited the rich levels of meaning of the original in the light of his Christian convictions (as related to Israel, to Christ and to the church and its mission). His hearers/readers would be expected to pick up the resonances within the passage he had written.

The second line of the quotation is explanatory of the εἰς φῶς ἐθνῶν in the first line: τοῦ with the infinitive expresses purpose as does εἰς with φῶς ἐθνῶν. Thus, φῶς and σωτηρία are set in parallelism, and this suggests that "to the ends of the earth" parallels "Gentiles," even if "ends of the earth" is not a precise verbal equivalent.

---

218. Deutschmann, *Synagoge*, 102-5, 116-18

219. A little later, Radl, "Rettung," 46, stressed that contemporary Judaism interpreted the Servant of Isa. 40–55 collectively, and he approached Acts 13.47 from this standpoint. Deutschmann, *Synagoge*, 117-18, followed him.

220. Koet, *Five Studies*, 112-14.

As to the quotation, Luke has omitted εἰς διαθήκην γένους, which the LXX has perhaps brought in from Isa. 42.6, if this is the correct text.[221] If this is the LXX reading, either Luke omitted this phrase to concentrate on the Gentiles or he was following a tradition which was akin to the MT. The announcement of turning to the Gentiles is the first of three such statements in Acts. The second occasion is when Paul was rejected by the Jews at Corinth (18.6) and the last occasion is when Paul criticised the Jews at Rome for not accepting his message. We have already touched on these pronouncements and shall return to them later. Suffice to say at this point that before this Barnabas and Paul had already preached to Gentiles,[222] so that this moment is certainly not a "first" turning to Gentiles.

When the Gentiles heard these words, "they rejoiced and glorified the word of the Lord and those who had been appointed to eternal life believed" (v. 48). "God's action—this time in Paul's decision to address the Gentiles—is recognized as part of his saving plan, so glory is ascribed to him."[223]

Jervell assumes that the Gentiles mentioned in v. 48 are God-Fearers, in accordance with his belief that in Acts Luke does not narrate major conversions of Gentiles.[224] He may be right, but Luke does not appear to be interested in making that specific distinction. Clearly, not all Gentiles were open to the offer of salvation through the gospel of Jesus the savior, for Luke goes on to say that the non-believing Jews were able to enlist the support of God-fearing women of high social standing and leading men of the city[225] (vv. 44–49).

Deutschmann[226] has rightly pointed out that Luke has used the term "Jews" to cover three different groups: some believe (v. 43); some do not

---

221. Ziegler judged that it was not original (quoted and followed by Holtz, *Zitate*, 33), but Swete and Rahlfs did; cf. Rahlfs-Hanhart (followed by Barrett, *Acts*, 1:657 and Fitzmyer, *Acts*, 521).

222. As Cadbury, *Beginnings*, 4:159, and Barrett, *Acts*, 1:657, rightly point out.

223. Doble, *Salvation*, 62. Doble, *Salvation*, 25–69, has argued successfully that the phrase "to glorify God" "acts as a Lukan signal for those moments when God's purposes, revealed in scripture, to save his people—purposes expressed also in Jesus' programme outlined in the Nazareth sermon—are being fulfilled in Jesus' activity" (26). The phrase in Acts 13.48 ("they glorified the word of the Lord") is rightly included by him within his other category (Jesus' kerygmatic program), even if the wording is slightly different, since, as Barrett, *Acts*, 1:658 says, it can hardly mean anything other than that they gave glory to God for the word which they had heard.

224. Jervell, *Apg.*, 364. So also, Deutschmann, *Synagoge*, 126,

225. It is a reasonable assumption that the leading men were the husbands of the God-fearing women, and that the non-believing Jews were able to influence the husbands through their wives—so Deutschmann, *Synagoge*, 78–81, 132, 137.

226. Deutschmann, *Synagoge*, 67–82. He points out that Luke can use general concepts to describe a group or special circle (82).

believe and verbally dispute the message of Paul and Barnabas (v. 45); while others took their rejection so far as to organise violent measures against Paul and Barnabas and secured their ejection from the city (v. 50). "Gentiles" is used three times in vv. 46-48. In the quotation from Isa. 49.6, "Gentiles" seems to be used with a general sense. That would seem to control the sense of Gentiles in the words of Paul and Barnabas that they would turn to the Gentiles (v. 46). The Gentiles who believed the message (v. 48) may well have been those already in contact with the Synagogue. Of course, the God-fearing women and the leading men of the city (v. 50), who side with the non-believing Jews, are also Gentiles. There is, therefore, division within both Jews and Gentiles towards the preaching of the gospel.

Thrown out of the city, Paul and Barnabas respond with a gesture of prophetic symbolism. They shake the dust from off their feet. This is hardly, as some commentators suggest,[227] a gesture shaking off (as it were) the uncleanness of Gentile territory. Such an interpretation hardly befits the assertion that God wills the taking of the light of the gospel to Gentile lands! It is, rather, a gesture which invokes the threat of the Last Judgment,[228] and is directed not just at non-believing Jews but also non-believing Gentiles as well.

At the end of his account Luke says that "the disciples were filled with joy and the Holy Spirit" (v. 52). Paul and Barnabas and the issue of whether salvation may be extended out beyond "Israel" to non-Jewish peoples have been central to Luke's narrative. Now, in a concluding brief sentence, he mentions the Christian community[229] that has come into being as a result of the preaching of the gospel in PA. There is no reflection on their status. There is no honorific title used to designate them. They are here simply referred to as disciples. They include Jewish as well as Gentile believers.

That the disciples were filled with the Holy Spirit recalls the events of the first Pentecost. There Peter claimed that the promise that God would pour out His Spirit "on all flesh" in the passage from Joel 2.28-32 was being fulfilled, and he ended his appeal with the words "The promise is to you and your children and to all who far off, whom the Lord our God calls" (2.16-21, 39; cf. 5.32; 8.17; 9.17; 10.44-48; 11.15-17). Both Jews and Gentiles on believing receive the Holy Spirit.

Joy is a mark of the new era in which God has visited earth with His salvation in Jesus and with the gift of the Spirit. Joy was promised by the

---

227. E.g., Deutschmann, *Synagoge*, 135.

228. Cf. Caird, "Uncomfortable Words," 40-43; Jeremias, *NT Theology*, 238, and Evans, *Saint Luke*, 396, on Luke 9.5.

229. Hardly a reference to Paul and Barnabas—*pace* Fitzmyer, *Acts*, 522.

angel in the message to the shepherds about the birth of Jesus at Luke 2.10. Even before Pentecost, but after they had witnessed Jesus' ascension, Luke says that the disciples returned to Jerusalem with great joy (Luke 24.52). There was great joy in the city of Samaria after Philip had proclaimed the gospel and the performed many miracles of healing (Acts 8.4-8). It is surely in line with this that the report of Paul and Barnabas about the conversion of the Gentiles to the churches in Phoenicia and Samaria brought them great joy (Acts 15.3). Joy is a mark of the experience of salvation.[230]

Odile Flichy appositely remarks about the conclusion to the account of the mission at PA: the opponents may persecute the missionaries, but they cannot hinder God's plan accomplishing itself.[231]

---

230. Conzelmann, χαίρω χαρά, συγχαίρω κτλ., *TWNT* 9.366–72, does not deal with the occurrences in Acts.

231. Flichy, *Figure*, 220.

Chapter 5

The Theological Emphases of the Speech

THEOLOGY AND THE PLAN OF GOD

"Theology," in the strictest sense of the word, is "talk about God," and of that there is plenty in the PA speech. But, first, let us note how the speech is itself framed by references to the "word of God" or its equivalent, the "word of the Lord." The readers enter the section Acts 13–14 with the refrain echoing in our ears from 12.24: "The word of the Lord continued to spread[1] and gained converts." On reaching the island of Cyprus, Paul and Barnabas went to Salamis and preached "the word of God in the synagogues of the Jews" (13.5). At Paphos, the Roman proconsul, Sergius Paulus, summoned Paul and Barnabas because he wanted to "hear the word of God." Clearly, then, when the synagogue leaders at PA ask if Paul and Barnabas had a "word of exhortation" to pass on to the people, the readers/hearers will think of "the word of God."

After the PA speech, Luke tells us that the following Sabbath almost the whole city was gathered "to hear the word of God" (v. 44). Faced with opposition from the Jews, Paul and Barnabas said that it was necessary that "the word of God" should have been spoken first to them (v. 46). As God's chosen people they had a prior claim on hearing that word. In the face of their resistance to the word and the command of God in scripture, Paul and Barnabas would now turn to the Gentiles. The Gentiles rejoiced and "glorified the word of the Lord" (v. 48). In another refrain like comment, Luke

---

1. ηὔξανεν imperfect indicative active!

says that "the word of the Lord continued to spread[2] throughout the whole of the district" (v. 49).

Thus, before and after the PA speech, the author has drawn our attention to the theme of the "word of God" and to its triumphal progression. It spreads despite opposition! Precisely because it is the word of God, there is something unstoppable about it.

In the speech itself, it is no exaggeration to say that *God is the main subject*.[3] In the first section of the speech (vv. 17–23), leaving aside the final two verses which speak about John the Baptist specifically (vv. 24–25), God is the subject of 14 verbs (3 of which are participles and 11 are finite verbs). Of only 2 verbs is God not the subject.[4] God elected the fathers; exalted the people in Egypt, led them out of that country, cared for them in the desert, destroyed the Canaanite nations and settled the people in the land; He gave them judges and, later, at their request, gave them a king. He removed Saul and raised up in his place David to whom He bore witness when He said that He had found in David a man after His own heart. God brought on the scene a savior for Israel, as He had promised, from David's descendants.[5] This survey of Israel's story is basically the story of *"the mighty deeds" of God for His people*. He is the actor in Israel's history.

The second section (vv. 26–37) opens with a reverential passive which conceals the action of God, viz "the word of this salvation has been sent to us" (v. 26). No less than four times God is the subject of raising Jesus from the dead (vv. 31; 33; 34; and 37). The speech asserts that God has fulfilled the promise which He made to the ancestors of Israel (v. 32). Twice, God is said to have spoken in the Scriptures (vv. 34 and 35).

The final section, which offers both salvation and a warning, contains two reverential passives, behind which God is the real actor: the verb "is justified" (v. 39) and the phrase "what has been spoken of in the prophets" (v. 40). In the concluding verse, God addresses the hearers through the quotation from Hab. 1.5: God warns the scoffers not to despise the astonishing work which He is doing in their midst (v. 41).

2. As at 12.24, Luke here uses the imperfect indicative active—διεφέρετο.

3. Rightly stressed among others by Jeska, *Geschichte*, 221, 224, 231, who points to the absence of names of individuals in vv. 17–20a, while even where names of individuals are mentioned in vv. 20b–22, God's action is still to the fore. Cf. also Zwang, *Paul*, 128. Here we might mention the observation of Marguerat, *First Christian Historian*, 90, that outside of the speeches God becomes a subject only in the words of a character (e.g., 9.27; 10.15; 12.11, 17). The sequel of the speech is really too small to base any conclusions of this nature, but such as it is, it bears out Marguerat's comment.

4. At v. 21 the people *asked for* a king; and at v. 22 David is said to be a man who *will do* God's will.

5. The verbs in participial form are "destroyed," "removed," and "bore witness."

The Theological Emphases of the Speech

"Promise" is a key concept in the speech, and, though it only occurs twice, those two occurrences are highly significant. In what we have described as a pivotal verse (v. 23), it is said that, in accordance with His promise, God has brought on the scene from among the descendants of David a Savior for Israel, viz. Jesus. A second time in the speech (v. 32), the theme of God's fulfilling His promise is articulated: Paul and Barnabas are bringing to the congregation the good news that God has fulfilled the promise made to the ancestors by raising Jesus from the dead. Here, the fulfillment is linked firmly to the act of resurrection.

God is the God of promises and the God who fulfills what He has promised. He is, therefore, the reliable, faithful, and trustworthy God. What He promises, that He will do, He does do.

The PA speech takes up many of the themes associated with God in the OT. God is the electing God—He has chosen Israel to be His people. He is the God of mighty deeds. He led Israel out of Egypt "with an outstretched arm." He drove out the nations of Canaan and enabled Israel to settle in the land as its inheritance (vv. 17–19). In recent times, He has raised Jesus from the dead, even though Jerusalem and its leaders had hung Jesus "on a tree" (vv. 29b–30). God is the God of resurrection and new life. He did not let Jesus, His "Holy One," "see corruption" (vv. 35, 37).

At crucial points in the speech, we see that God is the God of salvation. In two pivotal verses in the speech, this theme is overt. In v. 23, God brings on the scene a savior for Israel. Then, in v. 26, Paul announces that the message of God's salvation has been sent to the hearers. Through the savior appointed by God, the preacher can announce the "forgiveness of sins," that is to say the state of being declared in the right before God (vv. 38–39). Afterwards, while leaving the synagogue, Paul and Barnabas encouraged those favourably disposed to the message to continue "in the grace of God" (v. 43). The scriptural quotation (Isa. 49.6), which is used to support the decision by Paul and Barnabas to turn to the Gentiles, includes a reference to salvation which should be taken to the ends of the earth. As servants of the Servant of the Lord God, men like Paul and Barnabas by their preaching become the means of spreading the message of salvation to the uttermost parts of the earth. Luke records that "those who were destined for eternal life believed," another reverential passive (v. 48b).

God is the God of history, the God who purposefully pursues His plans within history. Egypt cannot thwart His plans—He is able to exalt His people there and He led them out of their enslavement. The Canaanite nations cannot withstand His purpose for Israel. He leads through the generations until David, a man after His own heart, who will do His will, comes on the scene. Then across the generations, God brings Jesus, a descendant of David, on the scene. He overrules the human act of rejection and killing of Jesus, and through resurrection installs him as His Son and the one who can dispense the blessings originally promised to David.

In v. 36 we meet the phrase the βουλή τοῦ Θεοῦ (the will, purpose or plan of God). David, described earlier as one who would do God's will (v. 22), is said Ἰδίᾳ γενεᾷ ὑπηρετήσας τῇ τοῦ Θεοῦ βουλῇ ἐκοιμήθη. As already indicated, various translations of this are possible,[6] but it seems best to take "his own generation" as a locative dative of time and "the purpose of God" as the object of "served:"[7] "For after David had served God's purpose in his own generation, he died." (It seems rather highfalutin to say that David served his generation and then died by the will of God—after all, all of us die by the will of God!) Even though both the ancestor and his descendant share the characteristic of obeying God's will and carrying out His plan (David was a man after God's own heart who would do God's will and Jesus has just been described as God's Holy One), nonetheless, in the context, there is a contrast between Jesus who was raised from the dead without seeing corruption and David who died and did see corruption. There is another contrast too, not as obvious but probably present: David's service lasted only for his own generation, whereas the risen Jesus goes on serving the purpose of God.

The purpose and plan of God is certainly an important concept in LA.[8] The term occurs once in Luke: the teachers of the law rejected God's purpose for themselves, by refusing the baptism of John the Baptist, whereas the people and the tax-collectors had submitted to his baptism (7.30).

Twice in Acts, the arrest, passion and death of Jesus are traced back to God's βουλή. In an important statement during his sermon on the day of Pentecost, Peter said that Jesus of Nazareth had been delivered up by the predetermined plan and foreknowledge of God and that the Jerusalemites "had crucified and killed [him] by the hands of lawless men" (2.23). The death of Jesus was not some tragic, unforeseen event, but an event which lay deep in the plan of the omniscient God. Then, in the prayer offered to God by the Jerusalem believers after the release of Peter and John from arrest by the Sanhedrin, this conviction is stated just as powerfully. Herod and Pilate, Gentiles and the people of Israel, had colluded together to act against God's anointed Servant, Jesus, but in fact they only did what God's plan had already determined should take place (4.27–28). There is a broader use of the term in Paul's speech at Miletus to the Ephesian Elders. Paul said that he

6. See 123–24n175.
7. See 123n175.
8. See Squires, *Plan of God*, 1.

had not shrunk back from declaring to them the whole βουλή τοῦ Θεοῦ (20.27). Here, the term seems to include the entire plan of salvation before and including Jesus and the fruit of the messianic suffering, death and resurrection in the life of the community of Jesus' followers.

The theme of divine necessity emerges in the sequel to the PA speech, when Paul and Barnabas declare that it was necessary that the word of God should be declared to the Jewish community first. This alludes to the election of Israel by God and her place in what we might call the initial saving plan of God. Now the time has come for the people of God to be widened to embrace peoples at earth's farthest bounds. The divine plan includes the mission to the Gentiles, as the risen Jesus made clear to his disciples on Easter evening (Lk. 24.47) and reiterated later according to Acts 1.8.

In concluding this survey, we might say that overall the thrust of the PA speech is theocentric. Where it emphasises Jesus, its Christocentricity (vv. 26–40), if one likes so to describe it, is contained within an overarching theocentricity.[9] Forgiveness of sins and justification may come through Jesus, but this state enjoyed by those who believe is described as "the grace of God" in which they should continue (v. 43).[10] With that basis, we turn now to the Christological message of the PA speech.

CHRISTOLOGY

Where once titles dominated the approach in studies on the theme of Christology, we now recognise that this, while important, is not sufficient on its own.[11] Thus, we are immediately confronted by this issue in the first section of the PA speech, the selective account of God's dealings with the people of Israel whom He had chosen. What is the implication of placing Jesus alongside of, or rather, at the head of this account? It surely implies two things: that Jesus is the climax of this story and that the story is incomplete and not fully intelligible without him. The story reaches a fulfillment in his appearance on the scene, and in turn he reflects a coherence back on to the story. Twice, as we have seen, God's action through Jesus is described as fulfilling a promise which He had made. At v. 23, God brought Jesus on the

---

9. We prefer to state the matter in this way, rather than the more sharply put "Luke is theocentric rather than Christocentric" of Ravens, *Restoration*, 137. See Flebbe, "Israels Gott," 101–39, who argues persuasively that Luke shows that the separation between Judaism and Christianity was due to theological rather than Christological reasons—i.e., Judaism's failure to understand properly its own God.

10. Flebbe, "Israels Gott," 115.

11. For criticism of the title-approach to Christology, see Keck, "Renewal of NT Christology," 321–40.

scene "in accordance with (His) promise," while at v. 32 Paul said that "we bring you good news that God has fulfilled the promise made to the fathers, to us the children." The past was the era of promise; the present was seen as its fulfillment. God had guided the story to this climactic point. Jesus and his resurrection was the fulfillment of what God had promised in the past. One thus cannot speak of Jesus apart from God, nor, indeed, of God apart from Jesus. This coheres with the idea expressed elsewhere in Acts that Jesus did what he did do because God was with him or God worked through him (Luke 7.16; Acts 2.22; 10.38-39; cf. Luke 24.19).[12]

The speech makes it clear that Jesus is a descendant of David. It is from David's seed that God has brought Jesus on the scene. The point is not elaborated—it did not need to be. Luke had already made the point clear right from the start, in the Annunciation scene in Gabriel's message to Mary (Luke 1.32-33); in the Benedictus (Luke 1.69); in the angelic announcement to the shepherds (Luke 2.10-11); and in the genealogy of Jesus (Luke 3.23-38, David being mentioned at v. 31).[13] Peter referred to it in his Pentecost sermon (2.30-31), while James at the Jerusalem Council will refer to the restoration of David's fallen tabernacle (15.16).[14]

Whether there was a continuous reflection and discussion on the promise to David during the post-exilic period[15] or whether there was, after a long period of dormant messianism, a renewed interest in and commitment to the Davidic messianic hope in reaction to either the Hasmonean rule[16] or the Herodian rule[17] or both[18] in the first century BC, the expectation of a descendant of David to save Israel was certainly around at the time of the NT era. This is shown by the Pss Sol. 17-18 and by a number of Qumran texts, in addition to 4 Q Floregium. For our purposes, we need not get involved in this debate. Suffice to say that early Christians would need to have responded to this expectation on the part of so many Jews. We can see from the genealogies of Matthew (1.1-16) and Luke (3.23-38), together

---

12. Cf. Flebbe, "Israels Gott," 106-7, 108-9, 112, 115, 125.

13. For a discussion of some of the issues connected with the genealogy in Luke, see especially Johnson, *Biblical Genealogies*, 229-52; Burger, *Jesus als Davidssohn*, 116-27.

14. Burger, *Davidssohn*, 138, commented on how at decisive points in "church history" Peter, Paul and James stress the promise to David in astonishing unanimity. He sees this unanimity as due to the work of Luke himself (142-52).

15. Laato, *A Star is Rising* [not available to me]; Schniedewind, *Society and Promise to David*; Pietsch, *Sprotz Davids*.

16. Pomykala, *Davidic Dynasty Tradition*; Strauss, *Davidic Messiah*, 38-45.

17. Collins, *Scepter and the Star*; Atkinson, "Use of Scripture," 106-23. Atkinson (109) dates the Psalm of Solomon 17 to between 37 and 30 BC.

18. Freyne, *Jesus*, 131-33.

with the use of the title "Root of David" in Rev. 5.5 and 22.16; the use of Isa. 7 and 11 behind the virgin birth story in Matt. 1.23 and the annunciation to Mary scene in Luke 1.26-38; the testimonium quoted in Rom. 15.12; and the confessional formula "born of the seed of David" at Rom. 1.3; 2 Tim. 2.8, that Jesus' Davidic descent did figure prominently in early Christian evangelism, apologetic, instruction and worship. What is said in the PA speech fits well into this background. Enough is made of Jesus' Davidic descent in the PA speech, even if it is not laboured.

Jesus is greater than John the Baptist. Josephus' writings show that John the Baptist was a highly respected figure in contemporary Judaism. There is a widespread conviction among NT scholars that a John the Baptist movement existed and survived his execution by Herod Antipas. Part of the evidence for this is the account given by Luke of twelve disciples of John the Baptist[19] whom Paul met at Ephesus, brought to faith in Jesus and baptised (Acts 19.1-7). While historically it is not implausible that Paul did come across some disciples of John the Baptist at Ephesus and that he would seek to bring them to faith in Jesus,[20] at the level of Luke's writing Luke could be using this episode (plus that of Apollos in the preceding paragraph) to give an indication of how to tackle the problem of what one did with disciples of John the Baptist.[21]

As we now have the story, a significant figure in first century Judaism is claimed as a witness to the greatness of Jesus. John the Baptist's role is that of a forerunner. He himself is not the expected one, but prepares for his coming. As in Luke's Gospel John the Baptist denies that he is the messiah (3.15-18), so also by implication in the PA speech (13.24-25).[22]

By implication, Jesus was innocent of the charges brought against him. The people of Jerusalem and their rulers, although they found no cause of

---

19. On the other hand, many scholars still think that, since Luke always uses μαθηται elsewhere of Christians, he must have been in his own mind describing Christians with a defective faith at Acts 19.1-7 (see e.g., Dunn, *Baptism*, 83-89, esp. 84-85, who stresses that this is the only time in Acts that μαθηται is used without the definite article).

20. Firstly, what Paul said at Rom. 8.9 reveals that for Paul the essence of being a Christian was to have the Spirit of Christ. Secondly, what is reported as Paul's instruction at Acts 19.4 could be his Christianised version of John the Baptist's teaching. Finally, baptism was important for him (Rom. 6.1-11), even if not his primary aim (1 Cor. 1.17).

21. See Barrett, *Acts*, 2:885 and, in more detail, "*Apollos*," 29-39.

22. See 99-100, for a discussion of the different ways in which the phrase at Acts 13.25b, τί ἐμὲ ὑπονοεῖτε εἶναι οὐκ εἰμὶ ἐγώ, could be translated: either "I am not what you think me to be" [the Coming One/Messiah] or "What do you think me to be? I am not he" [the Coming One/the Messiah]. On either translation, the meaning amounts to the same.

death in him, nevertheless requested Pilate that he should be put to death (13.28). This is putting matters negatively, as it were—he was not guilty of any capital offense (the positive side comes out later at v. 35 through the quotation from Psalm 16: in the language of the Psalm, Jesus is the Holy One of God). The innocence of the righteous sufferer is a well-known motif in the Psalms and other literature like Isa. 53 and Wisd. 2–5. It was one way in which early Christians might seek to overcome the scandal of the cross.

When the speech says that the rulers failed to understand the prophetic voices and yet paradoxically fulfilled them and goes on to say that they had accomplished all that was written about him, it is saying that Jesus' Passion was "in accordance with the Scriptures" (cf. 1 Cor. 15.3), in accordance with God's purpose and plan (cf. Acts 2.23; 4.28). Not only his appearance on the earthly scene (13.23), but also his death on the tree (= the cross) was foreseen in God's purpose. The reference to the cross as "tree" may be a reflection of an early Christian or specifically Pauline use of Deut. 21.22–23, though there is nothing of the Pauline idea of atonement as in Gal. 3. 13–14.[23]

The resurrection of Jesus is a crucial event and is prominent in the speech, not only in terms of its being a divine act which vindicated Jesus and reversed what humans had done to him (13.29–30), but also because of its significance in other ways. By raising Jesus from the dead, God has fulfilled the promise made to the fathers (13.32, 33). How could this be so? In the first place, the resurrection meant the enhancement of his dignity and status. The resurrection is his birthday to a new life and position. "You are My Son; I have begotten you today" (13.33). Where in Peter's Pentecost speech, Ps. 110.1 "Sit at My right hand" is quoted and used to interpret the resurrection as session at God's right hand, here in the PA speech Ps. 2 is used to interpret the resurrection. The resurrection is Jesus' "coronation"— he is the royal Son of God. This is the moment when Gabriel's promise about Jesus made to Mary is fulfilled.[24] Through resurrection, Jesus enters upon a never-dying, eternal reign.

Is this a relic of a very early Christology in which Jesus "became" Son of God at his resurrection (to which the term "adoptionist" Christology is often, though anachronistically, given[25])? Or could it be that the earliest Christians could think of Jesus as God's Son during his ministry and yet also at his resurrection (interpreted as exaltation)? Paradoxical as it may

---

23. See 187–89, for a discussion of this theme.

24. Cf. Pietsch, *Sprotz Davids*, 268–69.

25. Cf. the judgment of Vielhauer, "Paulinism," 44 and 48 resp.: "This Christology is adoptionistic, not a Christology of preexistence" and "the author of Acts in his Christology is pre-Pauline." Dunn, *Acts*, 180, also brands this anachronistic.

seem, we think that the latter could be the case. It was so with the heir to the throne: he was "the firstborn" and was important and special to Yahweh. Yet at his coronation, he became God's son. We might compare the way in which Wisdom is both created by God (Prov. 8.22; Sir. 1.4; 24.9) and yet also is the agent through whom or by which God created the worlds in Hebrew-Jewish thinking (Ps. 104.5, 24; Prov. 3.19; Wisd. 8.5; Philo, *Quod Deteriors* 54, etc.).

If Luke himself could attach Jesus' Sonship to his birth (Luke 1.32, 35) and to his baptism (3.22) and still include passages in Acts like 13.33 and 2.36, why could not Christians before him? We cannot have it both ways: viz. to argue that Luke is a theologian who moulds his sources to his theological beliefs, and then dismiss Acts 13.33 and 2.36 as relics of the tradition and included either through momentary carelessness or the occasional nod in the direction of the tradition! Dunn has noted this feature of Luke: "the fact that Luke retains these earlier emphases suggests that he saw no contradiction between them. Both Paul (Rom. 1.3f) and Luke here supplement earlier formulations concerning Jesus as Son of God without thereby denying the significance of the resurrection for Jesus' divine Sonship."[26]

It may smack too much of Western logic to get a neat linear progression—belief in Jesus' sonship is first located at the resurrection (Acts 13.33), is then pushed back to his baptism (Mark 1.11), and then to his birth (Luke 1.32, 35), and finally, into eternity (John 1.1–18). Early Christians were obviously deeply impressed by the resurrection of Jesus by God. They were also deeply impressed by his sense of God as Abba, as Gal. 4.5 and Rom. 8.14 reveal, since this Aramaic word had found its way into the worship of Greek-speaking congregations (and, indeed, at the church at Rome which was not founded by Paul). Even if formally they did not confess him Son of God in his earthly lifetime, it is not too bold to claim *both* that the combined impact of the resurrection and Jesus' use of Abba would have led to such a confession, especially as the important 2 Sam. 7, interpreted messianically within Jewish circles, contained the promise that Yahweh would be a father to David's son and David's son a son to Yahweh, *and* that they made that confession within a relatively short period.[27]

The prominence of the resurrection has drawn with it a glimpse of early Christian use of the OT. In general terms, 2 Sam. 7 is behind the whole sermon and the verb ἀνιστάναι is exploited for its potential to refer to resurrection from the dead, while specifically Ps. 2.7; Isa. 55.3 and Ps. 16.10 are

---

26. Dunn, *Christology*, 51, and also 61.

27. Cf. Hengel, *Son of God*, 63–64. On the speed of this development, see his comment, *Son of God*, 2.

quoted to explain the significance and meaning of the resurrection of Jesus. That is to say, the resurrection lay within the purpose and plan of God. One could say that it was not an "emergency" act, because things had gone desperately wrong when God's people rejected their own messiah. Scripture had foreseen the resurrection all along. It was part and parcel of God's plan for His messiah.

We come now to consider the speech's description of Jesus as Savior (13.23; cf. v. 26 and also v. 47). We have already seen that the word group "salvation, savior, to save" figures prominently in LA. In the birth stories, Zechariah speaks of the "horn of salvation" (= the powerful or mighty savior), who will bring about salvation from Israel's enemies and those who hate her (vv. 69, 71), an idea repeated in v. 74 in different words—"to rescue us from the hand of our enemies" in order that "we might serve Him without fear in holiness and righteousness all our days" (vv. 70–73). This is quite clearly a this-worldly salvation, however much the peace which results enables a high ethical lifestyle pleasing to God. Yet a little later, a more spiritual concept of salvation emerges when Zachariah predicts what will be the role of his own son, as prophet of the Most High, to prepare the way of the Lord, "to give knowledge of salvation to His people in the forgiveness of their sins" (vv. 76–77). The salvation consists in the forgiveness of sins.[28]

When Jesus said that salvation had come to Zaccheus' house, salvation there has the connotation of a renewal of a right relationship with the God of the covenant and would include forgiveness for past sins and the motivation to live in a way pleasing to God as a true son of Abraham (19.9), freed from the desire for wealth.

This sense of a restoration of relationship, of restoring wholeness to the relationship with God, is surely the sense in Acts 4.12. While the context is that of whose or what power made the crippled beggar whole (4.9–10), yet at the same time the Sanhedrin is reminded of its share in the crucifixion of Jesus. They are like the builders who rejected a stone which turned out to be the right cornerstone (4.11 = Ps. 118.22).[29] Nevertheless, even members of the Sanhedrin could receive salvation—a restoration of relationship with God.[30] But it is only received through Jesus, and so a revolution in their

---

28. Marshall, *Luke*, 93; Evans, *Luke*, 186; Fitzmyer, *Luke*, 1:386. In the Hebrew mind, the forgiveness of sins would have repurcussions, so that too rigid a separation of inner-spiritual and external-political would be wrong.

29. Note the ὑφ' ὑμῶν inserted into the Psalm quotation, thus personalising the application in a very direct way.

30. That this would include a corporate dimension—that of belonging to the eschatological people of God—is maintained by Barrett, *Acts*, 1:231.

attitude is by implication being demanded (4.12).³¹ If they refuse that, they will be condemned in the coming judgment.

All this provides a useful background for the statements about salvation in the PA speech. Jesus is the savior for Israel (13.23; cf. 5.31). Nothing is said in explanation, nor, when a little later, Paul asserts "the word of this salvation has been sent to you," which includes those who fear God as well as Jews, sons of Abraham (v. 26), though clearly the "word of salvation" picks up "savior" of v. 23. It is when we come to the end of the speech that we could say that we learn something of what is involved in "salvation." "Let it be known to you, therefore, brothers, that through this man [Jesus] the forgiveness of sins is proclaimed to you" (v. 38) and then in the next verse this is explained in terms of justification (acquittal or being declared in the right): "through this man [Jesus] . . . everyone who believes will be justified"³² (v. 38) (a position which the Mosaic Law could not confer). If 13.23 spoke of Jesus' being a savior for Israel, there is surely a universalism implicit in 13.38 in the phrase "everyone who believes," and this is borne out both by the fact that the Gentiles believe the message a week later (13.48) and that Paul and Barnabas use Isa. 49.6 with its reference to salvation being taken to the ends of the earth (13.47).

Summarising, we may say that Jesus is presented in the PA speech as the culmination and climax of Israel's story in fulfillment of God's promise to the ancestors; as both a descendant of David and the Son of God through the resurrection; as savior both for Israel and for everyone who believes; as the Holy One whose passion is the fulfillment of God's plan revealed in the scriptures; and as the one who has obtained forgiveness of sins and justification for men and women.

3. THE USE OF THE OT

The importance of the OT in the PA speech is seen by several facts. Firstly, an albeit selective account of the story of Israel up to David is given to open the speech. The account begins with the election of the patriarchs by God. This central affirmation of the OT is thus assumed from the very start. When the story reaches David, at least two OT passages are utilised to describe David—Ps. 89.20 and 1 Sam. 13.14 (and some would say a third

---

31. cf. Marshall, *Acts*, 100.

32. The verb δικαιοῦται could be a genuine present or a present with a future connotation (for this phenomenon, see BDF, para. 323; Moule, *Idiom Book*, 7; Brooks and Wimbery, *Syntax of NT Greek*, 80–81), though all commentators seems to assume the former.

passage, Isa. 44.28, as well). Secondly, the passage 2 Sam. 7 is probably in mind, even though not formally quoted. Thirdly, the second section of the speech (vv. 26–37) opens with language drawn from Ps. 107.20 ("He sent forth His word") and then, in its closing sentences, specifically quotes Ps. 2.7; Isa. 55.3; and Ps. 16.10, which are designed to explain what are the benefits of the resurrection seen as the "birthday" of the resurrected Jesus and his rescue from the normal process of corruption, and, who, as such, is able to bestow the holy and reliable blessings, originally promised to David, on all who respond to the message of salvation. Fourthly, the speech closes with a warning on all who fail to respond in faith, a warning drawn from Hab. 1.5. Finally, on the following sabbath, when many Jews had shown an active hostility to Paul and Barnabas and their message, the two respond by quoting the passage about the appointment of the Servant of the Lord to be a light to the nations, to take God's salvation to the ends of the earth (Isa. 49.6). These facts alone would indicate that the OT holds a place of considerable importance.

The use of the idea of "promise" indicates that the OT is, however, regarded as incomplete. Whatever may have been God's mighty deeds in the past, the story of Israel was looking for something beyond itself. This is signalled clearly in v. 23: "From this man's seed, according to the promise, God has brought a Savior, Jesus, to Israel." Verse 32 takes this idea up: "We bring to you the good news that God has fulfilled the very promise made to the fathers, for us, the children, by raising Jesus." This is reinforced by the fact that the kerygma about Jesus is "bolted on" to the (selective) story of Israel. The two belong together. Jesus is the climax, culmination and crown of Israel's story; without him, the story would be incomplete. But equally, the story enables Jesus to be fully understood.

For Luke, David is a highly significant figure. In the speech, Abraham is not mentioned by name in the story of Israel, neither is Moses nor is Joshua. Saul gets brief mention, but only as a backdrop to the choice of David as king. David is the chosen ancestor of the messiah for Israel. This role of David picks up what has been communicated to the reader/hearer at the beginning of Luke's work: the angel Gabriel said that God would give the child to be born the throne of his father David and he would reign over the house of Jacob forever and his kingdom would have no end (Lk. 1.32–33).

But David is not only important as a king, but also as a prophet. The reader/hearer knows that from Peter's description of him to that effect in the Pentecost speech (Acts 2.30). Peter's description of David as a prophet was related to Ps. 16 (Davidic authorship being assumed), which was interpreted in terms of a reference to the resurrection of the messiah. Acts 13.36 is really a highly condensed version of the longer argument of 2.25–35. Since David died and was buried ("gathered to his fathers"), Ps. 16 can not apply to him personally, but must refer to the coming messiah. Jesus was raised from the dead; he must be the messiah.

David's role in pointing to the one who should be God's chosen messiah is not unique. For Luke, the whole of the OT is "prophetic" in that it is about Jesus the messiah. This comes out in the kerygmatic section twice. Paul says that the inhabitants of Jerusalem and their leaders failed to recognise both Jesus and the voices of the prophets which are read every sabbath.[33] They failed to recognise who Jesus was *because* they did not understand the prophetic voices in scripture. Properly grasped, the OT witnesses prophetically to Jesus. This way of putting things is probably not meant to refer to readings specifically from the prophets, but rather that all the OT, whatever part of it may be under consideration, whether the law, prophets, or the writings, spoke of Jesus.

The passion and death of Jesus were announced in the OT. "When they had completed everything written about him, they took him down from the tree and laid him in a grave" (v. 29). The reference to the tree could indicate that Deut. 21.22-23 would be one such passage, while the Psalms of the Righteous Sufferer and Isa. 53 would also be areas of the OT where early Christians saw the passion of Jesus adumbrated.[34]

The important group of OT quotations in vv. 33-35 is concerned with the resurrection. Paul claims that God has fulfilled the promise made to the fathers by raising Jesus from the dead (ἀναστήσας Ἰησοῦν). A significant part of the promise is, then, resurrection—resurrection in the first place of the messiah, but also the messiah as the forerunner of the general resurrection.

Later, in the trial speeches of Paul, he maintained that resurrection was at the heart of the Christian message and that this actually corresponded to, and was the fulfillment of, "the hope of Israel." Before the Sanhedrin, Paul asserts:"I am a Pharisee, the son of Pharisees: I am on trial for the hope of the resurrection of the dead" (23.6).[35] When Paul appeared before the pre-

---

33. See chapter 4 for discussion of the fact that the sentence is somewhat overloaded. See Ropes, "Detached Note on xiii. 27-29," 261-63; Metzger, *Textual Commentary*, 409-10; Barrett, *Acts*, 1:642-43, for discussion of attempts to reconstruct the original "Western" text, which, as reconstructed, simplifies the sentence construction by not having any reference to not recognising Jesus but having μὴ συνιέντες τὰς γραφὰς τῶν προφητῶν . . . ἐπλήρωσαν in v. 27 and placing κρίναντες in v. 28.

34. See Lindars, *NT Apologetic*, 75-137; Juel, *Messianic Exegesis*, 89-133.

35. Most translations take the phrase περὶ ἐλπίδος καὶ ἀναστάσεως νεκρῶν as hendiadys (and BDF, 442 (16) treats it in this way), though Haenchen, *Acts*, 638, 643, takes it as (messianic) hope and the resurrection of the dead. For a discussion, see Haacker, "Bekenntnis des Paulus," 437-51.

fect, Felix, at Caesarea, he claimed that he, as a follower of what he described as the Way, believed everything written in the law and the prophets. He shared with his Jewish accusers hope in God, which he described as being the belief that there would be a resurrection of the righteous and the wicked (24.14-15).

The final trial speech was before King Agrippa II with his partner, Berenice, in the presence of Festus. Once again Paul claims that he is on trial for the hope of the promise made by God to the fathers. The twelve tribes of Israel hope to attain that hope. And he appeals to Agrippa: "Why is it judged by you something beyond belief that God raises the dead?" (26.6-8). He claimed to have preached nothing except what the prophets and Moses said should happen—"that the messiah should suffer and that as the first to be raised from the dead, he should proclaim light both to the people and the nations" (26.22-23).

In this series of statements, the hope of Israel is interpreted as both general resurrection and resurrection of the messiah, Jesus. The latter is a Christian perspective: the resurrection of Jesus is an anticipation of the general resurrection and confirms it. For Luke, the hope of Israel is that God will bring history to an end and usher in His kingdom via the general resurrection and the Last Judgment. God has inaugurated the last era and the resurrection of Jesus is the guarantee that He will consummate what He has started. Jesus is both the inaugurator of the Kingdom and God's agent to usher in the glorious Kingdom. At the moment he has been exalted to heaven and waits the moment in the Father's plan for him to return to complete what he had started (cf. Acts 3.20-21).

This is the salvation which far exceeds any deliverance from earthly enemies. This salvation is experienced partly now in forgiveness and renewed fellowship with God and will be fully realised in the future Kingdom (Acts 13.23, 26, 47; see Lk.18.30b; 20.34-38).

Scripture (the OT) contains what God has said and through which He continues to speak.[36] The composite quotation in 13.22 is introduced by εἶπεν μαρτυρήσας. While Psalm 2.7 is introduced by γέγραπται (written in the past but continuing to have a message), the other two quotations in vv. 33-35 are introduced by οὕτως εἴρηκεν "He has spoken in this way" (and what He said has continuing relevance) at v. 34 (Isa. 55.3) and ἐν ἑτέρῳ λέγει ("In another place He says") at v. 35 (Ps. 16.10). The concluding quotation from Hab. 1.5 is introduced by τὸ εἰρημένον ἐν τοῖς προφήταις ("What has been said in the prophets" in the past continues to speak a message). Finally, the Isa. 49.6 passage is preceded by οὕτως γὰρ ἐντέ

---

36. Cf. Jervell, *Unknown Paul*, 124.

ταλται ἡμῖν ὁ Κύριος ("For thus has the Lord commanded us"—again, a perfect tense is used with the implication that the command uttered in the past continues to have ongoing significance). This brief survey of the introductory formulae shows that with the exception of 13.22, four use a perfect tense (indicative or participle) and one the present tense. God has spoken and is still speaking.

Here is a convenient place to mention the reference to the Law in the PA speech. Acts 13.38 declares that no one can be justified by the Law of Moses. The phrase ἐν νόμῳ Μωυσέως means "by doing what the Law of Moses prescribes." No reason is here given why not, but we may reach a conclusion in the light of what has been said previously in LA and what will be said by Peter at the Jerusalem Conference referring to the Cornelius episode.

John the Baptist did not mince his words about the state of his Jewish contemporaries in the sight of God (Luke 3.7–17), while Jesus could be just as forthright—see his denunciation of the Pharisees and teachers of the Law (Luke 11.37–52) and his general condemnation of "this generation" (Luke 7.31–35; 9.41; cf. 10.13–15; 11.29–32; cf. 11.13; 13.24–30). Stephen sees the history of Israel as a story of massive disobedience towards God, illustrated in the rejection of a leader like Moses appointed by God; and the erection of and/or attitude towards a man-made building as a temple; and in the idolatrous worship which resulted in the end in the Babylonian exile. In his peroration he accused those in front of him of following in the footsteps of their ancestors: they have always resisted the Holy Spirit. Their ancestors had murdered the prophets who announced the coming of God's Righteous One and now they had aligned themselves with those ancestors by actually killing the Righteous One himself. They had received the Law, but they had not kept it (Acts 7.51–53).

Following Paul's and Barnabas' first mission, a number of Judean Christians had come to Antioch and taught that circumcision was necessary for salvation (15.1), a point of view which caused considerable dissension between them and Paul and Barnabas. As a result, a delegation was sent from the Antioch church to Jerusalem to discuss the matter (15.2). In Jerusalem, some Pharisaically inclined Christians also said that converts must be circumcised and ordered to keep the Law of Moses (15.5). Clearly, they believed that once "saved," there was an obligation to keep the Law. The issue is not only one of "getting in" but also of "staying in."

Peter at the Jerusalem Conference mentioned that, on the occasion when he personally had preached to Cornelius and his household, God had made no distinction between non-Jews and Jews, and had cleansed the hearts of the former by faith. Jew and Gentile are equal in faith before God (15.8–9). He continued: "And now why put God to the test, by placing a yoke on the necks of the disciples which neither our fathers nor we could carry? But we believe that we, in the same way as they, will be saved by the grace of the Lord Jesus" (15.9–11). The Law's demands are too heavy a burden for humans to shoulder.[37] To seek to impose the Law's demands on Gentile converts would be equivalent to the way the wilderness generation had put God to the test.[38]

While Stephen's position is set forth with more aggression and passionate vehemence, Peter speaks in calmer and more measured tones. But their conclusions are basically the same.

Add to all this the fact that Luke would be well aware from the Scriptures of the way the prophets had accused their nation of a massive failure to keep the covenant Law.[39] Thus we may say that the OT prophets, John the Baptist, Jesus, Stephen, Paul and Peter all afford ample support for the kind of statement that the chosen people, past and present, had found the demands of the Law to be something which they had been unable to shoulder, whether through weakness or deliberate disobedience, and that the Law is inadequate for and powerless to achieve salvation.

Klinghardt has argued that Peter's statement at the Jerusalem Conference should not be taken in the sense that the Law is unfulfillable.[40] Rather, Peter concedes that the Jews have not in fact kept the law and that they need cleansing/salvation the same as the Gentiles. Both Jews and Gentiles need to be converted to be saved.[41]

---

37. What Peter says in 15.10 is also in line with his description of the present generation of Jews as a crooked generation from which his hearers should dissociate themselves and repent (2.38, 40; cf. the warnings of 3.23 and the mention of their evil deeds at 3.26). They had fulfilled the role of the enemies of the Lord's anointed as mentioned in Psalm 2.1–2 (4.25–27) and needed repentance and forgiveness (5.31). Tyson, *Images of Judaism*, 147, made the observation, "Within the narrative world of Acts, Torah is therefore a theologically ineffective burden that includes commands that have not and cannot be obeyed."

38. Such is the implication of the use of the verb πειράζειν at v. 10a. The verb is used at Exod. 17.2, 7; Num. 14.22; Pss. 77.41, 56 (EV 78.41, 56); 94.9 (EV 95.9); 105.14 (EV 106.14); while the noun πειρασμός is used at Exod. 17.7; Ps. 105.14 (EV 106.14), of Israel's putting God to the test.

39. The prophetic denunciation of their own nation must be set against the voices of those responsible for Pss. 1 and 119, who delighted in the Law. We might say that the latter correspond in the Lucan narrative to the pious, godly people in Luke 1–2.

40. Klinghardt, *Gesetz*, 109–113. Compare the earlier article by Nolland, "Fresh Look," 105–15, arguing that βαστάσαι is not used in a bad sense but simply to "carry."

41. See Stenschke, *Luke's Portrait of Gentiles*, 108, for this in relation to Gentiles.

He is right in what he affirms, but may go too far in what he denies. If neither the ancestors nor the present generation "had been able" (ἰσχύσαμεν) to bear the yoke of the Law, that comes pretty close to saying that factually it was unfulfillable. If the Jews could not cope with the Law's demands, how much less the Gentiles? Later, James said that the gathering *should not cause difficulty* (παρενοχλεῖν) for the Gentiles by acceding to the demands of those mentioned earlier in the story at 15.1, 5, while the letter accompanying the decree denied that these people had received authority from the Jerusalem church leaders and apologised that they *had disturbed* (ἐτάραξαν) the new converts by what they had said. The two verbs used here seem fairly strong ones to use!

The so-called apostolic decree seems to be a compromise solution: it aims at Gentiles' keeping certain "purity" rules which would both enable them to be part of God's people and facilitate table-fellowship with Jewish believers. In this way the holiness of the community would be preserved. The four prohibitions laid upon Gentiles, according to Acts 15.21, are those that they will have or could have heard read in the law of Moses sabbath by sabbath in the synagogues.[42] This reference to "Moses" points us to the regulations imposed on strangers living in Israel in such passages as Lev. 17–18 (though there are actually more commands there than the four mentioned in the apostolic decree).[43]

Thus we may say that both Jews and Gentiles need to believe in Jesus for salvation. Both observe the law within the people of God constituted by God's action through Jesus and faith in him: Jewish believers observing what they had been accustomed to observe (less, of course, offering any sacrifice for sins),[44] and Gentile believers observing what was laid down in the "apostolic decree" which encapsulated the demands made on "strangers" in the midst of Israel.[45]

Into this pattern, we can fit the following features in LA:

---

42. Cf. Klinghardt, *Gesetz*, 179, 204.

43. While Wilson, *Law*, 86, stresses this, Klinghardt, *Gesetz*, 186, 204, counters by pointing out that these four are associated with an exclusion formula in Leviticus, and Luke was acquainted with such in the early church (cf. Acts 3.22-23; 5.1-11). Pao, *Isaianic New Exodus*, 241, argues that the injunctions in Lev. 17–18 only applied to people residing in the land of Israel. While this may be true of the text as it stands, that does not preclude its being taken as a model for governing relations between Jewish and Gentile believers in Jesus wherever they lived together.

44. This seems an obvious deduction to make from the stress on the once-for-allness and universal efficacy of Jesus' death for us.

45. Klinghardt, *Gesetz*, 205, 217, sees this as a model of relating Jews and Gentiles which is different from that which underlies the strategy of Paul behind the collection for the Jerusalem Christians.

1) Luke tells us that Paul had Timothy circumcised (16.1–3); and that Paul himself observed certain Jewish ritual practices (18.18; 21.23–24, 26). Paul is portrayed in the trial speeches of chapters 22–26 as a loyal and faithful Jew, indeed a Pharisaic Jew (e.g., 22.3). He claimed to have done nothing contrary to his nation's customs (28.17).

2) Mention is made of the large number of Jewish believers who are zealous for the Law (21.20: ζηλωταὶ τοῦ νόμου).

3) People like Cornelius who fear God and do good are acceptable to God, for there is no partiality with Him (Acts 10.1–4, 35). The experience given to Peter in connection with the Roman centurion showed him that God determines who is clean and unclean, and that is not related to the observance of the food laws.[46]

4) Once people like Cornelius have been accepted (11.18), however, there is no grounds for refusing table fellowship to them.[47] The decision proposed by James and accepted by the Jerusalem conference recognises this, and seeks to regulate it so that Jewish Christian sensitivities are acknowledged and catered for.

5) We may briefly refer to the Gospel. There Luke records the saying of Jesus criticising the Pharisees for tithing mint, rue, and every kind of herb, while neglecting justice and the love of God: they ought to have carried out the latter without, however, passing over the former (Luke 11.42; cf.16.17 "It is easier for heaven and earth to pass away than for one letter to become invalid from the Law" and the reference to Moses and the prophets as sufficient to guide the lives of Dives' brothers in 16.29).[48] At the same time, in two other episodes, there is concentration on the ethical aspects of the Law. Jesus commends the lawyer for summarising the Law in the double Love Command (10.25–28), to which is then appended the parable of the Good Samaritan (vv. 30–37). When asked by the ruler what must he do to inherit eternal life, Jesus replies by mentioning three ethical injunctions from the Decalogue, plus the command to honour one's parents (18.20).[49]

---

46. There is a helpful discussion of this episode in Gaventa, *Conversion*, 107–22. She (as others) points out that both Cornelius and Peter needed to be converted!

47. Gaventa, *Conversion*, 109, correctly notes the connection between conversion and the issue of hospitality in the Cornelius story.

48. Cf. Prieur, *Gottesherrschaft*, 231–232, 283. Prieur believes that this emphasis within LA is due to Luke's aim to combat the antinomian tendencies of the false teachers of his own day who are mentioned in Paul's farewell speech to the Ephesian elders in Acts 20.17–35.

49. Marguerat, *First Christian Historian*, 62, comments "It is these values that Luke

In total, one could say that this duality in the Gospel is not too dissimilar to that found in Acts. We may agree with the suggestion that while any soteriological function of the Law is abrogated, the Law still retains a function both as a witness to God's plan of salvation and as an ethical guide[50] and to indicate continuity between Israel and the followers of Jesus in the people of God.[51]

THE POSITION OF ISRAEL[52]

We cannot discuss this theme in chapter 13 in isolation, but need to set it in its context in the whole of LA. The major impression from the Lucan birth stories is that the ensuing story is primarily going to be concerned with Israel. Not only are the characters the "pious" in Israel, but the preponderance of the statements concern Israel. John the Baptist is to go in the spirit of Elijah to prepare God's people for Him (Luke 1.15-17). Mary's son, to be called Jesus, will receive the throne of his father David and he will reign over the house of Jacob forever (1.32-33). The Magnificat speaks of God's help to His servant, Israel, in order to fulfill a promise made to Abraham and his seed (1.54-55). Similarly, the Benedictus celebrates the redemption with which God has visited His people by raising up a savior from within the ranks of David's descendants (again, in fulfillment of His oath to Abraham). John the Baptist's task is to prepare the ways of the Lord and to impart knowledge of salvation to His people (1.68-69, 73, 76-77). The angel's message to the shepherds is good news for all the people, and in context that can only mean the entire people of Israel (2.10).[53] The prophetess Anna spoke about the infant Jesus "to all those who were looking for the redemption of Jerusalem" (2.38).

---

admires in Cornelius, the God-Fearer from Caesarea."

50. Prieur, *Gottesherrschaft*, 241, 283.

51. This is stressed by Marguerat, *First Christian Historian*, 62; see also his treatment "*Paul et la Torah*," 81-100.

52. There has been a considerable literature on this topic in recent years. We may mention the following as among some of the significant contributions: Jervell, *People of God*; Lohfink, *Sammlung Israels*; Franklin, *Christ the Lord*; Tiede, *Prophecy and History*; Tannehill, *Israel in LA*, 69-85; Brawley, *LA and the Jews*; Sanders, *Jews*; Tyson, *LA and the Jewish People*; Merkel, *Israel im lukanischen Werk*, 19-38; Weatherly, *Jewish Responsibility*; Ravens, *Restoration of Israel*; Wasserberg, *Aus Israels Mitte*; Moessner, *Heritage of Israel*; Deutschmann, *Synagoge*; Pao, *Acts and the Isaianic New Exodus*; Marguerat, *First Christian Historian*, 129-54.

53. Wilson, *Gentiles*, 35, and Wassenberg, *Aus Israels Mitte*, 125, 132, both conclude that this is the most likely interpretation.

It is really only in the canticle of Simeon, a man inspired by the Holy Spirit, that there is a lifting of our thoughts beyond Israel. The Nunc Dimittis speaks of a salvation prepared by God before all the peoples and proclaims Jesus as both a light for revelation to the Gentiles and the glory of God's people, Israel (2.31-32). This dual role is reminiscent of the task of the Servant in Isa. 49.1-6, a task which embraces both Israel and the nations. Even after this, Simeon returns to Israel when he makes the solemn prediction that the child is appointed for the rise and fall of many in Israel and a sign which will be spoken against (2.34, 36).

The reference to salvation for all peoples in Simeon's canticle seems to be picked up again when Luke extends the quotation from Isa. 40 in reference to John the Baptist to include the line "And all people[54] will see the salvation of God."[55] There is a strong hint that the benefits of Jesus' ministry will go to the Gentiles, in the conversation between Jesus and the members of the Nazareth synagogue. When his fellowtownsfolk requested that Jesus performs miracles in Nazareth comparable to those which he had done in Capernaum, Jesus said that no prophet was acceptable in his own country, and followed this up by saying that though there were many widows in Israel in Elijah's time, he was not sent to any of them, but to a widow in Zareptah in Sidon. Though there were many lepers in Israel in Elisha's day; he was not sent to any of them, but he healed Naaman the Syrian (Luke 4.24-27). While it is true that in the flow of the narrative, it could be claimed that vv. 25-27 explain why no miracles will be done in Nazareth as they have been done in Capernaum (v. 23c),[56] nevertheless, the fact that the recipients of what Elijah and Elisha did were both foreigners is still significant. Read in the light of Simeon's prophecy and the attempt of the Nazareth folk to kill Jesus, it is a pointer of what may happen in the future.[57]

From this point on, however, any pursuit of an interest in Gentiles seems to recede somewhat.[58] Luke has Jesus confine his ministry to Israel

---

54. Literally, "all flesh."

55. In agreement with the LXX. The Hebrew runs "and all flesh will see it [the glory of Yahweh] together."

56. As Wassenberg, *Aus Israels Mitte*, 161-62, stresses.

57. Even Wassenberg, *Aus Israels Mitte*, 163, in his summary of his discussion of Luke 4.16-30, concedes that where Israel refuses salvation (and the reaction of the Nazareth folk is a foretaste of what Jesus has to expect from his own people), it goes over to the nations.

58. Without going as far as many of the specific interpretations of King, "Universalism," 199-205, King (205) spoke of a "partial krypsis of his [Luke's] universalism while he is writing his Gospel."

(e.g., he drops the references to Jesus' journeys outside Israel at Mark 7.24[59] and the mention of Caesarea Philippi when copying Mark 8.27). There are, however, hints that the Gentiles will share in the future Kingdom of God. Of these, we may mention Jesus' remark that he had not found faith in Israel to equal that of the centurion (7.9) and the warning that the queen of the south and the men of Nineveh would both stand up and bring about the condemnation[60] of the Israelite people of Jesus' generation because of the latter's lack of response to his preaching, whereas the queen of the South had travelled from afar to hear the wisdom of Solomon and the Ninevites had responded to the preaching of Jonah (Luke 11.31–32; cf. the woes against the Galilean towns in 10.13–15). There is another warning which predicted the exclusion of "the sons of the kingdom" and the coming of people from east and west and north and south to dine with the patriarchs in the banquet of the Kingdom (13.28–29). The parable of the Great Supper (14.16–24), with its *two* invitations after the first guests had all refused, may point to the call to those who were marginalised in Jewish society and then the Gentile mission.[61] It is quite possible that Luke saw the centurion of Capernaum and the Samaritan, "the foreigner," who was the only one out of the ten lepers cured by Jesus and who returned to give thanks to God (17. 12–19), as prototypes of future Gentile and Samaritan believers.[62]

After the resurrection, however, the risen Jesus opens up the OT scriptures to the disciples and commissions them with these words:
"Thus it is written that the messiah should suffer and rise from the dead on the third day and that repentance leading to the forgiveness of sins should be proclaimed in his name to all the nations, beginning from Jerusalem. You are my witnesses." (24.46–48). This speech shows that the Gentile mission

---

59. Mark 7.24, of course, occurs within the so-called "Great Omission," for which there may be other explanations than a desire not to have Jesus meet non-Israelites during his earthly ministry.

60. So we should translate the verbs κατακρινεῖ and κατακρινοῦσιν. See the apt comment of BAG 413: "The conduct of one person, since it sets a standard, can result in the condemnation before God of another person whose conduct is inferior."

61. This is a widespread view, but it has to be said that it is possible to see the two invitations as illustrating the point that the house must be filled (v. 23c).

62. Some (e.g., Creed, *Luke*, 144; Grundmann, *Lukas*, 207; Marshall, *Luke*, 413: "possible"; Ellis, *Luke*, 155 "perhaps" Nolland, *Luke*, 2:558; Prast, *Presbyter und Evangelium*, 341–43) argue that Luke's account of the mission of the 70/72 in Luke 10, after the mission of the 12 in chapter 9, is meant to indicate a foreshadowing of the Gentile mission (based on an assumed reference to 70/72 nations in Gen. 10). Among others, on the other hand, Wilson, *Gentiles,* 45–47, maintained that if a symbolic reference is intended, it is to the appointment of 70 elders by Moses in Num. 11. But see now the careful examination of both these views and a negative assessment of them by Prieur, *Gottesherrschaft*, 212–20.

was contained in Scripture. It was not an after-thought, but was part of God's plan from the beginning. The Gentile mission was not an illegitimate development, but was within the divine purpose all along.

We can now also understand why Luke has not pursued the theme of Gentiles in his Gospel. The time for the Gentile mission is *after* the suffering and resurrection of Jesus. After those events, at the specifically appointed time, it can get underway.

Luke has a commissioning scene also in Acts, after the disciples have asked the risen Lord "Is it at this time that you will restore the Kingdom to Israel?" (Acts 1.6). We learn that there are two things wrong with this question. In the first place, there is a mistake concerning time. Verse 7 sets this right: "It is not for you to know the times and seasons which the Father has fixed by his own authority." And there is a mistaken preoccupation with Israel as such—that is to say, a too narrowly nationalistic perspective. This in turn is corrected by verse 8: "But you will receive power when the Holy Spirit comes upon you, and you will be my witnesses in Jerusalem and in all Judea and Samaria and to the ends of the earth." There is an allusion here (as in the Nunc Dimittis) to the task of the Servant in Isa. 49.6: the servant has a task not just to Israel but to the nations. So also the disciples of Jesus have a task not just to Israel but to the ends of the earth.

Thus, these two commissioning scenes set the major themes for Luke's second volume. The Gentile mission will be a major concern, but that does not mean that Israel is neglected.

The first real episode recorded by Luke after Jesus' ascension is the restoration of the full complement of the twelve by the choice of Matthias (1.15–26). The symbolism of the "twelve" had been put before us in Jesus' words in the Lucan account of the Last Supper: the twelve will sit on thrones judging the twelve tribes of Israel (22.30). Because Judas had apostasised, his place had to be filled (The martyred James, son of Zebedee, by contrast, does not appear to have been replaced—Acts 12.1–2). The apostolic band is at full strength before the outpouring of the Spirit. It is as if the core of the newly constituted Israel has been re-established, and the Spirit can be poured out as a renewal and restoration of Israel.[63]

The conclusion of Peter's Pentecost speech is revealing. He wants "the whole house of Israel" to know that the crucified Jesus is Lord and Messiah (2.36; cf. 4.10 "Be it known to you [the Sanhedrin] and the whole house of Israel. . ."). He regards the present generation as "crooked" (2.40) and encourages his listeners to step outside its attitude. There is a promise of forgiveness and the Holy Spirit "to you and your children and to all who are

---

63. Cf. Franklin, *Christ the Lord*, 97–98.

afar off, those whom the Lord our God will call" (2.39). The phrase "those afar off" can hardly be limited to Jews in the Diaspora, for the following reasons. In the first place, the relative clause which acts as an explanation would be inappropriate in respect of Jews—they are already within the covenant people. Secondly, after Acts 1.8, the speech clearly has in mind those beyond the confines of Israel. Thirdly, the phrase evokes Joel 2.32, already quoted at Acts 2.21, which has a latent universalism about it. So, then, the people of Israel are very much in mind, but there are indicators that others too may be called by God.

Following the Pentecost speech, Luke gives a description of the life of the Christian group, a noteworthy feature being the sale of possessions and the distribution to those in need (2.43-44), and this description is repeated in more detail in 4.32-37 (5.1-11). While Luke's language undoubtedly draws on Greek philosophical pronouncements on friendship and the sharing between friends,[64] we ought not to exclude the possible influence also of the OT, that is, Deut. 15.4.[65] There, in a section on the remission of debts after every seven years, it states that "there shall not be any poor with you if you obey the Lord your God by keeping carefully these commandments which I lay upon you this day." Obedience will result in blessing, specifically, the eradication of poverty. At Acts 4.34, Luke says "For there was no one among them who was poor" (ἐνδεής). The Mosaic promise was being fulfilled among Christians who are the obedient messianic community in Israel.[66]

The offer of forgiveness was made by Peter at the end of his Pentecost speech, with an appeal to dissociate themselves from the present crooked generation. But what will happen if hearers refuse to dissociate themselves? Peter's second speech in Acts indicates the dreadful consequences of refusing to listen to the prophet like Moses whom God has sent: "But every one who does not listen to that prophet will be exterminated from the people" (3.23, quoting Lev. 23.29). We are reminded of Simeon's prediction that Jesus was appointed for the rise and fall of many in Israel: he would be a sign from God, which would be rejected and spoken against (Luke 2.34).

If Peter's words using Lev. 23.29 are a sombre warning, he nonetheless addresses the crowd: "You are the sons of the prophets and of the Covenant which God made with your fathers, as He said to Abraham 'All families of the earth will be blessed through your seed.' To you first God has raised up

---

64. See, e.g., Johnson, *Possessions*, 2-3, 5, building on the work of scholars before him.

65. Dupont, *Études*, 503-19; Johnson, *Possessions*, 2-4, 183-90, 198-204, esp. 200.

66. Cf. Dupont, *Études*, 509-10; Johnson, *Possessions*, 200.

His servant and sent him to bless you by turning each of you away from your wrongdoings" (3.25-26). The phrase "sons of the prophets" seems to be unique.[67] The καὶ which links it with "of the Covenant" is probably epexegetic (explanatory), and thus "sons of the prophets" means sons of the Covenant which God had made with the fathers. It is, therefore, only right that God should send His servant first to them. But "first" implies others afterwards, and the quotation from Gen. 12.3 at verse 25 is a reminder that blessing is intended for "all families" the world over. But to receive this blessing Israelites must turn from their wicked deeds.

The concern for Israel continues when Peter and the other apostles had been released from prison by the angel of the Lord and told "Go, stand and speak in the temple to the people all the words of this life" (5.20). Then, when they appear before the Sanhedrin, Peter asserted that God had exalted the Jesus whom they had killed "to be Leader and Savior, to give repentance to Israel and forgiveness of sins" (5.31).

Thus far in Acts, we meet both a recognition of Israel's unique position as the covenant people of God; a concern that the message of Jesus raised and exalted by God be accepted and the blessings which God still offers to Israel be received; and a warning that refusal of this offer carries with it divine rejection. Lohfink has pointed out that Luke has taken great care to show in Acts 1–5 that all Israel has been confronted by the preaching of the apostles (2.14, 22, 36; 3.12; 4.10; 5.16, 25, 28, 42), and how large numbers of people have joined the community of Jesus' disciples (2.41, 47b; 4. 4; 5.14; 6.1, 7; cf. later 15.5; 21.20), even though the chief priests remain implacably opposed to the apostles and their teaching (Acts 4–5).[68]

Most scholars accept that Stephen's speech and martyrdom marks a significant change.[69] Luke is at pains to point out that the charges brought against Stephen are false (6.11–13): they concern the Law and the Temple. In the speech before the Sanhedrin, there is no criticism of the Law; indeed, it is described as "living oracles" from God (v. 38) and "delivered by angels" (v. 53), and Stephen denounced his judges for their failure to keep the Law (vv. 51–53). While many scholars believe that Stephen did reject the idea of a Temple (this view is usually accompanied by the conviction that he saw in the movable Tent of Meeting a more fitting symbol of the dynamic character of the God who is ever moving on), other scholars do not think that the criticism of the Temple is actually as forthright as might

67. Jervell, *Unknown Paul*, 176n56; Schneider, *Apg.*, 1.330n127.

68. Lohfink, *Sammlung Israels*, 47–55.

69. The current trend is towards seeing Stephen's speech as a Lucan composition, yet there are several scholars who still think that Luke is here passing on material which had come to him and which may not have tallied completely with his own standpoint.

have been expected, and query whether the Temple is in fact being denied[70] or that Solomon is actually being criticised[71] (this involves taking the δὲ in a weakened rather than a strongly adversative sense). The quotation from Isa. 66. 1-2 could be taken as a criticism of *a wrong attitude* towards the temple rather than the building of a temple as such, or as a relativizing of the importance of the temple in the sense that God's dwelling is in heaven and not in any earthly building.[72]

Which of these viewpoints is the better grounded? We note that at a number of points early in the speech, there is a stress on the fact that God revealed Himself and was encountered *outside* the promised land. Thus, He appeared to Abraham in Mesopotamia (v. 2), and, indeed, though God promised land to Abraham, He did not give him any of it in his lifetime (v. 5); God was with Joseph in Egypt (v. 9b); God's angel (= God, as v. 32 shows "I am the God of your fathers") appeared to Moses in the wilderness of mount Sinai (vv. 30-34). This motif must be taken account of when considering the impact of vv. 46-50.

After mentioning that Abraham had not possessed any of the promised land, Stephen's speech goes on to refer to the prediction that Abraham's descendants would become strangers in Egypt and would be severely maltreated and oppressed, but that God would judge the nation that oppressed them. As a result, the people would come out of Egypt and would worship Him "in this place" (v. 7). There are good reasons for assuming that this refers to the Temple rather than being a general reference to the land as a whole: both before and after this verse there are clear references to the Temple in the phrases "this holy place/this place" in 6.13-14 in contrast to "this land in which you now live" (7.4) and the subsequent reference to

---

70. E.g. Schneider, *Apg.*, 1:467; Franklin, *Christ the Lord*, 105; Brawley, *The Jews*, 121-22; Hill, *Hellenists and Hebrews*, 70-81; Wasserberg, *Aus Israels Mitte*, 242-43; Miura, *David*, 177.

71. E.g. Witherington, *Acts*, 273.

72. Bruce, *Acts*, 159, having first stated that v. 47 "expresses plain disapproval" of the temple, then goes on to say "Yet it is not Solomon's own act that Stephen deprecates... It was rather the state of mind to which the temple gave rise... that Stephen reprobates"; Franklin, *Christ the Lord*, 105-8; Koet, *Five Studies*, 78-80; Jervell, "Gottes Treue," 20; Brawley, "God of Promises," 290. Bachmann, "Stephanusepisode," 551-52, points out that according to v. 46 David asked to find a place of worship (eine gottesdienstliche Stätte) for the house of Jacob (Jews)—where Luke has altered the wording borrowed from LXX Ps. 131.5, from σκήκωμα τῷ θεῷ Ιακωβ to σκήνωμα τῳ οἴκῳ Ιακωβ. He also points out that already in v. 44 there had been a reference to the heavenly model which Moses had seen and on the basis of which he was to erect the "tent of witness," and emphasises that the critics of Stephen have wrongly assessed the relation between the Jerusalem temple and the heavenly Temple, with the result that their accusation rebounds on themselves.

"place" in God's words quoted from Isa. 66.1-2 at 7.49d. Accordingly, we assume a reference to the Temple rather than to the land despite the advocacy of the latter position by many scholars.[73] That being so, as Wasserberg tellingly points out, it is hardly possible to interpret the later building of the Temple by Solomon as a violation of God's will.[74]

Further, if it is said that David "found favour with God" (v. 46), it is hardly likely that this would be followed by a reference to a scheme which was regarded as totally contrary to the will of God.

Then again, while the idea that the Temple was something "made with hands" would certainly be offensive to Jewish ears,[75] the scriptural quotation from Isa. 66.1-2 with its assertion that God does not dwell in earthly temples says the same as Solomon's prayer placed at the occasion of the dedication of the Temple (1 Kgs. 8).[76] The same point is also made in the Areopagus speech of Paul, where it is said that the Creator God "does not dwell in temples made with hands, nor is He served by human hands as if He needs anything" (17.24-25).

We may also ask whether, if Luke were himself totally opposed to Temple worship, he would have depicted the earliest disciples frequenting the Temple or would he have recorded in such detail that Paul was involved in a Nazarite vow and paid the expenses of other Jews who were involved in such a vow, which involved a sacrifice at the end of the period of the vow (Acts 21.26-27; 24.18; 25.8)?

---

73. Those who take the Temple or city and Temple as the referent include Schneider, *Apg.*, 1:455; Roloff, *Apg.*, 120; Pesch, *Apg.*, 1:249; Lüdemann, *Early Christianity*, 86; Barrett, *Acts*, 1:345; Jervell, *Apg.*, 234 n. 687; Bihler, *Stephenusgeschichte*, 43; Holtz, *Zitate*, 99; Tannehill, *Narrative Unity*, 2:93; Klinghardt, *Gesetz*, 296; Wasserberg, *Aus Israels Mitte*, 245-46; Sterling, "Opening the Scriptures," 213; Bachmann, "Stephanusepisode," 551; Pietsch, *Sprotz Davids*, 316.

Those who take the referent to be the land include Bruce, *Acts*, 147; Marshall, *Acts*, 136; Fitzmyer, *Acts*, 372; Johnson, *Acts*, 116; Witherington, *Acts*, 262-64, 266 (though not seeing the speech as a whole as critical of the temple); Kee, *Acts*, 96; Jeske, *Geschichte*, 143-44 (emphasising the link with 1 Sam. 12.8, but there the verb "to dwell" is used so that only the land can be in question).

Haenchen, *Acts*, 279, is undecided, while Scharlemann, *Singular Saint*, 38, 50, refers to Shechem. Penner, *Christian Origins*, 96 and 318 resp., seems to waver between temple and land.

74. Wasserberg, *Aus Israels Mitte*, 246.

75. Barrett, *Acts*, 1:373; cf. too Pesch, *Apg.*, 1:257.

76. In the theology of the Deuteronomists, it is "the Name" of Yahweh which dwells in the Temple: see Rad, *Studies*, 37-41, for a discussion of this ("Deuteronomy is replacing the old crude idea of Jahweh's presence and dwelling at the shrine by a theologically sublimated idea," 39).

Arguably, the main aim of Stephen's speech, and the reason why Luke set it here, is that, through defending by counter-attacking,[77] it makes a severe charge of disobedience in various forms throughout Israel's history. There was the rejection of those sent by God in the past like Moses (vv. 27-29, 35, 39).[78] There was the disobedience to the command not to worship idols: the Israelites had worshipped the golden calf, brought sacrifice to it and rejoiced in what their hands had made (ἐν τοῖς ἔργοις τῶν χειρῶν αὐτῶν), and they worshipped the host of heaven, vv. 40-42. The charge of idolatry is supported by Amos 5.25-27, with its reproach that the people were idolaters, even in the desert, even after Yahweh's mighty act of redemption from Egypt, and they did not offer sacrifices to Him but rather they took up the tabernacle of Moloch and the star of the god Rephan. With this prior charge backed up by a scriptural quotation in mind, it is possible that the implication of vv. 47-50 is that the people of Israel had confused the Temple building with God's dwelling and had thereby not fully appreciated His transcendence over His own creation. Both in the wilderness and in the land, the people of Israel had not truly appreciated what God had done for them nor had they truly grasped the nature of God.

This could explain why the speech then leaps from this mention of the Temple in vv. 47-50 to its climax in the fierce charge of being stiff-necked, uncircumcised in heart and ears, and always resistant to the Holy Spirit. Like fathers, like sons: the past Israelites killed the prophets, the present generation has killed the Righteous One. Israel past and present has received the Law, but has never kept it.[79]

One might think that this would mark a definitive end to any mission to Israel, particularly as Luke reports a persecution directed against Christians in Jerusalem which led to their being scattered into Judea and Samaria and beyond.[80] But that is in fact not the case. Luke tells of the conversion of

---

77. Note how Wassenberg, *Aus Israels Mitte*, 251, speaks of Stephen's going over to verbal attack, the accused becoming the accuser, though he is thinking of the speech from v. 51. From the point of view of narrative criticism, the attack has begun before this and vv. 51-53 represents the climax.

78. Before Moses, Joseph had been initially rejected by his brothers and sold into slavery (7.9), but the fact that God was with him ensured his rise to high office under the Pharaoh.

79. Holtz, *Zitate*, 109, went so far as to attribute vv. 51-53 to Luke. For him, they introduced an entirely new thought—a sharp accusation against the Jews, and helped to explain the death of Stephen by placing him within the series of the prophets. To call this an entirely new thought, however, underestimates the undercurrent of the speech as a whole.

80. Luke adds that the apostles were exempt from this persecution (8.1). It seems difficult to imagine only the Twelve left in Jerusalem. Most scholars assume that it was

the arch-persecutor, Saul. We learn from this account that Saul is a "chosen vessel" to take the name of Jesus before the nations and kings and *the sons of Israel* (9.15). Indeed, what Saul did straightaway was to preach Jesus as messiah, Son of God, in the Damascus synagogues. By the time the converted Saul found his way back to Jerusalem, there were certainly disciples present in Jerusalem (despite 8.1b), including Barnabas, previously mentioned as an example of tremendous generosity (4.36–37). Through the good offices of Barnabas, Saul was accepted by the Jerusalem church, and, like Stephen, he engaged in disputations with the Hellenistic Jews in Jerusalem (9.28–29).

Meantime, Peter seems to be engaged in a preaching mission in western Palestine (Lydda and the coastal plain, Joppa, Caesarea). Luke has placed here a story which occupied central significance for Christianity in his story: the conversion of Cornelius, a Roman centurion, his household and friends. Cornelius was a Gentile, one who feared God (10.2, 4, 31). Peter mentioned to Cornelius what God had revealed to him: firstly, that he must call no one common or unclean (10.28), and, secondly, that God is no respecter of persons, but that in every nation the person who fears Him and does what is right is acceptable to God. (It must be stressed that "acceptable to Him" does not mean "saved," for Peter preached Jesus to Cornelius[81]). When we turn to what Peter said, we note that God sent His word to the sons of Israel, preaching peace by Jesus Christ, though this is followed by the assertion that "he is Lord of all," which could be said to pick up the phrase "in every nation" of v. 35 and anticipate the "everyone who believes in him will receive the forgiveness of sins" (v. 43).[82] Luke does not attempt here to explain why someone sent to "the sons of Israel" is "Lord of all." The reader/hearer is expected to remember that Jesus has been exalted to the right hand of God (2.33).

As Peter was speaking, the Holy Spirit fell on Cornelius and his friends. The Jewish Christians were amazed that the gift of the Holy Spirit had been poured out on the Gentiles (vv. 44–45). God made His will abundantly clear. As a result, no one challenged their right to be baptised (vv. 47–48).

---

the Hellenist group which was persecuted and that the Aramaic-speaking Christians escaped, although that is not what Luke actually says. The suggestion of Penner, *Christian Origins*, 301, that Acts 8.1 is not a literary device to get the gospel moving out beyond Jerusalem, but a signal that persecution has eroded the fraternal bonds between Jews of differing religious commitments, does not solve the problem of why the apostolic leaders of the Christians were exempt. Luke is probably emphasising the commitment of the apostles to Jerusalem and the link between the Christian faith and Jerusalem.

81. Stenschke, *Luke's Portrait of Gentiles*, 153–54, 239n622, 273, 313–14, 329, 384, 387, stresses this very forcibly.

82. The point being made here is not affected by the awkward Greek of v. 36 and the problems of translation associated with it.

When he got back to Jerusalem, Peter is called upon to explain his association with Gentiles (11.2-3). He gave a summary of what had happened. The gift of the Holy Spirit is the clinching argument: "The Holy Spirit fell on them as also on us at the beginning" (v. 15) and "If God gave them the same gift as also to us when we believed on the Lord Jesus Christ, who was I to be able to withstand God?" (11.17). Luke tells us that Peter's critics among the Jerusalem Christians were silenced and indeed glorified God: "Then God has given repentance leading to life to the Gentiles also"[83]

We now have the context for the PA speech and its sequel in respect of our theme. The Antioch church or perhaps its five leaders—the text of Acts 13.1-3 is not absolutely clear[84]—became convinced that the Holy Spirit of God was calling Barnabas and Saul to a mission and, accordingly, set them apart. This church was itself a mixed church—indeed, the original preachers of the gospel in Antioch were the first to address Gentiles in any place (11.19-21). Barnabas, as an envoy of the Jerusalem church, had recognized that what had happened was a genuine work of the grace of God, and it was he who persuaded Saul, then back in Tarsus, to join him at Antioch and to minister to the church (11.22-26).

The first "port of call" was the island of Cyprus, and at Salamis the two preached in the synagogues (13.5). At the western end of the island in the town of Paphos, seat of the proconsul, Barnabas and Saul have the opportunity of preaching to the proconsul himself, Sergius Paulus, at his invitation (v. 7). The invitation, apparently, presents no problems to the missionary pair. The punitive miracle performed by Paul on the court magician

---

83. We are concerned here with the flow of Luke's story as the background to Paul's PA speech. It may be that, historically speaking, what the objectors said was a more grudging acceptance of what had taken place: "Then even to these Gentiles whom you met, God has granted repentance leading to life." This translation assumes that the article τοῖς does not refer to Gentiles as a class (as e.g., Barrett, *Acts*, 1:543, takes it), but to the specific Gentiles mentioned in the previous discussion (i.e., the so-called anaphoric use of the article, for which see BDF, para. 252). This could go some way towards explaining what happened before and at the Jerusalem Council. It was one thing to accept an incident like the Cornelius episode as a "one off" event; quite another matter, if of set and deliberate policy, a mission was undertaken to bring in Gentiles into the Christian community without circumcision, on the basis of faith in Jesus and baptism. I am well aware that such speculation would be regarded by some as illegitimate and irresponsible, but, on the other hand, see Jervell, *Unknown Paul*, 26-38, for the idea that Jewish Christianity began to be theologically articulate around and at the time of the Jerusalem Council.

84. That Paul and Barnabas reported back to *the church as a whole* (14.27) might indicate that the whole church was involved in their being sent, but, it must be admitted, this is not entirely conclusive.

reinforces the impression made by the teaching given, and Sergius Paulus believed.

From Cyprus, Paul and Barnabas passed over to the mainland and pressed on into the interior to PA. There, on the sabbath, they once again went to the synagogue. As we have seen, the speech was addressed to Israelites, the sons of Abraham, plus proselytes, described as those who fear God.[85] The speech is about God's promise, made to the fathers and renewed to David (vv. 23, 32, 34) and about its fulfillment in Jesus (vv. 23, 32–33), especially through his resurrection: "God has fulfilled the promise made to the fathers for us the children by raising Jesus." The reliable and holy things, promised to David, are being given by God "to you" (v. 34). Forgiveness of sins is proclaimed "to you" (v. 38). Fulfillment of scripture (vv. 27, 29, 33–35), God's prophetic word in the past, is an important and vital motif running through the speech. The closing warning is expressed through a prophetic word, Hab. 1.5.

The sequel shows an Israel (in the Diaspora) divided, as Simeon had predicted (Luke 2.34). Some Jews accepted the message (v. 43), but others resisted forcefully (v. 45), and then stirred up trouble which led to the expulsion of Paul and Barnabas from the town (v. 50).

The announcement made by Paul and Barnabas, that they intended to go to the Gentiles, is obviously significant for two reasons. We note, firstly, the priority of Israel: she had first claim on hearing "the word of God." This is due to her election by God (v. 17). Then, secondly, turning to the Gentiles is justified by Scripture and, thereby, shown to be in God's plan from of old (Isa. 49.6), as well as part of the risen Jesus' commission (Luke 24.47; Acts 1.8). Simeon's prophecy had already marked Jesus as "light" for the nations (Luke 2.22) and Luke had at 3.4–6 extended the quotation from Isa. 40 to include "all people shall see the salvation of God."

What had happened during the rest of the journey shows that the solemn announcement of Paul and Barnabas was not absolute, for the two went to the synagogue at the very next town, Iconium (14.1). Again, we have a picture of division: "a great crowd" of Jews and Gentiles believed, but there were disobedient Jews who stirred up trouble for Paul and Barnabas (14.1–2). Indeed, the city was divided (14.4). In the end, Paul and Barnabas had to move on (14.5–6). After the encounter with pagans at Lystra (14.6–20), Luke hurriedly passes over the rest of the journey, and brings Paul and Barnabas back to Antioch where they reported on what God had done with them and how He had opened the door of faith to the Gentiles (14.27).

---

85. See 69–73 (beginning of chap. 4).

If Luke has shown that, despite 13.46-47, Paul and Barnabas still had exercised a ministry to Jews in the synagogue, his comment at 14.27 indicates a recognition that the mission of Paul and Barnabas was something of a turning point in the fulfilling of Jesus' commission. If in Luke's story the Cornelius episode in principle settled the issue of how Gentiles should be received into the people of God, the mission of Paul and Barnabas indicated a definite outreach to Gentiles as well as to Jews.

Luke's selection and presentation of speeches in chapters 13-14 is illuminating. He gives a "full scale" speech of Paul in the synagogue at PA (the Jews have the right to hear the word of God first) and he gives a "first sketch" of an approach to addressing Gentiles in Lystra (the "full scale" speech will come in the highly symbolic setting at Athens, 17.22-31). Here, then, we have the twin poles of Paul's ministry in Acts: he was called to bear the name of Jesus "before the Gentiles and kings and the sons of Israel" (9.15).[86]

We move on to the crucial Jerusalem Council which Luke presents as ultimately due to and provoked by the mission of Paul and Barnabas. Luke says that certain people came from Judea to Antioch and taught that circumcision was necessary to be saved (later James repudiated these people and denied that they were authorised by him, 15.24). When the Antioch church decided to send Paul and Barnabas to Jerusalem to discuss the matter, certain believers in Jerusalem of a Pharisaic persuasion—presumably of the same outlook as the τινές of 15.1—raised the issue of circumcision and keeping the law of Moses as a divinely required necessity (δεῖ).[87]

In the discussion, Peter sides with Paul and Barnabas. First, Peter recalls the Cornelius episode. This was the occasion that God had used to bring Gentiles to faith and God had given those Gentiles present the Holy Spirit as He had to Jewish believers earlier. God had thus made no distinction between the two racial groups and had cleansed the hearts of the Gentiles through faith (15.7-9).[88] Secondly, Peter asserted that the Law was a

---

86. A major—in length as well as content—speech is accorded to each of these "categories:" sons of Israel (chapter 13), Gentiles (chapter 17), and Kings (chapter 26).

87. Barrett, *Acts*, 2:705, thinks that v. 5 is Luke's addition to make clear that there really was an issue to debate.

88. Although it is often said that Peter "supports" Paul or that Peter becomes the guarantor of Paul, it should be noted that "to cleanse the heart" is not a Pauline phrase (as Hanson, *Acts*, 160, and Sabine Nagele, *Laubhütte Davids*, 74, point out). In fact, Paul only uses καθαρίζειν once in the undisputed Paulines, at 2 Corinthians 7.1: "Let us cleanse ourselves from every defilement of flesh and spirit." καθαρίζειν is used at Eph. 5.26 [where the church is the understood object] and Titus 2.14 [with "us as a people which is for him a costly possession" as the object—for this rather cumbersome translation, see Preisker, περιούσιος, *TDNT* 6.58]. Luke uses καθαρίζειν twice in Acts with the sense of to declare clean at 10.15; 11.9 (In the Gospel he uses it six times of

burdensome yoke which neither their ancestors nor the present generation could carry (v. 10). Finally, Peter asserted that salvation is by the grace of the Lord Jesus—for Jews just as for Gentiles (v. 11).

Luke does not give any detail of what Barnabas and Paul said in respect of the signs and wonders which God had done through them among the Gentiles (15.12b). Though not averse to repetition, Luke in this instance does not repeat what he has just reported in chapters 13-14. Then James makes his contribution. He refers to Peter's account of how God acted "to take a people for His name from the Gentiles." The significance of this phraseology, which never occurs in the. LXX,[89] though it is an Aramaic idiom, will be clarified when we look at the Amos 9.11-12 quotation by which James backs up the assertion: "With this (statement) the words of the prophets agree, as it is written: 'After these things, I will return and rebuild David's fallen σκηνή, and I will rebuild its ruins and set it up; in order that the rest of humanity may seek the Lord, that is[90] all the Gentiles on whom My name has been called.'" Since a literal restoration of the Davidic monarchy had not taken place, a metaphorical sense of David's fallen σκηνή has to be sought.

What sense, then, has the phrase τὴν σκηνὴν Δαυὶδ here? Let us first mention the view of some scholars who take this to be a reference to the resurrection of Jesus, whose body had been buried in a grave.[91] However, while there may be some ultimate reference to that event, it seems somewhat strained and unnatural to take the phrase as actually referring to the body of *Jesus*.[92]

---

the literal healing of lepers at 4.27; 5.12-13; 7.22; 17.14, 17; and once of ceremonial cleansing of vessels at 11.39).

89. It might be difficult, therefore, to see this as a Lucan creation on the basis of the LXX, as Dahl, "People," 322, claimed.

90. 15.17 is close to the LXX, with the addition of τὸν Κύριον as object of the verb to seek. Our translation assumes an epexegetic (explanatory) καὶ. The MT reads in Amos 9.12: "in order that they may possess the remnant of Edom and all the nations who are called by My name." Nägele, *Laubhütte Davids*, 101, sees two groups in v. 17: she takes "the rest of men" to be unbelieving Jews and "all nations" to be the Gentile nations, though she concedes that the interpretation espoused above is possible.

91. Bruce, *Acts*, 310; Haechen, *Acts*, 448; Schneider, *Apg.*, 2:183; Barrett, *Acts*, 2:725-26.

92. On the possible equation "tent" = body, it is true that at 2 Cor. 5.1 Paul speaks of his earthly body as ἡ ἐπίγειος ἡμῶν οἰκία τοῦ σκήνους. This paragraph is, however, the only occasion when he does compare the earthly body with a tent (see v. 4 also). Dupont, ΣΥΝ ΞΡΙΣΤΩΙ, 141-53, showed that this comparison was current in philosophical circles of Hellenism, as also the term "naked" of the post-mortem state, but that in 2 Cor. 5.1-5, Paul is also indebted for the "heavenly clothing" language to Jewish apocalyptic and to Jesus' words contrasting a temple made with hands and one not made with hands. There may be a borrowing of Hellenistic terminology behind

Secondly, there is the view proposed by other scholars who believe that it is probably better to assume that the reference is to the restoration of *Israel*, the nation of which David had been the head. We would have to assume on this interpretation that "tent" is being used *pars pro toto* (the part for the whole). Thus, this interpretation sees a reference to the establishment of the community of Jesus as the eschatological people of God, which will be open to accepting Gentiles[93] (which of course was based ultimately on the ministry of Jesus, culminating in his death, resurrection, and exaltation to glory). The purpose of this divine act is that non-Jews should seek God. The καὶ clause of v. 17b is epexegetic (explanatory) and interprets this human seeking from the divine side: God has caused His name to be called on them. Either this means all peoples, since in the act of creation God has called them into being, or there is a certain predestinarian ring and the sense of divine election to this phrase. The Gentiles will seek the Lord, and—this is the inference—become part of His people.[94] So, on this view, in verse 14, James must be saying that God has acted to take from among the nations those who should belong to Him, to His people. Lohfink maintains that the true Israel is attained when Gentiles have been brought into fellowship with God's people, those Jews who believe in Jesus.[95] Dahl has drawn attention to Zech. 2.11(LXX 2.15): "Many nations . . . will become His people"[96] (ἔθνη πολλὰ. . .ἔσονται αὐτῷ εἰς λαόν), which is an expression of the hope of the conversion of Gentiles who would join the faithful in Israel in the messianic age.[97] It is likely that some Jewish Christians enunciated this belief and drew on passages like Zech. 2.11 and Amos 9.11-12 in support of this view.[98]

"tent," but basically Paul's thought is dominated by Christian eschatological thinking. The fourth evangelist can speak of the temple of Jesus' body, but the word used at John 2.21 is ναός.

93. Roloff, *Apg.*, 232; Pesch, *Apg.*, 2.80; Lüdemann, *Early Christianity*, 168; Fitzmyer, *Acts*, 555; Jervell, *People of God*, 52–53; Lohfink, *Sammlung*, 59; Wilson, *Gentiles and Gentile Mission*, 224-25.

94. One is reminded of Isa. 11.10: a root of Jesse will be made into an ensign of the peoples, and the nations will seek him. Nägele, *Laubhütte Davids*, 98–99, 102, while acknowledging some influence from Zechariah 2.15 along with Isa. 55.5–6; 56.7, prefers to see Isa. 11.10 as the background for Acts 15.17 with the exegetical traditions of Qumran as a major catalyst.

95. Lohfink, *Sammlung*, 60. He thus dissents from the view of Jervell, *People of God*, 43, 49–69, that for Luke only the Jewish Christian part of the church is the true Israel.

96. The MT has "My people."

97. Dahl, "People," 321; Ravens, *Restoration*, 186, 211.

98. In the reprint of his original study, "ΛΑΟΣ ΕΧ ΕΘΝΩΝ," Dupont added a note in which he signified his agreement with Dahl's stress on Zech. 2.15 LXX (*Études*,

While there is much that is satisfying in this interpretation, some unease remains on the score of taking "the fallen and ruined tent of David" to refer to the restoration of Israel *per se*. Alternatively, a few scholars have suggested another alternative, viz. that there is a much more personal reference to David in the phrase "David's tent" than the previously outlined view. They suggest that in the first place the reference is to the restoration of David's "house,"[99] that is, his kingdom,[100] but in the sense that Luke has taken the promise made by Gabriel to Mary in the Annunciation scene. Jesus has entered his glory; he has been exalted to God's right hand; he is Lord. On this basis, the time has come for the people of God to be widened to include the rest of humanity, who, after all, belong to God as Creator.

A fourth line of interpretation takes the fallen tent of David to be Jerusalem-Temple and, in its state restored by God, to be the eschatological Jerusalem-Temple. This view was put forward independently of each other, by Sabine Nägele[101] and Bauckham.[102] Their views, though not identical, come close to each other. We shall set out their arguments for this interpretation. Both agree that the quotation from Amos has been adapted for its present context in Acts.[103] Both point to the use of Amos 9.11-12 in the Qumran

---

364-65). Bauckham, "James and the Gentiles," 170-72, on the other hand, appeals to Exod. 19.5; 23.22 (LXX); Deut. 7.6; 14.2; 26.18-19, and sees the phrase "a people for His name" as replacing λαὸν αὐτῷ περιούσιον and as anticipating the phrase about God's name in 15.17b.

99. σκηνή may be used in the sense of "dwelling" (see BAG 762; Michaelis, σκηνή, *TDNT* 7.368). Where Luke uses "house of David," however, he does not refer to the nation (Luke 1.27, 69; 2.4—against Jervell, *Apg.*, 95n274).

100. Dupont, *"Je batirai,"* 19-32; Tannehill, *Narrative Unity*, 2:188-89. Johnson, *Acts*, 265, speaks of "the restoration of David's kingdom (under the Messiah Jesus)."

101. Nägele, *Laubhütte Davids*, 71-107. Although Nägele's work is primarily focussed on Amos 9.11-12 and the history of its interpretation together with her own exegesis of the passage, she does devote the aforementioned pages to an interpretation of the use of Amos 9.11-12 in Acts 15.16-17. She also holds that the original reference of "the tent of David" in Amos 9.11 was to Jerusalem-Temple, arguing for a use of tabernacle to mean the temple in a few OT texts and then a broadening of the concept of "huts" from the wilderness time associated with the feast of Tabernacles, to the whole of Jerusalem (see *Laubhütte Davids*, 192-99). For this interpretation of David's tent, see also Pomykala, *Davidic Dynasty Tradition*, 61-62, who has argued that the original meaning of David's tent in Amos 9.11 was Jerusalem, not the Davidic dynasty or kingdom. He relied very heavily on Isa. 16.5 where he interpreted the phrase "David's tent" as meaning Jerusalem.

102. Bauckham, "James and the Gentiles," 154-84. He is followed by Witherington, *Acts*, 458-59. Bauckham shows no awareness of Nägele's work, presumably because his essay had been submitted around the time her book was being published.

103. Nägele, *Laubhütte*, 81, 97; Bauckham, "James and the Gentiles," 157.

community,¹⁰⁴ though probably Nägele lays greater emphasis on this factor, since she postulates early Christian knowledge of the Qumran exegesis on the basis of the proximity of the two religious groups in Jerusalem.¹⁰⁵

Both stress the fact that Luke uses ἀνοικοδομεῖν twice, where the LXX has ἀνιστάναι: since Luke uses ἀνιστάναι for the resurrection of Jesus, the fact that he has eschewed that verb here suggests that he does not have the resurrection of Jesus in mind, and his twofold use of ἀνοικοδομεῖν points to a building being in mind.¹⁰⁶ The opening phrase of the quotation μετὰ ταῦτα ἀναστρέψω points to the eschatological turning of God, from judgment, to a saving intervention on behalf of His people (cf. Hos. 3.4-5a; Zech. 8.3 LXX; possibly Jer. 12.15).¹⁰⁷

The early Christian community used Amos 9. 11-12 to support its basic conviction that it was itself the eschatological Jerusalem-Temple.¹⁰⁸ Coupled with this conviction was the belief that Gentiles might now be admitted to God's covenant people (unlike at Qumran, which envisaged the complete annihilation of Gentiles at the End). Various OT passages could be thought of as influential. Among these, Nägele stresses Isa. 11.10, but also includes Isa. 55.5-6; 56.7; Zech. 2.11 (LXX 2.15), while Bauckham points to Jer. 12.15-16; Zech. 8.22; Isa. 45.20-23.¹⁰⁹ The inclusion of the Gentiles was part of God's age-old plan, a point which Luke underlines by placing at the end of the quotation the phrase λέγει Κύριος ποιῶν ταῦτα γνωστὰ ἀπ' αἰῶνος. What was happening in the present is both a work of God (ποιῶν ταῦτα) and had been known by God ages ago (γνωστὰ ἀπ' αἰῶνος).

Whereas for Bauckham the phrase "on whom My name has been called" was most likely understood as a reference to baptism in the name of Jesus,¹¹⁰ Nägele points to passages in which God's name is called over

---

104. Nägele, *Laubhütte*, 77-80, 91, 99, 103; Bauckham, "James and the Gentiles," 158-59.

105. Nägele, *Laubhütte*, 80, 103, where she emphasises the proximity of the Jerusalem church to the Essene quarter in the south-west area of Jerusalem (relying on the research of B. Pixner and R. Riesener).

106. Nägele, *Laubhütte*, 82-86, 89 (We may note in passing that Nagele, *Laubhütte*, 92, thinks that Luke may have interpreted τὰ κατεσκαμμένα αὐτῆς ἀνοικοδομήσω as a reference to God's closing up the division between Jew [Christians] and Gentile [Christians]); Bauckham, "James and the Gentiles," 157.

107. Nägele, *Laubhütte*, 82; Bauckham, "James and the Gentiles," 162-64.

108. Nägele, *Laubhütte*, 91; Bauckham, "James and the Gentiles," 165-67.

109. Nägele, *Laubhütte*, 98, 102; Bauckham, "James and the Gentiles," 165.

110. Bauckham, "James and the Gentiles," 169-70. Cf. earlier Marshall, *Acts*, 252.

Jerusalem and also the Temple and sees this as confirmation that this is the referent in David's tent.[111]

Both scholars accept that Amos 9.11–12 played an important role in the Jerusalem Conference. For Nägele, the Amos 9.11–12 text answered all the questions under debate at the Conference: could Gentiles be accepted into the eschatological sanctuary, and, if so, what validity had the Torah?[112] Bauckham believes that it is plausible that Amos 9. 11–12 so interpreted could have played a decisive role in the Jerusalem church's debate and its decision about the status of Gentile Christians.[113]

What may be said about this interpretation of the restored fallen tent of David as the eschatological Temple, put forward by Nägele and Bauckham? While their point about the change of verbs (ἀνοικοδομεῖν in place of ἀνιστάναι) appears to be a telling argument, it should be observed that considerable abbreviation has taken place over against both the Hebrew and the LXX. Luke or his source has *retained* the verb ἀνοικοδομήσω twice (while dropping ἀναστήσω twice) and has produced a tauter sentence which is chiastically constructed (AB A'B' = verb—object—verb—object). Whoever was responsible for the abbreviation could have thought that the verb ἀνοικοδομεῖν was more appropriate for the imagery than ἀνιστάναι and, therefore, opted to keep it in preference to the latter. It is possible that this quotation came to Luke in the form before us, having arisen either in Jewish or Jewish Christian circles which looked for a renewal of the nation under a descendant of David.[114] If this was so, Luke himself may have been content to let the words stand as they were, without assimilating them to the LXX, and still have taken it as an allusion to the restoration of the Davidic kingdom and/or of Israel based on the resurrection and exaltation of Jesus to glory, especially in the light of the stress on the promise to David and the Davidic descent of Jesus in Paul's PA speech.

A major difficulty with the view under consideration is how the Temple, which is to be replaced by the eschatological Temple, could be described as "fallen" and "ruined" at the time *in Luke's story* of the Jerusalem Council. After all, later in the story, Paul is seized within the Temple precincts

---

111. Nägele, *Laubhutte*, 100. The references which she gives for the phrase are by no means exhaustive and in actual fact there are a few more references to individuals or to Israel over whom Yahweh's name has been called than the ones which she mentions (Deut. 28.10; Isa. 63. 19; Jer. 14.9; 2 Chron. 7.14), viz. Isa. 43.7; Jer. 15.16; Dan. 9.19; Bar. 2.15; and a "secular" example in Isa. 4.1.

112. Nägele, *Laubhütte Davids*, 70–107, esp. 105.

113. Bauckham, "James and the Gentiles," 167.

114. See Holtz, *Zitate*, 26. Cf. Schneider, *Apg.*, 2:182. Nägele, *Laubhütte*, 80, 103, appears to accept a pre-Lucan tradition behind the use of Amos 9.11–12.

and dragged outside with murderous intent in Acts 21.27-30.[115] (That the Temple may have been in ruins when Luke actually wrote Acts does not affect this point.)

Furthermore, would the Temple to be replaced be referred to as *David's tabernacle*? David did not build the tabernacle, and, while he brought the Ark into it in Jerusalem, would this of itself be sufficient for the tabernacle to be called David's tabernacle? The tabernacle was *God's* "house"—it did not "belong" to any human figure.[116] It is true that there is one place where in the LXX the phrase "David's tent" does occur—Isa. 16.5. This occurs in a section of prophecies concerning Moab. The aim of Isa. 16.1-5 seems to be contained in v. 5, where the establishment of the Davidic monarchy is in mind, and this seems to presuppose a time after the destruction of the state of Judah and the Davidic monarchy by the Babylonians. The help asked-for by Moab will be forthcoming when the Davidic monarchy has been restored. This Davidic descendant will rule with justice and righteousness. Clements takes the phrase "the tent of David" to refer to "the Davidic monarchy and kingdom."[117] Kaiser, on the other hand, assumes that "it is improbable that the 'tent of David' means more than David's dwelling place."[118] Neither scholar, however, takes the phrase to be Jerusalem as such.

Accordingly, in view of these points, the interpretation that David's tent in the quotation from Amos 9.11 in Acts 15.16 refers to the eschatological Temple is not wholly convincing.

The strongest arguments, then, seem to be in favour of taking Acts 15.16-17 to refer to a restoration of the Davidic kingdom *in the reinterpreted way in which Luke took it. This would naturally involve the establishment of a messianic community, a restored Israel.* This restored Israel under the leadership of messiah Jesus should now be prepared to open its membership to Gentiles who belong to God just as much as Israel with whom God had made His covenant.

---

115. Nägele, *Laubhütte Davids*, 32 mentions that in the eyes of the Qumran community the Jerusalem Temple was spiritually unclean and repudiated, but that at the end of time Zion will once again become a sacred place. It is, however, one thing for a Jewish group to regard the Temple as spiritually defiled and to repudiate it in that form; it would be another thing to describe it as "fallen and ruined." In any case, there is no evidence that the temple was regarded in those terms in earliest Christian circles, not even in Stephen's group (see 162-65).

116. These arguments also tell against the position of Busse, "Funktion der Vorgeschichte," 172, who refers the fallen tent of David to Jerusalem and the Temple, though without arguments.

117. Clements, *Isaiah 1-39*, 153-54.

118. Kaiser, *Isaiah 1-39*, 71. Kaiser presumably means David's palace by this phrase (cf. Wildberger, *Jesaja 13-27*, 622-23—mentioned by Nägele, *Laubhütte Davids*, 199).

This has been a rather lengthy discussion, and we may now move on. That the admission of Gentiles to the messianic community in the end raises the question of the terms of entry of Gentiles and, therefore, of the position of the Torah, has been rightly stressed by Nägele and Bauckham.[119] James' advice on how matters should be resolved then follows. Gentile Christians are asked to abstain from meat offered to idols; from marriage within the prohibited degrees; from what has been killed by strangling; and from blood (these two go closely together, because an animal killed by strangling would not have had the blood drained from it). These are some of the regulations imposed even upon foreigners living in Israel according to Leviticus and thus would facilitate common fellowship and sharing of meals in mixed congregations of Jewish and Gentile Christians. While it seems to be presumed that Jewish Christians would keep the Mosaic Law, though their salvation did not depend upon it (as Peter had pointed out in v. 11), Gentile Christians were asked to keep this minimum, though again their salvation would not depend on it.[120] According to Luke, the church at Antioch rejoiced on receiving the apostolic letter because of the encouragement which it conveyed (15.31).[121]

There can be no doubt that in Luke's story this meeting in Jerusalem was a significant moment in the life and history of the early church. The unity of the church was preserved: the Jerusalem church recognized fully the Gentile mission and the links of the Gentile church with the mother church were preserved. There was one people of God.

We have already seen that the pattern of Paul's ministry continues to be that of preaching first in the synagogue; the gaining of some Jewish converts, though Israel remains divided in its response to the gospel, as Simeon had predicted; then the preaching to the wider Gentile world. Paul continues to behave as a good Jew: he has Timothy circumcised before taking him on his second missionary journey (16.1–3); he shaved his head in pursuance of a vow at Cenchreae (18.18); he made certain travel arrangements[122] because he wanted to be in Jerusalem for the festival of Pentecost (20.16);

---

119. Nägele, *Laubhütte Davids*, 99–100, 105–7; Bauckham, "James and the Gentiles," 172–79.

120. Marguerat, *First Christian Historian*, 153, suggests that the apostolic decree represents the kind of universal Christianity which Luke had in mind, breaking with the exclusivity of Israel yet retaining enough practices to demonstrate continuity.

121. Luke uses the phrase ἐπὶ τῇ παρακλήσει. Cf. Acts 4.36; 9.31, for the use of the noun with this nuance.

122. We are not here concerned with whether those plans as set out in 20.16 would in fact have been the quickest ones, but with the picture Luke presents of Paul the loyal Jew anxious to get to Jerusalem for a particular festival.

he covers the expenses of four Jews involved in a Nazirite vow as well as his own (21.23–24, 26).

The Miletus speech to the Ephesian Elders indicated that Paul's ministry was directed to Jews as well as Gentiles: to both alike he declared the need of repentance toward God and faith in the Lord Jesus (20.21), even though he suffered a great deal at the hands of his fellow countrymen (20.19).

It is, however, in the series of trial speeches which dominate the closing chapters of Acts that we see the theme of Israel as *one of the most influential motifs of this final section of the book*. In his speech to the crowd outside the temple, Paul emphasises his strict Jewish upbringing in the law of the fathers and his zeal for God, which found expression in persecuting Christians (22.3–5). He stresses the devout character of Ananias, the first Christian to visit him in Damascus after his experience on the road there. This same Ananias had informed him that "the God of our fathers has appointed you to know His will and to see the Righteous One and to hear a voice from his mouth" (vv. 12–14) and he it was who had baptised him (v. 16). Finally, Paul reports that it was actually in the Temple precincts that he again had a vision of the risen Lord Jesus who ordered him to leave Jerusalem and go to the Gentiles (vv. 17–21). Dibelius commented, "There is no contradiction between the God of the temple and the God of the Gentiles."[123]

In Luke's account of Paul's appearance before the Sanhedrin, the theme of resurrection makes its appearance, and it will become one of the leading motifs henceforth under the rubric of "the hope of Israel." Paul created division in the meeting by maintaining that he was on trial for the hope of the resurrection of the dead, since the Sadducees did not hold that hope, whereas the Pharisees did (23.6). As a result of Paul's assertion, the Pharisaic component of the Sanhedrin was more favourably disposed towards Paul and not in favour of condemning him (23.6–9).

Next, Paul appeared before the Roman governor, Felix, when the Sanhedrin employed a professional orator, Tertullus, to put their case against Paul (24.1–9). Paul stoutly maintained that he has served "the God of our fathers" while following the "Way," believing everything in the Law and the prophets and sharing hope in God with his fellow Jews, and he defined this hope as a conviction that there would be a resurrection of the just and unjust (24.14–15). Thus, Paul is depicted as maintaining that resurrection is central to Judaism.

---

123. Dibelius, *Studies*, 161. Marguerat, "Saul's Conversion," 150–51, points out that the break with Jerusalem was not desired by Paul and that the new turn in the apostle's life takes place within a fundamental continuity with his Jewishness. Paul still has an impeccable and fanatical zeal toward the God of the fathers.

The final "trial scene," and the longest speech by Paul of the series, comes in chapter 26, when Paul appears before Festus and the Jewish King, Herod Agrippa II. Once more Paul stresses his strict upbringing according to Pharisaic standards (26.4–5). He then went on to the theme of hope and the resurrection from the dead. He was on trial for the hope of the promise made by God to the fathers (vv. 6–7) and then he made a direct appeal to Agrippa II—"Why should it be deemed incredible that God should raise the dead?" (26.8). Though this theme of resurrection is couched in general terms, the thought of how God raised Jesus from the dead is not far beneath the surface and is explicitly mentioned at what turns out to be the close of the speech at verse 23,[124] and the attentive reader would remember the assertion made in the PA speech that God had fulfilled the promise made to the fathers by raising Jesus from the dead (13.32–33).

In his account of his experience on the Damascus Road, considerable space is devoted to the direct conversation between Paul and the risen Jesus. He is promised that Jesus will rescue him from both the Jews and the Gentiles (v. 17). While he is sent to the Gentiles (v. 17), this clearly does not preclude a mission among his own people, for Paul said that immediately after his vision of Jesus, he proceeded to preach the need to repent and turn to God, "first to those who lived in Damascus and Jerusalem and all the district of Judea and to the Gentiles" (v. 20). To the present moment he had continued to testify to both small and great, and what he had said was in accordance with what the prophets and Moses had said should happen: namely, that the messiah should suffer and that, as the first to rise from the dead, he should proclaim light to the people and to the Gentiles (vv. 22–23). This is where the speech ends, or, at any rate, is broken off by a remark of Festus. The interruption of a speech is a device to emphasise the point being made at the time of the interruption.[125] The speech is interrupted at the moment where Paul was emphasising a ministry to both Israel and the Gentiles, a ministry in accordance with both the Law and the prophets.

There is no doubt that in these chapters Christianity is shown to be the true heir of the Old Testament.[126] What it stands for is in line with the Law and the Prophets, and so it can claim to be Israel, God's people comprising faithful, believing Jews and believing Gentiles. In its belief in

---

124. Gaventa, *Darkness to Light*, 80, followed by Marguerat, "Saul's Conversion," 153 (= *First Christian Historian*, 202), sees an inclusio between 26.6–8 and 26.23.

125. For this device, see Dibelius, *Studies*, 160–61.

126. Dibelius, *Studies*, 172: "The whole speech is drawn up in such a way as to show Christianity as the natural outcome of Judaism;" Luke is concerned to portray Christianity "as the completion of Judaism" (174).

resurrection—both in general terms and in particular the belief in Jesus' resurrection—Christianity stands in the mainstream of the faith and hope of Israel.

In the final scene of Acts, Paul invited the Jews of Rome to his hired quarters. He protested that he was innocent of having done anything to the detriment of his nation or contrary to their customs, and would have been set at liberty had he not been forced to appeal to Caesar (28.17-19). He said "I am bound with this chain because of the hope of Israel." On another day, they met Paul, who spent the whole day in discussion with them and in seeking to persuade them about Jesus from the Law of Moses and the prophets (28.23). Yet again, Israel is divided (28.24-25a). Paul quoted Isaiah 6.9-10 as a pronouncement of judgment against their unbelief and asserted that he would go with the message of God's salvation to the Gentiles (28.26-28). We have already discussed whether this final scene indicates that Luke has "written off" the Jewish nation, and we came to the conclusion that probably he thought that the obdurate part of the nation had forfeited its unique status for the time being but that individual Jews would be welcome if they responded to the gospel and that there are hints that he still hoped that the Jewish nation might find its place in the glorious Kingdom of God.[127]

What is clear from the closing chapters with their successive trial scenes is that for the moment Israel continues through the faithful, believing Jews and believing Gentiles. God's promises have not failed. Christians are the people of God, led by the messiah, the Lord Jesus. There is one people of God down the ages.[128]

All this material from LA chimes in with the main emphases of the PA speech and its sequel. In the speech, Israel's history is seen to climax in Jesus, descendant of David. What happened to Jesus in respect of his death and resurrection had been foreseen and foretold in the Scriptures of Israel. What had been promised by God to Israel had now been fulfilled in Jesus. Forgiveness of sins, justification, is now available, therefore, to all who believe, for, as the sequel to the speech reveals, though Israel has first claim on hearing all this good news, God had equally intended Israel to be a light to the nations that they might share in what Israel had been promised. Believing non-Jews join the believing Jews, and all are filled with joy inspired by the Holy Spirit, a sign of the eschatological people of God.

---

127. See 52-56.

128. Marguerat, *First Christian Historian*, 138-39, 153, stresses that while Luke emphasises that Gentiles are integrated into the people of God, enlarging it to world-wide dimensions, this does not deprive Israel of anything. Christianity is the true Jewish religion.

THE PICTURE OF PAUL[129]

As with our last theme, we cannot discuss this one in isolation from the rest of Acts nor in isolation from the letters of Paul. In pursuing this topic against the background of Paul's own letters, we have to face up to both the fact that we do not possess any direct record from Paul himself of how he actually preached to a congregation mainly comprised of fellow Jews and the fact that the letters themselves are addressed to fellow Christians. Perhaps Rom. 9–11 might give us some clues as to how Paul might approach his fellow Jews,[130] though obviously Rom. 9–11 is not attempting to prove anything directly concerned with Jesus, but is grappling with the problem of Jewish unbelief. Romans 4 and Gal. 3 defend the inclusion of Gentiles in God's people on the basis of divine grace and faith from men and women, and Gal. 3 stresses that Jesus the messiah was the seed of Abraham (3.16) and Gentile believers, incorporated into Jesus, become the seed of Abraham and heirs according to the promise. The focus on Abraham is due to various texts in Genesis—Gen. 15.6; 12.3 (18.18; 22.18); 17.5—which were a "gift" to Paul in terms of righteousness as a gift received by faith and the assertion of divine blessing intended for all. The Abraham saga was thus more useful to Paul to defend the inclusion of the Gentiles than the David saga (despite Isa. 11.10; 55.4-5). With these caveats in mind, we turn to the picture of Paul in Acts 13. The following points call for discussion.

(i)

In the first place, would Paul have stressed the Davidic descent of Jesus? Or would this have fallen under the charge of thinking too much "according to the flesh," given Paul's distinction between a Jew and circumcision κατὰ σάρκα and κατὰ πνεῦμα (Rom. 2.29)? This charge has some validity.

---

129. The issue of whether the Lucan Paul is the same as the Paul of the letters evoked a considerable body of scholarly literature, especially in the sixties and seventies and continues to exercise a fascination. A few of the notable contributions, apart from discussions in the commentaries, are Vielhauer, "Paulinism," 33–50; Borgen, "From Paul to Luke," 168–82; Barrett, *NT Essays*, 70–100; *On Paul*, 155–77; Stolle, *Der Zeuge*; Bruce, *Paul of Acts*, 282–305; Jervell, *People of God*, 153–83; *The Unknown Paul*, 52–95; Roloff, *Paulus-Darstellung des Lukas*, 510–31; Brawley, *LA and the Jews*, 68–83; Lentz, *Luke's Portrait*; Marie-Eloise Rosenblatt, *Paul the Accused*; Wassenberg, *Aus Israels Mitte*, 268–71; Porter, *Paul in Acts*; Walton, *Leadership and Lifestyle*; Parsons, *Luke. Storyteller*, 123–39; Flichy, *Figure*.

130. Indeed, Jervell, *Unknown Paul*, 74, claimed that Romans 9–11 confronts us with that part of Paul which is the basis and foundation of the Lucan Paul.

However, Paul did say at Rom. 9.5 that among the privileges and blessings enjoyed by Israelites are the patriarchs and the messiah:

> "whose (are) the patriarchs and from whom (comes) the Messiah as far as physical descent is concerned
>
> (ὧν οἱ πατέρες καὶ ἐξ ὧν ὁ Χριστὸς τὸ κατὰ σάρκα)."

In this phrase the τό is probably neuter because it includes both patriarchs and the messiah. The phrase τὸ κατὰ σάρκα implies that there is more to be said about the messiah than that he is the messiah of Israel. Dunn goes so far as to say that the restrictive sense denotes "a seriously inadequate understanding of the term or relation so qualified."[131] According to Dunn, Paul was in effect giving with one hand and taking away with the other. A less severe judgment, however, would be content with saying that, while it is a privilege for Israel that the messiah was born a Jew, he was from the start destined by God to be the savior of all the human race (cf. Rom. 5. 12-21).

Paul does utilise Isa. 11.10 at Rom. 15.12. The passage within which this occurs is interesting because it contains overall precisely the two facts just mentioned: Jesus was a "minister of the circumcision" (i.e., he came to minister to the Jewish people) "in order to confirm the promises made to the patriarchs and that the Gentiles might praise God for His mercy" (15.8-9). Then follow four OT quotations (Ps. 18. 49; Deut. 32.43; Ps. 117.1; Isa. 11.10), all designed to show that the OT foresaw this latter event and to encourage the nations of the world to praise God. The final quotation runs: "A root will arise from Jesse, the one who will arise to rule over the nations; the nations will hope in him." While the main purpose is to show the nations hoping in one who is a descendant of Jesse/David, the hopes are nonetheless directed to a Davidic figure. Particularly if Rom. 15.7-12 is Paul's own ad hoc composition,[132] the reference to Jesus' Davidic descent could not be dismissed as insignificant. If Paul had had serious misgivings about mentioning Jesus' Davidic descent, he could have either not chosen Isa. 11.10 or selected another passage with a similar theme of the praise of the Gentiles (even if Isa. 11.10 gave him a verbal link up via ἐλπιοῦσιν with the double use of ἐλπίς in the prayer-wish of 15.13).

We turn now to Rom. 1.3-4. This is accepted by probably the vast majority of scholars as a pre-Pauline formula edited or adapted by Paul. The disagreement comes on what may be Paul's additions or adaptations. The text runs:

---

131. Dunn, *Romans*, 2:528.

132. So Kasemann, *Romans*, 386; Dunn, *Romans*, 2:845 (held over from the collection of passages used in Rom. 9-11).

(περὶ τοῦ υἱοῦ αὐτοῦ)
τοῦ γενομένου ἐκ σπέρματος Δαυὶδ κατὰ σάρκα
τοῦ ὁρισθέντος υἱοῦ Θεοῦ ἐν δυνάμει κατὰ πνεῦμα ἁγιωσύνης
ἐξ ἀναστάσεως νεκρῶν

Some scholars believe that the two prepositional phrases with κατὰ are Pauline additions, but πνεῦμα ἁγιωσύνης is a phrase unique in Paul's letters, and is, therefore, hardly from Paul. It is another issue altogether whether the putative formula envisaged the two κατὰ phrases as complementary, whereas Paul read them through the lens of his own σάρξ-πνεῦμα antithesis.[133] The ἐν δυνάμει phrase is frequently held to be a Pauline addition. Two reasons have been suggested: firstly, it could "soften" what has thought to be the "adoptionist" flavour of ὁρισθέντος, and, secondly, because it seems to disturb the balance of the two members (two participles, two phrases with ἐκ and κατὰ). If this suggestion is accepted, the idea of being appointed with power could agree with the idea that Jesus became Lord at the resurrection, as at Rom. 14.9 (cf. Phil. 2. 9–11).

There is a "relic" of this confession at 2 Tim. 2.8: "Remember Jesus Christ, raised from the dead, of the seed of David." Here the two ideas of Davidic descent and raised from the dead are mentioned in the reverse order. Probably, the Trito-Paulinist wished to stress the resurrection from the dead, given that some were arguing for a spiritual type of resurrection according to 2.18. What the 2 Tim. 2.8 passage does show is that this formula was around in the Pauline congregations towards the end of the first century, so that, whatever may or may not have been Paul's views, his congregations had preserved the formula, and Davidic descent was important enough to retain. One might wonder whether that would have been so, if Paul had not been overly enthusiastic about it?

If this formula was a pre-Pauline formula, its likely origin would be in a Greek-speaking but Semitically influenced congregation. The formula was in Greek, but the phrase πνεῦμα ἁγιωσύνης is perhaps a literal translation of "Spirit of holiness" rather than τὸ πνεῦμα τὸ ἅγιον or τὸ ἅγιον πνεῦμα. It could have been taken to somewhere like Antioch by the Hellenists (cf. Acts 11.19–21), and Paul could have come across it there, but that is in the realms of conjecture.

One further comment may be made on the formula quoted in Rom. 1.3: it also shows that Paul did not entertain other messianic hopes than

---

133. So especially Dunn, "Jesus—Flesh and Spirit," 43–49; and *Romans*, 1:13.

a Davidic descendant.¹³⁴ That is a not unimportant point for us to bear in mind.

We need also to consider Paul's statement in 1 Corinthians about his mission practice, often referred to as the principle of accommodation:

"I became like a Jew to Jews, that I might win Jews;

> I became as under the law (though not under the law), that I might gain those under the law;
> (I became) like someone outside of the law to those outside the law . . . . .that I might gain those outside the law;
> I became weak to those who were weak, that I might gain the weak;
> I became all things to all people, that I might at least save some.
> I do all things for the sake of the gospel that I might be a sharer of it (with others¹³⁵)" (1 Cor. 9.20-23).

In other words, Paul adapted his mode of living to those among whom he lived. Jews are indicated by two phrases—"Jews" and "those under the law," while non-Jews are indicated by those who are οἱ ἀνόμοι. The "weak" may indicate those who had not yet been liberated from a legalistic approach to their faith (as in Rom. 14-15).¹³⁶

Thus, Paul's behavior and lifestyle were flexible in the interests of the gospel, i.e., winning men and women to believe in Jesus, flexible that is in what he would deem non-essential matters. It is not straining matters to assume that he would be *guided by the same sort of principle in preaching the message of the gospel*. While its heart and core could not be altered, the way in which it might be presented could be adapted to the hearers.¹³⁷

---

134. Paul maintained that he was "on matters of the law, a Pharisee" (Phil. 3.5). The Seventeenth Psalm of Solomon indicates a belief in a messiah who would be a "son of David" (See 17.23-51; cf. 18.6-10). The Psalms of Solomon are regarded as originating in Pharisaic circles in the middle of the first century BC—see Gray, *APOT* 2.628-30; Nickelsburg, *Jewish Literature*, 203, 212; Wright, *OTP* 2.641; cf. Winnige, *Sinners*, 13.

135. "With others" is probably implied, as is argued by Fee, *First Epistle*, 432, who comes down on the sense as Paul's "sharing with them [those mentioned in vv. 19-22] in its benefits." The translation of Barrett, *First Epistle*, 216, seems to share that interpretation—"that I too may have my share in it [the benefits of the gospel]."

136. With Barrett, *First Epistle*, 215, and against Fee, *First Epistle*, 431, who takes "weak" as more a sociological than a religious category.

137. An example could be that of the use or non-use of the title ὁ Χριστὸς and the preference for ὁ Κύριος. Pesch, *Apg.*, 2:98-99, defended the historicity of Luke's account of Paul's having had Timothy circumcised (Acts 16.4) on the basis of Paul's missionary accommodation clarified programmatically in 1 Cor. 9.20.

What, then, is the result of our enquiry? While it is unlikely that Paul placed tremendous emphasis on Jesus' Davidic descent—for him the nodal points[138] in the human story seem to have been Adam, Abraham, and Jesus,—it is equally true that he recognized it as a part of the tradition within the Christian community. It seems likely that he would have used it in preaching to a wholly or mainly Jewish audience, for, while it was not the only expression of Jewish messianism, it was probably one of its major expressions.

We cannot, therefore, rule out the possibility that Paul, in the kind of situation like that of a synagogue at PA, could have presented king David as a highly important moment in the story of Israel and set forth Jesus, as a Davidic descendant, as the climax of that story.[139]

(ii)

The discussion of the topic of Davidic descent leads us on to the wider topic of Christology. Does the Christology of the PA speech accord with Paul's Christology?

The letters nearest in time to the occasion when the PA speech is placed are probably 1 and 2 Thessalonians. In 1 Thessalonians, Jesus is the one who has been raised from the dead, is God's Son and will return from heaven to deliver his followers (i.e., save them) from the wrath to come at the Last Judgment (cf. 1 Thess. 1.10; 2.19; 3.13; 4.13–18; 5.9, 23). Jesus is described as Lord and is bracketed with the Father three times (1.1; 3.11; 5.8). The role of Jesus at the End is described with great vividness in 2 Thessalonians, especially 1.3–2.12.

It cannot be said that the Thessalonian correspondence has any material which is inherently incompatible with the PA speech, and yet there is a complete absence of the idea of the imminence of the End in the speech, and indeed in the speeches in Acts as a whole. Where the End is mentioned, there is no hint of its imminence (10.42; 17. 30–31). In all probability, Luke has played down this aspect of early Christian belief. While Luke has not eliminated the idea of an early parousia in the Gospel, in Acts that idea has disappeared. There will be a judgment, but the date of it is not under

---

138. The phrase is taken from Barrett, *From First Adam to Last*, 5: "Paul sees history gathering at nodal points, and crystallizing upon outstanding figures—men who are notable in themselves as individual persons, but even more notable as representative figures."

139. The choice of David would allow plenty of scope for emphasising the grace of God, e.g., 1 Sam. 16.1–13; 2 Sam. 17.5–16; 12.7–8.

consideration (It could be said that Jesus' warning at the beginning of the book, at 1.6–7, has given a ruling and settled the issue. The church is not to be preoccupied with "times and seasons," but to get on with the work of the mission to the world).

If Galatians were written before the Jerusalem Council, i.e., around the time after the PA speech, the same would have to be said. Here Paul uses the title Son of God three times. God raised Jesus from the dead (1.1) and revealed him as His Son to Paul on the Damascus Road (1.16). Paul's life is now centered on Christ—he lives by faith in this Son of God who lives in him (2.20) (we would not expect this idea of Christ's indwelling a believer to figure in a missionary sermon). Jesus is "the seed of Abraham" and those who are the followers of Jesus, who are "in him," are the (true) seed and heirs of the promise made to Abraham (3.16, 29 plus 3.13–14). We note the theme of the promise to Abraham. In the PA speech, this was renewed to David, and believers are the recipients of the blessings promised to David (13.23, 32, 34).

What of Galatians 4. 4–6? The expression "born of a woman" indicates the normal processes of human birth (and is not a reference to the virgin birth) and there is no reference in the PA speech about a special birth—Jesus is a descendant of David. Does the phrase "God sent forth His Son" (Gal. 4.4) indicate pre-existence, or does it say exactly the same as Acts 13.23 that God brought to Israel a Savior from David's seed, according to the promise, namely Jesus? While most scholars probably read this in terms of pre-existence[140]—God sent His Son from heaven to earth,—it could, however, be read to signify no more and no less than God sending a servant of His like the prophets and Dunn has argued for this sense here.[141] If Dunn were right, then, overall, once again there would be nothing inherently incompatible with the PA speech. If the majority of scholars are right, then there would be present in Galatians an idea not present in the PA speech. That stated, are Davidic descent and pre-existence contradictory models? If the coming of the pre-existent Son was in Paul's mind, then "born of a woman" firmly links the Son into the realm of flesh and demands human parents.

When we have said all, the truth remains that Paul's Christology was very much a functional rather than what we call an ontological Christology;

---

140. E.g., Lightfoot, *Galatians*, 166; Bruce, *Galatians*, 195; Mutzner, *Galaterbrief*, 272; Cerfaux, *Le Christ*, 332; Kramer, *Christ*, 114; Merk, *Handeln aus Glaube*, 153; Hengel, *Son of God*, 10–11. Schweizer, "Hintergrund," 199–210, and Betz, *Galatians*, 206–8, distinguish between a pre-Pauline formula not intending pre-existence and Paul's use of it in a pre-existence direction.

141. Dunn, *Christology in the Making*, 38–44. Bonnard, *Galates*, 86, urges caution in reading pre-existence into it.

that is, he was more interested in what Jesus had done and what he had obtained for us, rather than in questions relating to the nature or essence of Jesus. To that extent, with its emphasis on Jesus' role as Savior, the PA speech coheres with this functional approach.

(iii)

The third question to be discussed is whether the concept of "promise" in the PA speech (Acts 13.23, 32) agrees with Paul's use of promise? In the PA speech, the "promise" is probably the one promise made to the "fathers" (v. 32), renewed to David (v. 23), and fulfilled in the person of Jesus, above all in the resurrection of Jesus (v. 38). The double meaning of ἀνιστάναι (to raise up) enabled the speaker at 13.33 to see Jesus' resurrection as the fulfilment of 2 Sam. 7.12, as well as the explicit quotations of Ps. 2.7, Isa. 55.3 and Ps. 16.10.

What, then, was Paul's use of "promise"? Apart from two occurrences, both in the plural, in 2 Corinthians,[142] Paul uses promise(s) in Galatians and Romans. Basically, the promise is the promise or promises of God to Abraham (e.g., Gal. 3.16, 18; Rom. 4. 13): namely that Abraham and Sarah would have a son and heir (Gal. 4.23, 28; Rom. 4.20; 9.8-9) and that through this heir Abraham would become the ancestor of numerous descendants, indeed a nation (Gen. 15.5-6; 22.17), and, beyond that, the father of many nations (Gen. 17. 4-6) and the source of blessing to the world (Gen. 12.2-3; 22. 18).[143] Paul insists that this promise antedated the Law and was in no way abrogated by the Law (Gal. 3.17-18; Rom. 4.13-16). The Law was a secondary and temporary way in which God dealt with Israel until the time of promise, the time of Jesus and, therefore, the time of grace and faith (Gal. 3.21-25, 29). Those who display the kind of faith which Abraham exercised are his true descendants and heirs of the promise of blessing (Gal. 3.22, 29; cf. Rom. 4.11-12, 23-25). The promised blessing for Abraham's descendants is equated by Paul with the gift of the Holy Spirit (Gal 3.13-14).

---

142. 2 Corinthians 1.20 refers in general to God's promises being fulfilled in Christ, and 7.1 refers to the composite quotations in 6.16-18, which illustrate the privilege given to, and the responsibility placed on, believers by God of being His temple.

143. Renewed to Isaac (Gen. 26.24: descendants) and to Jacob (Gen. 28.14: descendants, land, and blessing for the world). See Williamson, *Abraham*, for a detailed study of the relation of especially Genesis 15 and 17 in their existing literary setting in Genesis. Williamson sees a second covenant promised in Gen. 17 and ratified in Gen. 22, a covenant different from but related to that in Gen. 15. Even if he is right for the final author of Genesis, it would still be possible that Luke in the first century AD thought of basically one covenant which God made with Abraham.

There is a difference between Paul's application of "promise" in Galatians-Romans and how "promise" is used in the PA speech. Are the differences complementary or on a different plane altogether? Could one and the same speaker utilise different applications of God's promise according to the context? Did the controversy over how Gentiles were set right with God and became part of God's people mean that Paul's argument in Galatians and Romans took a particular direction and focussed on Abraham, the father of the Jewish people, and a key figure in the debate? Could Paul in a more directly evangelistic-mission situation have applied "promise" in a different direction, focussing on the promise of royal descendants among Abraham's offspring ("I will make you very fruitful; I will make nations of you, and kings will come from you" Gen. 17.6)? Paul had interpreted the collective noun "seed" (σπέρμα) as referring to one descendant in Galatians 3.16, namely Jesus, so presumably the plural "kings" in Genesis 17.6 could be taken in a similarly restrictive manner or culminating in one special king.

Uncertainty must remain. Perhaps any judgment is bound to be subjective. But the use of "promise" in Galatians-Romans has such a special flavour and forcefulness that it makes one wonder whether Paul would have used it differently elsewhere, but this may be to put limits on his creative thought and imagination.

(iv)

The fourth issue to be discussed is whether Paul would have included some exposition of the meaning of Jesus' death when speaking to Jews in a synagogue situation? The PA speech stresses the involvement of the people of Jerusalem and their leaders in bringing about the death sentence for Jesus, despite Pilate's reluctance to sentence him. The terms "to crucify" and "cross" are not specifically used, and the actual putting to death is not mentioned in a main verb at 13.28.[144]

That the death of Jesus is within the purpose of God as revealed in Scripture is shown in the words "When they had fulfilled all that had been written about him" (v. 29), but there is no effort to elucidate this in the same way as Scripture is quoted in vv. 33–35 in respect of the resurrection and its consequences.

---

144. "They asked Pilate for a being-put-death in respect of him" is a literal translation where the passive infinitive ἀναιρεθῆναι is the object of the verb "to ask" and the αὐτόν [=Jesus] is an accusative of respect. A more natural English translation is, of course, "they asked Pilate for him to be put to death" or "they asked Pilate to have him executed."

The cross is referred to as "the tree:"[145] "When they had taken (him) down ἀπὸ τοῦ ξύλου" (v. 29). Reference to the cross as a tree clearly evokes Deut. 21.22-23. Paul himself used this passage to maintain that Jesus became a curse for us; he took the curse of the law upon himself and thereby exhausted its power against us; and, as a result, the blessing for the nations in the promise made to Abraham could come to pass, namely the Holy Spirit (Gal. 3.13-14). Of this approach there is no hint in the PA speech.[146] The same is true of the other uses of ξύλον at Acts 5.30; 10.39.

It looks as if Luke has taken over the terminology τὸ ξύλον without taking over the theological interpretation associated with it, namely an atoning view of the cross.[147] Scholars like Bruce,[148] Marshall[149] and Peterson[150] believe that Luke assumes the kind of theology propounded by Paul in Gal. 3.13-14, but this does seem to be reading into the passage more than is legitimate, since apart from Acts 20.28 Luke has not expressed anything like an atoning view of the death of Jesus, and even at Acts 20.28 the language is not completely typically Pauline.[151] What Paul says to the Ephesian elders at Miletus does reveal the extent to which God will go in order to obtain the church—it is through the blood of His Own (Son), and that indicates how precious the church is to God (as Peterson rightly stresses).[152] In the context of the speech, this fact becomes a motivation for the elders to be on

---

145. For the use of hanging on a tree to mean crucifixion, see Fitzmyer, *Acts*, 337.

146. Nor is there anything like "he bore our sins in his own body on the tree" of 1 Peter 2.24.

147. Cf. Barrett, *Acts*, 1:642: "There is no attempt here to bring out any theological significance in the choice of the word" (see also his comment on 5.30 at *Acts*, 1:289-90).

148. Bruce, *Acts*, 121, 227-28, 275.

149. Marshall, "Resurrection," 105, felt that the references to Jesus hanging on a tree, with Luke 22.19-20 (the longer text) and Acts 20.28, were "sufficient proof that Luke accepted the theory of Jesus' death as a means of atonement," but he was more cautious in *Acts*, 120: "One may wonder whether there is a hint of the idea developed by Paul..."

150. Peterson, "Atonement Theology," 64-65.

151. While Paul uses "blood" to refer to the death of Jesus, he never uses the verb περιποιεῖσθαι (The verb is used in the Trito-Pauline 1 Tim. 3.13 of deacons, who, by serving well, will *obtain* good standing and great boldness in the faith which is in Christ Jesus. Apart from Acts 20.28 and 1 Tim. 3.13, the verb only occurs elsewhere in the NT at Luke 17.33, and then with a different nuance—of the person who seeks to *preserve* life but ends up losing it), though Paul does use the cognate noun περιποίησις at 1 Thess. 5.9, in connection with the salvation intended for us by God through our Lord Jesus Christ who died for us. So, perhaps, this difference ought not to be exaggerated. Certainly Walton, *Leadership and Lifestyle*, 172-73, lays stress on this link between the Miletus speech and 1 Thessalonians.

152. Peterson, "Atonement Theology," 64.

The Theological Emphases of the Speech 189

the spiritual alert and to discharge faithfully their task of taking care of the church, particularly in the light of the rise of false teaching in the imminent future after Paul's death (20. 28–31).

We have to ask why, apart from Acts 20.28, does Paul in Acts nowhere refer to anything like Christ "dying for our sins," a truth in which he himself had been instructed (1 Cor. 15.3), or "Christ died for us" (1 Thess.5.10) and which was central to the gospel (e.g., 1 Cor. 1.17–2.5; cf. 8.11; 2 Cor. 5.14–15, 18–21, etc.)? We have earlier in chapter four rejected Wolter's attempt to get over the difficulty by saying that mission preaching did not include an explanation of the death of Jesus as unconvincing.

What dominates the speeches in Acts is the contrast scheme—"You did . . . but God did . . . ." "You put Jesus to death, but God raised him from the dead." The resurrection is the great act of divine intervention, reversing the verdict and action of human beings. The blessings which ensue from the fact that Jesus was raised from the dead, never to die again or to return to corruption, are developed in 13.32–39. The center in the PA speech is not the cross, not Christ crucified, but Christ raised from the dead and exalted, the Son of God, able to dispense the blessings of an eternal reign promised to David's descendant and in its realisation far eclipsing what had been originally envisaged by the tradents of the promise.[153] The conclusion seems to be that either that Luke did not fully share the particular standpoint by which Paul interpreted the cross of Jesus, or he chose not to do so in the PA speech or elsewhere with the modest exception of Acts 20.28.

All this said, it remains true that no less for Luke than for Paul[154] Jesus is unquestionably the Savior sent by God and that salvation is not to be found elsewhere in any one else (so Acts 4.12). We have already pointed out the predominance of vocabulary associated with the σωζ-root,[155] and there is no need to traverse that ground again. Jesus is designated Savior at his birth, and he proceeds from the beginning of his ministry to the task of seeking and saving the lost, those who are far from God. Note the assertion almost at the beginning of the ministry: "I have not come to call righteous

---

153. Cf. Wassenberg, *Aus Israels Mitte*, 312, who says that in the PA speech, similar to the Pentecost speech, the resurrection of Jesus is interpreted by means of Scripture "as the basic event of salvation surpassing David's story."

154. The statistics for Paul are as follows: the verb σῴζειν: in the undisputed Paulines 18x, 2 Thessalonians 1x, Ephesians 2x and the Pastorals 7x; the noun σωτήρ, in the undisputed Paulines 1x, Ephesians 1x, the Pastorals used of Jesus 4x and of God 6x; the noun σωτηρία in the undisputed Paulines, 12x, Ephesians 1x, 2 Thessalonians 1x; the Pastorals 2x; the noun σωτήριον, Ephesians 1x.

155. See particularly 58–59, but also 93–94.

people but sinners to repentance" (Luke 5.32[156]) and towards the end of his ministry "The Son of Man came to seek and to save the lost" (19.10—L material). On the cross Luke has Jesus both praying for the forgiveness of those who have brought about his death (23.34) and also admitting the penitent guerilla to paradise in the words: "Truly I say to you, Today you will be with me in paradise" (23.43).[157]

At this point it is convenient to mention that Böttrich has argued very strongly that for Luke Jesus' whole life as well as his dying is part of a comprehensive *Proexistenz,* which we may paraphrase as *life given over to help or serve others.*[158] Jesus died as he had lived. His death should not be observed in isolation, though his saving presence receives special concentration in death. Jesus' whole ministry received its fulfilment in his death, as the twofold "for you" at the Last Supper shows.[159] His death "for" others is the climax and center of a comprehensive *Proexistenz.*[160]

Böttrich urges us not to see Luke as an antipode to Paul. He points to their different literary strategies: Paul's argument needs an actual climactic point (Zuspitzung), whereas Luke's presentation lives from the wealth of facets contained in biographical narrative. Indeed, he claims that "the painter" Luke is not inferior to the "thinker" Paul.[161] This is a bold claim to make and certainly runs counter to the rather derogatory estimate of Luke held by so many of his fellow scholars from Germany! While many scholars would not accept the longer text of the Lucan account of the Last Supper and, if this were to be rejected, then one of the foundations, with its twofold "for you,"

---

156. Luke here alters Mark 2.17 by adding εἰς μετάνοιαν and also changing the tense of the main verb from the aorist (ἦλθον) to the perfect indicative active (ἐλήλυθα).

157. See Mittmann-Richert, *Sühnetod,* 89–93, who argues that the scene with the penitent guerilla is the centre of the crucifixion in Luke's passion story and that Luke portrays Jesus as atoning for the sins of this man who has no hope of redemption. In Jesus' death, the sinner experiences freedom from guilt and can enter paradise as the place of unbroken fellowship with God.

158. Here Böttrich is picking up a term used especially by H. Schürmann in connection with what he deemed a characteristic of the historical Jesus' ministry (though apparently G. Schmauch had used it earlier in 1957): see Böttrich, "Proexistenz," 415 n. 15. This seems to me to be a more fruitful approach than that which attempts to relate the general coverage in Luke's story of death, resurrection and the preaching of salvation to the Gentiles (cf. too Acts 26.23) to what Paul says in his letters, the view put forward by Moessner, "The Christ Must Suffer," 443–58, and accepted by Parsons, *Luke, Storyteller,* 135.

159. Mittmann-Richert, *Sühnetod,* strongly emphasises the significance for Luke of the twofold "for you" in the words of institution.

160. Böttrich, "Proexistenz," 413–16, 425, 431–36.

161. Ibid., 436.

for Böttrich's linking the life and the death would disappear; nevertheless, there would still remain in Jesus' prayer of forgiveness and his promise to the guerilla fighter the picture of Jesus as longing for the salvation of people even in his dying moments.

Sellner has also taken up the concept of *Proexistenz* in his explanaation of the meaning of salvation for Luke.[162] He suggests that Jesus' death is the most radical intensification of this feature of *Proexistenz*. Salvation is mediated through the immediate encounter with Jesus in his earthly ministry and then, in the new mode after Pentecost, through the work of the Exalted One, his Spirit and his Name.[163] Sellner's detailed examination of various stories in the Gospel suggests that forgiveness and healing are different aspects of the divine act of salvation: in the encounter with Jesus more than the possibility of bodily healing is available (e.g., 17.19).[164] Jesus has been sent by God for salvation, which is the restoration of our nearness to God.[165] Sellner accepts that renewed Israel is the place where salvation may be found by Jews, and when Israel has been "gathered," the way is open for the acceptance of Gentiles[166]

Just after Bottrich's and Sellner's works appeared, Ulrike Mittmann-Richert attacked the almost standard view that Luke had no atoning view of the cross.[167] She argues that Luke has been profoundly influenced by the Isaianic concept of the Servant of God, including the Suffering Servant picture of Isa. 53, and she sees many allusions to the Servant passages. She particularly stresses the twofold "for you" at the Last Supper and the scene with the penitent guerilla in Luke 23.39-43 as an indication of Jesus' taking the sins of others and enabling them to have life in fellowship with God. Space forbids a detailed examination of all her arguments, some of which may strike others as strained. While it is true that Luke does not quote Scripture in quite the way nor to anything like the same extent as (let us say) Matthew does, he does quote Scripture and he does quote passages from Isaiah, and it is still, therefore, a problem that he does not quote any sentence from Isaiah 53 which mentions the servant bearing the sins of others.[168]

162. Sellner, *Heil Gottes*, esp. 403-80 (He refers to Böttrich on 449 n. 239).
163. Ibid., 479.
164. Ibid., 190, 212.
165. Ibid., 124; cf. 5, where Sellner defines how he is using the phrase "God's saving activity"—God's action to remove the limiting and destructive aspects of human existence and to put our relation to Him on a new basis.
166. Ibid., 364-65, 394-95.
167. Mittmann-Richert, *Sühnetod*.
168. Ulrike Mittmann-Richert does not deal with the Acts of the Apostles (a second volume is promised).

In view of the twofold "for you" in the words of institution and the reference to the "blood of His own (Son)" in Acts 20.28, it would be unwise to deny to Luke any concept that the death of Jesus was instrumental in establishing the new covenant based on the forgiveness of sins.

The concept of *Proexistenz* certainly seems a fruitful one by which to express Luke's understanding of Jesus as the one who brings salvation. It is capable of holding together the ministry of Jesus and his death, the latter being the culmination of and the most concentrated expression of the existence-on-behalf-of-others which is such a feature of the Lucan picture of Jesus. If Luke was not as completely cross-centered as Paul was, if he does not stress the atoning meaning of the death of Jesus as much as Paul does, he does emphasise the theme of salvation through Jesus as much as Paul does. In terms of the variety of witness to the significance of Jesus as God's savior for men and women within the New Testament, Luke's voice finds a rightful place.[169]

(v)

Our next topic is whether the parallelism between forgiveness of sins and justification in the PA speech at 13.38–39 is sufficiently Pauline. There is widespread agreement that in these verses Luke is endeavouring to give a Pauline flavour to the speech and has brought in the term "justified," but many scholars have suggested that the thought expressed does not come near the depth and profundity of Pauline thought on the justification of the ungodly by a righteous God. Vielhauer argued that basically justification in the PA speech is equivalent to forgiveness of sins and this is not genuinely Pauline thought.[170] In the speech, Paul mentioned forgiveness of sins first in v. 38 as the message to be proclaimed. Then v. 39 begins with an explanatory/ epexegetic καὶ = "that is," and then comes the message that every one who believes (in Jesus) will be justified (a blessing which the Law could not procure for men and women[171]).

However, as certain scholars have pointed out, the interpretation of justification in terms of the forgiveness of sins is not so foreign to Paul as has been asserted by scholars like Vielhauer. Romans 4.1–8 does precisely

---

169. Probably in much Christian devotion there has been a blending of the two emphases: Jesus the Savior in his earthly ministry and the Savior in his death and resurrection.

170. Vielhauer, "Paulinism," 41

171. We have previously argued against the idea that a double standard of justification is being propounded in 13.38–39. See 126–28.

this! Paul turns to the story of Abraham and quotes Gen. 15.6—"Abraham believed God and it was reckoned to him for righteousness" (4.3). Then Paul draws an illustration from everyday life in v. 4: "A workman's wages are not reckoned to him on the basis of grace," i.e., he has earned his wages. At this point, Paul contrasts this (δὲ of v. 5) with an example which moves from the everyday world of workers and wages to the spiritual reality which he has in his sights: "but to the person who does not work but believes in Him who justifies the ungodly, that person's faith is reckoned as righteousness" (v. 5).

Then comes a quotation from Ps. 32.1-2 introduced by "Just as also David speaks of the blessedness of the person to whom God reckons righteousness apart from works: 'Blessed are those whose wicked deeds have been forgiven and whose sins the Lord will not reckon.'" The Psalm quotation which speaks of wicked deeds being forgiven, sins being covered or not reckoned, is used as an explanation of justification by grace through faith.[172]

This passage in Romans 4 may be linguistically unusual, since elsewhere in the undisputed Paulines Paul never uses ἄφεσις nor does he use ἀφιέναι with sin(s), transgressions,etc., as its object.[173] Nevertheless, the section in Romans 4 is carefully crafted and deliberately put together, as Paul applies the rabbinical exegetical principle known as 'gezerah shawa,' by which, when the same word occurs in two biblical passages, they can be used to illuminate each other mutually (λογίζεσθαι is the word common to Gen. 15.6 and Ps. 32.1-2).

We should also recall that at Rom. 11.26-27 Paul quotes a combination of Isa. 59.20-21 and 27.9 and applies it to Christ returning at the Parousia. "The deliverer will come from Zion; he will turn ungodliness away from Jacob. This is my covenant (which I will make) with them when I take away their sins." The removal of sins is the same as the forgiveness of sins. Paul is content to use this quotation to describe the final salvation of Israel. He is picking up on a hope that at the end through God's mercy Israel's sins would be forgiven and her relationship with God restored (e.g., Jer, 31.31-34).

Klinghardt has maintained that apart from Rom. 6.7, which, he accepts, is a Jewish legal precept, Paul never uses δικαιοῦν with ἀπό; that the use of δικαιοῦν ἀπό here in Acts 13.39 indicates "ein privatives Geschehen;"[174]

---

172. See Barrett, *Romans*, 89, and *Acts*, 1:651; O'Brien, "Was Paul Converted?" 380-81.

173. In the Deutero-Pauline letters, ἄφεσις is used to explain redemption at Col. 1.14 and Eph. 1.7, whereas δικαιοῦν is not used, and δικαιοσύνη is used only in Ephesians and then in an ethical sense at 4.24; 5.4; 6.14.

174. It is difficult to be sure what exactly Klinghardt, *Gesetz*, 100, means by the use of "privatives." He appears to have coined a neologism (German individuals whom I have consulted confess themselves baffled by it!), and I assume from the examples which

and that what is envisaged in verse 38 is not the positive gift of the new life.[175] While it is true that Romans 6.7 is the only occurrence of δικαιοῦν ἀπὸ in Paul's letters,[176] it is perhaps not completely fair to Paul's *total* picture to say, as Klinghardt does, that Paul uses the verb without a closer definition in a prepositional phrase indicating from what we are justified, since Paul charges the whole of humanity of being guilty under the power of sin before God and enumerates a whole list of sins of which people are guilty (e.g., Rom. 3.9–20, 23a; 1.28–32; Gal. 5.19–21). Furthermore, while the language of Romans 6.7 may be reminiscent of a Jewish legal precept (though this is not absolutely certain), there are strong arguments against assuming that Paul intended his words to mean that a person's death atoned for their sins and much to be said that he is taking the phrase "the one who has died" in the sense of the "one who has died with Christ" as in the statements in 6.1–11 as a whole.[177] If Klinghardt means by "ein privatives Geschehen" that at Acts 13.39 we do not have the Pauline idea of the (potential) incorporation into Christ crucified and risen of all humanity (e.g., Rom. 5.12–21; 2 Cor. 5.14–15, etc.), this must probably be conceded.[178] We have already seen that Luke has not really produced the depths of Paul's doctrine of the cross.

This linguistic data noted, it must be asked whether "forgiveness of sins" is such an impoverished idea in comparison with "justification by grace through faith"? Jeremias asserted "Justification is forgiveness, nothing but forgiveness for Christ's sake," but does go on to say "Yet this statement needs further clarification."[179] Later, he says "The forgiveness, the good pleasure which God grants, is not only negative, i.e., an effacement of the past, but it is an antedonation of God's final gift . . . justification is pardon in its

---

he quotes (see n. 175) that he is using "ein privatives Geschehen" in the sense of the removal of personal sins but not including the giving of new life which in Paul comes through union with the crucified and risen Christ and has corporate connotations.

175. Klinghardt, *Gesetz*, 99–109, esp. 99.

176. For other occurrences of δικαιουν ἀπὸ (τῆς) ἁμαρτίας, see *Sir.* 26.29 (referring to a merchant and a shop keeper) and *Test. Sim.* 6.1 (the reference is to Simeon personally), while in *The Shepherd of Hermas*, Vis. 3.9.1, the woman [= the church], addressing her children, says that she has brought them up "in great simplicity, innocence and reverence because of the mercy of the Lord who instilled righteousness into you that you might be justified and sanctified from all wickedness and from all deceit [δικαιωθῆτε καὶ ἁγιασθῆτε ἀπὸ πάσης σκολιότητος]."

177. Leenhardt, *Romans*, 162–63; Barrett, *Romans*, 125; Cranfield, *Romans*, 1:310-11; Morris, *Romans*, 252–53; Ziesler, *Romans*, 161. Dunn, *Romans*, 1:321 comments "The saying is, therefore, not Christian in itself . . . The Christian usage comes in what Paul does with it."

178. Although, that said, there are occasions when justification is expressed in personal terms, e.g., Rom. 3.28.

179. Jeremias, *Central Message*, 57.

fullest sense. It is the beginning of a new life, a new existence, a new creation through the gift of the Holy Spirit."[180] One thinks of a now old work by a doctrine specialist, justly famous in its day and well beyond it, *The Christian Experience of Forgiveness* by H. R. Mackintosh. Mackintosh amply pointed out that forgiveness was not to be confused with remission of penalty,[181] and he speaks of the gift of restored communion between God and us:[182] "to forgive, on God's part, is in pure love to draw the sinner, despite his sin, into communion with Himself."[183]

If forgiveness is thus understood, there could be no objection to seeing it rightly set in parallelism with justification. But, did Luke so understand forgiveness, or would it be a negative view of forgiveness which he held? Did Luke correlate repentance with forgiveness and faith with the positive blessings of salvation? We need to explore ἄφεσις and ἀφιέναι with sin(s) etc. in the Lucan writings.

The first two occurrences in the Gospel are, so to speak, pre-Christian. Zachariah says that his son will go before the Lord to prepare His ways, to give knowledge of salvation to His people ἐν ἀφέσει of their sins (1.77). Commentators are divided in the meaning which they give to ἐν: either by/through, or consisting of. If the latter is accepted and salvation consists of the forgiveness of sins, then the concept of forgiveness must be taken in a very positive and broad sense. At 3.3, Luke tells us that John the Baptist preached a baptism of repentance leading to the forgiveness of sins. Luke retained this phrase from Mark 1.4 without apparent embarrassment, even though it is Jesus the messiah who really obtains forgiveness for us. Forgiveness is necessary in order that people might survive the awesome judgment of the Coming One. It makes them ready for God's imminent reign.

The next relevant example occurs in the instructions of the risen Jesus to his disciples. They are to remain in the city until clothed with power from on high, whereupon they are to proclaim repentance leading to forgiveness of sins in the name of Jesus to all the nations (Luke 24. 47). Here the two ideas of repentance and forgiveness cover the negative and positive poles of salvation. Repentance means turning away from sins and to God, in order to receive from Him forgiveness through Jesus, that is the restored relationship with Him.

---

180. Jeremias, *Central Message*, 64 and 66. Compare how Hofius, *Paulusstudien*, 128, sees forgiveness of sins and new life linked inextricably in Paul's thought ("forgiveness of sins is for Paul only conceivable as the abolition of the fallenness into sin and as the person's becoming entirely *new*"); cf. 48.

181. Mackintish, *Forgiveness*, 23.

182. Ibid., 31–32, 34–36.

183. Ibid., 287.

We see Peter on behalf of the eleven carrying out this task in Jerusalem from the day of Pentecost onwards. At the end of Pentecost speech, he appeals to the crowd: "Repent and be baptised every one of you in the name of Jesus Christ [faith in him is subsumed under the act of submitting to baptism] for the forgiveness of sins and you will receive the gift of the Holy Spirit," and he follows this up with "Save yourselves from this crooked generation" (2.38, 40). To be saved is to receive the forgiveness of sins, i.e., a restored relationship with God, which will include also receiving the Holy Spirit and becoming a member of the messianic community. Later, to the Sanhedrin, Peter said that God raised and exalted the Jesus whom they "hung on a tree," to be "a Leader and Savior, to give repentance to Israel and the forgiveness of sins" (5. 30–31). The message is the same to the Roman centurion and his household: "All the prophets bear witness to him [Jesus], that everyone who believes in him should receive forgiveness of sins" (10.43). Here we could say that repentance is subsumed under believing in Jesus.

Luke portrays Paul as carrying on this task of preaching forgiveness of sins in the name of Jesus. In reporting to king Agrippa II his call from the risen Jesus on the road to Damascus, Paul says that the risen Jesus had appointed him as his own minister and witness and promised to rescue him from the people and from the Gentiles to whom he was sending Paul:

> "to open their eyes,
> to turn them from darkness to light and from the power of Satan to God,[184]
> that they might receive forgiveness of sins and a share among those sanctified by faith in me" (26.17–18) .

Barrett wisely warns against reading a rigid sequence of elements in the process of conversion here; rather, Luke is piling up a number of vivid images, any one of which would stand for the whole.[185]

---

184. So NIV, and very similarly NEB/REB: this translation assumes that Paul is to do the turning (so Schneider, *Apg.*, 2:374, whose comment differs from the translation which his commentary uses! Fitzmyer, Acts, 760. On the other hand, the RSV/NRSV translates "that they may turn from darkness to light, etc" (so also Barrett, *Acts*, 2:1162; Jervell, *Apg.*, 594; Witherington, *Acts*, 745; Gaventa, *Darkness to Light*, 85–86). If Luke had intended the "subject" of ἐπιστρέψαι (aorist infinitive active) to be those who responded to Paul's missionary preaching, why did he not use αὐτοὺς, as he does in the adjacent τοῦ λαβεῖν clause, and possibly also ἐπιστρεψασθαι (the aorist middle infinitive)? While it is true that at v. 20 the verb ἐπιστρέφειν refers to the action of those who respond, the context of vv. 15–18 is very much what is involved in the commission given to Paul himself.

185. Barrett, *Acts*, 2:1162.

The use of the verb ἀφιέναι in LA does not add to the picture already obtained. Apart from its appearance in the Lord's Prayer (11.4 twice), Jesus forgives sins (5.20; 7.48), which provokes criticism (5.21; 7.49) and he asserts his authority as Son of Man to forgive sins (5.23). He himself forgives his executioners (23.34) and enjoins unlimited forgiveness on his followers (17.3-4). Words spoken against the Son of Man may be forgiven, but not blasphemy against the Holy Spirit (12.10). The only occurrence in Acts is when Peter urges Simon Magus to pray to God so that his sinful intention might possibly be forgiven (Acts 8. 22).

We should note that repentance which is linked with receiving forgiveness is a turning away from sins to God to receive forgiveness/salvation, as is indicated at Acts 3.26, where the task of Jesus the servant of God is to turn people from their evil deeds and, thereby, also receive God's blessing (cf. 3.19), and in turn this leads to a changed way of life—producing works worthy of repentance, as Acts 26.20 maintains.[186]

This brief study confirms that forgiveness for Luke is a richer concept than his critics have sometimes made out. There is no need to be hypercritical of Luke's procedure at 13.38-39 in the PA speech, as if there was a serious lack in the way in which he has presented forgiveness and justification as parallel concepts.[187] As Koch put it, for Luke forgiveness is a soteriological concept.[188]

Before we move on to our next theme, it will be as well to say something briefly about the Lucan understanding of repentance. By some scholars, repentance has been taken to be something which humans do, as a result of which God "rewards" with salvation.[189] Such an interpretation is surely untenable[190] in the light of some clear statements in Acts, in which re-

186. The same could be said of Paul's appeal to the Lystrans to turn from the useless ways associated with paganism and to live for the living God (Acts 14.15-16). Nave, *Role and Function of Repentance*, 145-224, has amply demonstrated that for Luke repentance "entails changing one's way of thinking and living and adopting a new way of thinking and living consistent with the lifestyle prescribed in the teachings of Jesus" (169).

187. Note how Söding, "Sühne durch Stellvertetung," 379, can say, in interpreting Paul's thought in Rom. 3.21-26, that since sin is not only personal guilt but also the state of lack of salvation (Unheil) due to Adam's sin, "forgiveness can only be *an act of new creation*. It is anticipation of the state of perfection (Vollendung) and therefore God's very own work" (my italics).

188. Koch, "Proselyten," 98-99, criticises Klinghardt and Jervell for contrasting forgiveness and new life. He strongly asserts that at 13.38-39, forgiveness and justification mutually interpret each other.

189. So Taegar, *Mensch* (not available to me), 66-67 n. 255, quoted by Mittmann-Richert, *Sühnetod*, 242, n. 76.

190. See the convincing case made out in her excursus on "The μετάνοια of Israel

pentance itself is a gift of God (given both to Israel in Acts 5.31 and Gentiles according to Acts 11.18) or in which God opens people's "eyes" enabling them to repent and receive forgiveness/salvation (Part of Paul's task given to him by the risen Lord Jesus according to his speech before Agrippa in Acts 26.16–18).

(vi)

We must also address the question whether Paul would have spoken of the Jerusalem witnesses in such a way as Acts 13.31 represents. Paul seems to accept an inferior position vis-à-vis the original witnesses when it comes to witnessing to the risen Jesus. After his resurrection by God from the dead, Jesus "appeared over many days to those had come up with him from Galilee to Jerusalem, who are now his witnesses to the people."

The witness theme begins with the risen Jesus' words to the eleven both at the end of the Gospel and the beginning of Acts. At Luke 24.44–49, the risen Jesus explains the references to himself in the Old Testament. The messiah has to suffer and rise from the dead on the third day, and repentance leading to forgiveness has to be proclaimed in his name to all the nations, beginning from Jerusalem. "You are witnesses of these things." He will send what the Father has promised [= Holy Spirit] on them, but they must stay in the city until that happens, which will be a clothing with power.

In the opening scene of Acts, the disciples ask whether now is the moment when Jesus will restore the kingdom to Israel. Jesus brushes aside such a question relating to times and seasons. "You will receive power when the Holy Spirit comes upon you, and you will be my witnesses in Jerusalem and in the whole of Judea and Samaria and to the ends of the earth" (Acts 1. 6–8). Speculation about the end is dismissed; the disciples have a task for which they will be shortly equipped, and that is to be their main preoccupation.

But what is exactly involved in being one of Jesus' witnesses? The story of the choice of a successor to Judas is helpful here (1.15–26). The qualification of such a successor is to have accompanied the rest of the apostles during the whole period of the Lord Jesus' ministry: this encompasses the time from John the Baptist's ministry to Jesus' ascension.[191] Such a man can become a witness to Jesus' resurrection with the eleven.

---

and of the Gentiles," in Mittmann-Richert, *Sühnetod*, 242–45. Conzelmann, *Theology*, 226 and 228 resp., states that "faith and conversion are thought of as God's work," and "repentance is the condition of forgiveness"; the latter statement is acceptable taken in the light of the former.

191. We should note how Luke emphasises that the Galilean disciples (women as

The capacity of these disciples to be Jesus' witnesses is underlined in the speeches: "God raised this Jesus, of which we are all witnesses" (2.32, with virtually an identical statement at 3.15). At 5.32, the claim "We are witnesses of these things" includes crucifixion, resurrection, and exaltation by God, so that Jesus is Leader and Savior and can give repentance and forgiveness of sins to Israel. With the disciples, the Holy Spirit is conjoined as witness, presumably because the Holy Spirit is the power behind the disciples' witness (Luke 12.11-12; cf. 21.14-15), but also because he works visible signs and wonders which can authenticate the message, possibly also as he is given to those who respond to the preaching of the gospel (e.g., 10.44-46).[192]

In the speech to Cornelius, the witness theme occurs twice. Peter claims that "we are witnesses of all that he did [both his preaching and teaching and his healing and exorcism work] in the region of Judea and Jerusalem" (v. 39). Then, having mentioned how Jesus was killed but God raised him from the dead, Peter goes on to say that "God granted him to be seen, not by all the people, but by witnesses appointed beforehand by God, to us who ate and drank with him after he rose from the dead" (10.41).

Now, Paul could not be a witness on either of these levels so defined. He had not been a witness of the earthly Jesus' ministry nor had he been a witness of an appearance of Jesus before the ascension. This seems to be acknowledged in the PA speech quoted above. Acts 13.31-32 seems to draw a distinction: the original disciples, specifically the twelve, are Jesus' witnesses to the people, whereas Paul and Barnabas are those who preach the gospel to the synagogue congregation (13.32).

To this evidence must now be added the fact that Paul is never on his own called by Luke an apostle. He and Barnabas together are called apostles only at Acts 14.4, 14.[193]

---

well as men) witness major "moments" of the passion and resurrection. Luke 23.49 says that all his acquaintances (masculine πάντες οἱ γνωστοὶ αὐτῷ) and the women who had accompanied him *from Galilee* saw the events of the crucifixion. A few sentences later, we read "and the women who had accompanied him *from Galilee* . . . saw the tomb and how his body had been buried" (v. 55). These same women prepared spices and ointments, rested on the Sabbath (23.56) and then went early on the Sunday morning and discovered that the tomb was empty (24.1-3). Their Galilean origin is indirectly reiterated at 24.6. Peter verifies that the tomb was empty (24.12). Jesus appears to Peter and then to the eleven and others (24.34, 36). At the Ascension, the two angels addressed the eleven disciples: "You men *of Galilee*, why do you stand looking to heaven?" (Acts 1. 11).

192. Less likely that the gift of the Spirit is per se a witness to the fact that Jesus had been exalted and received the Spirit from the Father to pour out on believers as in Acts 2.33 (against Marshall, *Acts*, 120).

193. Possibly because the two were apostles sent out by the church at Antioch under

It seems *prima facie* that Luke places Paul on a level below that of the eleven/ twelve. Before we assume this, we need to take two other sets of facts into account. The first of these is that Luke seems to regard the task set out in Acts 1.8 to fall on Paul.[194] The basis for making this assertion is both the sheer fact that the bulk of the effort to take the Christian message outside Palestine in Luke's story is made by Paul and that in the sequel to the PA speech the important phrase in Acts 1.8, ἕως ἐσχάτου τῆς γῆς, recurs when Isa. 49.6 is quoted by Paul and Barnabas to justify their taking the message to the Gentiles.

The second fact is that the μαρτ-group of words are applied to Paul, especially in the last quarter of Acts, and once before, during the so-called second missionary journey—at Corinth Paul testified (διαμαρτυρόμενος) to the Jews that the messiah was Jesus (18.5). In the Miletus speech, which is part retrospect on his life's work and which is uttered at a point where Paul's service for Christ as a free man is really at an end, Paul said that he had testified (διαμαρτυρόμενος) to Jews and Gentiles the need of repentance towards God and faith in our Lord Jesus Christ (20.21). A little later, He declares that he places little worth on his own life so long as he can complete his course and ministry received from the Lord Jesus, to bear witness (διαμαρτύρασθαι) to the gospel of the grace of God (20.24).

While under arrest after the uproar in the temple when he was nearly lynched, Paul received an appearance from the risen Lord in the night. He said to Paul: "Take heart, for as you have borne witness (διεμαρτύρω) in Jerusalem about the things concerning me, so you must also bear witness (μαρτυρῆσαι) in Rome" (23. 11).[195]

In the speech delivered on the steps of the Antonia castle to the crowd who had nearly lynched him, Paul gave the story of his Damascus Road experience and how a devout Jew, Ananias, had come to him and said: "The God of our fathers has appointed you beforehand to know His will and to see the Righteous One and to hear his voice, because you will be his witness (μάρτυς) before all the people concerning the things which you have seen and heard" (22.14-15). Then Paul goes on to report a vision which he received in Jerusalem in the Temple when the risen Jesus told him to

---

the guidance of the Spirit. This with other reasons has persuaded many scholars that Luke got the material in chapters 13-14 from an Antiochene source.

194. Dupont, *Nouvelles Études*, 446-56, esp. 455-56, has stressed this point. Paul "appears as executor of the mission entrusted to the apostles" (455); also Ellis, "Ende der Erde," 283; Pokorny, *Theologie*, 76, 100, 104-5; Wassenberg, *Aus Israels Mitte*, 211, 265, 269; and Jervell, *Apg.*, 283, 288, 595, 639.

195. Strathmann, μάρτυς, *TDNT* 4.511: "There is hardly any difference in meaning between διαμαρτύρεσθαι and μαρτύρεσθαι."

depart from the city "because they will not accept your witness (μαρτυρί αν) concerning me" (v. 18).¹⁹⁶

When Paul appeared before King Agrippa II, he reports that he received his commission directly from the risen Jesus on the road to Damascus: "Get up and stand on your feet. For I have appeared to you for this very purpose to appoint you as a minister and witness (μάρτυρα), both of the events in which you have seen me and in which I will appear to you" (26. 16).

Acts concludes with a scene in which Paul meets representatives of the Roman Jews to discuss his contention that his message fulfills the hope of Israel. They came to where Paul was under house arrest and he "bore witness (διαμαρτυρόμενος) to the kingdom of God, seeking to persuade them concerning Jesus from the Law of Moses and the prophets, from dawn to dusk." (28. 23).

If Luke appears reticent about giving Paul the title "apostle," it is clear from his use of the μαρτ-group of words that he puts Paul on the same level as the twelve in terms of function.¹⁹⁷ Why, then, the differentiation in 13.31-32? As we have said, Paul could not bear witness to the earthly ministry of Jesus, and his ministry had taken him into areas far from Jerusalem. So, Luke may have wished to indicate that difference in the wording of 13.31—the original disciples are Jesus' "witnesses to the people," i.e., the people in the land of Israel, while Paul is a witness to all peoples.¹⁹⁸

Two further points have been made by Wassenberg on this issue. He has suggested that the phrase that Paul is "a chosen vessel" (σκεῦος ἐκλογῆς) for the risen Jesus (Acts 9.15) puts Paul "on an (almost) equal level" with the twelve.¹⁹⁹ (We note that Luke has Peter using the language of God's election: at the Jerusalem council: he said that God had chosen [ἐξελέξατο] him to be the one through whom the Gentiles should hear the word of the gospel and believe [Acts 15.7]). Wassenberg has also pointed to the fact that Paul is the only person in Acts to whom the exalted Lord gives a commission. The same heavenly Lord who indicated that Matthias should

---

196. A little later in this speech, when referring to the dialogue with the risen Jesus during which Paul had demurred about being sent out of the city because he was sure that the people would accept what he said, Paul mentions the fact that he was in full agreement with those who "shed the blood of Stephen your witness" (22.20). Here, then, Stephen is, by implication, ranked as a witness of Jesus alongside the twelve.

197. Cf. Burchard, *Der dreizehnte Zeuge*, 129-36, 173-76; Löning, *Saulustradition*, 126-63; Dillon, "Easter Revelation," 247.

198. So Schneider, *Apg.*, 2:136, and Pesch, *Apg.*, 2:38; cf. Marshall, *Acts*, 225.

199. Wassenberg, *Aus Israels Mitte*, 268.

become a member of the twelve commissioned Paul for his service.[200] These two observations help to increase the conviction that it is wrong to say that Luke saw Paul as inferior to the twelve; rather, he basically puts him on the same level.

How then did Paul in his letters describe himself and his experience of the risen Jesus? In 1 Cor. 15.3-11, he observes no distinction before and after the ascension (indeed Paul subsumes resurrection and exaltation to lordship in one), but slots the appearance given to him in the series of appearances mentioned in vv. 5-7.[201] He claims the title "apostle," albeit acknowledging that he is the least of the apostles and unfit to be called an apostle because he persecuted God's church (v. 9). Whatever may have been the disputes over his right to the apostolic office, functionally he has been superior to those before him: "I have laboured much more than all of them, though not I but God's grace (working) with me" (v.10). Actually, it is precisely the appearance of the risen Lord to him which grounds his claim to be an apostle: "Am I not an apostle? Have I not seen Jesus our Lord?" (1 Cor. 9.1).

It is in Galatians that we encounter the most passionate assertion of his independence as an apostle vis-a-vis the Jerusalem church. He did not receive his gospel from human agency (παρὰ ἀνθρώπου), nor was he taught it, but he received it through revelation of Jesus Christ (δι'ἀποκαλύψεως Ἰησοῦ Χριστοῦ, 1.12). In the light of 1.15, where God is said to have revealed His Son to Paul, we should probably take the genitive Ἰησοῦ Χριστοῦ as an objective genitive: it is a revelation made by God about His Son.[202] As a result of this revelation, Paul's life was changed. He received a commission and a message—a message about Jesus as God's Son to be preached to the Gentiles (1.16). This message, as the rest of Galatians shows, involves acceptance by God as a free gift of His grace through Jesus Christ to be received by faith, and not due to becoming part of a group obligated to keep the Law of Moses.

Paul was clearly sensitive about his position as an apostle, and Galatians is evidence that there were those who either challenged completely his right to be called an apostle or, at any rate, saw him as subordinate to the twelve and the mother church. He was, to put the matter colloquially,

---

200. Wassenberg, *Aus Israels Mitte*, 268-69.

201. We need not here go into the issue whether there were originally two lists with rival claims—a Peter one (vv. 5-6) and a James one (v. 7).

202. Dunn, *Galatians*, 53: "Jesus Christ is not thought of as the source of the revelation (GNB, NIV) but as its content." So also Bruce, *Galatians*, 89; Mutzner, *Galaterbrief*, 68; Betz, *Galatians*, 63; Witherington, *Grace in Galatia*, 92 (against Bonnard, *Galates*, 28, who takes it as a genitive of origin).

a "Johnny-come-lately," and, indeed, an ex-persecutor of Christ's followers. What he preached—a law-free gospel—added further "fuel to the fire" as far as his critics were concerned.

If the opponents behind 2 Corinthians were Jewish Christians from Palestine, this letter affords further evidence of such opposition.

We see, then, in a number of letters, Paul reacting sharply to critics of his position and role. To yield an inch would be to compromise the gospel and that Paul was not prepared to do. Might there be, however, situations outside of controversy, when his own position was not under threat or challenge, where Paul might have been more eirenical and less sensitive? I am inclined to doubt it, however, because the issue was not one which could go away. There were those who would always remember him as the persecutor, as probably Gal. 1.23 suggests. There, Paul says that the Judean churches were hearing reports from others that "he who once persecuted us now preaches the good news of the faith which he once was trying to destroy."

While a considerable number of scholars are prepared to say quite dogmatically that Paul could not have spoken as he does in Acts 13.31,[203] Jervell has argued that Paul was far more eirenical and non-controversial than we are inclined to give him credit.[204] Jervell's thesis is that Jewish Christianity became theologically active after the Jerusalem Council in 48 and it became consolidated after AD 70 (just as Pharisaism consolidated itself into Rabbinism).[205] The PA speech is set in the period before the council, i.e., the period before which Jewish Christianity became theologically active, according to Jervell. This is the period before which Paul's missionary activity and practice was challenged.[206] Opposition began to rear its head in the wake of the first missionary journey as the full implications of a law-free mission to the uncircumcised began to be apparent. Jervell sees a more conservative policy on the part of the Jerusalem church emerging at the Council (the Decree demands certain concessions from Gentile converts), and then afterwards a Jewish Christian counter mission invaded the churches founded by Paul.[207]

---

203. Haenchen, *Acts*, 441; Roloff, *Apg.*, 206; Johnson, *Acts*, 239; Dupont, *Nouvelles Etudes*, 72; Dumais, *Langage*, 245–46. More conservatively inclined scholars often just note that there is no mention of the appearance to Paul: Bruce, *Acts*, 275; Marshall, *Acts*, 225; Buss, *Missionspredigt*, 80.

204. Jervell, *Unknown Paul*, 10, and 52–67 (= the essay from which the book takes its title).

205. Ibid., 30, 63.

206. Ibid., 31, points to Gal. 1.23–24.

207. It hardly needs pointing out that if Galatians were to be dated before the Jerusalem Council, then Jervell's whole reconstruction would collapse.

It seems to me that the Achilles' heel of Jervell's construction may be a text to which he appeals, namely Gal. 1.23–24.[208] The period to which Paul's preaching the good news of the faith (εὐαγγελίζεται τὴν πίστιν) must refer is that when he was in "the regions of Syria and Cilicia" (Gal. 1.22), before Barnabas persuaded him to join him at Antioch. It is inconceivable, in the light of Galatians 1.15–17, that Paul was not preaching a law-free gospel in this period, while, furthermore, it is precisely on this score that Barnabas saw in him a suitable colleague and partner for the work at Antioch, which was a mixed congregation of Jews and Gentiles. It follows that the Judean churches, even if they had not seen Paul face to face, *could not have been uninformed of the kind of gospel which Paul was preaching.* Jervell's suggestion of a much later reaction against the preaching of a law-free gospel to Gentiles does not entirely carry conviction. While it is always good to have a new suggestion challenging old views and the stimulus provided by it, in this case the old views must still hold sway.

SUMMARY AND IMPLICATIONS

That Luke has written up the PA speech is to be accepted. We have examined whether he has used genuine Pauline material in his composition or whether he has totally composed the speech, in order to express his own views. Our discussion has shown that even where we may feel that Luke has "ploughed his own furrow," so to speak, there is quite often something (which we can observe) in the letters of Paul with which there is some accord. While Jervell probably goes too far in reacting against the views of those who see a different Paul in Acts, he has issued a timely warning, which should be heeded. The truth probably lies somewhere in between the two extremes. Luke has given us a portrait of Paul; it is recognisably Paul, but it is Paul as Luke saw him, and that is inevitable in the work of anyone writing any sort of history with the aim of helping his/her contemporaries. Why Luke presented Paul in the way in which he did will take us on to the theme of the next chapter.

My friend and former colleague and sometime Principal of Regent's Park College, Oxford, the Revd. Dr. B. R. White, a church historian with his specialisation in Baptist history, once said in my hearing: "You know, it is a remarkable thing, but you don't turn to Melanchthon for an understanding of Luther, nor to Beza for an appreciation of Calvin."[209] This was uttered, I

---

208. See note 206.

209. Melanchthon and Beza were very close associates of Luther and Calvin respectively.

may add, without any reference to Luke and Paul, but I have remembered the comment as an example of how a great man's associates may not always be his best interpreters.

Historians are well aware that it is impossible to write history without some bias obtruding in the interpreting of events, actions, and personalities, in the selection of evidence, etc. Herbert Butterfield's *The Whig Interpretation of History* showed a tendency on the part of British historians to portray those deemed to contribute to the advance of parliamentary democracy as the "good" people of British history. Maurice Ashley wrote three biographies of Oliver Cromwell in his career. The first was published in 1937 and was entitled *Oliver Cromwell, the Conservative Dictator* (the 30s saw the rise of dictators like Hitler, Mussolini, and Franco); then, in 1957 to mark the approaching tercentenary of Cromwell's death (1658—1958) he published *The Greatness of Oliver Cromwell*, in which Cromwell appeared as the parliamentary democrat; finally, he wrote *Oliver Cromwell and the Puritan Revolution* in the Teach Yourself History series, in 1958, where he portrayed Cromwell as a Puritan revolutionary. Three biographies of the same person by the same author and yet three different slants!

I would also like to mention that the Dutch Historian, Pieter Geyl, wrote a survey of scholarship on Napoleon, entitled *Napoleon: for and against* (London: Jonathan Cape, 1949. Rev. ed. 1964). Each French historian of the nineteenth century whose work on Napoleon was examined had a different understanding of him, which reflected the changes and disputes in French political life through the century. The facts were not in dispute; the interpretation of them differed. The scholarly methods of research were the same; the results obtained differed. The historian was deeply influenced by the situation in his own day.

I mention these examples from memory from my days as a history undergraduate at Oxford (1955-58). No doubt these examples could be extended from more recent writings. Even my examples are a warning to those of us who approach Biblical books. There is no such thing as wholly objective historical writing, neither in the past nor in the present. We should not expect Luke's portrait of Paul to be identical with Paul's own portrait of himself![210]

210. I have allowed this paragraph to stand, in spite of its inadequacies, but since penning it, I have at long last read Carr's *What is History?* Carr gives some examples of what I tried to illustrate, and from his far greater knowledge of historians of the past. He instances from the nineteenth century Grote's *History of Greece* and Mommsen's *History of Rome*; and from the twentieth century G. M. Trevelyan's *England under Queen Anne* and the German historian Meinecke, whose three histories of Germany written at different times reflected the different social and political fortunes of his country. Carr, *What is History?*, 44, made the comment: "Before you study the historian, study his historical and social environment" (36-44 are well worth reading).

Chapter 6

The Speech and Luke's Community

A final probe of the PA speech is to be directed to the issue of whether the speech throws any light on the situation of the congregation (s) for whom Luke wrote. Can we draw any conclusions as to the nature and composition of the congregation (s)? Obviously, care must be taken not to exaggerate the amount of material which one section of a total work can offer, and, as with other themes, any pointers from the PA speech must be related to the totality of LA.

Given the outcome of the PA speech and the opposition of the majority of the Jews from the PA synagogue, it is highly unlikely that any Jew professing faith in Jesus as Saviour (13.23), never mind any non-Jew with such convictions, would be welcome in the synagogue in Luke's neighbourhood. The probability is that we should reckon with the formation of a group of Christians, Jews and non-Jews, in PA *on the narrative level*, even though this is not mentioned in so many words.[1] Luke significantly remarks, after mentioning that Paul and Barnabas shook the dust of PA from off their feet[2]

---

1. So Roloff, *Apg.*, 210: "What remains [after the departure of Paul and Barnabas] is a flourishing congregation"; Jervell, *Apg.*, 365: "A congregation of Jews and God-fearing Gentiles had come into being in Antioch." Johnson, *Acts*, 243–44, believes that "joy and Holy Spirit" are code words indicating that "this foundation is an authentic realization of the Church." Fitzmyer, *Acts*, 522, is surely incorrect to think that Paul and Barnabas are meant by "the disciples" in v. 52.

2. This is the gesture to be performed, on the recommendation of Jesus, when a town had refused the message of his disciples—see the Mission Charges at Mark 6.11/Luke 9.5 and in Q at Luke 10.11/Matt. 10.14. It is a minatory gesture, enacting a negative verdict at the Last Judgment. See the Marcan mission charge which has εἰς μαρ-τύριον αὐτοῖς, which is a dative of disadvantage (Mark 6.11; with Luke 9.5 having εἰς

and departed for Iconium, that "the *disciples* were filled with joy and the Holy Spirit" (13.52).[3]

Assuming this surmise to be correct, it chimes in with the picture observable elsewhere in Acts. As an example, we may take what happened in Ephesus. Luke tells us that Paul conducted a ministry in the synagogue for the space of three months, but when the Jews refused to believe his message and went so far as to speak evil of the Way, Paul left the synagogue and separated the disciples (ἀφώρισεν τοὺς μαθητάς), and thereafter conducted his ministry in the lecture hall of one Tyrannus (19.9). That is, Paul established a specific Christian group in Ephesus.

Furthermore, whatever the historical problems with Luke's statement that Paul and Barnabas appointed elders in every congregation[4] as they retraced their footsteps from Derbe to Perga (14.21-26a), the picture which Luke wants the readers to get is that Christian congregations were formed separate from the synagogue in the towns visited by Paul and Barnabas on the first missionary journey.

One of the major themes in the PA speech is that Jesus represents the climax of God's dealings with the people elected by God (13.23, 32). He is the goal of "sacred history" or "salvation history." This stress also agrees with one of the major themes which runs through the whole of LA. This stress can answer the concerns and/or needs of both ethnic groups represented in the congregation(s) to which Luke wrote. It could be a word of assurance to those Jewish Christians who had now been turned away from the synagogue and were no longer welcome among their former co-religionists. They would be reassured that their decision to believe in Jesus was not misplaced, but in line with the plan of God to bring His saving purposes to a climax in Jesus. In reality, they had not been expelled from God's people, but were part of that people whom God had chosen from Abraham.

On the other hand, the fact that Paul and Barnabas had asserted that God intended His salvation to reach peoples at the ends of the earth (13. 47) would be encouraging to Gentile Christians. God had had them in mind from time immemorial. Furthermore, they were part of a people whom

---

μαρτύριον ἐπ᾽ αὐτούς).

3. The imperfect ἐπληροῦντο suggests an ongoing experience. The phrase "joy and the Holy Spirit" is hendiadys and means "joy inspired by the Holy Spirit."

4. Elders are nowhere mentioned in the undisputed Paulines, and only appear in the Pastorals, which are probably Trito-Pauline. Where Paul does mention titles of church officers, it is "apostles, prophets and teachers" in 1 Cor. 12.28 or "bishops and deacons" in Phil. 1.1. This is not to deny that any group would have some form of leadership (see, e.g., 1 Thess. 5.12; 1 Cor. 16.15-16; Gal. 6.6), but simply to state the oft repeated fact that elders are nowhere referred to outside of the Pastorals in the Pauline corpus.

God had chosen back in Abraham's day. They had not joined some newly invented religion but one which had ancient roots.

In addition to this encouragement that Christianity was not something which had recently appeared on the scene but had an ancient pedigree, there is the other side to the coin; namely, that Christianity has its roots in ancient Israel and that must not be forgotten.[5] Jesus is only fully intelligible against the background of the Old Testament and the Jewish faith. If God's plan purposed to embrace all nations, nonetheless that plan began with Israel and reached its fulfilment within Israel. Christianity cannot deny that umbilical cord which links it with the Old Testament and the Jewish faith.

We have already seen in Chapter 5 (4) how important the issue of Israel was for Luke. What Paul's speech at PA affirms fits in with the emphases of Luke elsewhere and there is no need for us to traverse the same ground again. The PA speech is harmonious with what Luke sought to get across throughout his work. It, therefore, confirms the view that Luke wrote for a congregation or congregations where there was a mixture of Jewish and non-Jewish Christians. The PA speech fits in with the view that Luke was not writing simply and solely for Gentile Christians. The Jewish Christian element was by no means negligible in his congregation (s).

The contribution of the PA speech to our sociological knowledge of the Lucan *Sitz im Leben* is small but significant.

---

5. Hence the priority of Israel in hearing the message that God had fulfilled His ancient promise, as indicated in 13.46 (note the πρῶτον. Compare Paul's insistence on this in Rom. 1.16; 2.9).

Chapter 7

Summary and Conclusions

We have in this study examined from different angles the speech which in Acts 13 is delivered by Paul at PA—rather like holding up a jewel and revolving it round and letting the light strike it from different angles, so revealing different facets of beauty in the jewel.

We first reviewed scholarly discussion of the so-called kerygmatic speeches in general in Acts and the PA speech in particular. This survey showed that in the post-war era initially scholarship seemed to line up behind either Dodd or Dibelius: either the kerygmatic speeches were held to represent the gist of what the Jerusalem church preached (some even went further and claimed they represented summaries of what Peter or Paul had preached on certain occasions), or they represented compositions of Luke and represented what he thought the church of his day ought to be preaching. As time progressed, a mediating position was espoused by many scholars, namely that while the final form of the speeches as we have them was indeed the work of Luke, he had incorporated into them traditional material. By careful attention to detail, they believed that it was possible to distinguish between tradition and redaction. More recently, scholars pursuing a narrative criticism approach have moved away from any attempt to distinguish between tradition and redaction, and have emphasized author's intention and readers' reception.

Several monographs have been written on the PA speech, together with numerous articles, in addition to treatments of it in the several commentaries published in the past sixty years or so. The broad division of opinion about the kerygmatic speeches in general is true also of this particular speech. Some scholars see this speech as emanating from Paul; others attribute it to Luke. The use of the OT quotations has been of particular interest: do they represent the kind of use of the OT which we might expect of a trained rabbi in the setting of a sermon delivered in the synagogue, or has Luke who was clearly well acquainted with the Septuagint brought these OT quotations together himself, or has he here taken over some material which he found within the tradition of the churches among which he had moved? There is considerable agreement in seeing the speech as related to 2 Sam. 7, the promise from God to David mediated through the prophet Nathan and "the charter document" of the Davidic ideology behind the Davidic dynasty. More recently, there has been considerable interest in examining Luke's portrait of Paul from the perspective of the reception of Pauline tradition in the post-Pauline period.

Our second chapter endeavoured to set the speech in its immediate and further context. We examined first the place of the PA speech in the missionary work of Paul and Barnabas described in Acts 13–14, commonly referred to as Paul's first missionary journey. Unquestionably, the speech occupies a crucially significant role within this section. Luke gives us a first detailed account of the preaching to Jews of the one who is the hero of the second half of Acts. Then we examined successively the relation of the speech to what had preceded it (Acts 1–12), what succeeded it (Acts 15–28), and to the whole of LA. This survey revealed how many are the links between the PA speech and the rest of Luke's double volume. These links demonstrate the closeness to each other of the Lord Jesus and the apostles Peter and Paul in the message they proclaimed. This unity is part of the assurance which Luke aimed to mediate to his readers/hearers about the Christian message in which they had been instructed.

Then, in chapter three, we proceeded to examine the structure of the speech and the various suggestions which have been put forward. It seemed best to adhere to a tripartite division of the speech: vv. 16–25; vv. 26–37; vv. 38–41. This division fastened on certain recurring phrases which broke up the speech:

ἄνδρες Ἰσραηλῖται καὶ οἱ φοβούμενοι τὸν Θεόν (v. 16);

ἄνδρες ἀδελφοί . . . καὶ οἱ ἐν ὑμῖν φοβούμενοι τὸν Θεόν (v. 26);

and ἄνδρες ἀδελφοί (v. 38).

These phrases introduce natural divisions within the speech's flow of thought. Thus, vv. 16–25 offer a selective history of God's dealings with Israel, leading up to David and the promise of a savior for Israel from one of his descendants, whose arrival had been announced by John the Baptist, namely Jesus. The next section, vv. 26–37, concentrates on how the rulers of Israel and the people of Jerusalem had rejected this promised savior, but God had raised him from the dead and bestowed on him incorruptible life so that he could dispense the blessings promised to David. This contrasting destiny at the hands of human beings and of God is in fact grounded on the will of God disclosed in the Scriptures. The third section, vv. 38–41, proclaims that as a result of the resurrection of Jesus, forgiveness of sins and justification before God can be offered through him to everyone who believes. But a stern warning is issued to those who refuse to acknowledge what God has done through Jesus and is doing in the present.

In this way, form and content dovetail into each other to produce a division of the speech which seems superior to other suggestions.

We also examined the links which seemed to exist between these three sections and which suggested a careful intention to link them together to assist the flow of thought.

Chapter Four took up the task of examining the speech section by section in order to see how far it is possible to determine whether Luke had made use of traditions available to him or whether he had freely composed the entire speech.

The selective survey of Israel's history running from the election of the patriarchs to the choice of king David, and passing from David to the promise and arrival of a descendant of his as the promised savior, Jesus, proved to be unlike any existing survey of Israel's history in the OT, the intertestamental literature or Jewish literature contemporaneous with or slightly later than the NT literature. Most covered from Egypt to Canaan, from the Exodus to entry into the land. That the survey should climax in David and the promise of a savior from his descendants proved virtually unique, with only Ps. 78 approaching the PA speech in this respect, with its climax in the choice of Judah (an anti-northern bias revealing itself in the idea of God's rejection of Joseph), Mount Zion, and David (78.68–72). But the whole ethos of Ps. 78 is very different from that of the PA speech. Although composition by Luke could not be ruled out completely, a case could be made out for its pre-Lucan composition.

The short sub-section on the role of John the Baptist (Acts 13.24–25) exhibited some variation from Luke's account of this in his Gospel. This could be due to a wish for stylistic variation, but could also be attributable to Luke's use of a slightly different tradition.

The second major section (vv. 26–37) begins with the account of the proceedings of the Jewish leaders and the people of Jerusalem against Jesus and their request to Pilate for his death. Clearly, Luke's hand is obvious here, as preaching to a completely strange congregation in a synagogue for the first time about Jesus would not commence with the last few hours of his life. Some account of his appearance on the scene, his preaching, his activity, the reasons for his clash with and ultimate rejection by the leadership of the nation and execution by the Romans would be absolutely necessary. This drastic abbreviation must be put down to Luke's account. The absence of any explanation of the atoning meaning of the death of Jesus, even along the lines of 1 Cor. 15.3 (a very old Christian confession), together with the non-exploitation of the "hung on a tree" motif, fits in with the general lack of such an interpretation throughout Luke's double volume, although the Lucan stress on Jesus as the fulfillment of the Isaianic Servant of the Lord and the twofold "for you" in the account of the institution of the Lord's Supper ought not to be underplayed either.

The emphasis on his Galilean disciples as witnesses (13.31) fitted in with the evidence elsewhere in LA on apostolic witness. Lucan shaping at this point seems evident, particularly in the light of the passionate defence in Paul's own letters of his equality with the original disciples in apostleship.

The block of OT quotations in the resurrection section, viz. Ps. 2.7; Isa. 55.3; and Ps. 16.10, is a striking feature of the speech. Here the arguments seemed tilted in favour of Luke's use of an earlier series of testimonia on the theme of the resurrection. The early Christian confession at 1 Cor. 15.4 asserted that the resurrection of Jesus by God was in accordance with the scriptures, and it is not surprising to come across an indication of early Christian work on the OT scriptures in an endeavour to convince fellow Jews that Jesus' resurrection was foretold in their scriptures. The brevity of the quotation from Ps. 16 might be due to Luke's having already used it extensively in Peter's speech on the day of Pentecost in Acts 2.

The final section of the speech (13.38-41) combines a positive and negative note. On the positive side, the hearers are assured that through this Jesus the forgiveness of sins, defined as justification (which the Law of Moses could not confer on anyone), is offered to everyone who believes. Here a Pauline flavour is given with the mention of justification, but, while claims that justification is set forth in an unPauline manner are somewhat exaggerated, nonetheless this is not quite typically Pauline in its mode of expression. The use of Hab. 1.5 to express a warning to the hearers against failing to discern the fact that God is doing a work in their midst is unique in the NT. While Paul made great use of Hab. 2.2 in both Galatians and Romans, and, therefore, would be acquainted with what was said at 1.5, he does not make use of this verse in his letters when dealing with the topic of either unbelief towards the preaching of the gospel about God's redeeming work in Jesus, or lack of response towards his particular interpretation of the implications of God's salvation within his congregations.

Lucan shaping of the PA speech is evident, not just at the level of language, but in abbreviation and compression, and in various emphasises or absence of them. At the same time, a case can be made out for Luke's use of older material in the survey of the God's dealings with Israel; in a contrast scheme between what humans did to Jesus and what God did to him in raising him from the dead; and in the use of the OT in connection with the resurrection of Jesus.

All this said in respect of Lucan shaping, it cannot be said that what we have before us is in all respects positively unPauline. If we miss the atoning understanding of the death of Jesus and if we would expect a reference to Paul's own experience of his encounter with the risen Jesus alongside the other appearances, we cannot rule out the possibility that in preaching to fellow Jews Paul might exploit the Davidic descent of Jesus and use the promise of 2 Sam. 7 in seeking to persuade fellow Jews that Jesus was God's promised saviour, or that he might emphasise forgiveness of sins in contexts where the issue of Gentile acceptance into the people of God was not at stake. The use of the OT, not just in the review of Israel's history, but also in connection with the resurrection and the warning not to ignore God's work, faithfully portray Paul as one steeped in the Scriptures of Israel and an able expositor of them.

Our fifth chapter was devoted to examining various theological themes which emerge from the PA speech and their relation to how Luke develops his message elsewhere in LA. We dealt with theology, christology, the use of the OT, the position of Israel, and the picture of Paul. We found that the themes developed in the PA speech cohere with what emerges about these same themes elsewhere in LA. Overall, the PA speech is theocentric. God is the God of history. His mighty acts are visible in the story of Israel, His people. He is the God whose plan is operating within history. What God has promised He has fulfilled. He is the God who saves and has done so pre-eminently through Jesus. He is the God of resurrection, who raised Jesus from the dead and intends His salvation to go to the ends of the earth. Any Christology is to be set within this overarching theocentricity.

Jesus is presented as the climax of God's dealings with Israel and the fulfillment of God's ancient promise to the fathers of the nation. He is a descendant of David; he is greater than John the Baptist; and through his resurrection God has declared that he is His Son. Completely innocent of the charges brought against him, he is in fact the Holy One and through the resurrection is permanently alive, free from corruption to which the rest of human beings are subject. He is the savior through whom every one who believes can receive forgiveness of sins and justification.

The use of the OT was our next theme. Though not formally quoted, there are substantial reasons for believing that 2 Sam. 7 underlies the PA speech. It may well determine what particular moments of Israel's history find a mention, and it is probably a fundamental part of what is understood by the reference to the "promise" in verses 23 and 26. The three quotations in the resurrection section of vv. 33–37 almost certainly are related to the promise made by God to David through Nathan. David is not only the ancestor of the promised savior but by implication in the PA speech he had prophetically foreseen the resurrection from the dead of his greater descendant. Given the prominence of the term "promise" in the PA speech, it is reasonable to think of the OT in terms of promise—i.e., it was pointing beyond itself and looking for its completion and fulfillment. The emphasis on the resurrection of Jesus is in harmony with the stress in later speeches by Paul that Israel's hope is precisely summed up in resurrection. Interestingly, of the six introductory formulae to quotations, four use the perfect tense and one the present (one uses the aorist), in this way pointing to the ongoing significance of the OT. The speech starts with the selective review of Israel's history and ends with the warning drawn from Hab. 1.5 not to ignore the work which God is doing in the present time. We also had a brief look at the theme of the Law of Moses. The PA speech indicates that the Law cannot grant a person justification before God; a person can only receive forgiveness and justification through Jesus and faith in him.

The theme of Israel in LA is a hotly debated issue and continues to elicit diametrically opposite assessments of how Luke regarded the Jewish people. In our discussion, we ranged over the whole of LA, and claimed that for Luke believing Jews together with believing Gentiles now comprise the true Israel. Though that phrase is not actually used, the substance of it seems to be present. As Simeon predicted, Israel has been divided by the coming and preaching of Jesus. That is true of what happened after the PA speech. We believe that the final scene of Acts is not recording a definite rejection of the Jewish people.

Our last section in this chapter was devoted to looking at Luke's picture of Paul. We concluded that while there are some differences between Luke's portrait of Paul compared with the picture of Paul which emerges from his letters, we cannot dismiss Luke's portrait out of hand. What Luke gives us is how he saw Paul, and that does not necessarily mean the way Paul saw himself. The fact that we have no record of how Paul might preach the Gospel to his fellow Jews is a major handicap for us in our attempt to assess the PA speech.

Our penultimate chapter was an exploration of whether the PA speech offered us any clues to the nature of the congregation or congregations to which Luke was writing. We argued that on the narrative level we could assume the formation of a Christian congregation separate from the synagogue as a result of the PA speech (a pattern repeated elsewhere in the Pauline mission as recorded in Acts) and led by elders. Judging by the sequel to the speech, it would be a mixed congregation of both Jewish and Gentile Christians. To Jewish Christians in Luke's congregation or congregations, who would no longer be welcome in the synagogue, the PA speech would bring assurance and comfort. Faith in Jesus was in line with God's ancient purpose and His saving acts for Israel. Jesus was in fact the fulfillment of what God had promised in the past. They were still part of God's people. But for Gentile Christians, the PA speech would also bring encouragement. In believing in Jesus and joining the community of believers, they were becoming part of the people of God which stretched back centuries and which had an ancient pedigree. They would also be reminded that there was a link with Israel, its history, and the acts and promises of God contained within it, and that link could not be set aside. This is part of what has recently been called "the reception of the Pauline tradition" in the era after Paul's death.

In its theological themes, the PA speech fits in nicely with Luke's theological emphasises discernible throughout LA. It occupies a key place in Luke's strategy in his double volume.

Appendix

Other Summaries of Israel's History

We shall here briefly review the passages which involve some kind of a summary of Israel's history but which we excluded in our survey on pp. 79-82. This will, it is hoped, further underline the special character of the PA speech's review of Israel's history. It will act, therefore, as a justification for the earlier exclusion, but also give the reader the opportunity of looking at these passages for themselves and making their own verdict.

SIRACH[1]

Chapters 44-50 is a section in praise of the famous men in Israel's history. Enoch, Noah, Abraham, Moses, Aaron, Phinehas, Joshua, Caleb, Samuel, David, Solomon, Elijah, Elisha, Hezekiah, Josiah, Zerrubabel, and the high priest Simon, are mentioned. These are the people through whom God "established His renown and revealed His majesty." While God is mentioned a great deal, the focus of attention is not so much on His mighty deeds as on these great figures who are models to be imitated.

---

1. The Wisdom of Jesus ben Sirach or Ecclesiasticus was written by a professional scribe in Jerusalem during the first quarter of the second century BC (see 50.27). The original was in Hebrew and it was translated into Greek by his grandson in Egypt near the end of the second century BC, so he informs us in the Preface (Nickelsburg, *Jewish Literature*, 64-65).

Appendix

1 ENOCH

The section 93.1-14; 91.12-17² is referred to as *The Apocalypse of Weeks*.² The so-called weeks are periods of varying length. The first seven weeks are already past; the final three are still to come. Each of the seven weeks has been marked by some important event, often towards its close. The first period is up to and including the birth of Enoch (93.3); the second week is one of human wickedness with Noah being the exception (93.4); the third week sees the election of Abraham, "the plant of righteous judgment" (93.5). This is followed by the fourth week, which alludes to the time in Egypt and the giving of the Law (93.6). The fifth week ends with the building of the Temple (93.7). Wickedness during the divided kingdoms marks the sixth week, with Elijah's ascent, the burning of the Temple, and the captivity in Babylon (93.8). The seventh week is the apostasy from the exile to author's day, in which the elect righteous will arise (93.9-10). During week eight, the righteous will destroy the oppressors and build a new Temple (91.12-13). This is followed by the ninth week of righteous judgment and the destruction of all ungodliness from the earth (9.14). The final week is the destruction of the fallen angels and the creation of new heavens, and sin will be no more (91.15-17).

Although there may be a cursory run through of Israel's history, its difference from the PA speech is obvious straightway.

1 Enoch 83-93

Within this section of 1 Enoch, chapters 85-90 are the second dream-vision and are called the *"Animal Apocalypse."*³ They begin by describing the human characters of the early chapters of Genesis as bulls, heifers, cows, and oxen of various colors and the fallen angels as fallen stars. The first period of world history runs up to the Flood (85-89.9); then comes the period up to Jacob, Israel being depicted under the imagery of sheep (89.10-15). The third period is that of the history of Israel up to the fall of Jerusalem

---

2. 1 Enoch 91.12-17 clearly goes with 93, and this has been confirmed by the Aramaic fragments found at Qumran (Nickelsburg, *Jewish Literature*, 157 n. 140, referring to Milik, *Books of Enoch*, 260-70). Nickelsburg, *Jewish Literature*, 150, dates the so-called epistle of Enoch (chapters 92-105) to early in the second century BC and that together with chapters 1-36 it may have formed the major parts of an Enochic testament, with chapters 81-82 and 91 forming a narrative bridge between the two parts (*Jewish Literature*, 150).

3. Nickelsburg, *Jewish Literature*, 93, believes that the apocalypse was written or revised during the campaigns of Judas Maccabaeus, i.e., between 164 and 160.

(89.16–67). During this period, the sheep either go astray or are oppressed by wild beasts (= the Gentiles), seen as punishment for their apostasy. Fourthly, there is the period of the "exile" which runs from the destruction of Jerusalem to the Maccabean Revolt (89.68—90.15).[4] The fifth period is that of the Last Judgment and the Messianic Kingdom (90.20–42).

This review of Israel history is markedly different from that in Acts 13. It is considerably longer; it starts with Adam and ends with the Last Judgment and the Messianic Kingdom; it uses allegory (depicting characters by means of animals); the focus is not so much on God's mighty deeds as the fate of Israel, indeed, we meet the imagery of shepherds standing for angels to whom after the destruction of Jerusalem God delegates His rule over Israel.

1 MACCABEES[5]

2.52–60 is part of the dying Mattathias's speech to his sons, in which he exhorts them "Be zealous for the law and give your lives for the covenant of your fathers. Remember the deeds they did in their generations, and great glory and eternal fame shall be yours" (2.51). The names which follow are Abraham v. 52; Joseph v. 53; Phinehas, v. 54; Joshua, v. 55; Caleb, v. 56; David, v. 57; Elijah, v. 58; the three young men and Daniel, v. 60. While the sons are reminded that no one who trusts in heaven will ever lack strength, the stress is undoubtedly on the human figures worthy of imitation.

3 MACCABEES[6]

2.2–20 is part of the response of the high priest, Simon, to King Ptolemy of Egypt's desire to enter the Holy of Holies in the Jerusalem Temple. What we have is a number of examples from the past where similar incidents have aroused the anger of the God of Israel with dire consequences for those who transgressed God's law in this way. Simon declares that the Creator God is

---

4. Charles, *APOT*, 256–60, divides the period from the destruction of Jerusalem to the Maccabean Revolt into four periods, on the grounds that this is the time of the rule of the seventy shepherds.

5. Nickelsburg, *Jewish Literature*, 117, dates to ca. 104–63 BC. Our passage is more of a list of famous men, who were outstanding examples of steadfastness under trial and whose example is to be followed.

6. Nickelsburg, *Jewish Literature*, 171–72, dates it to either before 77 BC or 20–15 BC. Anderson, in Charlesworth, *OTP*, 2:512, suggests between 217 BC and 70 AD, while himself favouring early first century. Barclay, *Jews*, 448, suggests a date at the end of the first century BC (following Tcherikover, *Hellenistic Civilisation and the Jews*).

just (vv. 2–3); He punished the giants with the flood (v. 4); He destroyed Sodom by fire (v. 5); He defeated Pharaoh and destroyed his army at the Reed Sea (vv. 6–8); He chose Zion and sanctified the temple (v. 9).

DAMASCUS DOCUMENT (CD)[7]

At 2.14—6.11, the author indicates his intention to help his "sons" to understand the works of God, so that they might choose what pleases Him and reject what He hates. Even great men and mighty heroes have in the past gone astray and followed evil ways. A didactic intention is uppermost. The author's illustrations include the fall and punishment of the heavenly watchers and the giants and humanity. Even Noah's children went astray. By contrast, Abraham, Isaac, and Jacob obeyed, but Jacob's descendants disobeyed when they were in Egypt. At Kadesh God's anger was provoked and He punished them. God confirmed the covenant with those who were faithful and gave the law concerning the sabbath, established the priesthood [the Zadokites] and later confirmed it through Ezekiel. Later, faithful priests and Levites left Judah [and migrated to Damascus]. God raised up men of discernment from this group of priests who interpreted the Law and founded the community at Qumran.

This is a highly selective review of Israel's story (so selective indeed that one wonders whether really the passage ought to be included in this genre), designed to lead up to the founding of the community at Qumran. While this is God's purpose, nonetheless there is no reflection on the mighty act of redemption from Egypt. The attention is directed to a contrast between those who were disobedient and those who were faithful whom God rewarded with an understanding of His will.

2 BARUCH[8]

This work, written after the destruction of Jerusalem in 70 AD, grapples with some of the problems raised for a devout Jew by God's punishment and apparent abandonment of His people. Chapters 56–74 are the interpretation of a vision given to Baruch. Alternate black and white waters symbolise

---

7. Vermes, *DSSE*, 95, suggests a date of about 100 BC; Nickelsburg, *Jewish Literature*, 124, dates to 100–75 BC.

8. In view of the references to the destruction of Jerusalem, to be dated after AD 70: Nickelsburg, *Jewish Literature*, 287 ("toward the end of the first century"), while Klijn, in Charlesworth, *OTP*, 1:617, puts it slightly later, in the first or second decade of the second century.

periods of wickedness and righteousness during the history of the world and Israel. The pairs are the fall of Adam and the fall of the wicked angels (56) followed by the obedience of Abraham (57). The wickedness among the Egyptians and their oppression of Israelites (58) is suceeded by the advent of Moses, Aaron, Miriam, Joshua, and Caleb, and the gift of the law (59). Then comes infidelity in the time of the judges (60), after which there was the era of David and Solomon and the founding of Zion (61). From the reign of Jeroboam to the fall of the northern kingdom (62) is a period of idolatrous apostasy, contrasted with the reign of Hezekiah and the deliverance of Zion from Sennacherib (63). The wicked reign of Manasseh (64-65) is balanced by that of Josiah (66). The destruction of Zion by the king of Babylon is discussed (67), to be followed by the final "bright waters," which includes the evil times before the End, during which, however, the Holy Land will be protected (69-70) and then comes the glorious Reign of the Messiah (72-74).

The periodization of history under God's control is a means whereby the author seeks to encourage the faithful to hang on in the difficult days following the destruction of Jerusalem and the Temple in AD 70.

4 *EZRA* 3-14[9]

This Jewish Apocalypse opens with Ezra troubled and perplexed over "the desolation of Zion and the prosperity of those who lived in Babylon" and he turns in lament to God. In his prayer he reviews the story of humanity and Israel from Adam to the exile in Babylon. He begins with the creation of Adam who disobeyed the one command which God had given him (3.4-7). Later, he describes Adam as "burdened with a wicked heart; he sinned, and was overcome, and not only he but all his descendants. So the weakness became inveterate" (3.21-22a). Human beings sinned, and each nation went its own way, sinning against God, and God "did not stop them" (3.8), until He destroyed the earth by the Flood, sparing one man, Noah (3.7b-11). God then chose Abraham and made an everlasting covenant with him. God rescued Jacob's descendants from Egypt and on Mount Sinai gave them the Law. But God "did not take away their wicked heart and enable Your law to bear fruit in them . . . Although Your law was in your people's hearts, a rooted wickedness was there too; so that the good came to nothing and what

---

9. The Jewish Apocalypse, 4 Ezra 3-14, is, in view of the references to the destruction of Jerusalem, to be dated some time after AD 70. See Nicklesburg, *Jewish Literature*, 287, 293 ("the end of the first century") and Metzger, "The Fourth Book of Ezra" in Charlesworth, *OTP* 1:517 (1:520 - "at the latest not much after AD 120").

was bad persisted" (3.20, 22). Then Ezra mentions that God raised up David and ordered him to build the city which bears God's name and offer sacrifice there. Eventually its inhabitants went astray like Adam ("for they had the same wicked heart") and God gave over Jerusalem to its enemies (vv. 23–26). Ezra has personally experienced the greater moral wickedness of the inhabitants of Babylon (vv. 27–29), which raises for Ezra the acute problem of why God allows the wicked to flourish and why He has destroyed His own people: "Is Babylon more virtuous than Zion?" (v. 31), he asks God. "So weigh our sins in the balance against the sins of the rest of the world and it will be clear which way the scale tips" (v. 34).

Although certain historical events are mentioned, the real issue is theodicy. God's rule in this world seems called in question by what He has done or not done. There is no celebration of the mighty acts of the sovereign Lord. The logic behind His ways seems inscrutable.

4 *Ezra* 14.29–33 also includes a brief survey of Israel's history. Ezra is warned by God that he is nearing the end of his days (14.9), and also that nine and a half of the divisions of history have already passed, leaving two and a half only still to come (v. 12). The world is growing older, and evils will increase. Ezra should warn his people (vv. 13–18). Before he commits his visions and their interpretation to writing, Ezra summons the people and addresses them. He recalls that their ancestors lived in Egypt as foreigners (v. 29). They were rescued (by God), and were given the law, which, however, they disobeyed, and Ezra's contemporaries have followed their example (vv. 30–31a). They were given the land of Zion, but yet again Israel did not keep God's commands and God took the Land away from them, and so they find themselves in exile (vv. 31b–33). But if they will discipline themselves in God's ways, they will be kept safe in life and be raised to life hereafter (vv. 34–36).

In this short résumée, the stress is on Israel's disobedience and failure to keep God's commands, with the inevitable consequence of receiving God's just judgment. God's actions in Israel's favour are "concealed" within the "divine passive" (vv. 30–31), but Ezra is explicit about God's action as the just judge in imposing exile on His disobedient people.

In all these passages, the only references to David are those in 1 Maccabees 2.57 where his inner quality and reward are mentioned: he "was a man of loyalty and was granted the throne of an everlasting kingdom";[10] in the

10. See Pomykala, *Davidic Dynasty Tradition*, 152–59, for the arguments that "everlasting" is an incorrect translation and that εἰς αἰῶνας should be translated as "for a long time"—a supporter of the Hasmonean House would not wish to claim that the

Damascus Document, where, however, the sole mention is David's sin in sexual and marital matters, because he had not read the Book of the Law concealed in the Ark and not discovered till Josiah's reign; and in 2 Baruch and 4 Ezra, where he figures as the one who was associated with Zion/Jerusalem, where God's Temple was built.

Within the NT, there is in *Hebrews 11* a catalogue of the "faithful" of the OT era. The author prefaces each one with "by faith" (πίστει). He mentions Abel (over against Cain), v. 4; Enoch, vv. 5-6; Noah, v. 7; Abraham and Sarah,[11] vv. 8-12, 17-19; Isaac, Jacob, and Joseph, vv. 20-22; Moses, vv. 23-29; the fall of Jericho and Rahab, vv. 30-31. At this point, excusing himself on the grounds of lack of time, he simply mentions the names of Gideon, Barak, Samson, Jepththa, David, Samuel, and the prophets, and then summarises the exploits of others not mentioned by name in vv. 33-38. The list finally culminates in Jesus himself (12.2).[12] While at times the phrase "by faith" seems rather forced, nonetheless the focus is on what the individuals achieved by their sticking at it in the great race of faith.[13]

Hebrews 11, then, is really a catalogue of the heroes of Israel rather than God's mighty deeds. In its present form, "faith" is a *Leitmotiv* of the chapter. There is no stress on God's activity from Exodus to Conquest nor on the Davidic monarchy as such.

From the brief comments made on these passages, we feel justified in excluding them from our survey of the background of "reviews of Israel's history" as potential sources or inspiration for the review which we find in the PA speech in Acts 13.

Davidic dynasty was eternal.

11. Reading στεῖρα after καὶ αὐτὴ Σάρρα with P46 D* lat syr—"though Sarah herself was barren." See Black, *Aramaic Approach*, 83-89, on circumstantial clauses.

12. The translation which makes Jesus "the pioneer and perfecter of *our* faith" must be challenged. Not only is ἡμῶν not in the text, but this translation imports into πίστις a sense at variance with its meaning throughout chapter 11. In 12.2 Jesus is himself envisaged as one who exercised πίστις—he both began and completed the race of faith.

13. See Grasser, *Glaube im Hebraerbrief* for a discussion of the nuance of πίστις in the letter to the Hebrews.

Bibliography

Alexander, Loveday. *The Preface to Luke's Gospel: Literary Convention and Social Context in Luke 1.1-4 and Acts 1.1.* SNTSMS 78. Cambridge: Cambridge University Press, 1993.

Alexander, P. S. "Midrash and the Gospels." In *Synoptic Studies. The Ampleforth Conferences of 1982 and 1983*, edited by C. M. Tuckett, 1-18. JSNTSS 7. Sheffield: JSOT, 1984.

Anderson, K. *"'But God Raised Him from the Dead.' The Theology of Jesus's Resurrection in Luke-Acts."* PBM. Carlisle: Paternoster, 2006.

Atkinson, K. R. "On the Use of Scripture in the Development of Militant Davidic Messianism at Qumran: New Light from the Psalm of Solomon." In *The Interpretation of Scripture in Early Judaism and Christianity: Studies in Language and Tradition*, edited by C. Evans, 106-23. London: T. & T. Clark, 2004.

Aune, D. E. *The New Testament in Its Literary Environment.* Cambridge: James Clarke, 1988.

Bachmann, M. "Die Stephanusepisode (Apg. 6.1—8.3). Ihre Bedeutung für die lukanische Sicht des Jerusalemischen Tempels und des Judentums." In *The Unity of Luke-Acts*, edited by J. Verheyden, 545-62. BETL 142. Leuven: Leuven University Press, 1999.

Barrett, C. K. "Apollos and the Twelve Disciples at Ephesus." In *The New Testament Age: Essays in Honor of B. Reicke*, edited by W. C. Weinrich, 29-39. Macon, GA: Mercer University Press, 1984.

———. *A Critical and Exegetical Commentary on the Acts of the Apostles.* 2 vols. ICC. Edinburgh: T. & T. Clark, 1994, 1998.

———. *The Epistle to the Romans.* London: A. & C. Black, 1962.

———. *The First Epistle to the Corinthians.* London: A. & C. Black, 1968.

———. *From First Adam to Last: A Study in Pauline Theology.* London: A. & C. Black, 1962.

———. *Luke the Historian in Recent Study.* London: Epworth, 1961.

———. *New Testament Essays.* London: SPCK, 1972.

———. "Old Testament History according to Stephen and Paul." In *Studien zum Text und zur Ethik des Neuen Testaments. Festschrift für H. Greeven*, edited by W. Schrage, 57-69. New York: de Gruyter, 1986.

———. *On Paul: Essays on His Life, Work and Influence in the Early Church.* New York: T. & T. Clark, 2003.

———. "Theologia Crucis—in Acts?" In *Theologia Crucis—Signum Crucis. Festschrift für E. Dinkler,* edited by C. Andresen and G. Klein, 73-84, Tübingen: Mohr, 1979.

Bauckham, R. "Kerygmatic Summaries in the Speeches of Acts." In *History, Literature and Society in the Book of Acts,* edited by B. Witherington, 185-217. Cambridge: Cambridge University Press, 1996.

Bechard, D. P. *Paul Outside the Walls: A Study of Luke's Socio-Geographical Universalism in Acts 14.8-20.* AB 143. Rome: Pontifical Biblical Institute, 2000.

Best, E. *A Commentary on the First and Second Epistles to the Thessalonians.* BNTC. London: A. & C. Black, 1972.

Betz, H. D. *Galatians.* Hermeneia. Philadelphia: Fortress, 1979.

Beutler, J. "Die paulinische Heidenmission am Vorabend des Apostelkonzils. Zur Redaktionsgeschichte von Apg. 14.1-20." *TP* 43 (1968) 360-83.

Blass, F., and A. Debrunner. *A Greek Grammar of the New Testament.* Translated and revised by R. W. Funk. Chicago: University of Chicago Press, 1961.

Bock, D. L. *Proclamation from Prophecy and Pattern. Lucan Old Testament Christology.* JSNTSS 12. Sheffield: JSOT, 1987.

Bonnard, P. *L'Épitre de saint Paul aux Galates.* CNT 9. Neuchâtel-Paris: Delachaux & Niestlé, 1953.

Bonz, Marianne Palmer. *The Past as Legacy: Luke-Acts and Ancient Epic.* Minneapolis: Fortress, 2000.

Borgen P. *Early Christianity and Hellenistic Christianity.* Edinburgh: T. & T. Clark, 1996.

———. "From Paul to Luke: Observations toward Clarification of the Theology of Luke-Acts." *CBQ* 31 (1969) 168-82.

Böttrich, C. "Proexistenz im Leben und Sterben. Jesu Tod bei Lukas." In *Deutungen des Todes Jesu im Neuen Testament,* edited by J. Frey and J. Schröter, 413-36. WUNT 181. Tübingen: Mohr Siebeck, 2005.

Bovon, F. *Luke the Theologian: Thirty-Three Years of Research (1950-1983).* Allison Park, PA: Pickwick, 1987.

———. "'Schön hat der heilige Geist durch den Propheten Jesaja zu euren Vätern gesprochen' (Act 28.25)." *ZNW* 75 (1984) 226-32.

———. *Studies in Early Christianity.* Grand Rapids: Baker Academic, 2005.

Brawley, R. L. *Centering on God: Method and Message of Luke Acts.* Literary Currents in Biblical Interpretation. Louisville: Westminster John Knox, 1990.

———. "The God of Promises and the Jews in Luke-Acts." In *Literary Studies in Luke-Acts: Essays in Honor of J. B. Tyson,* edited by R. P. Thompson and T. E. Thomas, 279-96, Macon, GA: Mercer University Press, 1998.

———. *Luke-Acts and the Jews: Conflict, Apology, and Conciliation.* SBLMS 33. Atlanta: Scholars, 1987.

Brooke, G. J. *Exegesis at Qumran. 4 QFlorilegium in its Jewish Context.* JSOTSS 29. Atlanta: SBL, 2006.

Brooks, J. A., and C. L. Winbery. *Syntax of NT Greek.* Washington, DC: University Press of America, 1979.

Brown, S. *Apostasy and Perseverance in the Theology of Luke.* AB 36. Rome: Pontifical Biblical Institute, 1969.

Bruce, F. F. *The Book of Acts.* NLCNT. London: Marshall, Morgan & Scott, 1954.

———. *The Epistle to the Galatians.* NIGNC. Exeter: Paternoster, 1982.

———. "Is the Paul of Acts the Real Paul?" *BJRL* 58 (1976) 282-305.

———. "Paul's Use of the Old Testament in Acts." In *Tradition and Interpretation in the New Testament. Essays in Honor of E. Earle Ellis*, edited by G. F. Hawthorne with O. Betz, 71–79. Grand Rapids: Eerdmans, 1987.

———. "The Speeches in Acts—Thirty Years After." In *Reconciliation and Hope: New Testament Essays on Atonement and Eschatology Presented to L. Morris*, edited by R. Banks, 71–79. Exeter: Paternoster, 1974.

———. *The Speeches in the Acts of the Apostles*. Tyndale Lecture 1942. London: Tyndale, 1944.

Burchard, C. *Der dreizehnte Zeuge: traditions- und kompositionsgeschichtliche Untersuchungen zu Lukas' Darstellung der Fruhzeit des Paulus*. FRLANT 103. Göttingen: Vandenhoeck & Ruprecht, 1970.

Burger, C. *Jesus als Davidssohn. Eine traditionsgeschichtliche Untersuchung* FRLANT 98. Gottingen: Vandenhoeck & Ruprecht, 1970.

Buss, M. F.-J. *Die Missionspredigt des Apostels Paulus im Pisidischen Antiochen*. FzB 38. Stuttgart: KBW, 1980.

Busse, U. "Das 'Evangelium des Lukas.' Die Funktion der Vorgeschichte im lukanischen Doppelwerk." In *Der Treue Gottes trauen. Beiträge zum Werk des Lukas*, edited by C. Bussmann and W. Radl, 161–79. Freiburg-Basel-Wien: Herder, 1991.

Bussmann, C., and W. Radl. *Der Treue Gottes trauen. Beiträge zum Werk des Lukas*. Freiburg-Basel-Wien: Herder, 1991.

Butticaz, S. "'Has God Rejected His People?' (Romans 11.1). The Salvation of Israel in Acts: Narrative Claim of a Pauline Legacy." In *Paul and the Heritage of Israel: Paul's Claim upon Israel's Legacy in Luke and Acts in the Light of the Pauline Letters*, edited by D. P. Moessner et al., 148–64. LNTS 452. London: T. & T. Clark, 2012.

Cadbury, H. J. *The Book of Acts in History*. London: Adam & Charles Black, 1955.

———. *The Making of Luke-Acts*. London: SPCK, 1927.

———. "The Speeches in Acts." In *The Beginnings of Christianity, Part I: The Acts of the Apostles: Additional Notes to the Commentary*, edited by K. Lake and H. J. Cadbury, 5:402-27. London: Macmillan, 1933.

———. *The Style and Literary Method of Luke*. HTS 6. New York: Kraus Reprint, 1969.

Caird, G. B. "'Uncomfortable Words' II: Shake off the Dust from Your Feet." *ExT* 81 (1969) 40–43.

Callan, T. "The Preface of Luke-Acts and Historiography." *NTS* 31 (1985) 576–81.

Carr, E. H. *What is History?* Harmondsworth, UK: Penguin, 1990.

Carson, D. A., et al. *Justification and Variegated Nomism*. Vol. 1, *The Complexities of Second Temple Judaism*. Tübingen: Mohr Siebeck, 2001.

———. *Justification and Variegated Nomism*. Vol. 2, *The Paradoxes of Paul*. Tübingen: Mohr Siebeck, 2004.

Cassidy, R. J. *Society and Politics in the Acts of the Apostles*. Maryknoll, NY: Orbis, 1987.

Cassidy, R. J., and P. J. Scharper. *Political Issues in Luke-Acts*. Maryknoll, NY: Orbis, 1983.

Cerfaux, L. *Le Christ dans la Théologie de saint Paul*. LD 6. Paris: Les Éditions du Cerf, 1952.

Charles, R. H., ed. *The Apocrypha and Pseudepigrapha of the Old Testament in English*. 2 vols. Oxford: Clarendon, 1913.

Charlesworth, J. H., ed. *Old Testament Pseudepigrapha*. 2 vols. ABRL. New York: Doubleday, 1983, 1985.

Cifrak, M. *Die Beziehung zwischen Jesus und Gott nach den Petrusreden der Apostelgeschichte. Ein exegetischer Beitrag zur Christologie der Apostelgeschichte.* FzB 101. Würzburg: Echter, 2003.

Clark, A. C. *Parallel Lives: The Relation of Paul to the Apostles in the Lucan Perspective.* PBTM. Carlisle: Paternoster, 2001.

Clements, R. E. *Abraham and David: Genesis 15 and Its Meaning for Israelite Tradition.* SBT 2.5. London: SCM, 1967.

———. *Isaiah 1–39.* NCBC. Grand Rapids: Eerdmans, 1980.

Collins, J. J. *The Scepter and the Star: The Messiahs of the Dead Sea Scrolls and Other Ancient Literature.* New York: Doubleday, 1995.

Conzelmann, H. *Acts of the Apostles.* Hermeneia. Philadelphia: Fortress, 1987.

———. "The Address of Paul on the Areopagus." In *Studies in Luke-Acts: Essays Presented in Honor of Paul Schubert*, edited by L. E. Keck and J. L. Martyn, 217–30. Nashville: Abingdon, 1966.

———. *An Outline of New Testament Theology.* London: SCM, 1969.

———. *The Theology of Saint Luke.* London: Faber and Faber, 1960.

———. Χαίρω, κτλ. In *TDNT* 9.366-72.

Cosgrove, C. H. "The Divine DEI in Luke-Acts." *NT* 26 (1984) 168–90.

Cranfield, C. E. B. *Romans 1–8 and Romans 9–16.* ICC. Edinburgh: T. & T. Clark, 1975, 1979.

Cullmann, O. *The Christology of the New Testament.* London: SCM, 1959.

Dahl, N. A. "The Atonement—An Adequate Reward for the Akedah? (Ro 8:32)." In *Neotestamentica et Semitica: Studies in Honour of Matthew Black*, edited by E. E. Ellis and M. Wilcox, 15–29. Edinburgh: T. & T. Clark, 1969.

———. "The Story of Abraham in Luke-Acts." In *Studies in Luke-Acts*, edited by K. E. Keck and J. L. Martyn, 139–58. Nashville: Abingdon, 1966.

Delebecque, E. *Les Actes des Apôtres.* Paris: Belles Lettres, 1982.

De Boer, M. C. "God-Fearers in Luke-Acts." In *Luke's Literary Achievement. Collected Essays*, edited by C. M. Tuckett, 50–71. JSNTSS 116. Sheffield: Sheffield Academic Press, 1995.

Degenhardt, H.-J. *Lukas Evangelist der Armen: Besitz und Besitzverzicht in den lukanischen Schriften.* Stuttgart: KBS, 1965.

Delling, G. "Die Jesusgeschichte in der Verkündigung nach Acta." *NTS* 19 (1972–73) 373–89.

Denova, Rebecca. *The Things Accomplished among Us: Prophetic Tradition in the Structural Pattern of Luke-Acts.* JSNTSS 141. Sheffield: Sheffield Academic Press, 1997.

Deutschmann, A. *Synagoge und Gemeindebildung. Christliche Gemeinde und Israel am Beispiel von Apg 13, 42—52.* BU 30. Regensburg: Friedrich Pustet, 2001.

Dibelius, M. *From Tradition to Gospel.* Paperback ed. New York: Scribners, 1934.

———. *Studies in the Acts of the Apostles.* London: SCM, 1956.

Dietrich, W. *Das Petrusbild der lukanischen Schriften.* BWANT 5/14. Stuttgart: Kohlhammer, 1972.

Dietzfelbinger, C. *Der Abschied des Kommenden. Eine Auslegung der johanneischen Abschiedsreden.* WUNT 95. Tübingen: Mohr Siebeck, 1997.

———. *Die Berufung des Paulus als Ursprung seiner Theologie.* WMANT 58. Neukirchen-Vluyn: Neukirchener, 1985.

Dillistone, F. W. *C. H. Dodd: Interpreter of the New Testament*. Grand Rapids: Eerdmans, 1977.
Dillon, R. J. "Easter Revelation and Mission Program in Luke 24.46–48." In *Sin, Salvation and the Spirit*, edited by D. Durken, 240–70. Collegeville, MA: Liturgical, 1979.
———. "The Prophecy of Christ and His Witnesses according to the Discourses of Acts." *NTS* 32 (1986) 544–56.
Doble, P. *The Paradox of Salvation: Luke's Theology of the Cross*. SNTSMS 87. Cambridge: Cambridge University Press, 1996.
Dodd, C. H. *The Apostolic Preaching and Its Developments*. London: Hodder & Stoughton, 1944.
———. *Historical Tradition in the Fourth Gospel*. Cambridge: Cambridge University Press, 1963.
Doeve, J. W. *Jewish Hermeneutics in the Synoptic Gospels and Acts*. Assen: Van Gorcum, 1953.
Dömer, M. *Das Heil Gottes. Studien zur Theologie des lukanischen Doppelwerkes*. BBB 51. Köln-Bonn: Peter Hanstein, 1978.
Downing, F. G. "Common Ground with Paganism in Luke and Josephus." *NTS* 28 (1982) 546–60.
———. "Ethical Pagan Theism and the Speeches in Acts." *NTS* 27 (1980–81) 544–63.
Duling, D. C. "The Promises to David and their Entrance into Christianity—Nailing Down a Likely Hypothesis." *NTS* 20 (1973–74) 55–77.
Dumais, M. *Le Langage de l'Évangélisation: l'annonce missionaire en milieu juif (Actes 13, 16–41)*. TR 16. Montreal: Bellarmin, 1976.
Dunn, J. D. G. *The Acts of the Apostles*. Epworth Commentaries. Peterborough: Epworth, 1996.
———. *Baptism in the Holy Spirit*. SBT 2/15. London: SCM, 1970.
———. *Christianity in the Making*. Vol. 1, *Jesus Remembered*. Grand Rapids: Eerdmans, 2003.
———. *Christianity in the Making*. Vol. 2, *Beginning from Jerusalem*. Grand Rapids: Eerdmans, 2009.
———. *Christology in the Making*. London: SCM, 1975.
———. "Jesus—Flesh and Spirit: An Exposition of Romans 1.3–4." *JTS* 24 (1973) 40–68.
———. *The New Perspective on Paul*. Rev. ed. Grand Rapids: Eerdmans, 2008.
———. *Romans 1–8* and *Romans 9–16*. WBC 38A and B. Dallas: Word, 1988.
Dupont, J. *Études sur les Actes des Apôtres*. LD 45. Paris: Les Editions du Cerf, 1967.
———. "Je batirai la cabane de David qui est tombée (Ac 15, 16 = Am 9, 11)." In *Glaube und Eschatologie: Festschrift für Werner Georg Kümmel*, edited by E. Grässer and O. Merk, 19–32. Tübingen: Mohr, 1985.
———. *Nouvelles Études sur les Actes des Apôtres*. LD 118. Paris: Les Editions du Cerf, 1984.
———. "Le Salut des Gentiles et la significance théologique du Livre des Actes." *NTS* 6 (1959–60) 132–55 (= *Études*, 393–415).
———. "'Le Seigneur de tous' (Ac 10: 36; Rom 10: 12): Arrière-fond scripturaire d'une formule christologique." In *Tradition and Interpretation in the New Testament: Essays in Honor of E. Earle Ellis*, edited by G. F. Hawthorne with O. Betz, 229–36. Grand Rapids: Eerdmans, 1987.
———. *The Sources of Acts*. London: Darton, Longman & Todd, 1964.

———. "La structure oratoire du discours d'Étienne (Actes 7)." *Bib* 66 (1985) 153–67.
———. *SUN CRISTWI: L'Union avec le Christ suivant saint Paul*. Bruges: Éditions de l'Abbaye de saint-André, 1952.
Durken, D., ed. *Sin, Salvation and the Spirit: Commemorating the Fiftieth Year of the Liturgical Press*. Collegeville, MA: Liturgical, 1979.
Ellis, E.E., "Das Ende der Erde (Apg.1.8)." In *Der treue Gottes trauen. Beiträge zum Werke des Lukas. Für Gerhard Schneider*, edited by C. Busse and W. Radl, 277–87. Freiburg-Basel-Wien: Herder, 1991.
———. "Midrash, Targum and New Testament Quotations." In *Neotestamentica et Semitica: Studies in Honour of M. Black*, edited by E. E. Ellis and M. Wilcox, 61–69. Edinburgh: T. & T. Clark, 1969.
———. "Midrashic Features in the Speeches of Acts." In *Mélanges Bibliques en hommage au B. Rigaux*, edited by A. Descamps and A. de Halleux, 303–12. Gembloux: Duculot, 1970.
———. *Prophecy and Hermeneutic in Early Christianity: New Testament Essays*. WUNT 18. Tübingen: Mohr, 1978.
Epp, E. J. *The Theological Tendency of Codex Bezae Cantabrigiensis in Acts*. SNTSMS 3. Cambridge: Cambridge University Press, 1966.
Esler, P. F. *Community and Gospel in Luke-Acts: the Social and Political Motivations of Lucan Theology*. SNTSMS 57. Cambridge: Cambridge University Press, 1987.
Evans, C.A. "Is Luke's View of the Jewish Rejection of Jesus Anti-Semitic?" In *Reimaging the Death of the Lukan Jesus*, edited by D. D. Sylva, 29–56. BBB 73. Frankfurt am Main: Anton Hain, 1990.
Evans, C. A., and James A. Sanders. *Luke and Scripture: The Function of Sacred Tradition in Luke-Acts*. Minneapolis: Fortress, 1993.
Evans, C. F. "The Kerygma." *JTS* 7 (1956) 25–41.
———. "'Speeches' in Acts." In *Mélanges Bibliques. Festschrift for B. Rigaux*, edited by A. Descamps and A. de Halleux, 287–302. Glemboux: Duculot, 1970.
———. *St. Luke*. TPINTC. Philadelphia: Trinity, 1990.
Farris, S. *The Hymns of Luke's Infancy Narrative: Their Origin, Meaning and Significance*. JSNTSS 9. Sheffield: JSOT, 1985.
Fee, G. D. *The First Epistle to the Corinthians*. NICNT. Grand Rapids: Eerdmans, 1987.
Fitzmyer, J. A. *The Acts of the Apostles*. AB 31. New York: Doubleday, 1998.
———. *The Gospel according to Luke I-IX*. AB 28. New York: Doubleday, 1981.
———. *The Gospel according to Luke X-XXIV*. AB 28A. New York: Doubleday, 1985.
———. *Luke the Theologian: Aspects of his Teaching*. London: Geoffrey Chapman, 1989.
Flebbe, J. "Israels Gott der Auferwecking. Zur Bedeutung und zum paulinische Charakter der Rede von Gott in der Apostelgeschichte." In *Reception of Paulinism in Acts/Réception du Paulisme dans les Actes des Apôtres*, edited by D. Marguerat, 101–39. BETL 229. Leuven: Peeters, 2009.
Flichy, Odile. *La figure de Paul dans les Actes des Apôtres. Un phénomène de réception de la tradition paulinienne à la fin du 1er siècle*. LD. Paris: Cerf, 2007.
———. "The Paul of Luke. A Survey of Research." In *Paul and the Heritage of Israel*, edited by D. P. Moessner et al., 18–34. London: T. & T. Clark, 2012.
Foakes Jackson, F. J., and K. Lake, eds. *The Beginnings of Christianity, Part I: The Acts of the Apostles*. 5 vols. London: Macmillan, 1920–1933.
Franklin, E. *Christ the Lord: A Study in the Purpose and Theology of Luke-Acts*. London: SPCK, 1975.

Freyne, S. *Jesus a Jewish Galilean: A New Reading of the Jesus Story*. London: T. & T. Clark, 2004.
Friedrich, G. κῆρυξ, κηρύσσω, κτλ. In *TDNT* 3.683–718.
Frohlich, Ida. *Time and Times and Half a Time: Historical Consciousness in the Jewish Literature of the Persian and Hellenistic Eras*. JSPSS 19. Sheffield: Sheffield Academic, 1996.
Fuller, R. H. *The Formation of the Resurrection Narratives*. London: SPCK, 1972.
Gamble, H. Y. *Books and Readers in the Early Church: A History of Early Christian Texts*. New Haven: Yale University Press, 1995.
Garrett, Susan R. *The Demise of the Devil: Magic and the Demonic in Luke's Writings*. Minneapolis: Fortress, 1989.
Gathercole, S. J. *Where is Boasting? Early Jewish Soteriology and Paul's Response in Romans 1–5*. Grand Rapids: Eerdmans, 2002.
Gaventa, Beverly R. *From Darkness to Light: Aspects of Conversion in the New Testament*. OBT 20. Philadelphia: Fortress, 1986.
———. "Initiatives Divine and Human in the Lukan Story World." In *The Holy Spirit and Christian Origins: Essays in Honor of James D. G. Dunn*, edited by G. N. Stanton et al., 79–89. Grand Rapids: Eerdmans, 2004.
Gempf, C. H. "The 'God-Fearers.'" In *The Book of Acts in the Setting of Hellenistic History*, edited by C. J. Hemer and C. H. Gempf, 444–48. WUNT 49. Tübingen: Mohr Siebeck, 1989.
———. "Public Speaking and Published Accounts." In *The Book of Acts in Its First Century Setting*. Vol. 1, *Ancient Literary Setting*, edited by B. W. Winter and A. D. Clarke, 259–303. Grand Rapids: Eerdmans, 1993.
George, A. "Le sens de la mort Jésus pour Luc." *RB* 80 (1973) 186–217.
———. "L'emploi chez Luc du vocabulaire de salut." *NTS* 23 (1977) 308–20.
Gertner, M. "Midrashim in the New Testament." *JSS* 7 (1962) 267–92.
Giles, K. N. "Luke's Use of the Term ΕΚΚΛΗΣΙΑ with special reference to Acts 20.28 and 9.31." *NTS* 31 (1985) 135–42.
Glasson, T. F. "The Kerygma: Is Our Version Correct?" *HJ* 51 (1953) 29–32.
———. "The Speeches in Acts and Thucydides." *ExT* 76 (1964–65) 165.
Glöckner, R. *Die Verkündigung des Heils beim Evangelisten Lukas*. WS Theologische Reihe 9. Mainz: Matthias-Grünewald, 1975.
Gnilka, J. *Die Verstockung Israaels. Isaias 6. 9–10 in der Theologie der Synoptiker*. SANT 3. München: Kosel, 1963.
Goldsmith, D. "Acts 13.33–37: A Pesher on 2 Samuel 7." *JBL* 87 (1968) 321–24.
Gordon, R. P. "Targumic Parallels to Acts XIII.18 and Didache XIV.3." *NTS* 16 (1974) 285–89.
Goguel, M. *La foi à la résurrection de Jésus dans le christianisme primitif*. Sciences Religieuses 47. Paris: Leroux, 1933.
Gray, G. B. "The Psalms of Solomon." In *APT* 2, edited by R. H. Charles, 628–30. Oxford: Clarendon, 1913.
Green, J. B. *The Theology of the Gospel of Luke*. Cambridge: Cambridge University Press, 1995.
Guilding, Aileen. *The Fourth Gospel and Jewish Worship*. Oxford: Clarendon, 1960.
Gundry, R. H. *Matthew: A Commentary on His Literary and Theological Art*. Grand Rapids: Eerdmans, 1982.

Haacker, K. "Das Bekenntnis des Paulus zur Hoffnung Israels nach der Apostelgeschichte des Lukas." *NTS* 31 (1985) 437–51.

Haenchen, E. *The Acts of the Apostles: A Commentary.* Oxford: Blackwell, 1971.

———. "'We' in Acts and the Itinerary." In *The Bultmann School of Biblical Interpretation: New Directions?*, edited by R. W. Funk, 65–99. New York: Harper & Row, 1965.

Hagene, Sylvia. *Zeiten der Wiederherstellung. Studien zur lukanischen Geschichtstheologie als Soteriologie.* NA n.f. 47. Münster: Aschendorff, 2003.

Hall, R. C. *Revealed Histories: Techniques for Ancient Jewish and Christian Historiography.* JSPSS 6. Sheffield: Sheffield Academic Press, 1991.

Hansen, G. W. "The Preaching and Defence of Paul." In *Witness to the Gospel: The Theology of Acts*, edited by I. H. Marshall and D. Peterson, 295–324. Grand Rapids: Eerdmans, 1998.

Hayes, R. B. "The Paulinism of Acts, Intertextually Reconsidered." In *Paul and the Heritage of Israel*, edited by D. P. Moessner et al., 35–48. LNTS 452. London: T. & T. Clark, 2012.

Hays, R. B. *Echoes of Scripture in the Letters of Paul.* New Haven: Yale University Press, 1989.

———. *The Faith of Jesus Christ: The Narrative Substructure of Galatians 3.1–4.11.* 2nd ed. BRS. Grand Rapids: Eerdmans, 2002.

Hemer, C. J. *The Book of Acts in the Setting of Hellenistic History.* WUNT 49. Tubingen: Mohr, 1989.

Hengel, M. *Acts and the History of Earliest Christianity.* Philadelphia: Fortress, 1980.

———. "'Schriftauslegung' and 'Schriftwerdung' in der Zeit des Zweiten Tempels." In *Schriftauslegung im antiken Judentum und im Urchristentum*, edited by M. Hengel and H. Löhr, 1–71. WUNT 73. Tübingen: Mohr, 1994.

———. *The Son of God.* London: SCM, 1976.

———. *The Zealots: Investigations into the Jewish Freedom Movement in the Period from Herod I until 70 A.D.* Edinburgh: T. & T. Clark, 1989.

Hermison, H.-J. "The Fourth Servant Song in the Context of Deutero-Isaiah." In *The Suffering Servant: Isaiah 53 in Jewish and Christian Sources*, edited by B. Janowski and P. Stuhlmacher, 16–47. Translated by D. P. Bailey. Grand Rapids: Eerdmans, 1996.

Hill, C. C. *Hellenists and Hebrews: Reappraising Division within the Earliest Church.* Minneapolis: Fortress, 1992.

Hirschberg, P. *Das eschatologische Israel. Untersuchungen zum Gottesvolkverständnis der Johannesoffenbarung.* WMANT 84. Neukirchen-Vluyn: Neukirchener, 1999.

Hoffmann, P. *Studien zur Theologie der Logienquelle.* NA n.f. 8. Münster: Aschendorff, 1971.

Hofius, O. *Paulusstudien.* 2nd ed. WUNT 51. Tübingen: Mohr Siebeck, 1994.

Holtz, T. *Untersuchungen über die alttestamentlichen Zitate bei Lukas.* TU 104. Berlin: Akademie, 1968.

Horsley, G. H. R. "Speeches and Dialogue in Acts." *NTS* 32 (1986) 609–14.

Janowski, B., and P. Stuhlmacher. *The Suffering Servant: Isaiah 53 in Jewish and Christian Sources.* Grand Rapids: Eerdmans, 2004.

Jeremias, J. *The Central Message of the New Testament.* London: SCM, 1965.

———. *The Eucharistic Words of Jesus.* Rev. ed. London: SCM, 1966.

Jervell, J. *Die Apostelgeschichte.* KEK Band 3. Göttingen: Vandenhoeck & Ruprecht, 1998.

———. *Luke and the People of God: A New Look at Luke-Acts*. Minneapolis: Fortress, 1972.
———. *The Theology of the Acts of the Apostles*. Cambridge: Cambridge University Press, 1996.
———. *The Unknown Paul: Essays on Luke-Acts and Early Christian History*. Minneapolis: Augsburg, 1984.
Jeska, J. *Die Geschichte Israels in der Sicht des Lukas. Apg 7.2b-53 und 13.17-25 im Kontext antik-jüdischer Summarien der Geschichte Israels*. FRLANT 195. Göttingen: Vandenhoeck & Ruprecht, 2001.
Johnson, L. J. *The Acts of the Apostles*. SP 5. Collegeville, MN: Liturgical, 1992.
———. *The Literary Function of Possessions in Luke-Acts*. SBLDS 39. Missoula, MT: Scholars, 1977.
———. *Septuagintal Midrash in the Speeches of Acts*. Milwaukee, WI: Marquette University Press, 2002.
Johnson, M. D. *The Purpose of the Biblical Genealogies, with Special Reference to the Setting of the Genealogies of Jesus*. SNTSMS 8. Cambridge: Cambridge University Press, 1969.
Juel, D. *Luke-Acts*. London: SCM, 1984.
———. *Messianic Exegesis: Christological Interpretation of the Old Testament in Early Christianity*. Philadelphia: Fortress, 1988.
Kaiser, O. *Isaiah 1-39*. OTL. London: SCM, 1974.
Karris, R. J. *Luke: Artist and Theologian. Luke's Passion Account as Literature*. New York: Paulist, 1985.
———. "Luke 23.47 and the Lucan View of Jesus' Death." JBL 105 (1986) 65-74. [Reprinted in *Reimaging the Death of the Lukan Jesus*, edited by D. D. Sylva, 68-78, 187-89. BBB 73. Frankfurt am Main: Anton Hain, 1990].
Käsemann, E. *Commentary on Romans*. London: SCM, 1980.
Keathley, N. H. *With Steadfast Purpose: Essays on Acts in Honor of Henry Jackson Flanders, Jr.* Waco, TX: Baylor University Press, 1990.
Keck, L. E. "Toward the Renewal of New Testament Christology." In *From Jesus to John: Essays on Jesus and New Testament Christology in Honour of Marinus de Jonge*, edited by M. C. de Boer, 321-40. JSNTSS 84. Sheffield: JSOT, 1993.
Keck, L. E., and J. L. Martyn. *Studies in Luke-Acts*. Nashville: Abingdon, 1966.
Kee, H. C. *To Every Nation under Heaven: The Acts of the Apostles*. Harrisburg, PA: Trinity, 1997.
Kennedy, G. A. *New Testament Interpretation through Rhetorical Criticism*. Chapel Hill: University of North Carolina Press, 1984.
Kezbere, Ilze. *Umstrittener Monotheismus: Wahre und falsche Apotheose im lukanischen Doppelwerk*. NTOA 60. Göttingen: Vandenhoeck & Ruprecht: Academic Press Fribourg, 2007.
Kilgallen, J. "Acts 13.38-39: Culmination of Paul's Speech in Pisidia." Bib 69 (1988) 480-506.
———. *The Stephen Speech: A Literary and Redactional Study of Acts 7, 2-53*. AB 67. Rome: Pontifical Biblical Institute, 1976.
King, N. Q. "Universalism in the Third Gospel." *Studia Evangelica I*. TU 73 (1959) 199-205.
Klauck, H.-J. *Magic and Paganism in Early Christianity: The World of the Acts of the Apostles*. Edinburgh: T. & T. Clark, 2000.

Kliesch, K. *Das heilsgeschichtliche Credo in den Reden der Apostelgeschichte.* BBB 44. Köhn-Bonn: Peter Hanstein, 1975.

Klinghardt, M. *Gesetz und Volk Gottes: das lukanische Verständnis des Gesetzes nach Herkunft, Funktion und seinem Ort in der Geschichte des Urchristentums.* WUNT 2/32. Mohr: Tübingen, 1988.

Kloppenborg-Verbin, J. S. *Excavating Q: The History and Setting of the Sayings Gospel.* Minneapolis: Fortress, 2000.

Koch, D.-A. "Kollektenbericht, 'Wir'-Bericht and Itinerar. Neue (?) Uberlegungen zu einem alten Problem." *NTS* 45 (1999) 367–90.

———. "Proselyten und Gottesfürchtige als Hörer der Reden von Apostelgeschichte 2.14–29 und 13.16–41." In *Die Apostelgeschichte und die hellenistische Geschichtsschreibung*, edited by C. Breytenbach and J. Schröter, 83–107. AJEC 57. Leiden: Brill, 2004.

Koet, B. J. *Five Studies on Interpretation of Scripture in Luke-Acts.* SNTA 14. Louvain: Leuven University/Peeters, 1989.

Korn, M. *Die Geschichte Jesu in veränderter Zeit: Studien zur bleibenden Bedeutung Jesu im lukanischen Doppelwerk.* WUNT 2/51. Tübingen: Mohr, 1993.

Kraabel, A. T. "The Disappearance of the God-Fearers." *Numen* 28 (1981) 113–26.

Kramer, *Christ, Lord, Son of God.* SBT 50. London: SCM, 1966.

Krankl, E. *Jesus der Knecht Gottes: die heilsgeschichtliche Stellung Jesu in den Reden der Apostelgeschichte.* BU 8. Regensburg: Pustet, 1972.

Krodel, G. *Acts.* Augsburg Commentary on the New Testament. Minneapolis: Augsburg, 1986.

Kuhn, K.G. προσήλυτος. In *TDNT* 6.727-44.

Kümmel, W. G. "'Das Gesetz und die Propheten gehen bis Johannes'—Lukas 16.16 im Zusammenhang der heilsgeschichtlichen Theologie der Lukasschriften." In *Verborum Veritas: Festschrift für G. Stählin*, edited by O. Bocher and K. Haacker, 398–415. Wuppertal: Brockhaus, 1970.

Laato, A. *A Star is Rising: The Historical Development of the Old Testament Royal Ideology and the Rise of Jewish Messianic Developments.* Atlanta: Scholars, 1997.

Lampe, G. W. H. *St. Luke and the Church of Jerusalem.* 1969 Ethel Wood Lecture. London: Athlone, 1969.

Leenhardt, F. J. *The Epistle to the Romans.* London: Lutterworth, 1961.

Lehre, E. "Die Predigt in Lystra (Acta xiv.15–18)." *NTS* 7 (1960–61) 46–55.

Lentz, J. C. *Luke's Portrait of Paul.* SNTSMS 77. Cambridge: Cambridge University Press, 1993.

Levinskaya, Irina. *Diaspora Setting.* Vol 5 of *The Book of Acts in its First Century Setting.* Edited by B. W. Winter. Grand Rapids: Eerdmans, 1996.

Lightfoot, J. B. *St. Paul's Epistle to the Galatians.* London: Macmillan, 1874.

Lindars, B. *New Testament Apologetic: The Doctrinal Significance of the Old Testament Quotations.* London: SCM, 1961.

Lohfink, G. *Die Himmelfahrt Jesu: Untersuchungen zu den Himmelsfahrts- und Erhohungstexten bei Lukas.* SANT 26. Munich: Kosel, 1971.

———. *Die Sammlung Israels: eine Untersuchung zur lukanischen Ekklesiologie.* SANT 39. Munich: Kösel, 1975.

Löning, K. *Das Geschichtswerk des Lukas. Band 1: Israels Hoffnung und Gottes Geheimnisse.* Kohlhammer Urban-Taschenbucher 455. Stuttgart: Kohlhammer, 1997.

———. *Die Saulustradition in der Apostelgeschichte.* NA 9. Munster: Aschendorff, 1973.
Lövestam, E. *Son and Saviour: A Study of Acts 13, 32–37.* CN 18. Lund: Gleerup, 1961.
Lüdemann, G. *Early Christianity according to the Traditions in Acts: A Commentary.* London: SCM, 1987.
Luomanen, P., ed. *Luke-Acts: Scandinavian Perspectives.* PFES 54. Göttingen: Vandenhoeck & Ruprech, 1991.
Maddox, R. *The Purpose of Luke-Acts.* Edinburgh: T. & T. Clark, 1982.
Malherbe, A. J. *The Letters to the Thessalonians.* AB 32B. New York: Doubleday, 2000.
Maloney, Linda M. *"All that God had Done with Them": The Narration of the Works of God in the Early Christian Community as Described in the Acts of the Apostles.* American University Studies: Theology and Religion 91. New York: Peter Lang, 1991.
Manson, T. W. *The Sayings of Jesus.* London: SCM, 1949.
Marguerat, D. "The Enigma of the Silent Closing of Acts (28.16–31)." In *Jesus and the Heritage of Israel: Luke's Narrative Claim upon Israel's Legacy,* edited by D. P. Moessner, 284–304. Harrisburg, PA: Trinity, 1999.
———. *The First Christian Historian: Writing the "Acts of the Apostles."* SNTSMS 121. Cambridge: Cambridge University Press, 2002.
———. "Paul after Paul: A (Hi)story of Reception." In *Paul and the Heritage of Israel,* edited by D. P. Moessner et al., 70–89. LNTS 452. London: T. & T. Clark, 2012.
———. *Reception of Paulinism in Acts/Réception du Paulinisme dans les Actes des Apôtres.* BETL 229. Leuven: Uitgeverij Peeters, 2009.
———. "Saul's Conversion (Acts 9-22-26) and the Multiplication of Narrative in Acts." In *Luke's Literary Achievenent,* edited by C. M. Tuckett, 127–55. JSNTSS 116. Sheffield: Sheffield Academic Press, 1995.
Marshall, I. H. *The Acts of the Apostles.* TNTC. Leicester: InterVarsity, 1980.
———. *The Gospel of Luke.* NIGTC. Exeter: Paternoster, 1978.
———. *Last Supper and Lord's Supper.* Exeter: Paternoster, 1980.
———. *Luke: Historian and Theologian.* Exeter: Paternoster, 1970.
———. "The Resurrection in the Acts of the Apostles." In *Apostolic History and the Gospel: Biblical and Historical Essays Presented to F. F. Bruce,* edited by W. W. Gasque and R. P. Martin, 92–107. Exeter: Paternoster, 1970.
Marshall, I. H., and D. Peterson. *Witness to the Gospel: The Theology of Acts.* Grand Rapids: Eerdmans, 1998.
McDonald, J. I. H. *Kerygma and Didache: The Articulation and Structure of the Earliest Christian Message.* SNTSMS 37. Cambridge: Cambridge University Press, 1980.
Merk, O. *Handeln aus Glauben.* MTS 5. Marburg: Elwart, 1968.
Merkel, H. "Israel im lukanischen Werk." *NTS* 40 (1994) 371–98.
Metzger, B. M. *A Textuary Commentary on the Greek New Testament.* New York: United Bible Societies, 1975.
Michaelis, W. σκηνή σκῆνος. In *TDNT* 7.368–94.
Michel, O. *Der Brief an die Hebräer.* KEKNT. Göttingen: Vandenhoeck & Ruprecht, 1960.
———. *Paulus und seine Bibel.* Gutersloh: Bertelsmann, 1929.
Milik, J. *Books of Enoch: Aramaic Fragments of Qumran Cave 4.* Oxford: Clarendon, 1976.

Minear, P. S. *To Heal and to Reveal: The Prophetic Vocation according to Luke*. New York: Seabury, 1976.
Mittmann-Richert, Ulrike. *Der Sühnetod des Gottesknechts. Jesaja 53 im Lukasevangelium*. WUNT 220. Tübingen: Mohr Siebeck, 2008.
Miura, Y. *David in Luke-Acts*. WUNT 2/232. Tübingen: Mohr Siebeck, 2007.
Moessner, D. P. "'The Christ Must Suffer,' The Church Must Suffer: Rethinking the Theology of the Cross in Luke-Acts." *Society of Biblical Literature Seminar Papers* 29 (1990) 443–58.
———. "Luke's 'Witness of Witnesses': Paul as Definer and Defender of the Tradition of the Apostles—'From the Beginning.'" In *Luke the Interpreter of Israel*, edited by D. P. Moessner et al., 117–47. LNTS 452. London: T. & T. Clark, 2012.
Moessner, D. P., ed. *Jesus and the Heritage of Israel: Luke's Narrative Claim upon Israel's Heritage*. Vol. 1, *Luke the Interpreter of Israel*. Harrisburg, PA: Trinity, 1999.
Moessner, D. P., et al., eds. *Paul and the Heritage of Israel: Paul's Claim upon Israel's Legacy in Luke and Acts in the Light of the Pauline Letters*. Vol. 2, *Luke the Interpreter of Israel*. LNTS 452. London: T. & T. Clark, 2012.
Morris, L. The *Epistle to the Romans*. Grand Rapids: Eerdmans, 1988.
Moule, C. F. D. *An Idiom Book of New Testament Greek*. 2nd ed. Cambridge: Cambridge University Press, 1959.
Mutzner, F. "Die Erzählintention des Lukas in der Apostelgeschichte." In *Der Treue Gottes Trauen. Beiträge zum Werk des Lukas. Für G. Schneider*, edited by C. Bussmann and W. Radl, 29–41. Freiburg: Herder, 1991.
———. *Galaterbrief*. HTKNT 9. Freiburg: Herder, 1974.
Nägele, Sabrine. *Laubhütte Davids und Wolkenssohn. Eine ausgeschichtliche Studie zu Amos 9.11 in der jüdischen und christlichen Exegese*. AGAJU 24. Leiden: Brill, 1995.
Nanos, M. D. *The Mystery of Romans: The Jewish Context of Paul's Letter*. Minneapolis: Fortress, 1996.
Nave, G. D. *The Role and Function of Repentance in Luke-Acts*. Ac.Bib. 4. Atlanta: Society for Biblical Literature, 2002.
Neyrey, J. *The Passion according to Luke: A Redaction Study of Luke's Soteriology*. New York: Paulist, 1985.
———. *The Social World of Luke-Acts: Models for Interpretation*. Peabody, MA: Hendrickson, 1991.
Neusner, J., et al. *Judaisms and their Messiahs at the Turn of the Christian Era*. Cambridge: Cambridge University Press, 1987.
Nickelsburg, G. W. E. "The Genre and Function of the Markan Passion Narrative." *HTR* 73 (1960) 153–84.
———. *Jewish Literature between the Bible and the Mishnah*. London: SCM, 1981.
Nolland, J. "A Fresh Look at Acts 15.10." *NTS* 27 (1981) 105–15.
———. *Luke 1–9.20*. WBC 35A. Dallas: Word, 1989.
———. *Luke 9.21—18.34*. WBC 35B. Dallas: Word, 1993.
———. *Luke 18.35—24.53*. WBC 35C. Dallas Word, 1993.
O'Brien, P. T. "Was Paul Converted?" In *Justification and Variegated Nomism II: The Paradoxes of Paul*, edited by D. A. Carson et al., 361–91. Tübingen: Mohr Siebeck, 2004.
Omerzu, Heiki. "Apostelgeschichte als Theologiegeschichte: Apg 19 als Beispiel konstruktiver Paulusrezeption." In *Reception of Paulinism in Acts/Réception du*

Paulisme dans les Actes des Apôtres, edited by D. Marguerat, 157–174. BETL 229. Leuven: Uitgeveru Peeters, 2009.

O'Neill, J. C. *The Theology of Acts in its Historical Setting*. London: SPCK, 1961.

O'Toole, R. F. "The Activity of the Risen Jesus in Luke-Acts." *Bib.* 62 (1981) 471–98.

———. *The Christological Climax of Paul's Defense*. AB 78. Rome: Pontifical Biblical Institute, 1978.

———. "Christ's Resurrection in Acts 13.13–52." *Bib* 60 (1979) 361–72.

———. "How Does Luke Portray Jesus as the Servant of Yahweh?" *Bib* 81 (2000) 328–46.

———. *The Unity of Luke's Theology: An Analysis of Luke-Acts*. GNS 9. Wilmington, DE: Michael Glazier, 1984.

Ott, W. *Gebet und Heil: die Bedeutung der Gebetparanese in der lukanischen Theologie*. SANT 12. Munich: Kösel, 1965.

Palmer, D. W. "The Literary Background of Acts 1.1–14." *NTS* 33 (1987) 427–38.

Pao, D. W. *Acts and the Isaianic New Exodus*. BSL. Grand Rapids: Baker Academic: 2002. Originally WUNT 2/130. Tübingen: Mohr, 2000.

Parsons, M. C. *Body and Character in Luke and Acts: The Subversion of Physiognomy in Early Christianity*. Grand Rapids: Baker Academic, 2006.

———. *The Departure of Jesus in Luke-Acts: The Ascension Narratives in Context*. JSNTSS 21. Sheffield: JSOT, 1987.

———. *Luke: Storyteller, Interpreter, Evangelist*. Peabody, MA: Hendrickson, 2007.

Parsons, M. C., and R. I. Pervo. *Rethinking the Unity of Luke and Acts*. Minneapolis: Fortress, 1993.

Penner, T. *In Praise of Christian Origins: Stephen and the Hellenists in Lukan Apologetic Historiography*. ESEC 10. Edinburgh: T. & T. Clark, 2004.

Pesch R. *Die Apostelgeschichte Band 1: Apg. 1–12*. EKK 5/1. Neukirchener: Neukirchen-Vluyn, 1986.

———. *Die Apostelgeschichte Band 2: Apg. 13–28*. EKK 5/2. Neukirchener: Neukirchen-Vluyn, 1986.

Peterson, D. "Atonement Theology in Luke-Acts: Reflections on its Background." In *The New Testament in its First Century Setting. Essays on Context and Background*, edited by P. J. Williams et al., 56–71. Grand Rapids: Eerdmans: 2004.

Pichler, J. *Paulusrezeption in der Apostelgeschichte: Untersuchungen zur Rede im pisidischen Antiochien*. ITS 50. Innsbruck-Wien: Tyrolia, 1997.

Pietsch, M. *"Dieser is der Sprotz Davids . . ." Studien zur Rezeptionsgeschichte der Nathanverheitzung im alttestamentlichen, zwischentestamentlichen und neutestamentlichen Schrifttum*. WMANT 100. Neukirchen-Vluyn: Neukirchener, 2003.

Pillai, C. A. J. *Apostolic Interpretation of History: A Commentary on Acts 13.16–41*. Hicksville, NY: Exposition, 1980.

———. *Early Missionary Preaching: A Study of Luke's Report in Acts 13*. Hicksville, NY: Exposition, 1979.

Plumacher, E. *Lukas als hellenistischer Schriftsteller*. SUNT 9. Göttingen: Vandenhoeck & Ruprecht, 1972.

Pokorny, P. *Theologie der lukanischen Schriften*. FRLANT 174. Göttingen: Vandenhoeck & Ruprecht, 1998.

Pomykala, K. E. *The Davidic Dynasty Tradition in Early Judaism: Its History and Significance*. EJIL. Atlanta: Scholars, 1995.

Porter, S. E. *Paul in Acts*. Peabody, MA: Hendrickson, 2001. Originally published WUNT 115, Tübingen: Mohr, 1999.

———. "Thucydides 1.22.1 and the Speeches in Acts: Is There a Thucydidean View?" *NT* 32 (1990) 121–42.

Prast, F. *Presbyter und Evangelium in nachapostolischer Zeit. Die Abschiedsrede des Paulus in Milet (Apg 20.17–38) im Rahmen der lukanischen Konzeption der Evangeliumsverkündigung*. FzB 29. Stuttgart: Katholisches Bibelwerk, 1979.

Preisker, H. περιούσιος. In *TDNT* 6.57–58.

Prieur, A. *Die Verkündigung der Gottesherrschaft. Exegetische Studien zum lukanischen Verständnis von βασιλεία τοῦ θεοῦ*. WUNT 2/89. Tübingen: Mohr, 1996.

Rad, G. von. *Old Testament Theology: The Theology of Israel's Historical Traditions*. Translated by D. M. G. Stalker. Edinburgh: Oliver & Boyd, 1962.

———. *The Problem of the Hexateuch and Other Essays*. Translated by E. W. Trueman Dicken. Edinburgh: Oliver & Boyd, 1966.

———. *Studies in Deuternomy*. SBT 9. London: SCM, 1953.

Radl, W. "Jesu Tod und Sundenvergebung bei Lukas und Paulus". In *Reception of Paulinism in Acts*, edited by D. Marguerat, 15–35. BETL 229. Leuven-Paris: Peeters, 2009.

———. "Rettung in Israel." In *Der Treue Gottes trauen. Beiträge zum Werke des Lukas. Für Gerhard Schneider*, edited by C. Busse and W. Radl, 43-60. Freiburg-Basel-Wien: Herder, 1991.

Räisänen, H. *Paul and the Law*. WUNT 29. Tübingen: Mohr, 1983.

———. "The Redemption of Israel: A Salvation-History Problem in Luke-Acts." In *Luke-Acts: Scandinavian Perspectives*, edited by P. Luomanen, 94–114. PFES 54. Göttingen: Vandenhoeck & Ruprecht, 1991.

Rampling, K. "Gepriesen sei der Herr, der Gott Israels." In *Der lebendige Gott. Studien zur Theologie des Neuen Testaments. Festschrift für Wilhelm Thüsing zum 75. Geburtstag*, edited by T Söding, 149–79. NA 31. Münster: Aschendorff, 1996.

Ramsay, W. M. *St. Paul the Traveller and the Roman Citizen*. 3rd ed. London: Hodder and Stoughton, 1908.

Rau, G. "Das Volk in der lukanischen Passionsgeschichte, eine Konjektur zu Lc.23.13." *ZNW* 56 (1965) 41–51.

Ravens, D. *Luke and the Restoration of Israel*. JSNTSS 119. Sheffield: Sheffield Academic Press, 1995.

Rengstorff, K. ὑπηρέτης, ὑπηρετέω, κτλ. In *TDNT* 8.530–44.

Rese, M. "Die Aussagen über Jesu Tod und Auferstehung in der Apostelgeschichte—altestes Kerygma oder lukanische Theologumena?" *NTS* 30 (1984) 335–54.

———. "Die Funktion der alttestamentliche Zitate und Anspielungen in den Reden der Apostelgeschichte." In *Les Actes des Apôtres*, edited by J. Kremer, 61–79. Gembloux: Louvain, 1979.

Richard, E. "The Creative Use of Amos by the author of Acts." *NT* 24 (1982) 37–53.

———. *New Views on Luke and Acts*. Collegeville, MN: Liturgical, 1990.

Ridderbos, H. N. *The Speeches of Peter in the Acts of the Apostles*. Tyndale NT Lecture, 1961. London: Tyndale, 1962.

Riesenfeld, H. *Jésus Transfiguré*. ASNU 16. Copenhagen: Ejnar Munksgaard, 1947.

Riesner, R. *Paul's Early Period: Chronology, Mission Strategy, Theology*. Grand Rapids: Eerdmans, 1998.

Robinson, W. C. *Der Weg des Herrn. Studien zur Geschichte und Eschatologie im Lukas-Evangelium. Ein Gespräch mit Hans Conzelmann*. TF 36. Hamburg-Bergstedt: Herbert Reich Evangelischer, 1964.

Roloff, J. *Die Apostelgeschichte*. NTD Band 5. Göttingen: Vandenhoeck & Ruprecht, 1981.

———. "Die Paulus-Darstellung des Lukas: ihre geschichtlichen Voraussetzungen und ihr theologisches Ziel." *Ev.Th*. 6 (1979) 510–31.

Ropes, J. H. "Detached Note on xiii.27–29." In *The Beginnings of Christianity, Part I, The Acts of the Apostles: The Text of Acts*, edited by J. H. Ropes, 3:261–63. London: Macmillan, 1926.

Rosenblatt, Marie-Eloise. *Paul the Accused: His Portrait in the Acts of the Apostles*. ZSNT. Collegeville, MN: Liturgical, 1995.

Rothschild, Clare K. *Luke-Acts and the Rhetoric of History*. WUNT 2.175. Tübingen: Mohr Siebeck, 2004.

Ruppert, L. *Jesus als der leidende Gerechte? Der Weg Jesu im Lichte eines alt- und zwischentestamentlichen Motivs*. SBS 59. Stuttgart: KBW, 1972.

Sanders, E. P. *Paul and Palestinian Judaism*. London: SCM, 1977.

Sanders, J. T. *The Jews in Luke-Acts*. London: SCM, 1987.

Schenke, L. "Die Kontrastformel Apg. 4.10b." *BZ* 26 (1982) 1–20.

Schmitt, J. "Kerygme pascal et lecture scripturaire dans l'instruction d'Antioche (Act. 13, 23–37)." In *Les Actes des Apôtres*, edited by J. Kremer, 155–67. Gembloux: Louvain, 1979.

Schneider, G. *Die Apostelgeschichte, 1 Teil (Apg. 1–8) 2 Teil (Apg. 9–28)*. HTKNT 5. Freiburg: Herder, 1980, 1982.

Schniedewind, W. M. *Society and Promise to David: The Reception History of 2 Samuel 7.1–17*. Oxford: Oxford University Press, 1999.

Schoeps, H. J. *Paul: The Theology of the Apostle in the Light of Jewish Religious History*. London: Lutterworth, 1961.

———. "The Sacrifice of Isaac in Paul's Theology." *JBL* 65 (1946) 385–92.

Schröter, J. "Heil für die Heiden und Israel. Zum Zusammenhang von Christologie und Volk Gottes bei Lukas." In *Die Apostelgeschichte und die hellenistische Geschichtsschreibung. Festschrift für E. Plümacher*, edited by C. Breytenbach and J. Schröter, 285–308. AJEC 57. Leiden: Brill, 2004.

———. "Paul the Founder of the Church: Reflections on the Reception of Paul in the Acts of the Apostles and the Pastoral Epistles." In *Paul and the Heritage of Israel: Paul's Claim upon Israel's Legacy in Luke and Acts in the Light of the Pauline Letters*, edited by D. P. Moessner et al., 195–219. LNTS 452. London: T. & T. Clark, 2012.

Schürmann, H. *Das Lukasevangelium I: Kommentar zu 1.1–9.50*. KTKNT 3. Freiburg: Herder, 1969.

———. "Lk 22.19b-20 als urspringliche Textuberlieferung." *Biblica* 32 (1951) 364–392, 522–41. Reprinted in *Traditionsgeschichtliche Untersuchungen zu den synoptischen Evangelien*. Düsseldorf: Patmos, 1968.

Schütz, F. *Der leidende Christus. Die anfochtene Gemeinde und das Christuskerygma der lukanischen Schriften*. BWANT 5/9. Stuttgart: Kohlhammer, 1969.

Schweizer, E. "The Concept of the Davidic 'Son of God' in Acts and Its Old Testament Background." In *Studies in Luke-Acts: Essays Presented in Honor of Paul Schubert*, edited by L. E. Keck and J. L. Martyn, 186–93. Nashville: Abingdon, 1966.

———. "Concerning the Speeches in Acts." In *Studies in Luke-Acts: Essays Presented in Honor of Paul Schubert*, edited by L. E. Keck and J. L. Martyn, 208–16. Nashville: Abingdon, 1966.
———. *Jesus*. London: SCM, 1971.
———. *Lordship and Discipleship*. SBT 28. London: SCM, 1960.
———. "Zur religionsgeschichtlichen Hintergrund der 'Sendungsformel' Gal 4.4f; Rom 8.3f; John 3.16; 1 John 4.9." *ZNW* 57 (1966) 199–210.
Seitz, Claudia. *Jewish Responses to Early Christians: History and Polemics, 30—150 C.E.* Minneapolis: Fortress, 1994.
Sellner, H. J. *Das Heil Gottes. Studien zur Soteriologie des lukanischen Doppelwerks*. BZNW 152. Berlin: Walter de Gruyter, 2007.
Sheeley, S. M. *Narrative Asides in Luke-Acts*. JSNTSS 72. Sheffield: JSOT, 1992.
Sherwin-White, A. N. *Roman Society and Roman Law in the New Testament*. Oxford: Clarendon, 1963.
Soards, M. L. *The Speeches in Acts: Their Content, Context, and Concerns*. Louisville: Westminster John Knox, 1994.
Söding, T. "Sühne durch Stellvertetung. Zur centralen Deutung des Todes Jesu im Römerbrief." In *Deutungen des Todes Jesu im Neuen Testament*, edited by J. Frey and J. Scröter, 375–96. WUNT 181. Tübingen: Mohr Siebeck, 2005.
Squires, J. T. *The Plan of God in Luke-Acts*. SNTSMS 76. Cambridge: Cambridge University Press, 1993.
Steck, O. *Israel und das gewaltsame Geschick der Propheten. Untersuchungen zur Überlierung des deuteronomistischen Geschichtsbildes im Alten Testament, Spätjudentum und Urchristentum*. WMANT 23. Neukirchen-Vluyn: Neukirchener, 1967.
Steeley, D. "Jesus' Death in Q." *NTS* 38 (1992) 222–34.
Stenschke, C.W. *Luke's Portrait of Gentiles Prior to Their Coming to Faith*. WUNT 2/108. Tübingen: Mohr Siebeck, 1999.
Sterling, G. "'Athletes of Virtue': An Analysis of the Summaries of Acts (2.41–47; 4.32–35; 5.12–16)." *JBL* 113 (1994), 679–96.
———. *Historiography and Self-Definition: Josephos, Luke-Acts and Apologetic Historiography*. SNT 64. Leiden: Brill, 1992.
———. "*Mors philosophi*: The Death of Jesus in Luke." *HTR* 84 (2001) 383–402.
Steyn, G. J. *Septuagint Quotations in the Context of the Petrine and Pauline Speeches of the Acta Apostolorum*. CBET 12. Kampen: Kok Pharos, 1995.
———, "Soteriological Perspectives in Luke's Gospel." In *Salvation in the New Testament: Perspectives on Soteriology*, edited by J. G. van der Watt, 67–99. SNT 121. Atlanta: Society of Biblical Literature, 2005.
Stolle, V. *Der Zeuge als Angeklagte. Untersuchungen zum Paulusbild des Lukas*. BWANT 6. Stuttgart: Kohlhammer, 1973.
Strathmann, H. μάρτυς, μαρτυρέω, κτλ. In *TWNT* 4.474–514.
Stuhlmacher, P. *Gerechtigkeit Gottes bei Paulus*. FRLANT 87. Göttingen: Vandenhoeck & Ruprecht, 1965.
Sylva D. D. *Reimaging the Death of the Lukan Jesus*. BBB 73. Frankfurt am Main: Anton Hain, 1990.
Taegar, J.-W. *Der Mensch und sein Heil. Studien zum Bild des Menschen und zur Sicht der Bekehrung bei Lukas*. SNT 14. Gütersloh: Mohn, 1982.

Talbert, C. H. *Literary Patterns, Theological Themes and the Genre of Luke-Acts.* SBLMS 20. Missoula, MT: Scholars, 1974.

———. *Luke and the Gnostics: An Examination of the Lucan Purpose.* Nashville: Abingdon, 1966.

———. "Martyrdom in Luke-Acts and the Lukan Social Ethic." In *Political Issues in Luke-Acts*, edited by R. J. Cassidy and P. J. Scharper, 99–110. Maryknoll NY: Orbis, 1983.

———. *Perspectives on Luke-Acts.* Danville, VA: Association of Baptist Professors of Religion, 1978.

———. *What is a Gospel? The Genre of the Canonical Gospels.* London: SPCK, 1978.

Tannehill, R. C. "The Functions of Peter's Mission Speeches in the Narrative of Acts." *NTS* 37 (1991) 400–414.

———. "Israel in Luke-Acts: A Tragic Story." *JBL* 104 (1985) 69–85.

———. *The Narrative Unity of Luke-Acts: A Literary Interpretation.* 2 vols. Minneapolis: Fortress, 1986, 1990.

Tcherikover, V. *Hellenistic Civilisation and the Jews.* Philadelphia: Jewish Publication Society of America, 1961.

Thompson, R. P. and T. E. Phillips. *Literary Studies in Luke-Acts: Essays in Honor of Joseph B. Tyson.* Macon, GA: Mercer University Press, 1998.

Thornton, C.-J. *Der Zeuge des Zeugen. Lukas als Historiker der Paulusreisen.* WUNT 56. Tübingen: Mohr, 1991.

Tiede, D. L. "The Exaltation of Jesus and the Restoration of Israel in Acts 1." *HTR* 79 (1986) 278–86.

———. *Prophecy and History in Luke-Acts.* Philadelphia: Fortress, 1980.

Trebilco, P. R. *Jewish Communities in Asia Minor.* SNTSMS 69. Cambridge: Cambridge University Press, 1991.

Trocmé, É. *Le "Livres des Actes" et l'Histoire.* EHPR 45. Paris: Presses Universitaires de France, 1957.

Tuckett, C. M. *Luke's Literary Achievement: Collected Essays.* JSNTSS 116. Sheffield: Sheffield Academic Press, 1995.

Turner, M. M. B. *Power from on High: The Spirit's Role in Israel's Restoration and Witness in Luke-Acts.* JPTSS 9. Sheffield: Sheffield Academic Press, 1996.

———. "The Spirit and Salvation in Luke-Acts." In *The Holy Spirit and Christian Origins: Essays in Honor of James D. G. Dunn*, edited by G. N. Stanton et al., 103–16. Grand Rapids: Eerdmans, 2004.

Tyson, J. B. *The Death of Jesus in Luke-Acts.* Columbia: University of South Carolina Press, 1986.

———. *Images of Judaism in Luke-Acts.* Columbia: University of South Carolina Press, 1992.

Tyson, J. B., ed. *Luke-Acts and the Jewish People: Eight Critical Perspectives.* Minneapolis: Augsburg, 1988.

Untergatzmair, F. G. *Kreuzweg und Kreuzigung Jesu. Ein Beitrag zur lukanischen Redaktionsgeschichte und zur Frage nach den lukanischen "Kreuzestheologie."* PTS 10. Zurich: Ferdinand Schöningh, 1980.

Van de Sandt, H. "The Quotations in Acts 13, 32–52 as a Reflection of Luke's LXX Interpretation." *Bib* 75 (1994) 26–58.

Van Zyl, H. C. "The Soteriology of Acts: Restoration to Life." In *Salvation in the New Testament: Perspectives on Soteriology*, edited by J. G. van der Watt, 133–60. SNT 121. Atlanta: Society of Biblical Literature, 2005.

Vermes, G. *Scripture and Tradition in Judaism: Haggadic Studies*. SPB 4. Leiden: Brill, 1973.

Vielhauer, P. "On the 'Paulinism' of Acts." In *Studies in Luke-Acts: Essays Presented in Honor of Paul Schubert*, edited by L. E. Keck and J. L. Martyn, 33–50. Nashville: Abingdon, 1966.

Von Bendemann, R. "Paulus und Israel in der Apostelgeschichte des Lukas." In *Christliche Theologie im Angesicht Israels. Festschrift zum 70. Geburtstag von Wolfgang Schrage*, edited by K. Wengst et al., 291–303. Neukirchen-Vluyn: Neukirchener, 1998.

Voss, P. G. *Die Christologie der lukanischen Schriften in Grundzügen*. SN 2. Paris: Desclée de Brouwer, 1965.

Wainwright, A. W. "Luke and the Restoration of the Kingdom to Israel." *ExT* 89 (1977–78) 76–79.

Walaskay, P. W. *"And So We Came to Rome": The Political Perspective of St. Luke*. SNTSMS 49. Cambridge: Cambridge University Press, 1983.

Walton, S. *Leadershp and Lifestyle: The Portrait of Paul in the Miletus Speech and 1 Thessalonians*. SNTSMS 108. Cambridge: Cambridge University Press, 2000.

Wander, B. *Gottesfürtige und Sympathisanten. Studien zum heidischen Umfeld von Diasporasynagogen*. WUNT 104. Tübingen: Mohr Siebeck, 1998.

Wasserberg, G. *Aus Israels Mitte—Heil für die Welt. Eine narrativ-exegetische Studie zur Theologie des Lukas*. BZNTW 92. Berlin: de Gruyter, 1998.

Watson, F. J. *Paul, Judaism and the Gentiles: Beyond the New Perspective*. 2nd ed., revised and enlarged. Grand Rapids: Eerdmans, 2007.

Weatherly, J. A. *Jewish Responsibility for the Death of Jesus in Luke-Acts*. JSNTSS 106. Sheffield: Sheffield Academic Press, 1994.

Wehnert, J. *Die Reinheit des "christlichen Gottesvolkes" aus Juden und Heiden. Studien zum historischen und theologischen Hintergrund des sogenannten Apostelkrets*. FRLANT 173. Göttingen: Vandenhoeck & Ruprecht, 1997.

―――. *Die Wir-Passagen der Apostelgeschichte: ein lukanisches Stilmittel aus judischer Tradition*. GTA 40. Göttingen: Vandenhoeck & Ruprecht, 1989.

Weiser, A. *Die Apostelgeschichte. Band 1: Apg.1–12 Band 2: Apg.13–28*. ÖTKNT 5/1–2. Gütersloh: Mohn, 1981, 1985.

Westermann, C. *Isaiah 40–66*. OTL. London: SCM, 1969.

Whybray, R. N. *Thanksgiving for a Liberated Prophet: An Interpretation of Isaiah Chapter 53*. Sheffield: JSOT, 1978.

Wilckens, U. *Die Missionsreden der Apostelgeschichte: Form- und traditionsgeschichtliche Untersuchungen*. 2nd ed. WMANT 5. Neukirchen-Vluyn: Neukirchener, 1963; reprinted with supplement, 1974.

Wilcox, M. "A Foreword to the Study of the Speeches in Acts." In *Christianity, Judaism and Other Greco-Roman Cults: Studies for Morton Smith*, edited by J. Neusner, 1:206–25. SJLA 12. Leiden: Brill, 1975.

―――. "The 'God-Fearers' in Acts—a Reconsideration." *JSNT* 13 (1981) 102–22.

―――. *The Semitisms of Acts*. Oxford: Clarendon, 1965.

―――. "'Upon the Tree'—Deut. 21.22–23 in the New Testament." *JBL* 96 (1977) 85–99.

Wildberger, H. *Jesaja 13–27*. 2nd ed. Neukirchen-Vluyn: Neukirchener, 1989.

Williamson, P. *Abraham, Israel and the Nations: The Patriarchal Promise and Its Covenantal Development in Genesis*. JSOTSS 315. Sheffield: Sheffield Academic, 2000.

Wills, L. "The Form of the Sermon in Hellenistic Judaism and Early Christianity." *HTR* 77 (1984) 277–99.

Wilson, S. G. *The Gentiles and the Gentile Mission in Luke-Acts*. SNTSMS 23. Cambridge: Cambridge University Press, 1973.

———. *Luke and the Law*. SNTSMS 50. Cambridge: Cambridge University Press, 1983.

Winnige, M. *Sinners and the Righteous: A Comparative Study of the Psalms of Solomon and Paul's Letters*. CB NT series 26. Stockholm: Almqvist & Wiksell, 1995.

Winter, B. W., series ed. *The Book of Acts in its First Century Setting*. 5 vols. Grand Rapids: Eerdmans, 1993–96.

Witherington, B., III. *The Acts of the Apostles: A Socio-Rhetorical Commentary*. Grand Rapids: Eerdmans, 1998.

Witherington, B., III., ed. *History, Literature, and Society in the Book of Acts*. Cambridge: Cambridge University Press, 1996.

Wolter, M. "Die Juden und die Obrigkeit bei Lukas." In *Christliche Theologie im Angesicht Israels. Festschrift zum 70. Geburtstag von Wolfgang Schrage*, edited by K. Wengst et al., 277–90. Neukirchen-Vluyn: Neukirchener, 1998.

———. "Jesu Tod und Sündenvergebung bei Lukas und Paulus." In *Reception of Paulinism in Acts*, edited by D. Marguerat, 15–35. Leuven-Paris-Walpole, MA: Peeters, 2009.

Wright, N. T. *The Climax of the Covenant: Christ and Law in Pauline Theology*. Edinburgh: T. & T. Clark, 1991.

Wright, R. B. "Psalms of Solomon." In *OTP 2*, edited by J. H. Charlesworth, 639-70. New York: Doubleday, 1985.

Ziesler, J. *Paul's Letter to the Romans*. TPINTC. London: SCM, 1989.

Biblical and Extra Biblical Writings Index

OLD TESTAMENT

Genesis

10	159
12	88
12.1–3	73
12.2–3	186
12.2	88
12.3	162, 180
13.18	88
15	88, 186
15.4–5	73
15.5–6	186
15.6	180, 193
15.18	88
17	88, 186
17.2, 6–7	91
17.4–6	186
17.5–6	73
17.5	180
17.6	88, 187
17.15–16	73
17.19–21	73
18.18	180
22	186
22.16	57
22.17	186
22.18	180, 186
23	88
25.7–10	88
26.3	57
26.24	186
27.13–15	73
28.14	186
32.13	57
35.10–12	73

Exodus

1.6–10	73
6.1, 6	74
12.29–36	74
13.3, 9, 16	74
13.17–15.21	74
15.22–17.11	74
17.7	154
32.11	74

Leviticus

17–18	155
23.29	161

Numbers

11	159
14.22	154

Deuteronomy

1	90
1.31	74
2.7	74

Deuteronomy (continued)

3.24	74
4.25–46	89–90
4.25–26	21
4.31	57
4.39	74
5.15	74
6.20–24	79
6.21	74
7.1	74
7.6	172
7.8	74
7.8, 12	57
8.1, 15	57
9.26	74
14.2	172
15.4	161
20.17	74
21.22–23	24, 107–8, 146, 151, 188
21.22	125
21.23	107
23	35
26.5–9	79
26.18–19	172
28.10	174
32.10	74
32.43	181
32.48	85

Joshua

24.2–13	79

Judges

3.9, 15	75

Ruth

4.18–22	118

1 Samuel

4.18	74
8–10	75
11–31	75
12.8–13	80, 82
13.13–14	23
13.14	22, 75–76, 149
15.11–35	75
16.1–13	184
16.1	75

2 Samuel

2.1–4	88
5.1–5	88
7	19, 22–23, 25, 28–29, 77, 78, 84, 88, 90, 94, 120, 124–25, 147
7.1–16	20, 32, 89–90
7.5–16	121
7.6–16	19, 21, 77
7.6–9	23
7.6	77
7.7	77
7.9a	90, 159
7.9	88,
7.10	77
7.11–14	24
7.11–12	88
7.11	77
7.12–14	22
7.12	91, 119, 124–25, 186
7.14–15, 16	88
7.14a	19, 120
7.15	77
7.15a	90
12.7–8	184
17.5–16	184
23.1	75

1 Kings

4.21	88
6.1	74, 83
8	164

2 Chronicles

7.14	174

Nehemiah

9.6–31	80, 82
9.6	82

# Biblical and Extra Biblical Writings Index

Psalms

2	19–20, 119, 120, 146
2.1–2	154
2.7	20–24, 26, 28, 37, 57, 119–20, 124–25, 147, 150, 152, 186
16	21, 23, 44, 57
16.8	124
16.10	19–22, 26, 28, 37, 121–24, 147, 150–52, 186
18.49	85, 181
32.1–2	86, 193
38.11	114
78.	80, 83
78.1–8	83
78.12–72	82
78.41, 56	154
78.70–72	83
88.8	114
89	20, 23
89.1–37	88
89.3–4	88–89
89.20	76, 149
89.21	22, 75
89.28–29	91
89.29	89
89.30–35	91
89.33–37	89
89.36–37	91.
89.38–51	88
95.9	154
104.5, 24	147
105	80
106	80–81
106.6–46	82
106.14	154
107.19–20	15
107.20	15, 100, 150
110.1	146
117.1	85, 181
118.22	23, 148
132.2–9	88
132.5	83, 163
132.11–13	88
135	81
135.6–7	82
136	81
136.5–9	82

Proverbs

3.19	147
8.22	147

Isaiah

1	90
4.1	174
6.9–10	52, 55
7	145
9	89
11	89, 145
11.1, 10	22, 75
11.10	84–85, 171, 173, 180–81
16.1–5	175
16.5	172, 175
27.9	193
42.5	134
42.6–7	51
42.6	135
43.7	174
44.28	22, 75–76, 150
45.20–23	173
49	135
49.1–6	158
49.6	24, 28, 38, 42, 45, 51, 57–59, 61, 94, 130, 133–34, 149, 150, 152, 160, 168, 200
52.7	15, 101, 117, 125
53	108, 111, 146, 151
53.9	107
55.3	19–24, 26, 28, 33, 37, 121, 123–24, 147, 150, 152, 186
55.4–5	180
55.5–6	171, 173
55.7a	122
55.11	101
56.1–8	35
56.7	171
59.20–21	193
61.1	15, 118, 125
63.19	174
66.1–2	83, 163–64

Jeremiah

12.15–16	173
12.15	173

Jeremiah (continued)

14.9	174
15.16	174
31.31–34	193

Ezekiel

20.5–9	82

Daniel

9.19	174

Hosea

3.4–5a	123
13.5	74

Joel

2.32	161

Amos

9.11–12	46, 94, 130, 170–74
9.11	46, 172, 175
9.12	46, 170

Habbakuk

1.5	42, 128, 140, 150, 152, 168
2.4	25

Zechariah

2.11	171, 173
2.15	171
8.3	173
8.22	173
9.11	74

APOCRYPHA

Judith

5.6–18	79, 81

1 Maccabees

2.52–60	78
2.57	24

Sirach

1.4	147
24.9	147
26.29	194
45–50	78
47.11, 22	24

Wisdom of Solomon

2–5	110, 146
8.5	147

PSEUDEPIGRAPHA

2 Baruch

56–74	78

1 Enoch

85–90	79
93; 91.12–17	79

3 Maccabees

2.2–20	79

Psalms of Solomon

17–18	89, 144
17.5, 23–51	89
17.23–51	183
17.26	120
18.6–10	183
18.6	89

Testament of Simeon

6.1	194

DEAD SEA SCROLLS

Damascus Document 2.14-6.11	79
4Q Floregium	144
4Q PB 1. 2, 4	24

EARLY JEWISH WRITINGS

Josephus: Jewish Antiquities

3.86	81
4.43-45	82
6.378	75
10.143	75

Philo: Quod Deterius

54	147

Pseudo-Philo: Biblical Antiquities

20.9	74

NEW TESTAMENT

Matthew

1.1-17	86
1.1-16	144
1.20	87
1.23	120, 145
2.15	120
3.7-10	98
3.9	101
3.11	96
23.34-39	110
26.28	96

Mark

1.1	98
1.4	96.98, 195
1.11	120, 147
2.17	190
3.6	104
7.24	159
8.27-33	6
8.27	159
8.34	112
10.33	106
10.34	113
12.1-11	105
14.24	96
15.40-41	113
16.6	112

Luke

1-2	54, 56-57, 154
1.2-4	12
1.4	114
1.15-17	157
1.17	98
1.26-38	145
1.27	87
1.30-35	120
1.32-33	57, 87, 144, 150, 157
1.32	147
1.35	57, 147
1.54-55	93, 157
1.54b-55	57
1.54b	57
1.68-79	93
1.68-69	157
1.68	58
1.69	94, 119, 144, 148
1.70-73	148
1.71	94, 148
1.72	121
1.73-74	57
1.73	157
1.74-75	122
1.76-77	148, 157
1.77	195
2	98
2.4	87
2.10-11	144
2.10	137
2.11	58, 87, 94
2.22	168
2.28-32	134
2.28	36

Luke (continued)

2.30–32a	93
2.30–31	58
2.30	58
2.31–32	158
2.31	57, 87, 144
2.32	53, 58, 133
2.32b	93
2.34	158, 168
2.36	158
2.38	157
3.3	95, 98, 195
3.4–6	98.168
3.6	53, 58, 93, 95, 133
3.7–17	153
3.7–9	98
3.8	101
3.9	98
3.15–18	145
3.15	97
3.16	97
3.18	98
3.19–20	96
3.22	147
3.23–38	86, 144
3.31	87
4.18–21	44, 98
4.18	61, 98, 118
4.23c	158
4.24–27	158
4.25–27	61, 93, 158
4.27	170
4.43	98
5.12–13	170
5.20	197
5.21	197
5.23	197
5.32	190
6.11	104
6.24	36
7.9	159
7.16	144
7.22	98, 170
7.26–28a	98
7.30	142
7.31–35	153
7.35	29
7.48	197
7.49	197
7.50	59
8.1	98
8.12	59
8.48	59
8.50	59
9	159
9.5	138, 206–7
9.6	98
9.10	190
9.22	112
9.41	153
10.11	206
10.13–15	153, 159
10.25–28	156
10.30–37	156
11.4	197
11.13	153
11.29–32	153
11.31–32	159
11.39–52	153
11.39	170
11.42	156
11.47–51	105
11.49–51	110
12.10	197
12.11–12	199
13.24–30	153
13.28–29	159
13.31–35	110
13.34–35	105
13.34	135
13.35	56
14.16–24	159
16.15	29
16.16	97, 98
16.17	156
16.29	156
16.31	53
17.3–4	197
17.12–19	159
17.14	170
17.17	170
17.19	59, 191
18.9–14	29
18.20	156
18.30b	152
18.31	106

18.33	113
18.42	59
19.9–10	59
19.9	148
19.47	104
20.1	98
20.6	53
20.19–20	104
20.27	52
20.34–38	152
21.14–15	199
21.24	56
22.2	104
22.19b-20	111
22.28–30	56
22.30	160
22.35–38	98
22.66–70	104
22.67	104
22.70	104
22.71	104
23.1	104
23.2, 5	104–5
23.4	104
23.13–23	106
23.13	105
23.14–19	105
23.14	104
23.20–21	105
23.22	104
23.27	105
23.34	190, 197
23.39–43	191
23.43	190
23.47	110
23.48	105
23.49	113
23.50–53	107
23.55	114, 199
23.56	199
24.1–3	199
24.6	112, 199
24.10–12	114
24.12	199
24.13–53	114
24.19	144
24.22–24	114
24.25–27	106
24.34	112, 199
24.36	199
24.41–43	115
24.44–49	106, 198
24.45–49	35
24.46–48	159
24.46–47	54, 60, 93
24.46	113
24.47	134, 143, 168, 195
24.52	138

John

1.1–18	120, 147
1.6–8, 15	98
1.19–34	98
1.19–28	97
1.27	97

Acts of the Apostles[1]

1–5	162
1.3	45
1.6	160
1.6–8	198
1.6–7	185
1.8	59, 143, 160, 168, 200
1.15–26	160, 198
2.16–38	44
2.21	59, 161
2.22	144
2.23	142, 146
2.30–31	144
2.30	150
2.32	199
2.33	166
2.36	160
2.38	60
2.39–40	160–61
2.40	59
2.43–44	161
3.20–21	152
3.23	161
3.25–26	93, 161–62

1. In view of the numerous verses of Acts, referred to, only the most significant have been included.

Acts of the Apostles (continued)

4.10	160
4.10, 11–12	93
4.12	148–49, 189
4.27–28	142
4.28	146
4.32–37	161
4.36–37	166
5.20	162, 198
5.31	60, 93, 162
5.32	199
6.11–13	162
6.13–14	163
7.1–53	82–83
7.2, 7, 30–34	163
7.27–29, 35, 39	165
7.38	162
7.40–42	165
7.46	164
7.47–50	165
7.51–53	153, 162, 165
9.15–17	43
9.15	35, 43, 48, 50, 166, 201
9.16	44
9.20–22	43
9.28–29	166
10.28	166
10.35	166
10.36, 42	43
10.39	199
10.41	199
10.42	184
10.43	60, 166
10.44–46	199
10.44–45	166
10.47–48	166
11.2–3	167
11.14	59
11.17	167
11.18	198
11.19–21	167
11.22–26	167
12	36
12.24	139
13.16–52	41–42, 69–138
13.16b-25	36–37
13.16	69–73
13.17–23	73–91, 140
13.17	73–74
13.18–21	74–75
13.22	75–76
13.23	91–95, 141
13.23	32–33, 38–39, 67–68, 141, 143–44, 149–50, 186
13.24–25	37, 95–100
13.24	92, 95
13.25	96–97
13.26–40	143
13.26–37	140
13.26	94, 100–1, 141
13.27–31	102–17
13.27–29	103
13.29	106–12, 151, 187–88
13.30	112
13.31	60, 113–17, 198–204
13.32–33a	117–19, 146–47
13.33b-37	119–125
13.33–35	152
13.33b	119–20
13.34	120–23
13.35	123, 146
13.36–37	123–24, 142
13.36	123, 150
13.38–41	125–31, 140
13.38–39	192–195, 197
13.38	61, 125–28, 149, 153–57
13.39	128
13.40–41	128–31
13.42–52	131–38
13.42–43	131–32
13.44–45	132
13.44	38, 139
13.45	52
13.46–47	132–36, 141
13.46	42, 48, 139, 208
13.47	51, 207–8
13.48–50	136–37, 139–40
13.51–52	137–38, 206–7
13.52	207
14.4	168
14.4, 14	199
14.6–20	168
14.8–14	39–40
14.15–17	40–41

14.21–26a 207
14.27 168–69
15.1–31 45–48, 169
15.1–5 153
15.7 201
15.8–9 154
15.9–11 154
15.14 171
15.15–17 94
15.16–17 170–75
15.21 155
17.2–3, 11 49
17.22–31 49, 169
17.24–25 164
17.30–31 184
18.5 200
18.6 42, 48
19.1–7 145
19.9 207
20.17–35 49–50
20.21 177, 200
20.24 200
20.27 143
20.28 188
21.26–27 164
22.3–5 177
22.12–14 177
22.14–15 60, 200
22.17–21 177
22.18 200
22.21 50–51
23.6 51, 151, 177
23.11 200
24.14–15 51, 152, 177
24.17–35 49–50
24.18 164
25.8 164
26.4–23 178
26.6–8 152
26.16–18 198
26.16–17 51
26.17–18 51, 196
26.18 60
26.20 51
26.22–23 51, 152, 178
28.17–31 52–56
28.17–19 179
28.19 52
28.23 201
28.26–28 179
28.28 42, 48, 58

Romans

1.2 106
1.3 2–3, 84–85, 145, 182
1.3–4 3, 84, 147, 181
1.4 3, 119–20
1.5 50
1.16 132
1.28–32 194
2.9–10 132
2.28–29 85, 101
3.1–2 85
3.9–20, 23a 194
3.21–26 197
3.24–25 111
3.28 194
4 101, 180, 193
4.1–9 86
4.3–5 193
4.3 186
4.6–8 86
4.7–8 86
4.11–12 186
4.13–16 186
4.20 186
4.23–25 186
4.24 112
5.12–21 181, 194
6.1–11 194
6.7 193
8.14 147
8.32 111
8.34 2
9–11 180–81
9.5 84–85, 181
9.8–9 186
10.9–13 84
10.9 112
10.15 117
11.13–14 50
11.13 50
11.26–27 193
11.26 50
14–15 183

Romans (continued)

14.9	182
15	84
15.7–12	181
15.8–9, 12	85
15.8–9	181
15.9–12	85
15.12	3, 145, 181

1 Corinthians

1.17–2.5	189
6.14	112
8.6	120
8.11	189
9	3, 116
9.1	114, 202
9.19–23	50, 86, 183
9.19–22	183
9.20	183
10.4	120
15	112, 113
15.3–11	202
15.3–7	3, 107
15.3–4	2, 106
15.3	108–9, 146, 189
15.5–7	114, 202
15.5	112
15.8	114
15.9, 10	202
15.11	4, 44
15.14–17	109

2 Corinthians

1.20	186
4.14	112
5.1–5	170
5.1, 4	170
5.14–15	189, 194
5.18–21	189
6.16–18	186
7.1	169, 186
8.9	120
10–13	3

Galatians

1–2	3, 116
1.1	112, 185
1.10–12	114
1.12, 15	202
1.15–17	204
1.16	50, 185, 202
1.18	99
1.23–24	203–4
1.23	203
2.1–10	44
2.6	44
2.11–16	45
2.20	185
3	101, 180
3.13–14	111, 146, 185–86, 188
3.14	85, 108
3.16, 29	185
3.16	180, 186–87
3.17–18	186
3.18	186
3.21–25, 29	186
3.22, 29	186
4.4–6	185
4.5	147
5.19–21	194

Ephesians

3.8	117
5.26	169

Philippians

2.5–11	120
2.9–11	182
3	126
3.5	183

Colossians

1.15–17	120
2.12	112

1 Thessalonians

1.1	184
1.9–10	9, 110

1.10	2, 112, 184
2.14–16	106
2.15–16	105
2.19	184
3.11	184
3.13	184
4.13–5.10	110
4.13–18	184
5.8	184
5.9–10	110
5.9	184, 188
5.10	189
5..23	184

2 Thessalonians

1.3–2.12	184

1 Timothy

3.13	111, 188

2 Timothy

2.8	3, 84, 145, 182
2.18	182
4.7	96

Titus

2.14	169

Hebrews

1.5	119–20
5.5	119–20
6.1–2	9
11	78

1 Peter

1.10–12	106
1.21	112
2.21–25	6
2.24	108, 188

Revelation

3.7	87
5.5	87, 145
22.16	87, 145

APOSTOLIC FATHERS

1 Clement

18.1	76

The Shepherd of Hermas

Vision 3.9.1	194

Authors Index

Alexander, P. S., 124
Anderson, H., 219
Anderson, K. L., 56, 63, 65, 122, 124, 129
Atkinson, K. R., 144
Aune, D. E., 90

Bachmann, M., 163–64
Barclay, J. M.G., 70, 219
Barrett, C. K., 15–16, 27, 35–36, 39, 48, 53–54, 60, 62, 65, 70–71, 73–74, 76–78, 83, 85, 92, 99–101, 103, 115–16, 118, 123, 126, 128–29, 131, 136, 145, 148, 151, 164, 169–70, 180, 183–84, 188, 193–94, 196.
Bauckham, R., 7, 172–74, 176
Bechard, D. P., 39–41
Berger, K., 63
Best, E., 110
Betz, H. D., 26, 185, 202
Black, M., 22, 85, 223
Beutler, J., 41
Blaiklock, E. M., 6
Bihler, J., 83, 164
Blass, F., A.Debrunner, and R. W. Funck, 36, 73, 113, 115, 121–22, 129, 159, 172
Bock, D. L., 55–56, 76, 110, 118
Bonnard, P., 185, 202
Borgen, P., 56, 180
Böttrich, C., 111, 190
Bovon, F., 55
Bowker, J. W., 21–22, 89–90, 124

Brawley, R. L., 53, 55, 131, 157, 163, 180
Brooks, J. A., and C. L.Wimberry, 149
Bruce, F. F., 5–6, 63, 71, 76, 99, 103, 107, 115, 118, 123, 129, 163–64, 170, 180, 185, 188, 202–3
Burchard, C., 201
Buss, M-J, 25, 40, 65, 71, 74–76, 90, 92, 94–95, 101, 103, 107, 113, 116, 118, 127, 129, 131, 133, 203
Busse, U., 175
Butticaz, S., 16–17, 55, 91

Cadbury, H. J., 1, 90, 92, 119, 136
Caird, G. B., 56, 137
Carr, E. H., 205
Carson, D. A., 127
Chance, J. H., 56
Cerfaux, L., 185
Charles, R. H., 219
Charlesworth, J. H., 219–221
Cifrak, M., 16
Clark, A. C., 44
Clements, R. E., 118, 175
Clivaz, Claire, 16
Conzelmann, H., 8, 10, 97, 126, 138, 198
Cranfield, C. E.B., 85, 194
Creed, J. M., 159
Collins, J. J., 144
Cullmann, O., 6

Dahl, N. A., 101, 111, 118, 170–71
De Boer, M. C., 70–71
Delebecque, E., 53

Authors Index

Delling, G., 12, 19
Dettwiler, A. 16
Deutschmann, A., 38, 53, 55–56, 70–71, 105, 130–37, 157
Dibelius, M., 4–5, 8–13, 49, 117, 178
Dietzfelbringer, C., 107
Dillistone, F. W., 5
Doble, P., 25, 136, 110–11
Dodd, C. H., 1–3, 5, 10, 13, 97
Doeve, J. W., 19, 22, 90, 124.
Dumais, M., 23–25, 62, 74, 77, 89–90, 95, 115, 124, 203
Dunn, J. D.G., 16, 38, 54, 56, 84–85, 97, 107, 127, 134, 145–47, 181–82, 185, 194, 202
Dupont, J., 5, 13, 21, 49, 53, 56, 60, 62, 116, 118–19, 122, 124, 133–34, 161, 170–72, 200, 203

Ellis, E. E., 22, 56, 90, 111, 114, 124, 159, 200
Evans, C. A., 53, 131
Evans, C. F., 9, 53–54, 56, 137

Farris, S., 54
Fee, G. D., 183.
Fitzmyer, J. A., 16, 39, 53, 56, 60, 62, 65, 70–71, 75–76, 83, 101, 103, 106, 111, 114, 118, 123, 128–29, 131, 133, 136–37, 148, 164, 171, 188, 196, 206
Flebbe, J., 143–44
Flichy, Odile, 16–18, 31–32, 36, 38–42, 63, 65, 73–74, 76, 91, 117, 134, 138, 180.
Franklin, E., 53–56, 157, 160, 163
Freyne, S., 144
Friedrich, G., 95
Fuller, R. H., 107, 112, 114.

Gamble, H. Y., 19
Gathercole, S. J., 127
Gaventa, Beverly R., 156, 178, 196.
Gempf, C. H., 7, 70
Glasson, T. F., 115
Gnilka, J., 52, 55
Goguel, M., 107
Goldsmith, D., 22, 90, 118, 124

Gordon, R. P., 74
Gray, G. B., 183.
Grässer, E., 223.
Grundmann, W., 56, 114, 159
Guilding, Aileen, 90
Gundry, R. H., 96

Haacker K., 151
Haenchen, E., 10, 39, 53, 60, 71, 74, 76, 83, 99, 101, 103, 115–16, 118, 123, 128–29, 131, 151, 164, 170, 203
Hall, R. G., 62, 74, 94.
Hansen, G. W., 29, 129
Hayes, R. B., 17, 86
Hengel, M., 38, 107, 147
Hermisson, H., 107
Hill, C. C., 163
Hirschberg, P., 70
Hoffmann, P., 110
Hofius, O., 195
Holtz, T., 22, 75–76, 82–84, 121, 123–24, 136, 164–65, 174

Jeremias, J., 109, 111, 114, 137, 194–95
Jervell, J., 8, 39–40, 45, 63, 103, 118, 126–28, 131, 133–34, 136, 152, 157, 162–64, 171–72, 180, 196–97, 200, 203
Jeska, J., 29–30, 75–76, 78, 82, 140, 164
Johnson, L. J., 13, 39, 60, 73–75, 83, 92, 100, 103, 121, 123, 131, 133, 161, 164, 172, 203, 206
Johnson, M. D., 144
Juel, D., 151

Kaiser, O., 175
Karrer, M., 55
Käsemann, E., 17, 85, 181
Keck, L. E., 143
Kee, H. C., 71, 164
Kennedy, G. A., 26, 64–66
Kezbere, Ilze, 46
King, N. Q., 158
Killgallen, J., 27, 83, 122
Kliesch, K., 14–15, 64

Klijn, A. F.J., 220
Klinghardt, M., 38, 63, 127, 131, 154-55, 164, 193-94, 197
Kloppenborg-Verbin, J. S., 110.
Knopf, R., 76
Koch, D-A., 71, 131, 197
Koet, B. J., 38, 53, 55-56, 133-35, 163
Korn, M., 40, 55, 61
Kraabel, A. T., 69
Krankl, E., 11, 107
Kuhn, K. G., 131
Kümmel, WG., 98

Lake, K., and H. J. Cadbury, 1, 103, 123.
Laato, A., 144
Landolt, J-F., 16
Leenhardt, F. J., 194
Lentz, J. C., 180
Lerle, E. 39
Levinskaya, Irma, 70
Lightfoot, J. B., 185
Lindars, B., 52, 107, 151
Lohfink, G., 105, 129, 157, 162, 171
Löning, K. 201
Lövestam, E., 20, 90, 118, 122, 124
Lüdemann, G., 15, 39, 62, 107, 126, 131, 164, 171

Mackintosh, H. R., 195
Maloney, Linda M., 129.
Malherbe, A. J., 110.
Manson, T. W., 5, 56
Marshall, I. H., 6, 39, 53, 56, 71, 73-74, 90, 94-95, 98, 103, 106, 111, 114-15, 123, 129, 148-49, 159, 164, 173, 188, 194, 199, 201, 203.
Marguerat, D., 16-18, 38, 51, 55, 104, 140, 156-57, 176-79
Martyn, J. L., 107
Marxsen, W., 17
Merk, O, 185
Merkel, H., 53, 157
Metzger, B. M., 103, 117, 151, 221.
Michaelis, W., 172
Michel, O., 78, 85.
Milik, J., 218

Minear, P. S., 98
Mittmann-Richert, Ulrika, 54, 56, 111, 190-91, 197-98
Miura, Y., 67, 76, 118, 124, 163
Moessner, D. P., 17-18, 157, 190
Moule, C. F.D., 99, 149
Mussner, F., 53, 185, 202

Nägele, Sabrine, 46, 169-76
Nanos, M. D., 130
Nave, G. D., 197
Neusner, J., 85.
Nickelsburg, G. W.E, 81, 110, 183, 217-21
Nolland, J., 56, 96, 154, 159

O'Brien, P. T., 193
O'Toole, R. F., 118

Pao, D. W., 133, 155, 157
Penner, T., 83, 164, 166
Pesch, R., 14, 38-39, 60, 62, 71, 73-74, 83, 89-91, 103, 115, 118, 123, 131, 164, 171, 183, 201.
Pichler, J., 29, 63, 65, 67, 73-74, 92, 122-23
Pietsch, M., 63, 67, 70, 74, 90, 103, 105, 107, 118, 122, 124, 129, 144, 146, 164
Phillips, J. B., 53
Pillai, C. A.J., 23, 25, 65, 74, 90, 100, 129.
Plumacher, E., 11-12.
Pokorny, P., 94, 200
Pomykala, K. E., 144, 172, 222
Porter, S. E., 180
Prast, F., 159
Preisker, H., 169.
Prieur, A., 53-55, 156-57, 159

Radl, W., 134-35
Räisänen, H., 107
Ramsey, W. M., 90
Rapske, B., 53
Rau, G., 105
Ravens, D., 53-54, 143, 157, 171
Reicke, B. 17
Rengstorff, K.123

Rese, M., 29, 61, 111, 118
Ridderbos, H. N., 6
Riesenfeld, H., 111
Riesner, R., 70
Robinson, W. C., 96
Roloff, J., 15, 38–39, 60, 64, 71, 73, 76, 83, 98, 103, 115–16, 118, 123, 126, 129, 133, 164, 171, 180, 203, 206
Ropes, J. H., 74, 103, 131
Ruppert, L., 110

Sanders, E. P., 127
Sanders, J. T., 157
Schenke, L., 103, 105
Schmauch, W., 190
Schmid, J., 111
Schmitt, J, 24, 124–25
Schneider, G., 7, 39, 53, 60, 70–71, 83, 95, 97, 99, 103, 118, 123, 126, 129, 131, 133, 162–64, 170, 174, 196, 201
Schneidewind, W. M., 144
Schoeps, H-J., 111
Schrage, W., 27
Schröter, J, 16–17, 31, 53, 63, 118
Schubert, K., 10
Schürmann, H., 106, 111, 190
Schweizer, E., 11, 110, 118, 185
Seitz, Claudia, 107
Sellner, H. J., 53, 56, 109, 191
Soards, M. L., 12, 63, 66, 118
Squires, J. T., 142.
Stanton, G. N., 15, 100, 125
Steck, O., 10, 110
Steeley, D., 110
Stenschke, C. W., 54, 154, 166
Sterling, G., 164
Steyn, G. J., 55, 64, 74, 76, 100.
Strathmann, H., 38, 200
Strauss, M. L., 28, 40, 62, 74, 76, 90, 92, 100, 119, 121–22, 124, 144
Stuhlmacher, P., 128

Taegar, J-W., 197
Talbert, C. H., 55
Tiede, D. L., 157
Trebilco, P. R., 70
Trocmé, E., 6
Turner, M. M., 118
Tyson, J. B., 40, 154, 157

Van der Sandt, H., 64, 122, 129
Vermes, G., 111, 220
Vielhauer, P., 17, 126, 128, 146, 180, 192
Von Rad, G., 79, 164

Wainwright, A. W., 53
Walton, S., 180, 188
Wander, B., 70–73
Wassenberg, G., 53, 70, 101, 157–58, 163–65, 180, 189, 200–2
Watson, F., 127
Weatherly, J. A., 104–7, 157
Weiser, A., 54, 64
Westermann, C., 107
Whybray, R. N., 107
Wilckens U., 9–11, 40, 48, 65, 95–98, 193, 106–7, 112, 118, 129
Wildberger, H., 175
Wilcox, M., 6, 24, 69, 75–76
Williams, C. C., 115
Williamson, P. R., 186
Wills, L., 63
Wilson, S. G., 128, 155, 157, 159, 171
Winnige, M., 183
Witherington, B., 8, 26, 39, 49, 53, 60, 64–66, 71, 73–75, 101, 103, 115–16, 118, 131, 163–64, 196, 202
Wolter, M., 54, 109
Wright, N. T., 86, 127
Wright, R. B., 183

Ziesler, J., 194

www.ingramcontent.com/pod-product-compliance
Lightning Source LLC
Chambersburg PA
CBHW050343230426
43663CB00010B/1971